Praise for *Down by the River*

"At his best, Bowden can write a little like van Gogh painted: a thick, dark impasto of short, violent phrases that make up a narrative of constant, seething movement where just as you think you're lost for good in the welter of names, places, dates and deeds, in the constant taking back of what was just stated, Bowden clears a little space, where, if only for a moment, something, even if it is disagreeable, makes sense."

—*Rocky Mountain News*

"Bowden has written his masterpiece, a book that combines research, narrative skill and clear-eyed observation and interpretation of facts."

—*The Sunday Oregonian*

"A must read for any student of recent Mexican history—as well as for anyone who wants to understand the motivations of U.S. leaders when they make policy concerning our southern neighbor."

—*The San Diego Union-Tribune*

"A parable for much larger issues about truth, justice, greed and conspiracy. . . . Bowden's writing . . . crackles with poetic brilliance."

—*The Denver Post*

"Bowden's reporting—sophisticated, robust and aggressively independent—will drop jaws; his writing—as frenzied and ferocious and penetrating as the automatic-weapons fire that peppers the narrative—will drop jaws even further. . . . Crazy twists, longing, dreams, familial history and the unmistakable odor of sheer madness pour from *Down by the River,* in streams shocking and profound, revealing and commanding."

—*The Atlanta Journal-Constitution*

Down by the River

Drugs, Money, Murder, and Family

CHARLES BOWDEN

Simon & Schuster Paperbacks

NEW YORK   LONDON   TORONTO   SYDNEY

SIMON & SCHUSTER PAPERBACKS
Rockefeller Center
1230 Avenue of the Americas
New York, NY 10020

First Simon & Schuster paperback edition 2004

SIMON & SCHUSTER PAPERBACKS and colophon are registered trademarks
of Simon & Schuster, Inc.

For information about special discounts for bulk purchases,
please contact Simon & Schuster Special Sales:
1-800-456-6798 or business@simonandschuster.com.

Manufactured in the United States of America

7   9   10   8

The Library of Congress has cataloged the hardcover edition as follows:

Bowden, Charles.
Down by the river / Charles Bowden.
p. cm.
Includes bibliographical references and index.
1. Drug traffic—Mexican-American Border Region. 2. Narcotics and crime—
Mexican-American Border Region. 3. Homicide—Mexican-American
Border Region. 4. Narcotics, Control of—Government policy—
Mexican-American Border Region. I. Title.
HV5825 .D692 2002
363.45'0972'1—dc21
2002070633

ISBN-13: 978-0-684-85343-7
ISBN-10:   0-684-85343-4
ISBN-13: 978-0-7432-4457-2 (Pbk)
ISBN-10:   0-7432-4457-5 (Pbk)

CONTENTS

For Mary Martha Miles

But was it the truth? Nowhere has the truth so short a lifespan . . . a fact has scarcely happened five minutes before its genuine kernel has vanished, been camouflaged, embellished, disfigured, annihilated by imagination and self-interest; shame, fear, generosity, malice, opportunism, charity, all the passions, good as well as evil, fling themselves on the fact and tear it to pieces; very soon it has vanished altogether. . . . The truth no longer existed. Precarious fact, though, had been replaced by irrefutable pain.

—GIUSEPPE TOMASI DI LAMPEDUSA, *THE LEOPARD*

the history of blank pages

*L*isten . . . *and you can hear them whispering a fable. Look and you can glimpse the shadows darting down the midnight streets. The old man does not get out much at eighty, but now they've brought him to the room and he is grilled for six hours. Luis Echeverría Álvarez ruled Mexico from 1970 to 1976 as the president, and before that he ran internal security. Hundreds and hundreds of people vanished under his watch and now, in the summer of 2002, there are questions. He is a small piece of a blank page torn from a secret history. Just as the hundreds of officially missing people are a pulse in a larger wave of gore.*

In the summer of 2002, the new reform government of Mexico opened the secret files accumulated by the state between 1952 and 1985. In 1952, Mexico had 27,846,000 souls, by 1985, this number had grown to 77,938,000. The secret files for this period number eighty million. They hold the screams of interrogations, the taps on phones, the details of executions and hidden graves. They have brought Echeverría into the light of day, an old man who is one footnote to this history of blank pages.

People line up in the streets of Mexico City to glimpse these secret files. They are searching for their own lives and the lives of husbands, wives, sons, daughters, and lovers who have vanished as if they had never existed. Of course, there are limits to what people can find out. For example, the height of barbarism in Mexico most likely occurred after 1985, when the partnership between certain members of the Mexican government and the drug industry flowered, and of course, these files are not made public.

And then there is an additional barrier, the millions of files accumulated by the U.S. government on the killings and tortures, files that remain sealed with no promise of ever being made public, files that chronicle the intimate connection between the United States government and the slaughter.

This book is about that world of secret files. Files never seen, files buried alive, files still sealed. When we are all dead, then, just maybe, these files will be opened. But for now, the work goes on despite the governments.

Grab a shovel, the work begins. Come, down by the river, the dead speak and they rattle their bones on both sides of the line. They are witnesses to our history, buried for sure, but still the voices of our history. The tale involves two countries, the United States and Mexico, fused together in one lie.

This book is the archeology of a nightmare. There will be music and laughter, salsa will flavor the gunfire. Some will say none of this ever happened. But the ground is quaking and in the hard cantinas the songs are spewing forth.

Come, the dead are crawling out of their holes.

another country

We are in the safe house. The sun bakes at ninety and the humidity keeps stride with the sun. Texas wobbles under the blows of summer, the storms threaten, the whiff of tornadoes gives a tang to the changing skies. The street is tree-clogged, narrow, and lined with stretch versions of ranch-style houses. Plano, hugging the north flank of Dallas, is one of the richest suburbs in the United States. This section of that sanctuary houses managers, the lower end of the Plano pecking order. Weekends reverberate with lawn mowers, weekdays find the street abandoned as couples work to pay for their homes.

The woman scrubs diligently in the kitchen. Not compulsively, she notes, just rigorously. She is short and friendly. She was born in Mexico and raised in the United States and most of her life has revolved around the Drug Enforcement Administration, DEA. This is not her home, she is just helping out. This could never be her home. Everything about the house is wrong. It reeks of a failed marriage, of depression. And of Anglos. This last failing is never mentioned, it is too obvious for mention. Anglos mean a cold world, a soulless world, a place where there may be money but something essential is always missing.

That is why she is here. He's gone now, doing errands, but she is here to fill this missing thing, unnamed, unmentioned, but obvious. Too obvious to discuss. She has been tied to him most of his life, through his single time, the second marriage, and now with the new divorce she is, well, back in the picture. She is bright and works hard. And she prides herself on being practical, on not succumbing to the fatal temptations of the imagination, and this house is not practical nor is this place. Nor is this thing about the death.

"They have to let Bruno go, leave him in peace," she offers.

"But that's hard when he's your own brother," I reply. I don't mention the glass of water and the candle.

She nods, but still she knows.

She has been busy telling me everything, about the details of the ruin, the little discrete acts, the betrayals, the hopes dashed. And the hopes once again renewed, just as the hopeless kitchen counter is being renewed as it emerges from months of neglect and begins to shine and smell fresh once again. She is preparing the playing field for her chicken tacos. It has not been easy. The cilantro, for example, sold in Plano is not really cilantro. Here, smell it. See? It is off, like something dead, something faint and lacking soul.

"Phillip," she announces, and she always calls him Phillip even though every one else calls him Phil, "has to stop this stuff about drugs. It is all he wants to talk about. I go to Mexico and I see hotels and nice businesses and at the trade conferences, no one talks about drugs. And I don't see drugs. He has to stop this."

"But that is not easy," I reply. "It is everywhere if you look, if you know how to look. It is too big to ignore."

And then I trail off because I understand her point. It is a healthy point.

I can't even produce a metaphor for the drug world anymore. I don't even like the phrase the drug world since the phrase implies that it is a separate world. And drugs are as basic and American as, say, Citibank. Mexico's three leading official sources of foreign exchange are oil, tourism, and the money sent home by Mexicans in the United States. Drugs bring Mexico more money than these three sources combined. The United States and Mexico share a common border more than 1,800 miles long. Its official, licit, World Bank–type economy is piddling—4.5 percent that of the United States. Both nations, along with Canada, are officially partners in a common market under the umbrella of NAFTA, the North American Free Trade Agreement. But Mexico and the United States are partners in an unofficial economy called the drug business.

The number for the money in the Mexican drug business, around

$30 billion annually, came from the Mexican attorney general's office in the mid-1990s, and is smaller than the current take. The number is roughly the same as that quietly issued from time to time by the agencies of the United States government.

When the drug industry does get mentioned, it gets dismissed by Mexicans blaming the United States for creating the drug market because of its vile habits and the United States blaming Mexico for permitting the drug industry because of its corrupt practices. I disagree with both positions. Drugs are a business, one of the largest on the surface of the earth, and this business exists for two reasons: the products are so very, very good and the profits are so very, very high. Nothing that creates hundreds of billions of dollars of income annually and is desired by millions of people will be stopped by any nation on this earth. A Mexican study by the nation's internal security agency, CISEN (Centro de Investigación y Seguridad Nacional), that has been leaked to the press speculates that if the drug business vanished, the U.S. economy would shrink 19 to 22 percent, the Mexican 63 percent.[1] I stare at these numbers and have no idea if they are sound or accurate. No one can really grapple with the numbers because illegal enterprises can be glimpsed but not measured. In 1995, one Mexican drug-trafficking expert guessed that half the hotel room revenues in his country were frauds, meaning empty rooms counted as sold in order to launder drug money.[2]

A part of me sympathizes with the woman cleaning the kitchen that is not hers, that is a relic of her lover's failed marriage. I can taste the desire to move on, to leave all the arrests, tortures, corrupt politicians and cops on both sides of the line, to abandon talk of deals and busts. To smell the roses and let the cocaine go to hell or the customers. Outside in the yard, a small dog lazes in the sun, a mongrel from El Paso. The dog is called Cokie, short for Cocaine. And here, the dog's world has been reduced to the decent order of bones, water, a food dish, and two rubber balls for play. The trick is to pretend Mexico does not exist. Or if it does exist, that it is very much like the United States, just with a different cuisine and language. For decades the man of this house kept Mexico at bay. And then, it came visiting in a form that trade agreements and folkloric dances tend to ignore.

The visit was violent. In Juárez, the Mexican city just across the Rio Grande from El Paso, the world has been reduced to this: between 1993 and 2001, at least 2,800 people were either murdered or raped or kidnapped or simply vanished.[3] In Mexico City, the attorney general's office has placed the mug shots of 1,400 federales on a Web site to better enable citizens to identify them when they rob or torture them or, perhaps, kill someone. A Mexico City suburb has followed suit with its police force so that, the mayor explains, the local citizens can protect themselves from the community's eight hundred cops. The mayor already had fired half of the force for corruption. Recently, one Mexican politician called for reinstating capital punishment in Mexico—solely for police offenders.[4]

The house is cluttered with DEA bric-a-brac—plaques, citations, photographs, the litter from a career. The woman wants such things gone, consigned to the past. She wants the breath of a fresh, new life. There is a logic to this since in the end this work with DEA has brought ruin. Yet, it is hard to let it go. It is hard to pretend it never happened. Others can do this, but for those who were involved in the blood rituals such an act requires personal mutilation. I understand this dread of burying the past at the very same instant I share her desire to erase it. Or better yet, to have never known it at all.

There are things—the gulag of slave labor camps in the former Soviet Union, the burning bodies of the Holocaust in Europe, the clanking chains of human bondage in the United States—that intelligent and honest people know occurred and yet grow weary of contemplating. The drug business is not like such things. Beyond some songs, a few action-packed movies, the drug business is never really acknowledged. Drugs may be the major American story of our era, the thing that did more to alter behavior and law, that redistributed income to the poor far more dramatically than any tinkering with tax codes, that jailed more people and killed more people than any U.S. foreign policy initiative since the Vietnam War. But this vital force, this full-tilt-boogie economic activity, is absent from our daily consciousness and only surfaces when discussed as a problem. And this problem is always placed on the other side of town or the other side of a line or the other side of the river.

Imagine over a quarter of a trillion dollars in a decade, imagine thousands of murders in a decade. Then imagine such things never existed. That is the drug business in one impoverished nation, Mexico. On the U.S. side of the line, all the numbers and consequences are larger.

The woman is right. Clear the house of this clutter, sell it, move on.

But there are these things, strands I think, yes, strands weaving together to form a tapestry. In this instance, the tapestry has these little loose ends that are visible, but the weave and tapestry themselves are not. One tiny strand involves Matamoros, the Mexican town facing Brownsville on the Rio Grande. A dozen or so men armed with automatic weapons took over the three-story state police station there one afternoon this season. They carried AK-47s, wore bulletproof vests and masks, and at first the state police thought it was nothing, simply some prank being played by the federal police. The men seized a Mexican soldier being held in a kidnapping case. When they finally left they showered the police station with bullets. In 1984, a similar group of men took over a Matamoros hospital where a business rival was being treated. They left five dead. Then there was a prison riot in 1991 when a drug group took over and burned the place to the ground. Or the time when Juan García Abrego, the business leader of Matamoros, caused some headlines by kidnapping an American and ritually sacrificing him in pursuit of insights.[5] García Abrego had lineage and was intertwined with the family that ruled Mexico, including the man then occupying the presidency. And then there was the matter of American FBI and DEA agents held down at gunpoint in broad daylight for twenty minutes on November 9, 1999, and the gunmen demanded they give up an informant, and some of the gunmen were cops and some were cartel members, and one gunman sported a gold-plated AK-47,[6] a problem that one of Phil's cousins, a man named Sal, had to investigate and try to iron out. All of this, these strands from an invisible tapestry, all of these strands are merely details in the life of a huge ongoing organism, something called the Gulf cartel, and the Gulf cartel is but a small part of the pattern of the giant tapestry itself, and like the other parts of the tapestry, the Gulf cartel comes and goes in official consciousness. It is said to be a criminal group and from time to time there are reports it is on the run. There is a fistful of such businesses, cartels, on the line and, most days, they barely exist in the newspapers or the government meetings or the idle chat at the counters of the coffee shops. This recent episode—where an entire state police station is seized—will pass and soon it will never have happened at all.[7]

Just as the songs that flutter across Mexican radio come and go seemingly without a trace. The safe house, the one owned by Phil Jordan on the quiet street just north of Dallas, is in a community where, for the past several years, the adolescents of all those affluent parents have been busy overdosing on heroin. For a while, this was news and then, like the narco songs of Mexico, the dying seemed to slip away and become forgotten. In Mexico, the songs remember,

> From Cuchillo Parado in the state of Chihuahua
> Flew a magnificent eagle
> Carrying a load as his master had ordered
> Wearing a bulletproof vest, like he was human
> And with a kilo of white powder in his talons
> In the city of Dallas, they were waiting for the eagle . . .

The woman is right, I know she is right.

So I ask her about chiles, which kind is she going to use in the tacos, and she says jalapeños and also some sweet yellow peppers. Plus, of course, a *salsa cruda* she will create. I can taste the chiles on my tongue, smell the meat frying in the pan, feel the warm tortillas. This is a better country, clearly she is right in this matter.

The drug business lacks any honest metaphors, as I have mentioned. The common ones such as drug lords and drug czars are falsely grand. It is simply a business and like all businesses it has merchants and like all merchants they have power and access to people in power. The merchants are natural lobbyists. They are strictly business. I do not think drug merchants would ever have come to any particular notice except for the fact that they sold a product which gives people pleasure and threatens the shackles of government control. Nor would even these conditions have mattered if they sold materials that had evolved in Europe and been slowly absorbed, like alcohol, into the fabric of governments and banks and capitalism. But of course, this is not how it all happened and so we are left with a secret commerce and secret events and a secret structure. And with enormous profits. We are left with a history unwritten, one almost erased as soon as it happens to hit the page.

This unwritten history takes place down by the river, on the fabled banks where two nations meet. The official history is about the corruption of Mexico. The unwritten history, or the one that is almost instantly erased, is about the corruption of both nations. In this unwritten history, the drug merchants are almost the only honest players: vicious, greedy, murderous, and candid about their behavior. They are also the only real defenders of cutthroat capitalism since they literally cut throats and employ people based on their talents and with little regard to their sex, race, class, color, or religion. They are also one of the few industries in the developing sectors of the earth that really do redistribute income and do so at a level without parallel in the thousands of assembly plants now employing the poor of the planet.

Phil will be back in a while, the kitchen will sparkle, the tacos will blaze on the tongue. The house will be cleaned, probably put up for sale, and what happened here will also be erased. And the tendrils of power and corruption and pain that reach into this house will be snipped and destroyed and no trace of their existence will be left. Sanity will be restored. The photo on the refrigerator, the one staring out at this very instant, will be gone. She has not gotten to the refrigerator yet, but she surely will. Bruno will go into a file, be remembered but seldom mentioned. He will become a brother lost to a secret time and business.

I can't argue with her, not at all. But like Phil, I just can't seem to live her way, follow this path of clarity and good sense. And I am not alone. There are cemeteries, official and unofficial, there are prisons in Mexico and the United States, there are guarded conversations by thousands of people in cafés and cantinas, conversations by people who find themselves in the same place where I now seem to live. They have tasted a world that others seem to feel either does not exist or has little importance to the greater world. We are all captives of a kind of black hole where people and events enter and then never seem to escape the power of the hole and are condemned to live in darkness and solitude.

I'm talking to an El Paso cop and he mentions the name of a detective and he says, "Never go near him. He's my uncle, he works for the Juárez cartel."

I'm talking to an undercover narc, one who has a contract on his head paid for by the Juárez cartel. The contract calls for him to be kidnapped, taken across the bridge to Juárez, and skinned alive. He says, "They've got a photograph of me, the one they are using to hunt me down. My nephew gave it to them."

So, I can't argue with the woman who tells me to let it all go. But it is not easy to forget everything.

It's like this. Long ago, there was a murder and I became interested in that murder. The murder was never solved. It is a cold case. That is not a problem. Unsolved murders are the essence of this particular black hole. The dirty laundry of two nations must be examined to understand this unsolved murder. That also is not a problem. This black hole teems with dirty laundry.

Here is the problem: once you enter this black hole and truly live in it and taste it, then you understand.

And this understanding does not matter at all. It becomes a curse and the curse never lifts. In the myth of Prometheus, he is punished for bringing fire down off the mountain by having eagles eat his liver each and every day.

In this black hole, no one ever brings fire down off the mountain, the guards prevent such escapes. But there are two eagles and they never stop tearing at your entrails. Not for a single second. The other people you know, your friends and neighbors, cannot see these eagles and are puzzled by the descriptions you bring back from this alleged black hole, this place you insist exists. After a while, you stop talking about it, cease mentioning the eagles, pretend the entrails are not being shredded.

I'll tell you how it happened. It will take a while, but I will tell you what I know.

There is a glass of water and a burning candle. I am in this black hole, with thousands of other lost souls. I am the one who watches and yet is incapable of doing anything. A child plays in the sunlight. The house is cardboard and salvaged wood, the yard light brown dirt without grass. The air sags with dust and exhaust and the sweet stench of sewage. Electricity comes from a cord snaking across the ground from a neighbor's house. Water is a hose from a neighbor's faucet. The privy leans. The child works. He stands on street corners and juggles, his face pancaked with white makeup. He is very short and slight. Hardly anyone notices him as he juggles various balls and the traffic stands waiting for the light to go green. On January 20, 1995, a man goes down in El Paso, Texas. His killer is arrested, tried, convicted, and sentenced to twenty years. This alleged killer is thirteen years old.

The case is closed.

flesh

crime

Where is he? A steady hum of traffic rises from the interstate, the clunk of car doors forms a mild staccato in the mall parking lot, as night moves across El Paso. The air tastes of chemicals, car fumes, refinery smells, the gases off the smelter, the raw sewage seeping.

But as the engine idles, Patricia can feel her irritation rising. She has made herself pretty, she is always pretty, her face fine-boned, her body trim, her hair brushed, her clothes well thought out. She makes this effort for him. And she is tired of being late because of him, it does not show her the proper respect. Her face tightens at the thought. She has brought him around but still, she can't break his blithe attitude about schedules. Bruno can't seem to ever be on time. It is almost seven, the night is cold, and they are supposed to be at the hospital for the death watch over his grandmother, be there with the rest of the family. Patricia sits waiting in the car, young and pretty with those fine bones in her face, plus a gleaming smile, and she thinks, yes, he should treat her with a little more respect. She's drummed order into Bruno, she's got him calling in regularly, reporting to her. She is determined to make this work and part of that task means remaking Bruno.

But he's still in the store and she's sitting in the parking lot in El Paso, Texas, as dusk turns into night. It is January 20, 1995, and she has an exact sense of time. They've been dating since last summer, now they've got a joint checking account, and this coming August they'll be married and then he'll enter law school. It is all planned. And Patricia is a planner, the hammer to keep Bruno in line. Last fall, Bruno even worked out a schedule: get a law degree in four to five years, retire by age forty-five with an annual income of, say, $60,000, own a home, and have good health—this last item he lists as goal number one. This is all possible, she thinks, that is, if he can ever be on time. She is twenty-three and she has had some missteps in life, boyfriends that were simply wrong, moves that did not work out, but now she is going to iron out all those wrinkles and have the life she always imagined, be married to a professional man, have a house and a family. Be settled.

She can't see him through the glass front of the Men's Wearhouse where he works selling suits. There is no telling what is keeping him. Lionel Bruno Jordan is enmeshed with others and always in a hurry and always late. For Patricia hooking up with Bruno has been like joining a galaxy. His family ties in El Paso run somewhere between five hundred and a thousand depending on who is counting. And these ties are hardly loose: he is twenty-seven years old and still lives at home in the barrio a few blocks from the Rio Grande. He was a high school basketball star and that adds another list of friends. He is a super salesman, and that adds hundreds more. And he is mellow, possibly the nicest guy she has ever met, the kind of guy who seems to never lose his temper and never make an enemy. And besides that, he can cook.

He is almost unflappable, the guy who says, hey, I'll take care of it. When he was a kid playing catch in the street, he once missed the ball and wound up mashing some of his mother's flowers. She flew out of the house and spanked him on the spot. Bruno stood up, turned around and said with a kind of dry wit, "Thank you, I needed that." Or there was the time he was about sixteen and his girlfriend put $200 down as a deposit at a used car lot and then had to back out of the deal because her father put his foot down. The dealer wouldn't give her the money back, just blew her off. Bruno went down and tore into him about how he was ripping off a minor who couldn't legally even enter into a contract and on and on. The guy was impressed, gave Bruno the two hundred bucks, and said, "Hey, you get out of high school, you come around, I could use a guy like you on the lot."

So she sits in the mall parking lot waiting for him to be late once again. She can see him in her mind rushing out, his briefcase in hand, his sport coat flapping, he will be smiling, in a hurry and full of expla-

nations and yet, and this is the part that always fascinates, oddly
relaxed. He is always relaxed, even in his rush to do things.

The city swallows dirt. On one side there is that smelter spewing gases,
on the other side that oil refinery. Next to downtown the railroad yards
rumble and then a few blocks away flows the Rio Grande (the Río
Bravo to the Mexicans on the opposite bank), a polluted snake that
rises and falls based on releases upstream calculated for agricultural
needs. Juárez, a city fast approaching two million, faces El Paso and
pours almost entirely untreated waste into the canals that feed fields
downstream. El Paso itself has around 700,000 people but no one
really has a grip on the number of illegals. They are everywhere, on
street corners juggling, washing windshields, tucked away in houses
invisibly cleaning. Tens of thousands of people in the El Paso area live
in wildcat colonias, instant slums, without sewage connections and
often without potable water. Border factories have changed El Paso. In
1960, about 20 percent of the population had incomes lower than the
national average. By 1991, with the boom in border factories just
across the line, 42 percent had incomes below the national average.
Wages in El Paso have always been crushed by cheap Mexican labor.
The town has also lived with a good dollop of crime. By the 1920s car
theft averaged one a day. There is a racist tinge also. In the 1920s, the
school board was taken over by the Ku Klux Klan. El Paso is a
Mexican-American city traditionally lorded over by an Anglo elite.

Just across the river is Juárez. It is at the moment a touted success
story. The North American Free Trade Agreement passed in late 1993
and the traditional border plants in Juárez suddenly began to mush-
room. Soon, the city had the lowest official unemployment in Mexico,
less than one percent. New industrial parks began go open up, major
American corporations flocked in. In Juárez the wage starts at about $3
a day—in the American-owned factories they run $25 to $40 for a five-
and-a-half-day week—and no one can live on this wage—the cost of
living in Juárez is 80 to 90 percent of the cost of living in El Paso. The
turnover in the border factories runs 100 percent to 200 percent a year.

But Juárez is booming in its own fashion and the wait for cars on the bridges connecting them can run more than an hour. U.S. Customs is determined to get the delay down to no more than forty-five minutes. Both cities are faced on the west and south with dunes and when the wind comes up both cities disappear into a wall of brown. In El Paso, the per capita consumption of water for all purposes is 210 gallons a day, in Juárez it is seventy gallons. A long drought rakes the land. In the past twelve months, half of Mexico's six million cattle have dropped dead. In the northern states such as Chihuahua the absence of rain is more severe. Much of the state has not seen rain in over seven hundred days. Trees are dying, whole orchards go under, and about half the farmland is not even tilled. The World Bank decides that 80 percent of Mexico lives in poverty.

To stand anywhere in El Paso requires looking at Juárez. Yet the local newspapers hardly ever mention the Mexican city, nor does the television news. El Paso lives isolated—as close to San Diego as to Austin—and ignored. Juárez lives in a deeper silence. Under the Aztecs, the tlatoani, or emperor, could not be questioned. To even look upon his face meant death. In Mexico City the Ibero-American University does a study on freedom of information and finds Mexico rates 182 out of 189 nations, only nudging out places like Libya, China, and North Korea.[1] Decades after the slaughter of hundreds of students on October 2, 1968, in Mexico City on the eve of the nation's hosting of the Olympics, Mexican scholars still seek information on that matter from U.S. intelligence. The files of their own government remain sealed. Between 1988 and 1994, forty-six Mexican reporters are officially listed as murdered.[2] *La Jornada,* the nation's leading newspaper critical of the regime, secretly gets 70 percent of its advertising from the Mexican government, and often runs government propaganda as news. The rest of the press is more servile.[3] Juárez is less open than the rest of Mexico.

Rumors fly across Mexico, facts crawl. The nation has a bookstore for every 170,000 people, a bar for every 2,150.[4]

But mainly, there is an eerie silence. Just a few weeks before the presidency of the nation had changed hands with Ernesto Zedillo replacing Carlos Salinas, the former president's own biography demonstrated the silence of Mexico. On December 18, 1951, the major Mexico City dailies reported that two children, Raúl, five, and Carlos, three, and a playmate, eight, found a .22 rifle in the closet of the house. They created a game with the twelve-year-old maid, Manuela. She kneeled and they executed her. The three-year-old, Carlos, said, "I killed her with one shot. I am a hero." He grew up to be president. During his six-year term of office, every newspaper account of the incident disappeared from libraries across Mexico. An official biography by his minister of the interior said the eight-year-old playmate of the family actually did the killing.

Everyone is waiting for Bruno. Beatrice and Antonio are used to their son being late. He joined the family late. Beatrice was forty-four when he was born, eleven years after they thought the family was finished with the arrival of their fourth child, Tony. They decided the birth was a miracle, shut down their used clothing store, and devoted their life to this new child, a quarter century younger than his oldest sibling.

The doting on Bruno has never ceased. When he was leaving the house this morning, his mother said, "Bruno, don't wear that sport coat, wear a different one." She had a feeling about the color, it was just not right. Beatrice has always worried about her miracle baby, worried that God would take him away. Or that she would die before he grew up to be a man. She is by nature an emotional woman and Bruno would regularly take her blood pressure, almost function as her doctor.

He humors her by saying, "No, this is my lucky coat. Don't you have faith in God? Nothing can happen to me."

Beatrice answers, by way of making amends, "You look so nice, so cute."

And off he goes. There is no arguing with Bruno, he smiles his way through every disagreement. When he came out of a nightclub about two weeks ago and found all his tires had been slashed by his ex-girlfriend's new guy, he shrugged and said, hey, the world's full of tires, no big deal.

But Beatrice paid a lot of attention to that tire slashing. She'd been on edge about Bruno. She regularly has the tarot cards read and this last time, the woman said the cards looked bad, that she saw danger for Bruno. So when the tires were slashed, Beatrice went back to the reader and asked if this was the bad thing she had seen. And the woman said, no, it was something else. For the past two weeks or so, Beatrice has sensed some worry in her son. When he gets up in the morning, even before he takes his shower, she can see him poring over the dream book looking for some kind of answer in its explanation of symbols. She asks him if something is bothering him, but he just brushes her off. So, she lets it go.

Bruno tends to get his way. Beatrice and Antonio have been living in the same house all of their married years, fifty years in the same house, one built by Beatrice's father right across the patio from his own home. And now with five children raised in the same house, Bruno has this idea to add a room where they can put their big television and some chairs and everyone can sit around and have a beer and maybe some of her tacos while they watch football, especially the Washington Redskins, Bruno's team in Cowboys-crazed Texas. He's so fixated on the Redskins that one of the main reasons he crosses over to Juárez is to place bets on their games. Sometimes when he is busy, he sends his father, Antonio, over to place his bets. And of course, Antonio crosses over and puts down Bruno's wagers. There is no denying him. So now he says, let's add this room. And she knows they will, that her son, who is to be married in August and start his own family, will still get this room because there is no way to say no to him. He's always been that way.

Still, Beatrice wishes he could be on time for once. She can't understand it: Christina, Tony, and Virginia are on time. But Bruno and his older brother Phil can be two or three hours late for anything. Once, Phil was almost three hours late for the supper she was cooking him and then he arrived with takeout food because he'd forgotten she was preparing his favorite meal.

But now, she patiently waits with Antonio and her daughter Virginia and other relatives. Beatrice is the woman who always carries her beauty with ease and age cannot touch her flirtatious nature. She has this inner sense of herself, of her dress and her makeup, and this sense is as sure and durable as iron. In her seventies, her hair is jet-black, her eyes flash, and her cheeks glow. Her husband is rail thin and the nervous energy of his wife is absent in him. He is firm and yet unruffled, the rock the family rests on. He too defies time with his sense of self, his head a full shock of hair, his face smooth and unworried. Only the eyes reveal a deeper self, the eyes that never rest and are sharp with vigilance. Virginia is the mother's child, the beautiful woman who almost swirls into a room with her scent, composed face, perfectly groomed hair, and designer clothes, often garments she has designed herself. She is the beauty who never loses this expectation that she will catch the eye of others. She and her mother visit each and every day.

Now they have gathered because this could well be the last night for Antonio's mother. This is a vigil and she knows Bruno will try to be on time this once. He'd called Beatrice twice that day and both times said, "Now, you wait for me. Be sure and wait for me."

So Beatrice sits there waiting with her family and they sit as a unit, a family without any estrangements, a thing as durable as a nation. Every time the hospital elevator door opens, she looks up expecting her son Bruno.

"What?" Bruno asks.

He's in a hurry. His briefcase is full of tax returns he is preparing, a little sideline of his. And he has to get to the hospital with Patricia and she is waiting out front in the parking lot right now. His grandmother, he can't be late for this one, she is dying. His eyes are bright, Bruno is always staring almost owlishly out at life and in his mind he is already out the door. But now María,* the manager of this outlet of the Men's Wearhouse, is talking to him. And she is part of the web he lives in. She's the boss but that is not why she has his attention. A year ago, he was the boss for a few months, planning the promotions, and hey, he had that great idea for the billboard by the house, the one that slaps Mexicans in the face as soon as they cross over from Juárez and the big sign shouts about the fine clothes at the Men's Wearhouse, and the idea

---

*María is not her real name.

was a natural for Bruno, his family home was a half block from the
bridge approach, and there was a lot of business to be had in Juárez.
Sure the city is dirt-poor but there are the managers in those factories
and they need fine suits and there is this new boom, the drug guys,
dripping gold chains and money and wanting the cuts, the fabrics, the
good taste Bruno knows cold, wanting the suit that says a person is
legitimate and has made it. And the drug guys from Mexico are always
easy to spot. You sell them a bunch of suits and shoes, the whole works,
and then you are at the cash register and you ask, cash or charge, and it
is always cash, hundreds usually. And then you ask for an address so
that they can get future mailings on specials at the store. And you
never get an address, never. And besides the drug guys, and boy, he
never asks about them, they are just valued customers, then there are
the narcs. The El Paso Intelligence Center (EPIC) is right in town at
Fort Bliss and there are over three hundred narcs stationed there alone
and they come in for suits also.

Phil, his own brother, is going to take over EPIC this coming
Monday after almost thirty years in DEA. Why, Bruno has had to talk
him into the job, telling him what a great tool EPIC could be, not just
for busting drug guys but for educating the public, how it has been
kept a secret from the world and Phil is the guy to use it as a pulpit in
order to teach the world about dope and the dope wars. Bruno's
inspired him with this mission during their phone calls every couple of
days, calls in which they also figure out what numbers to play in the
lottery. Just a week or so ago, Bruno got close, had five of the six numbers and even with this failure wound up winning over a thousand dollars. And with just one more number he would have won $40 million.
They took his picture, Bruno standing there as the winner, and posted
it at the local convenience store where he'd bought his ticket. Phil will
be arriving early Monday morning from his home in Dallas to take
command, and that'll be good, having him around for a change. Sure,
he keeps in touch, calls his mother every single day, but that's not the
same as being here. And it looks like Phil's going to be living at home
to save money and keep his family back in Dallas so the kids won't
have to change schools.

All these details, Bruno's head is full of details. He lives at a trot, always this hurly-burly about him as he moves from one engagement to the next. And now Bruno—and he ought to be gone, be on his way—has to listen to María. She is almost family. In a week or so, she'll marry one of his relatives, and it can't get much closer than that.

So he listens to María and her problem. He's been dealing with her problems for a long time. María and this one guy had been going together since she was fifteen. The guy had a hard edge. There were all these rumors. And the guy was supposed to have all these connections, they said, with the street kids, the ones from Juárez who begged at stoplights all over El Paso, the ones that juggled or maybe tried to wash a windshield and then held out their hands. Well, the boyfriend was supposed to be a regular Fagin to these kids and had them hanging around his house all the time. Bruno didn't really know, after all the guy lived with his mom, but a lot of guys lived with their families in El Paso. It is not a rich kind of town. And then María broke up with him after that, and by June, about the same time he hooked up with Patricia, she and his relative became an item and now, in just a few days, they'd be married, a big family occasion.

And Bruno likes to help out. Why, just the month before, María came to him and she was flat broke, not a dime, and so Bruno went down to the credit union with her and co-signed a note for the loan. After all, she was going to marry his relative and be family. And maybe that was part of why he never really got out of El Paso, it was all so tight and family. Tony was up in Las Vegas and he is fun to visit. And Phil has his empire running DEA in Dallas and that is a rush. But El Paso is home and now he has Patricia and she is so fine. Just a little over a year ago, his steady girl had left him cold, and he was down for a while, really down. He won a radio contest by writing a goodbye letter to that girlfriend, they even broadcast it, and he got the prize. He'd consulted tarot card readers, the same ones his mother used. Nothing wrong with looking for an edge. And he had his dream book to help him straighten out any messages that came to him in his sleep. But now things were looking up. Patricia filled the gap and hey, he's not bitter, life isn't that way, don't worry, it will be okay, that's what he always tells himself. And María, well, things are looking up for her. She's getting married for God's sake. In early December, she is flat broke and bingo! Here it is only January and she's got a brand-new Chevrolet Silverado truck, the thing is all tricked out with everything, primo, had to cost close to thirty grand.

So she is asking Bruno this favor. His relative is working over at the K-Mart less than a mile away, and she needs to get the Silverado to him but she can't leave the store. Could he like drop it off in the parking lot and give him the keys? María has already asked another salesman, Israel Reyes, but he's turned her down. He figures with his luck he'll get some scratch or something on the new truck, so, no thank you. And Bruno, he kind of starts to sputter, he's in a rush, gotta get to the hospital for his grandmother, the whole family is expecting him right now, and Patricia is waiting out front, got his briefcase in his hand, those tax returns, he's got to make some extra money, and, but it's family, so, sure, it's only a mile, can't take that long. He'll have Israel Reyes follow him and give him a ride back. No problem. He and Israel work together selling suits and hey, they've known each other since Bruno was about six, came up together in the barrio. They're tight. Sure, Israel has a different life, what with a wife and a fistful of kids. That's why he drives an old beat-up VW Beetle, but he'll help out, no problem. María hands Bruno the keys. She was just on the phone and he could tell she was agitated, anyone could tell that. Israel noticed the same thing while she was talking to someone. So, no problem. Besides, driving the new Silverado will feel good, all that new-car smell and all the automatic this and that. Nice color too, teal, a coming color and Bruno is into color, not just fabric. You gotta know what is coming so you can tip your customers the right way, keep them in pace with the style. That's what he sells, knowing what they need even if they don't know. He's always thinking of the store, putting time into planning office parties—great for morale—and going to the Men's Wearhouse conventions.

He was just up in Phoenix this last November at one, and saw his nephew Sean, Phil's son from his first marriage, but really more like a brother since they are almost the same age and were raised together a lot of the time when Phil had his kids for the summer and couldn't take care of them because of the job and all that undercover stuff. He'd always shipped Sean and his sister, Brigitte, to El Paso and they'd hang out with Bruno, right there on the little street by the bridge to Juárez. It was tight then, a dead-end street and everything was warehouses except for his home and his uncles' and a few others, a separate world in the middle of El Paso. Anyway, he'd taken Patricia to Phoenix and they'd partied hard.

Sean wasn't into much partying right then, too busy getting ready for his own marriage. But he was doing well, managing a music store, finally on track, which was a blessing after all the bad times when he'd lived with that woman, and she had to be selling drugs, and he moved in with her and cut off everyone in the family. The only thing that kind of struck Bruno was that Sean was skeptical of Bruno's upcoming marriage, kind of expressed doubts about it, not that he said anything, but still it was there. It was like hey, Bruno, sure, you're going to get married, just like all the other times you were madly in love with other girls and they were the one, the special one. Just like you're going to go to law school but never quite get there.

This is kind of a family thing, this law school stuff. Why his grandfather was going to be a lawyer and wound up a junkman. And Phil was going to be a lawyer and then when he was kind of warming up in graduate school and just before he started law school, he jumped at the chance to join the drug fight and now has spent his life in DEA. So now Bruno was going to finish the job, the one his grandfather had begun, why it must have been around 1900 when his grandfather dreamed of becoming a lawyer. In fact, Bruno is named after a brother of his grandfather's, one who died long ago in Italy. He is going to law school, right after he gets married this summer. It will be a neat package: he'll turn twenty-eight in August, get married and start his career. But when he was in Phoenix, he could sense this doubt in Sean, hear in his words that he, Bruno, would never really do it, that he was some kind of momma's boy and was never going to leave home. He could feel this same doubt in his friend Israel, but he'd show 'em.

Okay, let's get organized. In a hurry, but this small thing can be done. Doesn't want his relative ending his shift and having to walk a mile to get the truck. Bruno's got the keys in his hand, he's out the back door to fetch the Silverado, Israel is right behind him, can't take more than a few minutes, everything will work out fine, nothing to worry about, he'll barely be late for the hospital. Besides, things feel good, he's on a roll. He's just won that thousand dollars on the lottery. He hangs on to every ticket, keeps them in a shoebox at home and studies his numbers, looking for that lucky one, the workhorse that will win and win. Phil tries to figure out the same things. Plays his kids' birthday numbers, Sean and Brigitte from his first marriage, Kelly and Kenny from the second. If you look hard enough, you'll find the number. Bruno lately has been working out a system for roulette, studying the wheel hard. Last time he was in Vegas to see Tony, he gave the system a try and there is real hope. It is not perfect but he can sense he is getting closer, that he is on to something.

You can't deny luck, it is there and just as real as the city streets. Why without luck his people would still be in southern Italy, his mother's father would have wasted his life there, or his father's father would still be starving in Guadalajara. Or his grandmother who is now dying in the hospital would still be in Durango, a bleak outpost of the drug business. Instead they're in El Paso and everything is looking up, just look at his life, things are fine. And besides he's wearing his lucky sport coat and it never fails him.

Luck is part of the air on the border. Lottery tickets everywhere, both sides of the line. And now these Indian casinos are popping up with more action. There is more to life than just hard work and savings, you have to have luck. Light that special candle. Wear the right coat. His sister Virginia, she likes séances and that stuff. Phil worships the lottery and he's got a good job. Tony, well, he's in Vegas. Bruno is floored in two cultures, Italian and Mexican, that know you cannot trust the future, cannot trust the government, can't even for sure trust God unless you first take care of things at the church. Ruin can rain down at any moment. That's the deal. It's like basketball. You take your talent, you hone it, you work out, master plays, feel out the rhythms of your teammates, and still, some nights you hit the boards and everything goes wrong. And other nights, you can't miss, shoot blind from half court, just can't miss. It's luck and everyone knows it.

Just two weeks before, Phil's daughter Brigitte was in town and they had a really good time. She was kind of down in the dumps over a relationship, so she'd come home to Frutas Street and the good luck that lives there. Brigitte had kind of strayed from the family for a while, just like her brother, Sean, but the tug was too strong and the warmth was too attractive. And now she was back in a world where there was more Spanish spoken than English. Back home. One night, she and Bruno and his cousin from next door, they were out riding around and pulled into a convenience mart to buy some lottery tickets. And they won. So they went on to the next place and bought some more lottery tickets and they won again. They must have hit twenty places, and they just kept winning. Not every ticket, of course, but a bunch of them. It's about luck. Sometimes when Bruno feels he is hot, well, that is when he'll send his father, Antonio, just across the bridge to Juárez to place bets on games. When he's on a roll, and he can feel when it's right, his father will cross over with his wagers every day for a week or two at a time.

No time. He decides not to even pop out in front and tell Patricia. She'll just get upset over the delay, anyway. Doesn't need to hear any of that. He'll be back in a minute and she'll never even know he's been gone. He gets in the Silverado, and pulls out, Israel right behind him in that old Bug. The traffic is a little heavy—what can you expect on a frontage road right along the interstate by a mall?—but they hardly have to go a mile. He turns on to McRae, then pulls into the K-Mart lot and it's kind of full, shoppers piling in after work, and he slows, looking for that parking space, and he wants one near the entrance of the store, be better for his relative that way, and safer too, less chance of this fine new truck being stolen if he parks it right there by the door. But the place is really jammed.

Israel pokes along in his old Volkswagen. One more bullshit thing with Bruno. Christ, how can Bruno always be so damn happy? Hey, don't worry, be happy. Israel has watched a string of girlfriends clean Bruno out and then dump him, and Bruno doesn't seem to care at all. How does he do it? Israel has the wife and five kids and a check that gets vaporized as soon as he cashes it, and he's listened to Bruno talk a constant upbeat line. He's gotta watch every penny, and his buddy seems to always be happy to pay for the drinks.

A damn momma's boy. He follows the Silverado closely, damn near bumper to bumper, and then in the lot, he kind of falls behind as Bruno goes up and down a lane or two looking for that right parking slot. Finally, one meets Bruno's standards, and Israel pulls just past the Silverado, the rear bumper of his Bug right on the tailgate, and stops and waits for Bruno to hand the keys over to his relative so that they can both go back to the Men's Wearhouse.

Couldn't be better, Bruno thinks, right near the big doorway leading into the K-Mart. He turns out the lights, opens the door, and steps out. He's trying to remember something but can't quite nail down what it is. After all, he's in a hurry. His grandmother is dying just a few blocks from the K-Mart where he now stands in the cool night air.

He's standing there with the key in the door, when suddenly two things bring him up short. He's left his briefcase in the truck, and he's gotta have that, those tax returns can't wait. The extra money matters now that he is building a nest egg for his marriage. And then this other thing, two loud sounds, two pops.

The photographer holds the small slide up to the light in his apartment: a hand blackened by the sun reaches through the sand of the dune toward the sky. He smiles and explains they do that sometimes, leave a hand sticking up as if to say, hey, look at what we did.

He smiles and then says, "The hand says, come over here, guys!"

He's sitting in his apartment just a few blocks from the bridge that leads from his world in Juárez over to El Paso, the same bridge where Bruno has pasted that Men's Wearhouse billboard. He sips his beer and rolls into this story. He was on assignment with a bunch of other Mexican photographers and they went to this nice house in a good neighborhood in Juárez. Some men came out of the house with guns and said, hey, we don't want you here or any publicity about this place. They gave them some money. The photographer grabbed his share.

He thinks of that night as he sits in his bleak, small apartment with only two strangers there looking at his slide of the black hand reaching up from the sand.

"Amado," he says wistfully. Then he snaps alert, his eyes dart around the small room, and he says, "I shouldn't have said that."

The Mexican north rings with songs, corridos, celebrating the men and events in the drug trade. The government periodically makes gestures toward suppressing this music by banning it from the radio. None of the prohibited songs ever mention Amado Carrillo. Between 1991 and 1995 there are hundreds of drug murders in Juárez. There are no arrests. Not a single one.

A woman rolls into the K-Mart lot and pulls up along the curb by the front door. Her fourteen-year-old niece is with her and they notice a black truck following a teal-colored truck into the parking lot.

Renan Barroso, seventeen, has been working less than a week at the K-Mart. He's on a break and walks out to the front of the store to use the pay phone. He's a mild-mannered kind of kid, glasses, serious face, and watchful eyes. As he waits for someone to pick up on his call, he idly stands at the phone and looks out at the parking lot. It is almost seven, the big lights are on in the lot. A nice new truck rolls in, teal-colored, and pulls into a vacant slot. And then a little ways behind it, rolling quietly, is a dark pickup truck. Renan hears a voice, what sounds like a woman's voice, say, "No, no," and then he notices a short figure in dark clothing hop from the front seat of the still rolling dark truck. The figure is crouched and has something metallic in his hand, something that looks to Renan like a machine pistol, most likely an Uzi or a Mac-10. Yeah, one of those. He knows his guns, he's seen them at school. El Paso has the highest number of gangs per capita of any city in Texas. Renan is transfixed, though he can't really say why. Something about the crouching figure, the movements, it is all just a little off, a little strange. He hears two bangs, see puffs of smoke suddenly appear out of that metallic thing. Sees a guy go down hard on the pavement.

The woman parked near the front entrance with her niece hears shots also, two or three shots, and she shoves her niece down to safety. But the fourteen-year-old has already seen too much. The guy is down on the pavement, shot. She thinks he must be cold, it has to be cold out there on a January night.

Suddenly Israel hears two gunshots and he wheels around in his seat. He sees Bruno staggering along the side of the truck, and God, he's kind of leaning over, his face white and full of some kind of fear. And then Bruno reaches the tailgate and he's down on one knee, hanging on with one hand to the rear bumper, and then this person, this figure appears behind him, a small figure, and Israel can see the figure clearly but he can't make out the face, the whole scene is backlit by the K-Mart lights. Israel is half out of his car, he's got one foot down on the pavement, and he notices that the small figure, and hell, Bruno and this figure are ten, maybe twelve feet away, and Israel suddenly focuses on the gun in the small figure's hand. Then Bruno is up on his feet and moving, he staggers around the end of the truck and heads toward the passenger door. Israel puts his VW in gear, starts rolling down the lane in the parking lot, figures to swing around and come back up in the next lane and head Bruno off. He is not thinking now, he is just moving.

Bruno lurches out between two cars into the lane where Israel is creeping up, slams down on the sloping front hood of the VW and then falls to the ground. Israel stops and he looks up and sees the cab light on in the teal Silverado with some kid in the front seat, sees his face clearly, and this kid looks bewildered by the controls in the truck and then he gets it going, backs out, and drives away.

The fourteen-year-old girl breaks her aunt's hold, she just can't take this anymore, the guy has to be cold, she jumps out of her aunt's car parked along the curb in front of the K-Mart and runs over to the guy on the ground. He's gotta be cold. She takes off her coat and lays it on him.

•   •   •

Israel looks up and Bruno's relative is standing there and he is asking, "What happened to Bruno? Where's my truck?"

Amado means Beloved and there are signs of this love. On August 4, 1994, a French-built full-bodied jet lands at Sombrerete, Zacatecas. The cargo hold contains twenty thousand pounds of cocaine. A tire explodes on the plane. Sixty federal police truck the load away. Within days, the cocaine shows up on the streets of Southern California. Under U.S. pressure, the case is investigated by Mexican authorities but after some months, it is closed without coming to any conclusion. Mexican officials at the time are charging federal police comandantes a million dollars per assignment to major border cities. In Juárez, the price is higher.[5]

She is riding with her husband and son. Her husband's driving and they're going to do some quick shopping. She teaches school, and she has the authority and clarity that come from ruling a classroom. As they pull into the K-Mart parking lot, they're suddenly jammed right next to a teal-colored Silverado trying to leave the lot and the truck just came up on them, didn't even have its headlights on. She looks over, the other vehicle is only four or five feet away, and for ten or fifteen seconds she takes in the driver, a kid, real short, in fact he's staring through the steering wheel, and he's got some kind of dark clothing on. Then, the Silverado starts moving, slips out of the lot, and is gone. The schoolteacher rolls the scene around in her head for a second and thinks: I bet that truck is stolen.

Israel loses track of time. Suddenly there are sirens, police, ambulance. Bruno is a ghost on the ground and then people are loading him into an ambulance and taking him away, his relative riding in back with him.

María gets a call about the shooting back at the Men's Wearhouse. She goes out in the parking lot and finds Patricia still waiting impatiently in the car.

When she tells her, Patricia thinks to herself, "My honey is going to make it."

The police talk to about a dozen witnesses to the shooting in the K-Mart parking lot. They put out a description: a guy maybe five foot six wearing dark clothing. About two miles away, a squad car rolls down the street twenty minutes after the shooting. The two cops inside have heard the bulletin and they get alert. El Paso is a city of car thefts, not carjackings. And this one comes with a shooting. They see a kid on the sidewalk wearing dark clothes. The kid moves as if he notices the squad car and crosses over to the other side of the street. The cops are suspicious. So they wheel around, stop, and pick him up. He doesn't run or make any fuss. He's a Mexican kid, just turned thirteen, an illegal from Juárez named Miguel Angel Flores.

The cops put the kid in the rear seat and take him back to the K-Mart. They ask some of the witnesses if this is the shooter. There is a hesitation. Some say, yeah, he's the guy. Others say, no, it is not him. One witness insists the stolen teal Silverado is red. But this does not faze the cops. Witnesses always disagree, unless they've gotten together and cooked up a story. Besides, in El Paso publicly identifying someone can be risky. After all, just across the river, a drug cartel earns $200 million a week. In El Paso, there are hundreds of gangs. The city is a national center for car theft.

So the cops take the kid to the station house and there, several witnesses, now safe from public view, identify him. Renan Barroso comes with his father. He is frightened but he is sure as he identifies Flores. And he is finished with K-Mart. He has already quit his job in his head. He thinks if I go back, someone connected to this will come looking for me. Twice in the next twenty-four hours, Miguel Angel Flores allegedly blurts out to his jailers that he shot the guy. The truck itself and the weapon used do not turn up.

Yes, the bulldozer driver beams, yes, my machine turned up the body. Bernardo Rubio works in the dunes loading sand onto trucks. On November 16, 1994, he was working on the southern edge of Juárez when he turned up the body of Javier Lardizabal, thirty-three. In May 1993, Lardizabal, an investigator working for the Chihuahua attorney general's office, turned in a report ticking off ties between the police and drug dealers. He mentioned, among other matters, that one drug dealer in Juárez moved about the city with a police escort. The next day Lardizabal disappeared and remained out of sight until Rubio accidentally unearthed him.

Rubio is getting used to such surprises. Earlier, he'd turned up the corpse of Cuauhtémoc Ortiz, former head of the national security office in Juárez. Ortiz was found with a single dollar bill in his pocket. Amado Carrillo Fuentes was assumed to be behind the murder. The reporter busily makes notes for his Dallas newspaper when the bulldozer operator offers that perfect quote, "Every time I go to work I think I might find another body."

So far seven have turned up accidentally where he works.

Lardizabal's sister, Rosa María, struggles to have her brother's death investigated. She appeals to the president of Mexico, the governor of Chihuahua, the police. The Mexican police tell her they are understaffed and overwhelmed and can hardly afford to spend time on the case. She takes out a loan on her house and gives the police $8,000 to pay for an investigation but she believes they actually wind up doing nothing. Eventually, she loses her house.

She says, "This has to go on until justice is done."

And then she adds, "You have to live with fear."[6]

Sometimes the bodies turn up with yellow bows wrapped around their heads. DEA wonders if this means they arc being offered as gifts to the agency.

The family waits and waits for Bruno at the hospital. He is impossible. And no Patricia either. That's odd, since she tends to keep him in line and make him show up on time. After an hour or so, they give up. Grandma is still hanging on. Before Beatrice leaves the hospital, she turns to a relative and says, "Be sure and tell Bruno we waited."

They will check in the morning and see if she makes it through the night. When they swing onto the dead-end street where the house is, they find neighbors standing out front. What's going on, they think. They get out, talk to the neighbors and that is when they learn Bruno had been shot near the very hospital where they waited.

When they wheel Bruno in, he tells the nurse, "Tell my mom I will be all right." Later, he tells his nurse, "I don't want to die."

At first, it looks okay. He has taken two rounds from a 9mm but the doctors think they can stabilize him. He is a hearty twenty-seven-year-old with no bad habits.

The police crowd around where Bruno was shot. The spot is exactly 105 feet north and sixty feet west of the southwest corner of the K-Mart. Two rounds are on the ground spaced three to four feet apart. At exactly 8:56 P.M. on January 20, 1995, the atomic absorption test is made on the hands of the defendant Miguel Angel Flores. There are three elements (barium, antimony, and lead) to the test and Flores's results show two of them at a sufficient level to legally register. This means he more than likely has fired a gun. It also means the test cannot be used in court because all three elements must be present at a legally determined level to meet the standard for evidence. Barium and antimony are commonly found in fertilizers and paper products, and at any given moment about one percent of the American population will test positive for them.[7] The police never secure the crime scene and soon everything there is willy-nilly.

Phil Jordan is driving home from his son's high school basketball game in Plano, the rich suburb on the northern edge of Dallas. His wife and daughter have gone ahead in another car, and Jordan is following his ninth-grade son's bus in order to give him a ride home. He is concerned. He thinks his son has failed to concentrate in the game. For Phil, basketball is a religion. It got him that scholarship to a university and was his ticket out of the barrio in El Paso. He's a self-made man. He can pick up his car phone and call Ross Perot and Perot will take the call. Or he can call Senator Phil Gramm and get him on the line. For a decade he has headed the Dallas bureau of DEA. Starting Monday, he will run EPIC, the intelligence center for the U.S. global War on Drugs. He has the nice house in the rich suburb, the two kids from the second marriage. He can retire anytime he wants at close to his real salary. In fact, he tells himself he is working for two hundred bucks a month, since that is all he would lose if he pulled the pin at this very instant. But his mind is focused on the game, on missed opportunities, on a failure to concentrate. Jordan is the head of a drug-free basketball league in Texas. The game for him is life itself. He has never smoked a cigarette, taken a drug, or been drunk. Not once.

Concentration has been his salvation. It translated him from Felipe Jordan in El Paso to Phillip Jordan in Dallas. But tonight, my God, his son's team had a twenty-point lead at the half and let it slip away. The game was supposed to be a lock and they've blown it. Concentrate, damn it, concentrate. Jordan remembers a practice when he was in college when another starter showed up with beer on his breath. He couldn't believe it. It doesn't matter how good you are, you can't give up that much of an edge to anybody. Concentrate. Just like tonight. He'd sat there quietly, his face a blank, but inside he'd thought: this is a game you shouldn't lose for any reason. He's going to have to have a hard talk with his son about tonight.

Basketball has been his great teacher in life. It is a team sport and it is a sport of movement, a fluid and beautiful thing. He took to it early, he grew to the size, six foot three, that allowed him to dream of a career in the sport. In high school, he played center-forward. In the college game, he was a guard-forward but essentially a playmaking guard. And what he learned is deceit, fraud, fakery. Basketball is not simply about points, but about moves and the key to every move is to make the other player go the wrong way, look the wrong way, think the wrong way, to destroy balance in the other player and leave him floundering, flat-footed and out of the real play. The basket itself is merely recognition of the game, of this fraud perpetrated. Even the eyes. He had to teach his eyes not to give away his moves, not to reveal his thoughts. Baseball is stand around and wait for your chance at bat. That's why players are dismissed for being all glove and no bat. Football is about muscle, forget the chalkboard plays, the bullshit laterals, it is muscle. Beat the other guy up, knock him out of position, trample him under your feet. But basketball is about moves and all the moves are deceptions. He has never left basketball, and for years has coached and led leagues, a way to keep kids off drugs, a way to teach sound habits, a way to induct people into a special way of thinking, a world where left means right, up means down, the feint for a shot turns into a lightning pass. In basketball no one ever knows what you are thinking until it is too late. And that is the sweet part. Moving from basketball to DEA was as simple as changing courts, leaving regular league play for pickup games in the street.

The phone rings. It's his wife, Debbie, and she says, "Your mom just called. Bruno's been shot—he's alive, he's talking." Jordan hangs up. He thinks it must have been a drive-by and Bruno accidentally got caught in the crossfire. That has to be it. Or maybe it's that store where he works, maybe someone came in and tried to rob it. And then he thinks: no one in his family has ever been shot. We're not that kind of people. Besides, he knows his brother. Bruno would never risk his life for the money in his wallet or for his car. He'd just hand over whatever anyone demanded. And then Phil Jordan thinks one other thing: that the shooting has something to do with him. He swiftly erases this thought from his mind. But it lingers. He accelerates. And he can't concentrate at all.

Things blur once he pulls into his driveway. He is used to giving commands, to being in control. He runs other agents, has secretaries, takes care of his informants. He lives a life where other people do what he tells them to do. He starts manning the phone as if he were in his DEA office. Calls the hospital, gets through, his brother is in surgery, he'll be out in a while. Then his sister Virginia calls, tells him again Bruno has been shot, that he's in surgery right now. Then she puts a detective on the line who tells Jordan it is a carjacking and they already have the shooter. Carjacking? Jordan can't imagine one in sleepy El Paso. The detective is rattling on, something about a dark truck following the Silverado into the parking lot, about a kid jumping out and shooting, and the police have an idea who owns that dark truck and drove, this guy they know who knows all the street kids. They're going to look him up, you can be sure of it.

Jordan is in the kitchen of his ranch-style home, the fluorescent lights making everything white, the counter cluttered with stuff, his son's iguana on his tree limb down near the breakfast table. The house is large, got the family room with bar, a hallway lined with bedrooms, the big living room. It is neutral, as if it came packaged from some safe place. The house is Jordan's security blanket. He lost his first home in that divorce and he does not intend to ever let that happen to him again. He's firm on family and this one is going to stay together and the house is going to stay in his hands.

Jordan stands, he keeps dialing numbers, hitting all those police connections he's piled up over the years, getting a short course in shootings, checking back in El Paso with the local police. He is almost hypnotized by the phone. Calling calms him. He is doing an investigation. He is on the familiar ground of thirty years of making cases. He is safe.

And he is ignorant. He doesn't do murders, he does drug busts. He doesn't know anything about car thefts either. In fact, he's a very limited cop, trained to handle one kind of case, drugs. And in this specialty, he pretty much does one thing: buys. Cut the deal, have the stuff on the table, then make the collar. He doesn't get into forensic evidence or detailed financial investigations or fences or ballistics. Or chop shops. Just dope deals.

Debbie watches and wants to help. She is the second wife, Anglo just like the first one, and El Paso is a place where she visits her in-laws but it feels almost like a foreign country to her. She is not Catholic. She speaks no Spanish. She can't keep straight the hundreds of relatives in the Jordan family. And now, as her husband works the phone, she is shut out. He has taken Bruno's shooting into his police world and that is a world she only knows by grunts or nods when she asks him questions. That is when he is home and most of the time he is gone. And half the time when he is gone, she doesn't even know where. If he tells her, she only half believes him. She goes down the hall to her son, Kenny's, room and sits with him. Kenny spends part of his summers in El Paso and for him Bruno is less an uncle than a buddy. They decide to walk to the nearby Catholic church, St. Elizabeth's, and light a candle.

They don't know quite how to do it, but they sense it is what people should do in such moments.

When they get back, Jordan is still on the phone. He's checking with the hospital, he's booking a flight on an airline. He is tracking down his two grown children from his first marriage, Sean and Brigitte.

They share the uselessness that comes with waiting for someone in surgery. Beatrice speaks as if nothing has happened. She fights the fear she has felt for weeks, ever since the reading of the cards. Virginia works the phone reaching out to family members. Antonio keeps saying, "Don't worry, don't worry. Everything will be okay."

As Bruno awaits surgery he suddenly begins choking and says to his nurses, "Please help me, I can't breathe."

After they get him clear again, he says, "Thank you."

He remains invincibly good-natured.

Then he says again, "Don't let me die."

Brigitte, Phil's daughter from his first marriage, feels like she has just gotten back to her own home in Tucson, hardly settled into her own bed. She's spent two weeks in El Paso with Bruno and her grandparents on Frutas Street, been there kind of taking stock of her life and trying to figure things out. She'd hung out with Bruno a lot, and with his friend Albert. They'd been together on the basketball team together in high school, though Albert had been the big star.

In the evening, her grandfather Antonio would teach them card tricks, and then later Bruno would pull the tricks on his fiancée, Patricia, just to dazzle her. She never could catch on just how the trick was done, and she'd get kind of flustered by it all. And then Brigitte and Albert drifted into a thing together. It wasn't serious. Just once. But it was that kind of a two weeks.

She remembered one night just before she left, they were sitting in the house on Frutas Street and it was shut up tight as a drum against the winter night. Suddenly, Brigitte, Bruno, and Albert felt this strong cold draft and it was like it came out of nowhere and it felt eerie. They all commented on it. And then when she was leaving, her grandmother said, "You'll be back in two weeks."

And that kind of stunned Brigitte. But she was used to her grandmother saying strange and prophetic things. She'd learned to pay attention to these statements.

Then, that night in Tucson, the phone rings and it is her father and he tells her about Bruno. She suddenly remembers the cold draft and her grandmother's prediction.

The slide is scratched and has never been published. The photographer makes this clear. It is taken some months before Bruno is shot in that parking lot. In the image, a man stands with his shirt half opened in an office. He is the center of attention even though he seems to show his contempt for the room by his dark sunglasses. Every eye in the room is upon him and there is this circle, this space right around the man, that no one appears willing to violate. He is called El Greñas, Mop-Top, for his carelessness about his grooming. In front of El Greñas a man in a suit stands behind his desk. His head is ever so slightly bent forward as a sign of respect. The slide is snapped inside a Mexican prison on the edge of Juárez. The man behind the desk is the warden of the prison. The man in the sunglasses, El Greñas, is an underboss of the Juárez cartel who has been incarcerated. He is technically the convict.

Sean, Phil's son from that first marriage, is a hotshot at selling musical instruments. Once he and his Uncle Tony were at a gas station filling up and Tony watched as Sean made a sale to a perfect stranger right there at the pumps. He thought, this kid is a natural. Sean is in L.A. for a trade show. He got there Thursday and it's in Anaheim at the Civic Center, right by Disneyland. Nothing but musical manufacturers and, naturally, they ply guys like Sean with free dinners and drinks, with invitations to swell parties. Friday is a workday. He gets up at seven, has breakfast, catches the bus at eight, and then starts hitting meetings and making buys. He's the manager of his store and is number one in the chain year after year. And that's just a sideline in his mind, since composing music is his real life. About noon, he eats right across the street from Disneyland and has a Reuben sandwich and a couple of beers. Everything is normal, the world is fine. He can look out and see the Magic Kingdom. He's thinking about the fine, hot parties the manufacturers are gonna put on that Friday night. But first he's got a dinner engagement at an exclusive restaurant, the thing paid for by a manufacturer because he buys so much from the guy.

But by late in the day, he's feeling kind of sick. It's raining outside, it's six o'clock, he's not in the mood to drink. He decides to limit his evening a little, skip any hard partying, and around eight sits down to eat lobster, prawns, and steak. His cell phone rings and it's his sister, Brigitte.

She asks, "Are you busy?"

And he says, "Yes," but what he's thinking is: why in the hell is she calling him on his cell phone in Anaheim when she hardly ever calls him when he's home in Phoenix? And hell, this is an important trade show, this is business.

He lets his irritation show.

Brigitte says, "Hey, I'll just call you back."

But Sean is curious and says, "What's up?"

She pulls away, saying, "No, no, no, I can tell you're busy. I'll just call you back."

"What in the hell is going on? You never call me at home and you're calling me in Anaheim?"

"Bruno's been shot."

"What?"

"Yeah, Bruno's been shot. He's okay, he's been shot a couple of times in the stomach at a K-Mart. His friend drove him to the hospital and he's talking and he's gonna be fine. He's talking."

Sean thinks, Holy shit! He's freaking out. He doesn't want to accept what she says. He thinks to himself, I'll give Bruno a call in the morning at the hospital, tell him a joke like the soup must be coming out, you know because he's shot in the belly.

Friday started out great for Phil's brother Tony. He bought a set of golf clubs, a tour model. Then he went out and hit some balls, got the feel of the new clubs. He's living in Las Vegas, and golf is his life. That afternoon he went and picked up the wife and someone cut him off in traffic and he got furious, was going to go up and tell the other driver off. But something made Tony hesitate. Maybe it was the mellow feeling from the golf, anyway, he swallowed his anger and continued on to the hotel where his wife works, and took her home. That evening, he and his wife and his wife's sister are all there. The sister takes care of his three-year-old son when his wife works her shift and Tony is just about to begin his graveyard turn in the counting room of a casino.

Phil calls, "Tony, Tony listen, listen to me good, some cholo just shot Bruno and took his truck."

"Shot Bruno!"

"He's in the operating room, he's okay. They're operating on him right now. But I don't want you to get excited. He's doing okay."

"Where did they shoot him?"

"They shot him right in the back I think. In the upper body."

"Those wounds to the body are very dangerous. There could be bleeding."

"Yes, I know. But I want you to maintain. I'll keep you informed of what's happening."

After Tony hangs up, Sean calls from L.A. and he asks, "Man, what is happening?"

The bullet wounds in Bruno at first seem manageable. No major organs seem damaged, the vital signs are good. But the initial diagnosis is deceptive. The two rounds entered the body and then wandered at high velocity, shredding him inside. The 9mm is a favored round in the drug business. The cartridges are small, so a clip in even a pistol can hold a dozen or more. The high velocity means a small bullet can wreak enormous havoc. As the staff fusses over Bruno Jordan, he is slowly bleeding to death. He dies in surgery at 9:45 P.M.

A call slips through Jordan's constant dialing. It is Virginia. He listens as his wife and son stand nearby watching him. Suddenly, he shouts, "No, no, no." He barks at his sister, "It can't be. Go back and make sure." He hands the phone to Debbie and smashes his fist into the kitchen cabinet. He turns to his son and tells him his Uncle Bruno is dead, and Kenny, fourteen, begins to sob. His daughter Kelly goes down the hall to her room and shuts the door. Then his mother, Beatrice, is on the line and keeps repeating that Bruno will be all right. His father refuses to come to the phone.

Tony calls in to the casino and says he won't be coming to work tonight. He sits in his apartment praying, and praying. Pacing up and down, pacing up and down. He is in shock, his wife tries to calm him. Then after about an hour, Phil calls and asks Tony how he thinks he should handle Sean. The brothers confer, they both know that Sean can fly off the handle. After that, Virginia calls. She is crying.

"Tony! Tony! Did Phil tell you?"

"No."

"He's gone."

"No, No. It can't be. Nooooooooooooo."

His mind races. This cannot be, he thinks. No, nooooooo. Not Bruno.

His wife looks at him. He is crying.

She asks, "What's happening?"

He starts praying even harder: "God, take care of him. I know he is with you."

He is not ready for this. He remembers back in '87 or '88, he was singing in Mexico down along the border with Guatemala. One day, a plane dropped a load of coke on an Indian village. Nobody there knew what it was or how it came to fall out of the sky. The Indians, Tony remembers, used the coke to make white lines on their ball field.

But Tony can't be that innocent. He knows what this is. He knows what it means when things fall from the sky in El Paso. He was raised there.

He thinks, it must have something to do with Phil.

A priest is in the hospital waiting room with the family when the doctors tell them Bruno Jordan is dead. He takes them home. Antonio walks into his house and sits down in a chair in the living room. He speaks to no one, not even his wife. A faint smile plays across his lips. No one disturbs him. No one wants to know what lurks behind his silence.

The light is on in Bruno's room. His Washington Redskins pennant hangs on the wall.

Beatrice keeps speaking of Bruno in the present tense. No one says anything about this. No one knows what to do now.

On November 27, 1994, they find José Refugio Ruvalcaba, fifty-nine, with his two sons, César and Alberto. Ruvalcaba is a former state police comandante with thirty-two years of service. The three bodies are found in the trunk of a 1991 Honda Accord. They have been beaten, strangled, and stabbed. The car is parked exactly midway on the bridge linking Juárez to El Paso. U.S. Customs recalls the car passing as it left El Paso. Both nations deny jurisdiction and so no one investigates the triple homicide.

The father had a yellow rope tied around his head. A big bow flowers out of his mouth.

His widow has three other children living and says she cannot understand the murder. Her husband was in law enforcement. A surviving son flips through a scrapbook of his father's career and there are all these photographs of his father posing with El Paso officials at the parties he would throw for them. But the son says that since the murders, no U.S. officials have ever called.

Phil Jordan is one of those U.S. officials who never called. From about 1985 through 1992, Jordan ran the Dallas bureau of DEA and in those years El Paso was part of his kingdom. He'd meet with Ruvalcaba, have dinner, talk. They'd meet in an office in El Paso, or in restaurants or parking lots in Juárez. The comandante was courteous, friendly, and serious. He had little tidbits for DEA. He was an encyclopedia of the Juárez cartel and in time an expert on Amado Carrillo. And he liked to come to El Paso to dine, in fact one place he liked to eat was at Phil Jordan's aunt's restaurant, a place called Forti's.[8]

The border is not so cut-and-dried. Things commingle. Ruvalcaba could glean information from his conversations with DEA that he could take back across the bridge. And the flow could go north also. Anyone can be more than one person.

Lines can go anywhere, dots can always be connected. Phil's aunt who owns the restaurant has a brother in prison. DEA sent him there. Phil's brother Tony had these relationships and problems. And then there is the stuff Sean got into. The mind can splinter into little pieces if it focuses on this kind of thing.

Anyone can be more than one person.

Phil Jordan knows this.

His grandfather taught him that much.

Jesus, Sal Martínez feels good. He's been intent on smelling all the roses lately. He can still feel the fear rise in his gorge when he thinks about that moment two weeks ago in Juárez. Then he pushes that thought away, locks it up in a compartment in his head.

He's spent his entire adult life as a cop and he loves the work. He loves being the man, carrying the gun. He comes from a belief in country that is absolute. When he was a kid in the barrio in El Paso, the neighbors would get irked at his grandmother Felipa, who lived in a little cottage in the family backyard. On September 16, Mexican Independence Day, almost everyone he knew hoisted up the Mexican flag in celebration. His grandmother refused and, my God, she'd been born in Mexico. She always flew the American flag on that day. The neighbors would ask her, "Felipa, why?" She'd say, "Because this is where my hunger ended."

Crazy, Sal thinks, these old people come from a different planet. But today is a good day to be alive. He can feel the rush of it all. Today is his wedding anniversary and so he and his wife have been celebrating with a good meal, champagne, the works. It goes perfectly, it being a Friday and all. Now they're back home and he kicks back and flicks on the evening news and there is something about a shooting and carjacking. He doesn't catch any names. That's odd, he thinks, a carjacking and shooting in El Paso. Car theft is like weather in El Paso, but not carjackings, those are things that happen in big cities like Dallas. And why would someone shoot to steal a car when they are boosted every day in El Paso as if the keys were left in them. No one has ever been shot in a carjacking in El Paso. Then the phone rings. He learns that the person shot has died. And that person is Bruno Jordan, his cousin.

Sal falls back. He is thirty-two years old, and he's known Bruno since childhood. His mother is Antonio's sister. He thinks, how can this happen? For Christsake, the guy just sells fucking suits.

Sal is one of Phil's little secrets. He is a DEA agent but Phil keeps the fact that they are cousins under wraps. He figures that if the kinship is known, it will just make life more difficult for Sal. Phil helped get him into DEA but after that, he has kept his hand hidden.

Sal's passion lies across the river in Juárez. He operates undercover there, sometimes alone. He is obsessed with one person: Amado Carrillo, the head of the Juárez cartel. Four times, Sal has almost been killed, and the last time, two weeks ago, was much too close. He barely made it back alive to El Paso.

And for what? His own agency officially doesn't admit he is even working over there. Much less carrying guns, operating undercover, and hanging out with lowlifes at all hours. He's chasing a goddamn phantom. No one even knows exactly how old Carrillo is. Or where he was born. Or what he looks like. DEA has some pictures but they don't even look like the same guy, much less prove that they are the face of Amado. Christ, some of the intelligence says Carrillo is a country bumpkin who speaks bad Spanish. And some of the reports say he is a college graduate. Sal has been in these meetings in the bad bars in Juárez and a bunch of the drug guys will be there and he'll look around the room and wonder is he that one or that one? But he can never be sure. He can't even be sure if the guy who's running things is really the person in charge. No one will even say Carrillo's name out loud. It never appears in the Juárez daily papers, or on the Juárez radio stations, or on the television. Carrillo has reached an arrangement with all media. He has offered them a customary choice: *plata o plomo,* silver or lead. He often moves surrounded by federal police. He carries credentials for the federal police that describe him as the leader of the special investigations section. He has a gold-colored federale badge also.[9] He lives in many houses. Sal's got lots of notes on all this stuff but he doesn't know which parts of his notes are true. Or if any of them are.

Carrillo is a secret, just as Sal is a secret. Carrillo is unknown outside of narc circles and even in those circles they have a hard time believing he exists at times. Then, they will find evidence. Carrillo has this thing about security. When he loses a load, he suspects everyone connected with that load. So everyone dies. The police will find some bodies littering the streets and the newspapers will comment on a settling of accounts, a culling of the herd. Mainly, the bodies were not found at all after Carrillo took over but vanished into secret grave sites around the city. But of course, Carrillo's name is never mentioned. No more than Sal's name is mentioned after hundreds of drug busts. Nor is his photograph ever in the newspapers. He does the buy, makes the bust, and then kind of vanishes. Can't really talk to many people about his work. He keeps his wife, Suzie, pretty much in the dark too. He'll get up, smile, have some coffee and head down to the office. He doesn't mention crossing the bridge to Juárez. She still doesn't know anything about that incident two weeks ago. But why tell her? She'll just get upset. Besides, the more people know about what you are up to, the more likely you are to get murdered.

That is the other world, the one kept separate from wedding anniversaries and family barbecues and mass on Sunday. But now Sal feels something breaking inside him as he absorbs the news of Bruno's murder. A fucking salesman, killed?

He reaches back to a place he feels comfortable, to a memory of being free and in control. He is riding his motorcycle coming back from San Antonio on the interstate. A big storm rolls in with sheets of rain. The trucks throw up walls of water obliterating him on the bike. He ratchets the machine up to ninety, pulls over to pass, accelerates toward the wall of water thrown up by the truck's wheels, hits it blind and slams through, not a wobble or a skid. Roars on down the road. He is okay at those moments on the bike in the thunderstorms of the night.

But he is not okay now.

•   •   •

Jordan talks to his son Sean again around midnight. He is careful because he knows his son is not at home but at some business thing in Los Angeles. Sean has been the problem child who drifted into drugs, and then for a while simply vanished from the family. He violates Jordan's sense of order and discipline. And he makes Jordan feel guilty about his divorce, about being the absentee father living in a distant city with a different wife. So, he thinks he'd better be careful tonight, not get his son upset when he is all alone in a strange city.

Jordan asks, "Hey, do you think you can make it to El Paso tomorrow morning?"

Sean says, "I think you're fucking right, sure I'll be there."

And then Sean asks, "Is Bruno okay?"

"Yeah," Jordan replies. "Everything is all right, but it'll be good if you can be there."

And then he hangs up. Like all DEA agents, Jordan is an accomplished liar. It is part of the job. He lies daily and without effort. If he calls his folks and they ask where he is, he just lies about the matter. They finally got a caller ID device for their phone so that they could actually know where he was. He can talk to people for hours and never actually say anything. Somehow in conversations he never actually answers a question but always manages to get the answers he wants. He is a fair-skinned man, and he passes in the anglo world of Dallas without an effort. He will go days without speaking Spanish and he knows people for years without giving a clue that he is from the barrio. Everything in his life is a double, or triple identity.

Including his name Phillip. On his birth certificate it is Felipe.

About 3:00 A.M. Antonio and Beatrice and Virginia and her husband, Isaac, are sitting in the house on Frutas Street. Beatrice cannot stop crying. Antonio can find nothing to say. The house almost sinks under the weight of silence. Suddenly, all four of them hear the jingle of keys at the door, a key going into the lock, the sound Bruno makes every night when he comes home.

And then, nothing.

• • •

For six years, from 1988 to 1994, two things characterize American coverage of Mexico: that Harvard-educated Carlos Salinas de Gortari is the future. And that Amado Carrillo is all but invisible and not fit to print. Salinas has achieved NAFTA and broken Mexico out of its isolation and tied it to the United States economy. During the campaign for U.S. congressional passage of NAFTA in the fall of 1993, Phil Jordan, along with the rest of the DEA agents concerned with Mexico, was told to keep his mouth shut about the links between the drug business and the Mexican government. In 1994, Salinas's partisans spent over $700 million—in a country where at least half the population lives in poverty—electing the next president and congress of what was at that moment the world's oldest continuously ruling party.

Salinas during 1994 plots his new career move when his six-year presidency ends that December. He is a leading candidate to direct the new World Trade Organization. He is one of the new masters of the universe, part of the group that grasps the new global unity of commerce. Within a week of his departure from office, he is giving a major address to policymakers in Washington, D.C., on the future of the world. He looks very serious and the applause rings out. He is the man who brought Mexico into the modern world.

Jordan sits alone through the night with his phone. The phone becomes the touchstone that convinces him he is doing something and making sense of what has happened. He checks in with his police connections. In El Paso, the cops tell him about a car theft ring that operates in the city and feeds the vehicles into Juárez. The cops can smell the ring's hand in this shooting and now that they've got the shooter, they're confident the kid will lead them right into the organization. The organization, the cops say, operates out of the Mexican consulate in El Paso, takes regular orders, and caters to the needs of the elite in Mexico City. To Jordan, it sounds like a done deal and he thinks they may wrap up this case in a few hours.

Still, he cannot make any sense of it. He is out of his league and he knows it. He does drug deals. He wears a suit, gains the trust of others, flashes money, and then when the other person believes him, he betrays the guy and arrests him. He has done this for years, in various U.S. cities and in Mexico. He has sent hundreds of people to prison for thousands of years and a lot of them never even learned his real name.

Late in the night, he has an El Paso cop on the phone and the cop says matter-of-factly, "Your brother was killed in cold blood."

This brings him up short. He does not like hearing something said out loud that has been ringing in his head for hours.

Jordan can't make sense of the murder. His brother did not do drugs. His brother did not hang out with lowlifes. His brother was so clean he squeaked. Cold blood? Jordan can't connect his brother to his world or to gangs. He knows his brother would never resist a carjacking, he can see him if someone pointed a gun and wanted that damn truck. Bruno would just hand over the keys instantly, with a look that said, hey, no problem.

But a thought keeps coming back and it hammers Jordan hour after hour. Bruno is dead because of him. Some bust he was in on, some killing he winked at, something he once said. Something he once did. Jordan's DEA career has been in stations facing Mexico—Albuquerque, Phoenix, Dallas—and now this assignment at EPIC. He's nailed down an indictment of Carrillo, the head of the Juárez cartel. He was in on the original case in the 1970s that tried to maim the original cartel, that first cell from which all the drug organizations grew. And he was in on that killing, in with a wink and a nod. He brushes this aside. It is all gauze in his mind, vague. Not like a case file with those discrete acts that are predicates to an indictment. He can't make it work, can't make it cross the river. But still the thought hammers him, hour after hour after hour. This is a payback, some kind of vengeance. But why? And then in tired moments, he realizes what a hall of mirrors he lives in and lies about. How he cannot seem to easily tell little truths, tell his parents where he is, even tell his own son that his Uncle Bruno has just died. And the work, well, the work is lots of lying.

He is going to El Paso to take over EPIC because for one brief instant his predecessor bluntly told the press, "Mexico is corrupt to the core." Boom, the guy was removed and Jordan was on his way. And now he will run an intelligence center in a city that stares at a cartel earning $200 million a week.

There was this moment a few years back that summed up the tissue of lies that Jordan lives within. He'd set up a good program at the Dallas–Fort Worth Airport, made every ticket agent and baggage clerk part of his hunt. He had them go on their instincts about customers, and for any tip that paid off, they got a cut of the money. Busts zoomed up. Basically, Jordan had harnessed the street smarts that any good waitress in a truck stop possesses. In 1992, a flight came in from Miami. The guy acted wrong. They took him down and he had $28 million in fifties and hundreds on him, eight duffel bags full of cash. DEA never even had time to count the money, the guy had blurted out the $28 million figure. Then Jordan got a call from Washington and the voice said, cut the guy loose and let the money go on its way. That's all. The caller was a high official in the Justice Department. And Jordan did as he was told. He thought he'd caught a whiff off the tail of the outfit, the CIA, someone like that. The guy with the cash said it was BCCI money, that funny bank out of Pakistan with two members of the Medellín cartel on its board. Hardly matters for Jordan, he takes the call from D.C. and does as he is ordered. And then, the silence. Jordan didn't tell anyone of the call or the bust or about giving the money back. He didn't pursue what it was really about.

The money is too big for Jordan to keep it clear in his mind. He tries to focus on his turf out of Dallas, where he is a baron with his patch of the kingdom. But once he gets into the cash flow of the industry his head spins. The State Department's Bureau of Intelligence and Research sends out this analysis of cocaine money: the leaf in Peru costs $650; by the time the labs have processed a kilo in Colombia the bill is $1,050; on arrival in Miami, the weight is now worth $23,000; by Chicago a kilo wholesales for $33,000; by ounce weight in Chicago, the kilo mushrooms to $188,000.[10] He'll look at these calculations but they never stick. They are too big to have a reality. And no pressure he applies really cuts into the money. This damn study out of the State Department puts forth this proposition: a pilot flies 250 kilos for a fee of $500,000. That only adds $2,000 to the per-kilo cost, 2 percent of the retail price on the street. Lose the whole plane to seizure after say one flight, that is just another $2,000 per kilo, another 2 percent.

Mexico just makes everything more efficient in this study. Moving a load across the 1,800-mile-border is dirt cheap. Peddling the stuff on the street also has low risk. The State Department study figures the chances of prison for a dealer making a quarter-gram sale are about one in three thousand. The chances of getting killed per unit run about one in seventy thousand. Jordan just has to think of the assholes he's busted to know these risks will never register in their calculus. And besides, the damn numbers they shove at him are all fake. In 1987, the experts tell all the agents like Jordan that Mexico is growing 5,700 tons of marijuana. Two years later, they claim the crop is 47,000 tons. Who can pay attention to this bullshit?

He fights something called the War on Drugs but he doesn't ask hard questions. It is a system, the justice system, and he is a believer. He has trained himself to keep things in their compartments. He keeps El Paso in a separate box from Dallas. He keeps the job isolated from the family. He keeps his thoughts separate from his words. He lives as his grandfather taught him to live, in a world where a man has many lives but only shows the life he wishes to have seen.

He keeps returning from this confusion of policies and information to the safe reality of building cases, noting discrete acts for indictments, cashing his check every two weeks. Lying to his folks over the phone. Living inside a puzzle and only dealing with the little pieces that fall into his own hands.

Jordan talks to himself in his mind and what he tells himself is simple: "My Bruno has this personality—you couldn't get him mad or riled. He never says anything bad about anybody."

And he is dead and there is no way to explain his cold-blooded murder. And it has to be cold-blooded because he knows his brother would never resist, would never try to be a hero. There is just no way he can explain to himself why Bruno is dead.

Except one way.

And Phillip Jordan does not want to go there. Nor does Felipe.

At 3:00 A.M. he finally tries to sleep. But the effort is useless.
He gets the first flight out of Dallas at 8:00 A.M.

Tony gets up about eight thinking he's got to get home to El Paso. He
takes a flight and then goes to the house. Two thoughts tumble
around in his mind: will his mother survive this blow and how to find
and kill those who murdered his brother. His father is almost mute,
he sits there brooding and has fallen inside of himself. The day begins
to blur for Tony. Phil's older daughter, Brigitte, is there, and they sit
at a table just off the kitchen in the big den where the television
squats. And they're talking about how could this happen, and my
God, Bruno, and how is he now? And where is he? Suddenly Tony
looks over at the television and sees the hanging lamp over it swaying
back and forth and back and forth. This isn't L.A., he thinks, there are
no earthquakes here, and yet in a perfectly still room inside the house
where he was raised on Frutas Street the lamp is swinging freely.
There's fifty or sixty of his kinfolk in the house and everyone is talking
and murmuring and weeping and he sees this lamp swaying and he
says, "Brigitte, Brigitte, look, look, it's Bruno telling us he's okay."
She looks and sees the lamp moving and is hypnotized. Tony calls his
mother, come, come here right now, and she does and he points to the
lamp and she looks and then with her glance, the lamp calms and
becomes still. Tony thinks, he's telling us he is all right, that he is in a
good place.

By Saturday morning, María's ex-boyfriend has allegedly gotten a
lawyer. Or so the Jordan family later hears. The cops have not talked to
him yet. Normally, he comes by María's father's house and drops off a
newspaper. But today, he never shows.

Sean meets his father at the El Paso airport and as they embrace
Jordan can feel in his son's body that he knows. He looks at him and
says, "He's gone." They walk past news racks headlining Bruno's murder. When they get in the car, Sean starts crying and then Phil starts
crying. Sean has never seen his father weep before. Sean wants to go

directly to the morgue and see his cousin, but his father tells him no. He tells his son he has to be strong for his grandmother.

At the family home on Frutas Street, Phil Jordan senses an unreality. His mother speaks of Bruno in the present tense. His father is out in back picking up tin cans and when he finally walks into the house he says nothing, nothing at all. And then he breaks and for the first time in his life Sean sees his grandfather cry. There are relatives and food has been brought in. As Jordan enters El Paso he becomes Felipe. Once in the house, he is Nono, grandfather in Italian, his childhood nickname.

The house breathes like a living thing. In the front room looms a baby grand piano with family pictures displayed on the closed lid—my God, there is Virginia when she was a beauty queen, there is Bruno on the high school basketball team. The walls feel cool. Off to one side, a row of bedrooms, all interconnected, and in Bruno's room, the sports pennants blaze on the wall and now, on a corner table, there is a candle burning. And a glass of water. The living room flows into the kitchen and this flows into the big room with the chairs and couches and television behind the blank back wall, the tracks where the rumble of passing trains vibrates through the house, day and night. Beatrice lights a candle the day after the murder so that her Bruno would not be cold. She put out a glass of water so that her Bruno would not be thirsty. Now, as the house fills with people, the water goes down dramatically.

He cannot stand it. He is useless, and in the family home he is expected to be useful. There is an unspoken thing in the air and it tells him, fix this. He is the oldest son. Fix this. And there is another thing, one even more silent: you are the reason Bruno is dead. You brought your world to this home. The rooms feel not so much planned as connected, an assembly much like the family itself. And the kitchen centers everything, the room where something is always on the stove, scents always in the air. Out front facing the street, a small smear of green lawn crouches next to a flowerbed. The bridge to Mexico begins rising a half block away, now as always clogged with traffic. Across the street, empty lots, industrial buildings. The air full of exhaust fumes and noise. The house is an island of calm trapped between the railroad and din of traffic in and out of Juárez. And no matter how often Jordan returns to his family's home, he cannot quite describe it. It is physical and yet it is not rooms or floor plans, it has this loose and almost elastic feeling like the huge extended family in El Paso that will claim him and pull him into a deep embrace if he should so much as pause for just a second.

Felipe Jordan never dared to try a cigarette because he feared one of his many uncles might see him and tell his father. His brother Tony is in from Las Vegas where he works in a casino. For years Tony traveled Latin America as a singer with the stage name of Tony Solo. He has hung out with gangsters, run a nightclub, had his times with cocaine. But he is still, even in his forties, hesitant to drink a beer in his father's presence.

Jordan looks at the old walls. He thinks back to when he was ten, maybe eleven or twelve. His grandfather is hosting a party. The family house is surrounded by the junkyard. It is in a no-man's-land near the tracks, a splash of ground between Barrio Segundo and Barrio Diablo but independent of any barrio, a turf without a name. There are a hundred people, two hundred. The band, five or ten guys with a black singer, is playing swing and now and then flings itself into deeper jazz. The afternoon melts into night and the party rages on. Tables of food, sausages, spaghetti, all kinds of Mexican food, meats alongside the Italian dishes. There is an open bar of wine and liquor and beer. The police are here, the leading politicians. El Paso throbs before his eyes. His grandfather circulates. He is not in a suit, he never wears a suit. But he dresses well, good slacks, crisp shirt. A pocket with a big wad of cash. The junkman. Someone comes in his store and maybe he has something worth a hundred dollars that he wants to sell. And his grandfather, the original Nono, looks at it coldly and offers ten. The man is disappointed, more than disappointed, angry, and he wheels around and leaves. Felipe's grandfather is unconcerned, and goes back about his business. A block, maybe a half a block from the store, the man offering the item for sale, he stops, he thinks, and he comes back and takes the ten dollars for the thing worth a hundred. Felipe's grandfather is always gracious in such moments. He never argues. He offers. That is all. He offers. He is the junkman, the man who has a store that buys and sells used things, old furniture, appliances, whatever. Sometimes the boy sees Italians come into the store, and then, all conversation hurls itself into Italian. Sometimes neighborhood people come in, they have problems, they talk to his grandfather. He says he will see. Now, tonight, the party is on, the police are here, the big guys, the pols, everyone is here in the junkyard near the river separating Mexico from the United States. The black singer offers up some scat. Music, food. Years later, when Nono becomes Felipe and Felipe disappears and becomes Phillip, he will see a movie called *The Godfather*, and those parties will suddenly come rushing back into his mind as he sits in the theater. Phil Jordan searches his mind, and he can never recall one instance, one second when his grandfather was indecisive. Not one. The walls close in, his mother is weeping, his father is someone he hardly knows, suddenly his father is an old man sobbing. Bruno is dead.

Jordan can feel something almost strangling him. He is back in the world he left, a world where Spanish is heard more than English, where the Rio Grande is five blocks away. Bruno's room is suddenly a shrine, a candle burning and a glass of water set by it. His parents have already found a burial plot in a cemetery a few blocks away. This way he will be close to home, they explain.

But this unspoken thing is the loudest thing in the hubbub of the house. Suzie, Sal's wife, is there helping out and she senses also an unreality in the family. She thinks the Jordans have not dealt with death, have not had enough problems. That they have lived as if they were exempt from tragedy, and now, with a son murdered, they are helpless. They cannot face the facts.

For Phil Jordan the problem is not a denial of death but of the consequences of the death. He is supposed to do something. He is supposed to avenge the death. He is supposed to find justice for the family. Not because he is a cop. But because he is Felipe. He cannot take it for one more minute. He sweeps up his son and his brother Tony and heads out to a pancake house.

When they enter the restaurant they run into María. Jordan embraces her and says, "Please, don't feel guilty."

• • •

That night Tony sleeps in Bruno's room—the walls festooned with pennants, and Redskins paraphernalia, a tick Bruno caught from Tony, who was determined to be the one guy in El Paso who did not root for the Dallas Cowboys. As he lies there, Tony thinks about it all and searches his own life and can't come up with anything he'd done that might lead to a hit, and he knows Bruno was as clean as a whistle. So that leaves Phil. It must have something to do with Phil and all the DEA stuff he's done. That looks like the reason to Tony.

And as he drifts toward sleep, he thinks about his family. The Jordan curse, yep, that's it, that's what the family jokingly calls it. His dad, he's so easygoing, God, the only time he's ever really seen him angry in that visible way, was when Christina, Tony's older sister, ran off and got married when she was sixteen. He cried then, it really hurt him. But Antonio, his father, has got this thing. He's not like his mom, she's real emotional. She lives in a world of mishaps and inattention. She has to put a glass of water in the center of a table to make sure it won't spill. His dad can set the glass right on the edge of the table, and someone will say, hey, watch out, the glass of water might get knocked off the table, and he'll say, the water? Oh, it's okay there. That's the way he is, careful, methodical, balanced.

Except when it comes to his family. If someone messes with them, or hurts them, he doesn't forget, no matter how long, and he gets back at whoever hurt his family. And he doesn't care about the price. If someone hurts his family, Antonio has no sense of proportion. That's the Jordan curse, Tony thinks as he drifts off to sleep.

Sal Martínez cannot do anything. He is stalled somehow by Bruno's killing. He has no questions about the murder. He takes it as a carjacking that went bad. But he cannot get past it. He keeps feeling his own death.

One of Sal's fellow DEA agents understands. All weekend, he clips the papers, makes videotapes of the television news broadcasts, copies and files local police radio transmissions about the case. When all this is over, the agent thinks, he'll give the files to Sal. Right now, he figures, Sal will be scattered, not able to do this. Christ, he's the guy who taught Sal to carry a day book and make notes of every call and meet, try and force a little order into Sal's crazy world.

There is this guy, a friend of Phil's, who has done a lot of things in DEA with him. And he has his own read on what has happened. And part of him considers Bruno's murder and says it doesn't add up, that it is surely an accident that has nothing to do with Jordan's career. That no one can make a real case in the matter, that the killing leads nowhere and doesn't mean anything except that a carjacking went bad.

But the guy also knows from his years in DEA and in Mexico that simple sense doesn't always explain things in the drug business. He thinks of Manuel Salcido Uzeta, El Cochi Loco, the Crazy Pig. He flourished in Sinaloa in the 1980s. The agent savors his memories of those days. He remembers El Cochi Loco had so much money, he was finally storing it in a cave on his ranch. He remembers trying to witness a meeting between the local governor and El Cochi Loco and being barred from entering the restaurant by federal police. Hell, he couldn't even get to the block the restaurant was on, the police had it all cordoned off. But he laughs at the memory since El Cochi Loco had a high rank in the federal police himself.

He remembers going to a comandante in Sinaloa about maybe arresting El Cochi Loco and the comandante threw up his hands and said, "If I do that, I will be killed. Besides, he holds a higher rank in the federal police than I do."

But the name, Crazy Pig, yes, that is the good part, earning the name. The agent drains his beer with satisfaction. El Cochi Loco had a tiff with another drug family and so he swept in and kidnapped a bunch of them, men and women together, probably even some of the kids, and took them to his ranch. Then he had them stand there while a backhoe dug a trench. Then he buried them alive. After that, he was El Cochi Loco.

Simple explanations can fail in that world. It operates on its own logic.

El Cochi Loco is dead now, of course. The agent is sure of it.

What about this rumor that he is alive and running a nightclub in Guadalajara?

The agent waves off such talk with contempt.

But still, an unease remains. Because you never get to know anything absolutely down there. So you can know someone is dead. But you can never be sure.

Jordan bolts. On Sunday, he gets a flight back to Dallas. The wake will be Tuesday, the funeral Wednesday. He needs some space in order to think things through.

He's got his own family to think about. His daughter Kelly, thirteen, is refusing to even go to the funeral. She sits down and writes a letter to her dead uncle, seals it, hands it to her mother and tells her to give it to Bruno. Her mother tries to coax her into going. Kelly says, "No. I'll say goodbye my way. I want to remember him bowling." And then Debbie remembers that only a month before Kelly and Kenny had been in El Paso and one night Bruno had taken them bowling at 11:00 P.M. and did not bring them back until 1:00 A.M., a signature event for a thirteen-year-old girl.

Jordan, Debbie, and Kenny fly into El Paso on Tuesday. As they walk up to the house on Frutas Street, Jordan sees María sitting on the porch. He stops to talk with her and suddenly she blurts out this stream of words and Jordan, the professional undercover guy, the agent, can't seem to understand her even though she is speaking clearly. He is hearing words but somehow he can't grasp their simple meaning. She says she knows it has something to do with her old boyfriend, she just knows. She'd go over to Juárez with him and they'd have fancy dinners there with a lawyer who was supposed to be part of some car theft ring. She's heard her boyfriend on the phone taking orders for cars from the lawyer. Or that is what it sounded like to her. She wants to help, she tells Jordan. She is sure her ex-boyfriend knows something about the carjacking.

Jordan does not push. He moves with delicacy. María has become the world he knows, the informant to be reeled in, cajoled, controlled. Besides, he already knows about the ring from the El Paso police and they are already eyeing her ex-boyfriend, who happens to own a dark pickup. He tells María she will be all right, that he can provide protection, that she should not worry, he will help her. He will get back to her, he promises.

Jordan walks into the house, the outburst still ringing in his ears. He smells his worst fears in her story.

He is now entering a place he will never manage to leave. He will be enveloped by a kind of weather, one created in part by the police telling him the night of Bruno's murder about a car theft ring, about a guy they know who has a dark truck and is a leader of the street kids and who they think is entangled in this car theft ring. A weather created by his recollection of this conversation with María. But this weather Phil Jordan enters will become a private universe for him, one slowly but surely denied by the rest of the world.

And he will never be certain if what María seemed to suggest in her panic is the truth, or simply the result of her panic. He will never really know if her boyfriend was guilty of anything but having an ex-girlfriend who was overwhelmed by the possibility that she may have brushed inadvertently against a murder.

Kelly stays at a girlfriend's house when her family goes to El Paso. She only cries when she is alone, or maybe back in a bedroom with her friend. She is on the basketball team and appears for the scheduled game. She dedicates it to her uncle and plays very hard. Afterward, she runs off the court. And sobs.

Suzie is in bed with Sal, she has a dream, or an almost dream, because the thing happens with her eyes closed, and yet with the sensation she is looking, staring right through her eyelids. Bruno is there, and she thinks this is odd, not because he is dead, but because she hardly knew him. And Bruno says, "I don't know anyone here," and he is in a gray suit and looks kind of scared. Suzie stares at Bruno and says, "Find my Uncle Chica, he'll be your friend," because her uncle had just died recently. She can see Bruno through her right eye, and then suddenly she sees her Uncle Chica through her left eye and they are both bathed in a white light and they look at her and smile, just like that, they smile, and my God, the white light is beautiful. Suzie is only three months older than Bruno, and, she thinks, maybe that is why he has come to her.

He lies there weary with his seventy-five years. Antonio is the quiet man who requires little speech. His life has been his marriage and his family. Beatrice is high-strung. But Antonio is a rock. And now he is all but mute. He cannot make sense out of his son's murder. Nor can he do something about his son's murder. He is used to doing things. He is the enforcer, the one who kept the children in line, the one who protected everyone. Now he is a failure.

The house has finally grown still, the constant streaming in and out of relatives has ended for a while. He can feel himself finally giving in to sleep. There is almost no sound except for the endless purring of cars and trucks over the bridge to Juárez, the rumble of a freight passing through on the tracks just behind the back wall of the house. But these are not sounds to Antonio, they are the normal music of his life. He has been semi-retired for twenty-seven years, ever since Bruno was born and he and Beatrice closed the store to raise this miracle. The block has changed. Once it was a pocket of houses and then the railroad expanded and took most of the back lot. The bridge came in and walled off this two-block section of Frutas Street from the rest of the world. The houses disappeared one by one and were replaced by warehouses. And now there are Antonio and Beatrice, her brother next door, the old man's abandoned house just across the courtyard from where Antonio lies in bed, and one or two other houses. The old man's house really doesn't count anymore since it is cursed and no one will live in it. Or even spend the night in it. Antonio smiles to himself every time he thinks of old man Forti and his junkyard and his shops and his steady manner. He always knew what to do. And did it.

Now, sleep comes. And he thinks he is dreaming. He is on the slopes of the Franklin Mountains, the range that knifes into El Paso and forces the city to spread as a U around its base. Every time Antonio is in his patio between his house and the old man's house, all he sees to the north is this wedge of the Franklins plowing into the city. Now the city has spread out, sprawled downstream to the east and south along the river, but the town, the one Antonio has spent his life in, simply curls around the base of the Franklins. In recent years with the strange money from border factories and drugs, mansions have crept up the slopes of the Franklins, some of the big houses on lots so steep they stand on huge stilts, but the mountain itself is pretty much unchanged from when he was a boy. Now it is a park looking down at the city. So he closes his eyes, and he is on the mountain and he sees his boy, Bruno, walking ahead of him up the slope. He wants to catch up, he makes his old bones clamber over the boulders, grabs at the desert scrub to help himself climb. Antonio blurts out, "Bruno, be careful, you have no friends." It is night, pitch-black and without hope of a moon.

Bruno turns to Antonio, and says, "I'll be all right. Don't worry."

He can't keep up, his son is moving away. He pauses and looks and sees Bruno vanish into a brilliant white light. A voice out of the light says, "Do not worry, I will protect him." The old man knows this is God.

From the parking lot at EPIC, the agents see Juárez just across the river sprawling in the dust. The hunters look at their prey and into a world foreign to their government checks and federal perks. Over there most of the streets are unpaved, two thirds of the houses lack any sewage connection. At least 200,000 people in the city live as squatters in shacks on land they do not own. At least 35,000 more poor people descend on Juárez each year. Or sixty thousand, no one is sure. They take jobs at $3 to $5 a day that cannot sustain them.[11] In the previous six years, the peso has lost 50 percent of its value. And now times finally are getting truly hard.[12]

In December 1994, the peso, battered for years, finally collapses and loses another 54 percent of its value. Unemployment explodes but no one knows the true extent. No accurate numbers are ever kept. For the next six months, inflation operates at a yearly rate of between 33 and 50 percent. Consumer loans hit 100 percent interest. Mexico's billionaires drop in six months from twenty-four to ten.[13] As President

Zedillo notes, "In the first days of 1995, massive withdrawals of investments left the country bordering on financial and productive collapse."[14] The average Mexican is not as optimistic. In Washington, D.C., the government begins pasting together a $50 billion international bailout, with $20 billion guaranteed by the U.S., a plan larger than any previous rescue scheme including the post–World War II Marshall Plan.

The government announces the economy will shrink 2 percent in 1995. Private economists estimate the decline at 4 percent. A year before in the presidential campaign, the government promised a 6 to 7 percent growth rate.[15] That was after the ruling party's candidate was shot dead. He'd been to Juárez shortly before his murder and local photographers noticed his security was feeble as if he'd been sent out in public with a bull's-eye painted on him. The Mexicans call this time *La Crisis,* the crisis. The Americans are entering the longest boom in their history. One thing holds steady: drugs.

By July 1995, five tons of cocaine are seized crossing the bridge in El Paso alone.[16] Meanwhile, Amado Carrillo moves at least 150 tons across the bridge in about a year. Or more. The government at the moment estimates U.S. consumption of cocaine at 260 tons a year but no one believes them. Carrillo is landing 727s at the Juárez International Airport, each carrying twenty thousand pounds of cocaine. DEA thinks they are being unloaded by Mexican federal police. In Juárez, cocaine is $5,000 a kilo (2.2 pounds). In El Paso, it is worth $20,000. Carrillo loses an estimated 7 percent of his loads to U.S. authorities and gains a fourfold increase in money for moving cocaine the width of the river.[17] The FBI through an informant discovers that on any given day Carrillo is storing between twenty and thirty tons of cocaine in Juárez. They also learn that federales are guarding his shipments into the Juárez airport.[18] The informant also notes that Carrillo is sometimes called El Señor, the term commonly used in Mexico to refer to God. Or the president. One day at 6:01 A.M. a U.S. Customs inspector on the bridge at El Paso waves through a truck carrying 2,200 pounds of cocaine. The task takes him thirty seconds. The inspector earns $1 million.[19]

These numbers and events and loads all blur. They exist beneath notice. One drug figure on Mexico's west coast allegedly pays government officials $40 million a month in protection. And he is not the largest player. He is guarded by a retinue of thirty-three federal police. During the election, two flights bring $40 million to the ruling party. After the election at the beginning of newly elected President Ernesto Zedillo's term of office in December 1994, cartels in Colombia ship Carrillo another $40 million to foster government support of the trade.[20] The attorney general of Mexico, boss of the federal police, has a budget of $200 million a year. A former attorney general, Jorge Carpizo McGregor, explained the challenge of his work by saying he was "surrounded by traitors."[21] In December 1994, Juan Pablo de Tavira, the new head of the federal police, is scheduled to meet with the new attorney general of Mexico to outline a purge of comandantes working for the cartels. He is poisoned by his bodyguard. He lives on paralyzed and unable to speak.[22]

Under President Carlos Salinas (1988–1994) five different attorney generals took a stab at law enforcement. The most esteemed, Jorge Carpizo McGregor, was estimated to control at most 35 percent of his agency, the rest was controlled by the drug cartels. The other four were estimated to control 5 percent of their agency.[23] In 1992, Bill Clinton runs for president by promising to put 100,000 more cops on the street. No one in Mexico has ever run for office by promising the long-suffering population more police.

There is not much law, there is less order, and there is no money. People stream into Juárez where there is work for impossibly low wages. And where a First World economy is the width of a river away. The Mexican border is the only place where the cyberspace world of a major economy rubs up against a world of raw sewage and mud huts. The world of mud is failing to sustain its people. In Chihuahua, the huge Mexican state facing El Paso, over a hundred Mennonite communities were planted in the 1920s at the invitation of President Alvaro Obregón, a general in the revolution. The Mennonites flourished and planted over a hundred colonies, each numbered rather than named lest they fall into the sin of pride. They planted apples, put up plain houses, and created a landscape that looked more like Iowa than the traditional stomping ground of Pancho Villa. They became famous for their cheeses and the fact that they prospered and yet did not spend their time or money in cantinas. They lived a life of cash, thrift, and peace. None of this is enough when the economy collapses around them. Their lands lap against the drug strongholds of the Sierra Madre. Now the members of the group begin to show up in drug arrests.[24]

At EPIC, radar readings are fed into the computer tracking flights out of Colombia. At EPIC, huge computers field 75,000 inquiries a week from U.S. agents checking out incoming people and vehicles. At EPIC, huge databases from the FBI, CIA, IRS, DEA, and dozens of foreign intelligence communities commingle. At EPIC, agents can stand in the parking lot and take in Juárez. They can stare into the dust of Mexico, where each year a million new faces hit the workforce and find there is no work.

But they can never see a thirteen-year-old boy coming with a gun.

They stand before the open casket in the funeral home and look down at Bruno. Brigitte has picked out the coffin and it is a silvery gray metallic and looks very modern. It has the feel of a new shiny automobile. She knows Bruno will be pleased. He understood style and modern lines. He lies in the coffin wearing a Redskins cap and is dressed in a suit he had put on layaway at the Men's Wearhouse.

Tony stands there and thinks of Juárez, where he used to sing in the nightclubs. A guy he went to high school with is said to be now number two in the Juárez cartel, the key assistant to Amado Carrillo. Tony knows what needs to be done. He wants vengeance. He wants someone to die for his brother's death. He is not impressed with the arrest of the thirteen-year-old. The kid is irrelevant, a fucking Kleenex to be used and tossed away. Tony wants the person behind the kid, the author of the murder. And he knows in his bones it is murder, not a carjacking gone bad.

There are no accidents in Tony's Mexico and he lived there for years playing the clubs. So he plans to go over, hit the bars, look guys up, shake the trees.

Sean knows the ground also. When he disappeared from the family, vanished from all contact, he was living all the time here in El Paso, shacked up with a drug dealer. They'd go over to Juárez and she'd do her business and they'd hang out and have a good time. And Sean also has little interest in the courts or their justice. He wants blood.

Phil Jordan feels their anger and knows it is directed at him. He is the cop. He is the family success story. He has the power. Fix it. Their eyes say fix it.

Phil takes Tony and Sean up to the casket, and there is Bruno in the nice suit he never quite paid off, and he's wearing that Redskins cap. Tony puts three tokens from the MGM Grand in his suit pocket so he can play the slots in heaven. Phil pins a DEA badge to Bruno's suit. Sean puts an Egyptian charm in his casket. Phil wraps his arms around Tony and Sean, pulls them both to his side and he talks to Bruno.

He says, "Bruno, I'll get whoever did this to you. And I'll get whoever was behind them."

Sal and Suzie Martínez attend the rosary at the funeral home. He is standing in the back behind the crowd and the place is packed with people. The family realizes at the rosary that the building will never be adequate for the funeral. Last-minute arrangements are made to secure a large church, St. Pius. Sal has been feeling strange for days now, ever since he heard that bulletin on the television on Friday night. He cannot quite put his finger on it, but there is this sense of dread that comes over him without warning. He thinks about nothing but Bruno but yet in a sense he never thinks about him. He's a busy guy, an active agent darting in and out of Juárez and his mind takes comfort in a series of compartments—marriage, family, job, and then within this last compartment there are many chambers for all the various false identities he parades before various rooms and people. His hair is long, he is living a role, but in this room the role fails him.

He sees his cousin Lionel Bruno Jordan in a box in the front of the room, the face strangely pale. He feels his knees buckle, things are spinning, he cannot seem to stand.

The wife of a fellow DEA agent comes to his aid and holds him up.

The guy is dead, and he just sold suits.

The room spins for Sal Martínez.

Virginia loses herself in all the things that must be done. She and Brigitte become the planners of rites, schedules, what to eat, where to be, what to wear, how should Bruno be dressed. It takes care of time and keeps things out of mind.

An old woman comes up to Virginia at the rosary and she cannot place her. The woman explains that she worked with Bruno at Forti's restaurant and he was very nice and so kind and so she felt she must come. A nurse comes up and Virginia cannot place her either. She says her son knew Bruno and when her son's girlfriend left him, he fell into despair and drink and considered suicide. Bruno talked him out of it and he is the reason her son is alive today.

The hours pass, people keep coming. Virginia learns Bruno's life now that he no longer has one.

But always, it is business as usual. And always, the business is quite normal, about cash flow, profit. And loss. In the songs of the border, the drug business is about bravos, about fine cars and fine women and automatic weapons and valiant deaths. But day by day, it is more humdrum, more like any other business. In 1995, Amado Carrillo and the Juárez cartel move to buy a Mexican bank. To represent them, they hire the brother of the new president of Mexico and the son of a former president of Mexico.[25] This is not known for years and when it becomes known, the Mexican government announces that, not to worry, it thwarted the deal. And that the transaction means nothing. A national labor leader was also involved in the purchase. This too is seen as insignificant.

But while the drug business is quite normal, a matter of accounts and of settling accounts, it is also different in scale from most businesses. The drug business is big business, very big business. Pemex, the nationalized oil industry, earns Mexico $7 to $8 billion a year, the largest official export. U.S. intelligence pegs Mexico's income from the drug industry at $27 to $32 billion a year, the figure varying because of squabbles between various analysts. And this is hard currency in a cash-and-carry business.

But nothing is said out loud. It is not done. And in the United States with its various agencies, talking out loud is forbidden.

As Virginia and her family busy themselves with grief and burial and prayers, business runs along in its relentless way. Bruno Jordan dies in a carjacking. Anything else is off the table. A carjacking can be solved by finding the carjacker. A carjacking leads nowhere. A carjacking stays on one side of the river. Before Bruno Jordan died in the hospital on the night he was twice shot, his case was functionally closed. The shooter was in custody and other matters did not matter. Talk of a car theft ring fell away and then suddenly no such ring existed to be discussed. The federal agencies, DEA and FBI, professed to find nothing in the incident in the K-Mart parking lot that brought the case within their mandate. So they never investigate any aspect of the murder.

Mexico is officially a mystery to American policy. Or a detail. In 1995, when Bruno Jordan dies, the U.S. State Department has nine people on its Mexico desk. It still assigns ninety to what was once called the Soviet Union.[26] All this is accomplished by careful use of language. A drug problem may call for a War on Drugs but still, it is contained, kept small and local by simply calling it a problem. But if drugs are seen as a business and this business is seen as a major industry, then no logic can contain it. Then it becomes elemental and part of the fabric of two nations.

Phil finally speaks with his father alone. He knew this was coming, this moment. He has known it for days, sensed it every time he tried to move. His legs feel like cast iron, he cannot lift his legs. There is this weight and it does not go away.

His father is silent. So Phil says what is on his mind. He tells him there will be no problem. That he will take care of it, take care of it legally within the justice system. He says, don't do anything stupid. And his father knows what he means: don't try personal vengeance. His father says nothing, nothing at all, but Phil can see a recognition of his words in his father's eyes. The look also says, take care of it, I am count-ing on you to take care of this.

Jordan thinks of how his legs can't move. He cannot imagine how his father's legs must feel.

Bruno is dead. There is no future in being normal. The future is with God and God is a mystery. Tony has to square his brother in a casket with the world he knows. And with the world he wants to believe in. He works in a city of dreams, Las Vegas, a place clogged with 150,000 visitors a day, a city that 38 percent of all Americans have visited. Tony is there as a refugee from troubles in El Paso and he no longer sings in clubs, he works in the money-counting room of a casino on the strip. He wears a smock with no pockets so that he cannot steal. He has a new wife from Chihuahua, small children, a nice apartment. The wife works in a big hotel changing sheets.

He also has these back pages and they will not go away now that his younger brother lies dead in a coffin. Tony has memories that take him into the world where murders occur. The memories can be exact: two men are kidnapped from Juárez and taken to Guadalajara and strapped to a table where their limbs are chopped off with an ax. Hard-edged memories.

But emotions boil within these compact memories. Once these memories come up and enter the mind, they never leave. The memo-ries hold the man who is sinking into a pit, and at the bottom of this pit—the sheer hard walls of this hole are terrifying—at the bottom of this pit a man is strapped faceup to an old table, the wood is amber from varnish and age and the black grain of the wood hunts through this glowing top, there are gouges, nicks, little cuts, and stains from perhaps thousands of hearty meals that have graced the wood and impregnated the old boards with love and grief and appetite. This table comes from all the childhoods, and it is in this memory round and seats multitudes and has room for platters and tureens and big bowls and racks of lamb and roasts of beef and veal and pork and Virginia hams and turkeys and a Christmas goose. It is the center of the human universe and now a man is strapped down to its top and he is staring up into the circular eye of a fluorescent light that bathes his face with white light and this light dances across the beads of sweat on his worried brow. In the mind this light off the sterile fluorescent bulb is the light of thousands of country kitchens huddled out on the land and this light smears the windows with a milky cast and helps keep at bay the darkness of the night, this light silences in the mind the howling of wind, the storm that robs people of any fantasy that they are one with the earth, that they are safe and in tune with the forces that wander the surface of the world, a storm that kills on contact, comes without warning, takes the power lines, shuts down the phone system, closes the schools, and sends drunks out at closing time to sidewalks where they will fall and then curl up and slowly disappear from life as dreams float across their minds as their dying brains sign off forever.

Tony has memories he cannot control. He tries but they ride with him.

Everyone has seen such storms, veritable warlocks that threaten our immortal souls, that rip down the walls of the flimsy homes and slobber against the panes of glass, gales that threaten all the dreams of safe homes and pleasant gardens, patios filled with partygoers, a band striking up and then the show tunes that bring such a cargo of fine memories and nights of love, a storm that takes everything before it, that snuffs out the barbecue, blows the band off its stand, kills the sound system, uproots the big tree that gives such generous shade, a storm that erases a world once seen as sure and solid, and at that moment everyone is left with just the hope implied by the white light cascading down from the circular fluorescent bulb, a light like the one light splashing down in the kitchen of the Jordan family home on Frutas Street, like the one in Tony's mind flowing across the reassuring old wooden table where the man lies strapped and looks upward, his eyes burning as they stare, reach past the glare of the light into the blackness waiting in the place called forever. Around the man strapped to the table are other men, and they hold axes, the blades whetstoned to a razor sharpness, the metal glistening with care. The men agree they will start with the arms. After that, they will see, but they will start with the arms.

There is a time when a person can think that all this is scattered and unconnected, part of the white noise that is the background for modern life and that seeks to deaden everyone. There is a time when the mind says, none of this has anything to do with real life. Safety comes from this way of thinking. The past is walled off and kept at bay. The little incidents stay little. And then there are moments like this weekend, a brother is dead in a casket, women are weeping, the rooms are crowded with family, and all the little incidents now come back and fill the mind and wander about and have a new mystery and importance.

Tony remembers. It is 1989 and Tony is in Mexico City sitting in his hotel room watching the World Series. On the screen the world is falling apart with a large San Francisco earthquake and when the camera pans away from the action in Candlestick Park there are scenes of fires erupting in the city and of freeways collapsing on travelers, hints of mayhem floor the television. At that moment, the phone rings in his room and he picks it up and hears his brother Bruno's voice, and Bruno says, "Enrique is dead. He was killed in a nightclub." Tony puts down the phone after talking with Bruno and calls his business partner, who explains that Enrique owed $100,000 and two men came to him one night while he was drinking in a nightclub and he dismissed them with a wave of the hand, told them he had no interest in talking with them. They fired machine pistols, stitched Enrique across the chest, then the groin. He thudded to the floor and then one man straddled his body, grabbed him by the hair and lifted his head and pumped a few rounds for good measure into his skull. The two men who did the killing were from Colombia and they fled El Paso and crossed the river and went into Juárez. Here they were captured and flown to Guadalajara and taken to the table. The pit.

The phone call floats in Tony's mind, the call that came while San Francisco collapsed on his television screen. His partner said that he had been invited down to Guadalajara to watch but had taken a pass. So the men with the axes cut off the killers' arms and then watched them bleed to death. Old business, something done and gone. Another case closed.

Tony has these back pages. And there is this storm sweeping over the land. The storm is a blizzard of money. The numbers must be repeated like the beads on a rosary or they will disappear. Most of the time, in fact, the simple numbers of economic reality are never mentioned either on the street or in the meetings of heads of state. A Mexico earning at least $15 billion a year from drugs and more likely $30 billion or more. At $15 billion this constitutes 5 percent of Mexico's gross domestic product, at $30 billion 10 percent. This blizzard of money means life or death for the nation. Take away $15 billion and Mexico goes from a growth rate of 4 percent to a recession of -1 percent. Take away the $30 billion and Mexico collapses. Have Mexico collapse and a border of almost two thousand miles shared with the United States becomes a place people march across as they flee a dying nation.[27] In December 1994, the new Mexican president, Ernesto Zedillo, has a secret report from his own National Institute for Combating Drugs land on his desk during his first week of office. The report notes dryly, "As a result of the financial capacity of these drug-trafficking organizations, the tendency to infiltrate the government and financial structures will continue. The power of the drug-trafficking organizations could lead to situations of ungovernability."[28] When a person enters this storm seeking facts or vengeance or just an explanation, the storm blinds the eyes and chills the heart. When a person enters this storm, the world as it is normally taken for granted, that world is left behind.

Tony forms a thought as he passes the hours waiting for his brother's funeral: "We always try to learn God's way and if we don't learn it all here on earth don't worry, you see to know it all is to have touched the face of God: Our Future."

And then he thinks: "If there is an afterlife."

The one good thing is the grave site they've found. Bruno used to jog right past where he will be buried. Close to home. Familiar. Safe. He will feel safe there.

Phil Jordan thinks: there has to be three. Three people. One to drive the truck into the K-Mart. One to leap from the truck and kill his brother and then drive the stolen truck away. And one to take the stolen truck and the gun and get them away from the scene. Three, an absolute minimum.

Carjacking means punks jumping someone in their car and stealing it. How many times does that mean three? And how many times are carjackings this organized with a driver, a shooter, and another person to hide the evidence?

He thinks: three.

And then he pushes the thought aside. If the case is solved as a carjacking, if the ring the police talk about is nailed, that is sufficient. It will stay on this side of the river.

It will stay out of his other life.

Still, there had to be three. At least three.

There are things back there and most of the time they stay there. Back, over with, things gotten past. The old man is like that, Beatrice's father, the immigrant, the founder. He had to leave Italy, came over, changed his name, invented a new life. He set everyone up, every child got his own business. A fresh start.

Beatrice has the clothing store. And right across the street, the old man has his kind of junk shop. He closes earlier than she and Antonio close, so every night he crosses the street and says good evening before he goes home.

He is getting old now, approaching seventy. It is a night in the late 1940s and he has crossed the street to say goodbye. Beatrice comes out on the sidewalk to speak to him. She sees a man coming up with a knife to stab her father and she grabs the man's arm, clamps down so hard the man winds up cutting himself.

Her father turns and takes his assailant down. The police come and it is cut-and-dried.

She never really learns what it is about. Just something about how the man was shiftless and of no consequence. How he was jealous of the old man.

But then her father lived in secret worlds within worlds. He would write things down and no one else could read them because he kept these special notes in classical Greek. He has businesses she only knows of by rumor. And she has brothers and sisters she only senses from whispers.

There is another world across the river, and her father has his fingers into it also. He is quietly everywhere. It is hard to put together. One of his friends is a young man in El Paso, a beginning judge named William Sessions. And then years later, Beatrice will read a newspaper and see the same man, Sessions, now heads the FBI. That fits also with her father. Her father would know who to watch. And who to know.

Sean is amazed at his father. He manages to keep control of things. He is constantly dealing with reporters. He is careful with his mother. He accepts condolences from relatives.

When he is alone, his father cries. Sean is still stunned by the fact that his father actually cries. He thinks maybe his father is the only honest man in El Paso. It is hard to follow the law on the border. Sean knows in his gut that local police are crooked. They can't be here, he thinks, and be straight.

The border for Sean is full of secrets, little worlds hidden from other worlds. Like the world he vanished into for a while.

And he thinks of Bruno's secrets. Unless you knew something about Bruno because you were around him and saw it, you would never know it. He would never tell you. Secrets.

There is a panic sweeping through the world across the river. A man will go out in the morning and find his goats dead, all the blood sucked out of them. The first reports come from Puerto Rico and then the sightings spread and come to Mexico and move north to Juárez. The thing, seldom seen, is called the chupacabra, the goat sucker. Reports suggest the animal is four to five feet tall, nocturnal in habit, possessing red eyes, large teeth, a gray skin, strong legs, quills on the spine and wings. In Mexico, dark things descend and cause havoc and these recurring stories explain why things are the way they are. Sometimes it is an invasion of chupacabras. Other times, children are being kidnapped and slaughtered in order to sell their organs. Always, it is really the same: outside forces are causing our misery and this reality explains why there is such suffering and also proves that Mexico matters, matters enough to have a host of foreign and occult enemies.

There are other matters. The littering of the streets with the dead from the drug business. And an almost silent dying, the sudden appearance of the bodies of young women in the desert outside Juárez, women who tend to work in the foreign, largely American-owned border factories called maquiladoras. Their numbers keep piling up. And no one knows what to do about them. And so hardly anyone speaks of them. Also people are disappearing in El Paso and Juárez, just vanishing from bars and restaurants and homes and streets. Sometimes witnesses say the vanished were last seen with the police or the military. Usually, there are no witnesses who will speak.

The deaths from chupacabras, from the police, from the army, from the drug cartel, from unknown kidnappers and rapists, pile up and still no one knows what to say.

When Bruno was a little boy he would ask Tony, his older brother, to sing his favorite song, "Cuando Tú Te Me Vayas."

Tony now thinks of the song he sang to his baby brother. It was just a silly thing he sang that Bruno liked. But when he runs it through his mind now he finally hears it. And he wonders does it mean something, could Bruno have sensed something long ago when the world was fine and everything seemed like a permanent summer?

But there is nowhere to go with such thoughts. They are like matters of faith, things not to be thought about but simply felt.

> *Nada se mira igual*
> Nothing looks the same
> *La vida es un castigo*
> Life is just a punishment
> *Todos me tratan mal*
> Everyone treats me bad
> *y no sé que voy hacer*
> and I don't know what I will do
> *cuando tú te me vayas*

when you leave me
cuando tú te me vayas
when you leave me
Entonces me iré yo también
At that point I'll leave myself
tras de ti, tras de ti.
after you, after you.

St. Pius sits just off the freeway and within reach of the smell coming off the nearby oil refinery. The funeral on Wednesday draws over a thousand people. The big white church is new, with the open altar dictated by Vatican II. Above the nave, stained glass windows flood the big sanctuary with light. The world of Bruno Jordan glows from this glass as the metallic coffin now centers the building. Christ is up there and his skin this time is brown and he wears a brown business suit, white shirt, and tie. He is the Mexican-American rising into the middle class. Or he is crucified, his face in this glass panel as old as the cross itself and as unforgiving. On the cross he wears two bandoliers of red chiles.

A Washington Redskins balloon floats up from the coffin. Outside at the door, Beatrice arrives with the family and there waiting for her are Bruno's teachers and his coaches from high school. The entire area is one big traffic jam and radio bulletins warn local citizens to stay clear of the mess. Patricia and Virginia and the rest of the women in the family wear black suits and black hats, formal, nice, just the way Bruno would have wanted it.

Phil Jordan sits in a pew and his mind goes absolutely blank. He can hear people speaking to him but he does not listen. His legs are still iron, his mind in a sense functions—he's just given sound bites to the press at the door—but it functions in a way he cannot control. His mind is on this thing he calls the case, his mind is full of tiny details of a car theft ring, of the tale of María and of María's ex-boyfriend, of slowly reeling in María like a new girlfriend, of making her comfortable and trusting, of filling her body with ease and small smiles, and then, when she is almost serene and talking and telling him everything, every little detail, all those names and dates, then, there will be this clang like a cell door slamming shut and she will be trapped and he will change, perhaps a very bright light will come on and blaze into her eyes, and she will hear this voice, a voice harsh and firm, grilling her hour after hour, probing her and dragging from her everything she knows including things she does not even think she knows.

This voice comforts Jordan in his mind, it takes him to the place he has spent decades, the busy work of DEA where he is in control, has forms and procedures, fills out documents, applies statutes to actions, knows every rule and the way around every rule, the place he thinks he belongs. Not this church, this grief, this black thing he cannot control, this Christ looking down on him with bandoliers of chiles and a brown face, this whole Mexican-American world he fled long ago, the prison where everyone calls him Felipe. There are a lot of DEA agents in the sanctuary, a showing of support. And of course, respect, since he is now the boss of EPIC and has hundreds of agents at his command. Jordan hears voices but cannot listen. Even when his wife, an anglo at that, says, "You should look at María," he hears but does not listen. He knows she is his resource, María, but he cannot quite get his mind around the idea that María, soon to marry into his family, is part of a murder.

Jordan has been away too long, he realizes that he has strayed from the hard truths of Frutas Street where he was raised. After the murder, he called an old informant, a guy he has done deals with in Mexico and the U.S., worked together on major busts for decades, and the guy, Mexican to his core, says it is about betrayal, look at that woman. Jordan can see his dark eyes in his mind and these eyes tell him something ancient and obvious and yet still hard for him to accept. *Venganza,* vengeance, the rules of blood, the eye for an eye, the tribal demands. His grandfather's world, so distant from the suit Jordan wears as he sits in his pew and the one Bruno wears as he lies in his coffin a few feet away.

Tony is singing, Jordan is sure of it, yes, he hears his brother singing "My Way," and he thinks the walls of the church may buckle from the booming of Tony's voice. Then he is singing that Italian song, "Aleila," something probably Jordan's grandfather liked, yes, it is Italian, the very same song Tony sang years ago at their grandfather's funeral. But his mind cannot stay in the church. He hears but does not listen. Now Patricia is speaking and saying something. Then Sean. Now Tony is saying something about how God needed a good angel and so took Bruno unto Himself. A priest looks out at the audience and says, look at all these people Lionel Bruno Jordan has brought together, what greater testament to his life can there be than this large gathering?

Men are up front, hoisting Bruno, now the coffin leaves the church. Yes, this thing is finally over, Jordan thinks as he stands.

Across the river a tiger purrs. Juárez lacks a public zoo. The large cat lives in the compound of Amado Carrillo. This is a growing tradition. Down in Sinaloa where Carrillo was born, an earlier player in the drug business, Rafael Caro Quintero, kept lions. At parties, he would entertain guests by tossing suspected informants into the lion pen and then all would watch them be devoured. In Juárez, yet another player, El Greñas, kept alligators or crocodiles, reports vary on this biological detail. In Tijuana, Jorge Hank Rhon keeps white Siberian tigers, hippos, cheetahs, and the like. His father, Carlos Hank González, is one of the most powerful men in the nation. A former schoolteacher, he has spent decades working for the government at a civil servant's salary. He and his family own many things in Mexico, a bank in Texas, a huge mansion in Connecticut. He is famous for having once said, "A politician who is poor is a poor politician." Señor Hank has a fortune estimated by *Forbes* at $1.3 billion. Among other things, he owns the largest private airline in Latin America, a fleet of jets. Or he does not own it. Señor Hank is vague on this matter. He admits he once owned it but now says his former personal pilot, a man of slender means, has bought it. In DEA files, there is no such vagary: the airline is stated to be owned by one Amado Carrillo of Juárez.

Across the river a tiger purrs in the privacy of a compound. No one goes near this place in the city. The press does not mention it, no photographs are taken. In DEA files, there is an aerial photograph, a picture with a slight tilt to it as if taken in great haste, even from the air. Outside the compound armed men keep watch. The police officially never come to this area. The compound where the tiger lives stares straight into El Paso, stares at the church where Bruno Jordan's funeral is breaking up. Stares straight at EPIC.

For half an hour, they cannot move Bruno's body. The traffic is impossible as a thousand people leave the church and head for the cemetery near the bridge into Juárez. The day is very cold and overcast and there has been a fear of rain. Finally, the hearse breaks free of the congestion at the church.

At the grave site, the clouds break apart briefly and a column of light falls down on the metallic coffin. Phillip Jordan looks around at the crowd and notices María's ex-boyfriend is in the throng paying his respects.

He hears but he does not listen. He goes back to that place in his mind where everything is a case and every case has regular procedures and produces sure patterns of evidence. Follow the ex-boyfriend, have him tailed, debrief María, let the FBI poke around. Yes, that will do it. The FBI has officially refused to look into the murder. True, there is now a federal carjacking statute but under this law, the perpetrator must be an adult and Miguel Angel Flores, thirteen, fails to qualify. That is what the agency has explained to Jordan but he does not believe them. For years, he thinks, he has worked comfortably with the FBI. They will find a way into the case, they always go anywhere they want to go. He is sure they are looking into it. Jordan looks over at his father and thinks about how he must feel standing helpless by a hole in the ground where in minutes they will lower his son. Suddenly, the leaden weight of his legs returns to Jordan. He tells himself that he got an indictment of Amado Carrillo. He got an indictment of Juan García Abrego, the head of a rival cartel on the Gulf of Mexico. Surely, he can solve this case, a carjacking and murder, in two or three weeks. That's it, he will take time off from EPIC, from assuming full command. He will pursue this matter of his brother. He will solve it, nail it down, follow the tracks from the parking lot to wherever they may lead.

At the house the world becomes food. Brigitte busies herself as a hostess as people flood into Frutas Street hour after hour. The restaurant of a family member, the place called Forti's, sends wave after wave of tamales, enchiladas, taquitos, chile con queso, chicken flautas with guacamole, and frijoles to the house. There is beer and wine. Aroma cuts through the stale air of death. The house rocks with talk as relatives mutter and remember good times. The gathering goes on until at least nine that night and then dwindles and finally ends.

That is when death slams everyone, when they are finally alone in the house on Frutas Street. Bruno is a few blocks away in a freshly dug hole in the ground. The sounds of the city are normal, the trains continue to rumble through El Paso right by the back wall of the house. The cars stream across the bridge linking El Paso and Juárez, the bridge that now separates the family from Bruno's grave.

Beatrice sets out the glass of water next to the candle kept burning in Bruno's room. She watches. Sometimes, the glass of water stays the same. Sometimes, it suddenly drops. Bruno is coming to her with his thirst. She stares at the glass and thinks of "what they did to my Bruno."

A mansion stands in Hermosillo, Sonora, the state bordering Chihuahua on the American line. The building takes up a block and is white. It has cost $3 million and is rumored to be for the owner's mistress. It has Moorish domes and arched windows. The locals call the house *Mil y Una Noches,* One Thousand and One Nights. It is a structural piece of magic in a provincial capital of half a million people. Geraldo Rivera in New York hears rumors of the structure and sends a film crew down to capture it. Armed guards swarm from the building and the crew flees. All this happens in midday with warm sunlight pouring down.

The strange mansion rising out of some fantasy of the Middle East fails to be mentioned in the American press. Nor is it publicized in Hermosillo. Everyone knows who is building the house, though no one

says just why it looks like something airlifted from Baghdad. His name
is Amado Carrillo. No one mentions his name either. Or they use a different name he has picked up: the Lord of the Skies.

When Phil Jordan allows himself the freedom and risk of thinking, one
word keeps coming into his mind, an ugly word, and this word keeps
returning and returning: humiliation. He cannot protect his own. He
cannot bring his brother back from the dead. He has to find some kind
of vengeance. There is a blood debt. The justice system is courts and
jails and that is good to Phillip Jordan. But it is not enough.

He is a middle-aged man, his gut slowly expanding, his face mild
and bland, his suits all bought at the Men's Wearhouse thanks to deals
Bruno would arrange. Jordan wears glasses, tends to sputter and wander around when he speaks, and all his sentences come out vague and
drifting. Sit by him on a plane, and instantly he is filed away as perhaps
an accountant, or some kind of middle manager in a dullish industry.
Jordan cultivates this image. He approaches declarative sentences as
potential minefields that can explode and injure one. He is a bureaucrat's bureaucrat.

When he stands in El Paso and looks across to Juárez this sense of
humiliation becomes more powerful. He knows they are over there.
And he can hear them laughing at him. They have created a special
place over there in Chihuahua. The governor of the state, a reformer
from a party said to be at odds with the nation's ruling party, has
recently told the press that big drug trafficking in Chihuahua is a
thing of the past and that American claims about the volume of the
cocaine traffic out of Juárez are untrue.[29] But then Jordan knows his
own DEA has just created a genealogical chart of the Mexican cartels
and on this family tree the Juárez cartel is a little box, the kind earned
by some spinster aunt or crazed uncle.

Jordan is a power in DEA. But now, as he looks and hears the
laughter, he realizes he is nothing.

Coca-Cola has penetrated the planet using a single slogan: "It's the real
thing." In Mexico, the company translates the slogan to *"Esta es la ver-*

dad," this is the truth. Focus groups of Mexicans recoil at the slogan. Marketing people learn that Mexicans believe the truth must be something bad, something constantly claimed by their government and therefore something very suspect. So they change the slogan to: *"La chispa de la vida,"* the spark of life.[30]

A few days after the funeral Phil Jordan returns to El Paso from Dallas. He has taken two or three weeks off from his official duties to privately explore his brother's murder. In Dallas, he talked with his friends in the police department on how best to look into a carjacking and murder. He is focused on María's ex-boyfriend because that is his only even tenuous lead. All he has to go on is some offhanded remarks made by the El Paso cops the night Bruno went down, glib cop references to the guy as being tangled up in hot cars and street kids. Jordan has two dreams. One is to catch the ex-boyfriend in a felony in El Paso. The second, and the one he really desires, is to catch him across the bridge in Juárez and have him busted. In Mexico, Jordan knows from experience, he can count on a serious interrogation.

He hires off-duty state troopers, calls on the help of friends in DEA. For about forty-five days, he keeps the boyfriend under surveillance. He pays the off-duty state troopers and soon has gone through somewhere between $5,000 and $7,000. He is afraid to really keep a tally. He does not tell his wife of this financial hemorrhaging. Nor his family. He hardly tells anyone what he is doing, especially the El Paso police. He thinks he'll see what the El Paso police can come up with and see what he comes up with independently. The El Paso police have already told him that the ex-boyfriend is their primary lead. Jordan figures the guy can't go too long without a mistake.

He still has María, the former girlfriend of the key lead and now the wife of his relative. María has told him she will give him everything—the times she listened in on a third phone while the guy talked to a guy in Juárez and took down orders for what models of cars to steal; her dinners over there with her boyfriend, the representative of the car theft ring and others; and she will give him her mother, who she says knows the guy in Juárez also. And Jordan has gone on bended knee to his relative asking his help, saying we must do this for Bruno. And to both he's made it clear that they will stay out of the picture, not be named, simply be tools to get him information so that he can move against the real culprits. They've gone ahead with their wedding to the amazement of the Jordan family but, while this rankles Phil Jordan, he cannot let it interfere with his investigation. For him, the wedding celebrated within ten days of his brother's funeral is a detail.

María has had only one request: a kind of cooling-off period, so that she can distance herself from the heat and rage of the murder. Then she will talk. She's taken that job at the Men's Wearhouse in Phoenix, though her husband is still in El Paso finishing up his work at K-Mart. But in Jordan's mind, María has become his ace in the hole, the one card he can play that will beat anything else on the table. He figures the murder can wait two or three weeks since he has such an ace to play. So he lets the El Paso police continue their investigation, and in two meetings they tell him two things: the ex-boyfriend, of course, is the primary lead. And that María is their number two lead. Jordan takes this as confirmation of his own instincts that he is on the right track.

He still feels the weight on him. He must fix this.

A week after the murder, the court assigns the defense of Miguel Angel Flores to Sam Medrano. He's thirty-two, jowly, and tends to blurt out sentences. He's spent two and a half years as a prosecutor, and now has gone private to see if he can get his share of the local white powder bar. El Paso's legal community is booming with drug cases. Medrano has burrowed into a loaned office in a law firm a half block from the courthouse and now he has a case that can earn him headlines and notice. The government has given him $500 for an investigator, a pittance. Medrano himself winds up putting at least 120 hours into the case.

He can see hope. True, he's discovered since the shooting that apparently half the city is related to Bruno Jordan but he can handle that in jury selection. On the plus side, the police picked up his client only fifteen or twenty minutes after the shooting and he had no truck, no gun, and only seven bucks in his pocket. The test for gunpowder on the boy's hands is inconclusive and thus off the table in court. True, his client was wearing dark clothing, an Oakland Raiders black sweatshirt with a hood, but that hardly fingers him as the shooter. Then, there is the family: the mother, Graciela, a stepfather who barely is in the picture, a sixteen-year-old brother, Juan Alfredo, and three younger siblings.

But the thing that catches Medrano's attention is the boy himself, and Medrano soon realizes "he's not a thirteen-year-old kid, he's thirty." He discovers that Miguel Angel stopped going to school when he was nine and started illegally coming over to El Paso to hustle. There is no police record on him and that's good. In El Paso, Miguel Angel hangs out at the house of two women, sisters, who live with their own batch of kids in a housing project about two miles from the K-Mart. He was only a few blocks from their place the night he was picked up. Sometimes he'd stay with the sisters for weeks at time. His brother, Juan Alfredo, though older, is instantly sized up by Medrano as weaker, a follower not a leader, the kind of kid no one would involve in a hit. Juan Alfredo has also found a place to bunk in El Paso on Webster Avenue and this leads to his street name, El Webster. Miguel Angel is called El Pitufo, the Spanish name for the popular Smurfs. He is four feet eleven inches tall. He has a small mutt he calls El Enano, the Dwarf.

Two weeks after Bruno dies, Sean dreams. He sees Bruno and in the course of the dream Bruno tells him that there are things he has to do, stuff he left up in the air. Sean knows Bruno is dead, and Bruno knows he is dead.

Bruno says, "I just got fifteen things to do."

Sean wants to hug him.

But Bruno balks and says, "Don't touch me, don't touch me."

While they talk, Bruno keeps repeating that he has got to do these fifteen more things. But somehow, he never spells out what these things are. Then he makes a motion with his hands like he is shooting a basketball, pivots and goes up for the shot. He is excited and he gestures toward that pole in front of the house on Frutas Street where Sean and he played as kids.

He says again, "I've just got fifteen more things."

Sean asks, "Yeah, what are they?"

But he just repeats, "I got fifteen more things."

And then, Bruno goes away. He comes back at times. But the dream is always the same, about things Bruno must do, things left unfinished. Sean thinks, Bruno is just trying to help me deal with this thing that has happened. After a while, he still visits Sean, just not as often.

Jordan knows one thing: he will not move his family from the Dallas area to El Paso. He explains this decision to others several ways. The kids are deep into high school and it would be disruptive for them. His wife is married to her life in Plano and why cause a fuss? Then there are the finances, the house and everything else, and why go through all that grief for a job that is a five-hundred-mile flight in Texas. Besides, he explains, his folks live in El Paso and he can stay at the house, there is plenty of room, and given the black times, it would be a good thing anyway to have him there to help fill the hole left by Bruno's death. After all, from the first night of the murder, he's wondered if his mother will even survive the ordeal. This splutter of explanations appears to satisfy everyone and he starts a routine of flying in Monday morning and taking a late afternoon flight home to Plano on Friday. The cost of these jaunts hurts but he's got lots on his mind and ignores the bills.

And one thing Jordan has on his mind is the real reason he won't move his family to El Paso. He can see this thing in his mind. His kids are in the high school cafeteria in El Paso. Suddenly, some kind of fight breaks out and there is a moment of general mayhem. Then it ends, everything is okay. Until they find a kid on the floor, shot, dead. And it is his son or daughter.

Virginia craves some kind of contact with her brother Bruno. And some kind of insight into what happened to him. She has his name made up in big gold letters, a charm, and wears it dangling from her necklace now. She works in the courthouse and tries to keep tabs on what is happening with the case. She talks it up with one of the assigned detectives but his only response is to flirt with her.

She wants the cops to look into this El Chino guy, María's ex-boyfriend, but they seem to shrug her off. Then María takes a job at the Men's Wearhouse in Phoenix and suddenly she and the relative vanish from the case.

Virginia is ravenous for something to solve the killing, something to give her some answers. She goes to a woman she knows, a woman who can see through the darkness. They sit and the woman peers and says she sees the Silverado, it is parked in a building in Juárez, there are a great many tires piled up, there is a brick wall. That is it, she can see no more. Not an address, not the outside of the building. Just the truck sitting in darkness inside this place.

Two or three hours a day, each day he is in El Paso, Jordan does surveillance. Sometimes he has a fellow agent with him, some guy helping out as a favor. Sometimes he is alone. Usually, the surveillance is at night, sometimes it is in the day. He will have a different car every time. DEA has such a large pool of machines seized from dopers. He will park a block, half a block down the street from the house where María's ex-boyfriend lives with his mother. Jordan knows the family well now, he's had everyone checked out by cop friends. All he has found is some minor busts for drugs, small stuff, just possession.

He is waiting for that felony. For the dark truck to leave, go somewhere, and maybe drop a kid off for a car theft. Or cross the bridge into Juárez. Or cross the bridge and go to the home of Miguel Angel Flores and visit his mother. He is prepared to videotape such a visit. Proof of a crime. Proof of a link. And of course, that ultimate hope, cross the bridge and commit a crime in Juárez and wind up in the eager hands of the Mexican police for questioning, a location where Miranda and other rights do not reach. And a place where Jordan thinks he can still exert pressure and call in favors.

Night after night, day after day. And nothing happens. The truck seldom moves. And when the truck does move it runs routine errands, and hardly breaks even minor traffic regulations. Once in a while, he

catches the driver failing to use a turn signal, but nothing worth noting. He drives two cars back from the truck, he is sure he is never
made. After all, he's been tailing people for decades. And the kids have
disappeared. The man initially described to Jordan as a local Fagin
with a herd of thieving Mexican kids at his command, well, now he is
isolated and there are no kids around.

Jordan tells no one of these nights. No one at the family home on
Frutas Street. This is his play, his return to the sure ground of the case.
And this ground slowly buckles underneath him, night after night.

One day just as dusk is falling, the truck is parked in the drive
when three or four Mexican kids come to the house. He knows the ex-
boyfriend is at home. The kids knock on the door but he cannot make
out any response. And after a while, the kids leave and head back to the
freeway where the K-Mart sprawls. Another night, the driver comes
out and heads carefully through the El Paso streets and goes to a
known doper bar. But nothing happens. He is in there a while, has a
drink and then goes home, careful as a deacon.

Night after night, Jordan sits there staring at the dark truck and
thinking that is the truck that helped kill my brother.

Brigitte is back in El Paso for a visit and goes with her grandmother to
a woman who has certain powers. The woman can cleanse the soul, and
the woman can reach over to the other side. She lights a candle and
then they ask questions of Bruno.

The answers come as yeses and nos. The candle's flame goes up and
down dramatically as the answers roll in. Sometimes it wavers from
side to side.

Brigitte is stunned as she watches the taper flame up and down
with replies. And she believes at that moment absolutely that they
have reached Bruno.

Medrano broods in his little office. A big glass golf club and ball sit on
his desk like an icon. Behind on a shelf, an opened but barely touched
bottle of Chivas Regal glows amber. He prides himself on not being a
handholding defense attorney. He does not go over to Juárez to visit

the family and has very little idea how they live and even less interest. He's a hired gun, not a damn social worker. But this professional distancing hardly prepares him for his client. He expects a child and gets the eyes of some ancient. He's got some assets: his client allegedly told the jailers after he was arrested that he shot Bruno because he thought he was reaching for a gun. But such statements will not be in the trial. Later, the prosecution will explain that they did not make any record of the confessions because they were afraid the defense would ask to see them, a statement of the mild idiocy produced by the assembly-line justice of the clogged modern court system.

A week after the murder, a Mexican reporter hangs out with the kids who know Miguel Angel and hustled with him near the K-Mart. The kids work the streets and cops are always trying to pick them up. They make $6 to $10 a day—maybe 35 cents a windshield. This looks good when a man in Juárez is likely to make no more than $5 a day. They tell the reporter they work in groups of three to five to protect themselves and that they sleep under bridges. They are *milusos*— people who in order to survive will do anything for a buck. They talk about some guy called El Chino who comes by and they all fear this one guy. They are also simply terrified of cops. They say they will never talk to the Mexican authorities, that if they talked the mafia would kill them. They insist Miguel Angel is innocent, though they admit he bragged about having mafia connections and sometimes claimed to work for the mafia as a mule carrying things into the U.S. This last matter, they wrote off as just an empty boast from a little kid. They say they were all in the parking lot of the K-Mart that night and saw the murder go down, the ambulance arrive and take Bruno Jordan away. But they soon fled since they figured the El Paso police would hassle them. The kids are jumpy as they tell the reporter these slivers of their world. And when he goes back, he is never able to find them again.

Medrano certainly wants to find them. He's got a string of street names—El Cuba, El Tolín, El Kala, El Moreno, and so forth—and he keeps coming up empty. He turns to the Mexican consulate in El Paso. After all, the consulate is legally Miguel Angel's guardian since he is a minor trapped in the American court system. Finally, the consulate produces El Cuba and El Cuba sits in Medrano's office as mute as a rock. But the consulate says it cannot find El Kala. Medrano has the kid's Juárez address but this gets him nowhere. El Kala told the El Paso police about El Chino, this shadowy Fagin-like figure, the day after the murder. As for his client, Miguel Angel consistently denies to Medrano that he was in the parking lot of the K-Mart on the night of the shooting.

Medrano senses he is in over his head. The Mexican consulate keeps having secret meetings with Miguel Angel and Medrano only learns of them because of jailhouse connections formed by his years as a local prosecutor. Besides this insult, the consulate keeps barging into his case and trying to tell him how to run his defense. Medrano thinks, What is this shit?

He knows that Mexican nationals get regularly ground up like sausage meat in the justice system of El Paso and no one ever hears from the Mexican consulate in these cases. Suddenly, they are all over Miguel Angel Flores's fate.

"I'm too American," he decides. "I can't get around that."

But a couple of things stick in his mind as the weeks slide by and he prepares his case for the front pages of the local newspapers, his shot at making some big legal bones. One is that he meets with his client at least ten times, meets with this thirteen-year-old who acts much older than Medrano himself. In all these meetings, he never gets an answer out of the kid that goes beyond yes or no. The kid is like a block of ice. Finally, in frustration, at one meeting Medrano whips out a mug shot of the guy said to be called El Chino, a photograph of María's former boyfriend. Suddenly, the kid starts crying. Medrano can see fear in the kid's eyes. In Medrano's mind, he can hear El Chino saying, if you talk, your mother dies, your brothers and sister die, your whole fucking family dies.

On February 7, 1995, Ross Perot is giving some of his ritual testimony in Congress against NAFTA and against the bailout of the Mexican economy when he suddenly ties together two things: this invisible Mexico and the murder of Phil Jordan's brother.

"How does Mexico define middle class?" he asks. "Middle class is having a paycheck large enough to buy food for one month. If you can buy it for more than one month, you're above middle class. How many people fall into this class which we would consider poverty? Only 4.3 million out of 91 million Mexicans. I'm sure you all are saying, Ross, where'd you get these numbers? From Mexico. The Mexican government.

"How many Mexicans fall into the category of living in poverty? Eighty million people live in poverty in Mexico. . . . Keep in mind, in Mexico you've got thirty-five people who own over half the country—thirty-five families. . . .

"Is the Mexican government honest? . . . Let's get down to plain talk. No. The politicians leave office much richer than when they were elected. In some of the cities, the police chief lives in the finest house in town. That sends a message. Mexico is now a huge shipment platform for cocaine to the United States. We have a tragic story . . . in the *Wall Street Journal* story. . . . It tells [about] the drug cartel in Mexico—it tells [that] they buy old U.S. planes from a big airline, gut them, carry as much as $120 million of cocaine for shipment, land them anywhere, abandon the airplanes because there's so much profit. It details the government officials that have been paid millions. It quotes one U.S. drug agent named Phil Jordan and the tragic end to this story—this story appeared on December 13. Two weeks later his brother was murdered by an illegal alien in El Paso. The good news is they captured him. The bad news is we still don't know what the ties are, but it's a sad coincidence. Here's a man who gives his life to try to clean it up and pays a price like that for having his name mentioned in the paper. When you read the details of that cartel and you read how brutal it is and you read the fact that it's wired to the Mexican government, I wouldn't give a nickel until they cleaned up their government because it's a government that's not responsive to the people."

Virginia and Beatrice are out shopping. They are waiting for the trial, for justice to arrive in their lives. They pull up to a red light at McRae, right by the K-Mart where Bruno was murdered. A Mexican kid is on the median hustling for some change.

They roll down the window and ask, "Do you know El Pitufo?"

The kid says, "Oh, yes."

They look at his little body and young eyes and the whole crime looks so very near and yet so far away. A mystery hidden in the world of children.

In February, Jordan flies to Phoenix. He figures the cooling-off period is over. It is time to get the information from María. She will surely feel safe in a city so far from El Paso. He takes his son Sean with him to the Men's Wearhouse so that he will have a solid witness. He has not told María he is coming.

He can sense that something is off as soon as they enter the store. He and Sean wait until the place empties of customers and while he waits, he idly looks for some signal of recognition from María and there is nothing. One thought crosses Jordan's mind: they have gotten to her, they have reached her.

Finally, the store is quiet and Jordan goes up to María.

"I'd like to talk to you for a minute," he begins. "Remember your promise? You will not be in any jeopardy. I'll make sure no one knows where the information comes from. I just want the killers behind Miguel Angel Flores."

María says, "I don't remember anything."

Jordan can feel the chill, see it in her rigid body language, hear it in her even voice that bites off words with almost a snapping undertone.

"What about your mother?"

"My mother doesn't know anything."

He scans her face and sees this mixture of distress, anger, irritation, and fear. He speaks softly, he contains himself, he will reel her in, coax her around.

She says, "Don't bother me again."

And then, she walks away.

Jordan keeps his calm face but he is taken aback. His ace has vanished. And he realizes something else. His power, his pull with cops, his command of EPIC, and the fabled sorcery of DEA, all these things have been outmatched. María is afraid of him, he can see that. But she is far more afraid of something else. And in his gut, Jordan knows exactly what that something else is.

When he gets back to El Paso, he discovers his relative, who had promised everything possible from María and her family, is now cool and distant. Jordan checks in with the El Paso police to see what, if anything, they have come up with on the ex-boyfriend and María. They have nothing to report. Except that María has called them and asked that charges be made against Phil Jordan for harassing her.

A deep regret fills him and it is over one small moment. That morning after the murder when he fled his parents' home because of pressure, took his son and brother Tony to the pancake house and they ran into María. And he hugged her and told her not to feel responsible for what had happened. He thinks now that he may have been hugging one of the people who helped get his brother murdered.

There will never be a shred of evidence to substantiate this feeling.

A man is detained by U.S. Customs at the Newark airport in March. Mario Ruiz Massieu is the former Mexican official heading the War on Drugs. At Newark, he was simply changing planes for a flight to Spain when $50,000 on his person was discovered, money he had failed to declare. Later, officials find he has a Houston bank account stuffed with $9,041,598. He says he saved this money from his earnings on the job. The Mexican government in the light of a growing scandal seeks to extradite him. First, Ruiz Massieu subpoenas former President Carlos Salinas. This causes a stir in Mexico where such a demand is unheard of and where trials are generally held in private before a judge without a jury. Then a U.S. federal judge discounts all the Mexican witnesses presented in their case for extradition. He rules that their testimony has been undercut by the fact that they have all been tortured.[31]

They have all been building up to this moment. Jordan found within EPIC a cell of analysts focusing on the intelligence coming out of

Mexico and he soon expanded this group to around twenty people. Now in late March, Attorney General Janet Reno visits the facility at Fort Bliss for a half-day briefing. EPIC's bunker on the military reservation is a testament to something the government seldom acknowledges publicly: its feebleness in its self-pronounced War on Drugs. Originally, the facility was on the edge of downtown El Paso but had to be moved when it was discovered that the Juárez cartel had penetrated its phones and was copying down the license plates of its agents. Even the name of the building, which honors DEA agent Enrique Camarena, contains a mixed message. Camarena, whom Jordan knew, was kidnapped in broad daylight in Guadalajara in 1985. His tortured body was found some weeks later. The subsequent scandal chilled relations between Mexico and the United States but DEA's own investigation was ultimately stopped when it kept leading to higher and higher officials in the Mexican government.

Jordan runs EPIC with a split consciousness: one side of him believes in the drug battles and the other side knows that no drug policy will ever overcome the demands of domestic politics and foreign policy. He cringes when he has to use the phrase War on Drugs since he knows it is not a war but at best a scattering of battles, skirmishes. And now he runs a place with over three hundred agents, with a massive computer that handles the raw intelligence from dozens of countries, and fields instantly those 75,000 inquiries a week from cops who have pulled over a car or Customs people running a license plate at a border crossing to see if it has a criminal tag. But he cannot trust even his own workplace since he assumes it has also been penetrated by the cartels.

But the arrival of Reno is a chance for Jordan and his Mexico unit to say in secret sessions what they are not allowed to say to the press. Reno herself is a bitter thing for Jordan. She never even called when his brother was murdered. He heard from the head of the FBI, the DEA, Customs, he got calls from Ross Perot, Senator Phil Gramm. But not from his boss, Janet Reno. And he'd done things for her: gotten her bumped up at the Dallas–Fort Worth Airport to first-class, walked the streets of Dallas with her on operations. It's not like they were strangers. It is simply not the way he was raised. You call when someone takes a loss like Bruno.

He sits beside her during the long briefings and he notices that after a while she begins to take notes furiously. The almost faceless analysts spare nothing. They quickly sketch the major cartels: the Juárez operation of Amado Carrillo, the Gulf cartel of Juan García Abrego, the Arrellano-Félix organization in Tijuana, the ghostly power of Félix Gallardo, in prison for years for his hand in the murder of Camarena and yet still easily running his Guadalajara organization from his palatial jail cell. Even back pages in the drug business, such as Rafael Caro Quintero, show up in the briefing. Quintero has been in prison since 1985 for his murder of Camarena and yet he lives in a luxurious cell block and periodically shows up in his home state of Sinaloa for family weddings and various parties. In Mexico, money can buy almost anything in or out of prison. Just recently, the director of Mexico's prisons announced he was outlawing private Jacuzzis in the cells of inmates. Few believe this change of policy will occur.

But what catches Jordan's attention is Reno's reaction. First, the constant note taking. Then as the analysts move up the food chain and trace the connections between the drug business and the government, questions are almost blurted out by the attorney general, questions that keep asking, "You mean to tell me . . . ?" Slowly, as the hours pass, the acid portrait of Mexico deepens with the ties between the former president of Mexico Carlos Salinas and the cartels, the role of his brother Raúl as bagman for the president, the all but complete corruption of the federal police and the army, and the successive powerlessness and corruption of Mexico's attorney generals. Various governors of states are also casually linked to cartel payrolls. And the analysis does not stop with the past administration but continues patiently to sketch the links between the drug business and the current Mexican government. Reno is taken aback when she is told that the people she deals with in Mexico work for and with the cartels. She is in a state of disbelief that asks: how can this be true if she has not been told before by briefings in Washington? Jordan is stunned. He suddenly realizes that she has been told essentially nothing before.

He can understand the denial he sees in her questions at the very same time she busily makes detailed notes of material she can hardly swallow. Just how does a person suddenly assimilate information like the fact that one player in the cartel world, Hector Palma, travels around Mexico with a squad of federales for protection and has a bribe budget that entails at least two $40 million payments to the authorities? There are, according to the Mexican government's own study, Nine hundred armed criminal gangs in Mexico. Over half are staffed with current or former cops.[32]

For Jordan this sensation of belief and yet disbelief is natural. He comes from a culture of authority within DEA. He drinks deeply of the agency's core myth: that after the reprisals for the murder of Enrique Camarena no cartel figure would dare to touch a U.S. narc. And yet a part of him, a growing part, knows this myth is a lie. His brother is dead and he has this feeling as the days slide by that nothing is being done about this fact. And he realizes that regardless of the limited proof he can crab together from his savings and part-time investigations the murder had to have come from across the river. In part he knows this, he thinks, because of the evidence of the car theft ring and its ties to Juárez. In part, he senses that nothing like a hit on his brother could occur so close to the absolute bedrock of the Juárez cartel's operations without its consent. But in the deepest sense, he knows this because it is exactly what he would do. It is in his blood. It is something beyond the calculus of business or tactics: it is about brothers and families. It is what he learned from his grandfather long ago.

For Jordan, it goes back in a logical, yet illogical way, to an incident in southern Italy around the turn of the century, an incident that is guarded in his family like an heirloom and yet one that is hardly ever mentioned lest it bring ruin and punishment upon them.

The half day with Reno is a holiday for Jordan from murder and he relishes it. He can see that the attorney general is stunned and listening, disbelieving at one level, but still making those notes on another level. He thinks his new expanded Mexico unit has scored big. He begins to hope, against his better judgment, that some piece of the worldview of the street agent will penetrate the policy levels of the U.S. government.

•   •   •

Jordan creates a fallback position after María and his relative move beyond easy reach and refuse to speak. He talks to the state prosecutors and they give him a green light. He gets the same reaction from the U.S. attorney's office, from Immigration. He privately meets with the U.S. ambassador to Mexico and he also signs on. He checks with the U.S. consulate and gets more approval. In a few days, he has his package: if Miguel Angel Flores is willing to talk, he can guarantee a deal.

He is running out of options. The El Paso police who told him the night of the murder that they had a prime lead, this guy who lords it over the kids and is part of a car theft ring run out of Juárez, well, they seem to have stalled and are coming up with nothing. His own surveillance efforts have failed and he has given up on them also. He is burning money, first the bundle he doled out for the surveillance. And now, every week, the flights to and from Dallas burn a bigger hole in his pocket. His wife has not found out yet, not discovered the looting of their savings, but he knows it is only a matter of time. God, she prides herself on never buying new clothes, on making sure everything is for the kids. He's going to have to make good on his expenses somehow, put the money back before she finds out.

And every night, he gets home late to Frutas Street and his parents are still up and supper is waiting for him. Spaghetti, or tacos, or enchiladas. Lots of food, the house is always rich with the aroma of something cooking. In Bruno's room, the candle is always glowing and right by it is that damned glass of water that goes up and down, a constant reminder of his brother's presence. And of unfinished matters. Jordan can feel this weight growing on him and he sometimes thinks his legs will buckle from this weight. His father says nothing. His mother searches his face with her eyes. He can give them nothing. This should have been settled weeks and weeks ago.

He is humiliated. He is nothing. He is at home on Frutas Street, and there he is Felipe. His is the failed son and brother.

But now he has this deal and surely this deal will change everything. No one in their right mind could turn down his deal. No one.

He calls a family meeting and outlines the deal and asks for their approval. And they give it. They depend on him, they trust him. Fix it.

•   •   •

There is a moment that stuns Medrano. Around March 20, the El Paso police relay an offer from Jordan to Medrano. The deal is simple: the government will drop all charges against Miguel Angel Flores, they will bring his entire family to the United States, give them citizenship, relocation, new identities, jobs. And all Miguel Angel must do is give up the name of the person who drove him into the K-Mart parking lot that night.

Jordan tells Medrano, "The United States government does not want Miguel Angel—he is merely a murder weapon."

So Medrano sets up a meeting down at the jail. A cop from the El Paso police is kept in one room while Medrano meets with the kid and outlines the offer. The kid says no.

Medrano thinks, Can you imagine a thirteen-year-old Mexican kid that can face down the fucking U.S. government? He must know something even more frightening, you know?

This is not a normal case. There is just too much strangeness for him. The intense interest of the Mexican consulate is like nothing he's ever seen before. And he can't forget the attitude of the kid, the coolness, the toughness, and then that outburst of weeping that one time. Whatever this kid knows, Medrano thinks, there is one thing he knows for certain: that there is something a hell of a lot scarier in the world than jail, prison, or the United States government.

At times, Medrano will sit alone in his office and try to spin theories about what happened that night in the K-Mart. He keeps coming back to the guy called El Chino and sees him as some kind of force who knows all the street kids and has them spooked. And El Chino is a jealous guy now that his former girlfriend is going to be married. So Medrano arrives at this theory that whoever drove the Silverado into the parking lot that night was going to die. Only it was supposed to be the guy she was going to marry, not Bruno. The crime was a kind of accident. And then Medrano sitting with his thoughts feels like he is floating off into space and retreats to the few gritty facts of the case that matter in court, what is admissible and what is not, how good are the eyewitnesses and how can they be undercut. This is his comfort zone. To hell with the theories. He's a lawyer and this is just one more case.

He tells himself once again what some people say the justice system is really about: "It's about twelve fucking people too fucking stupid to get out of jury duty."

Inflation for April rolls along at 23.66 percent. The Mexican government now projects growth in the GDP at one percent for the year. Since January 1, at least a half million workers have been laid off. Still, as always each and every year, yet another million young people hit the streets looking for work. Loans now cost around 70 percent per annum. In New York on the Stock Exchange, twenty-nine major Mexican corporations have seen 70 percent of their value vanish in five months. The national chamber of commerce thinks that about 40 percent of its 480,000 members are on the lip of bankruptcy. Factories creak along at maybe 30 or 40 percent of capacity. During the last good year, 1994, foreign debt ate up 32.8 percent of GDP. Now this bite grows yet larger.[33]

The county attorney's office is kind of puzzled. Teresa García, a young prosecutor, is handling the case against Miguel Angel Flores. She knows that the cartel in Juárez regularly uses kids in crimes since they can kill and not face an adult sentence. But what puzzles her is the Mexican consulate in El Paso. They've never paid any attention to a juvenile case in the past, not a one. Now, suddenly, they're constantly demanding information about the case and quoting the Geneva Convention to her. And the newspapers in Juárez have been blasting her and the case as the railroading of a Mexican boy by the DEA.[34]

Jordan goes to the Mexican consulate in El Paso. The building takes up a city block downtown, the consulate is a major installation because of the heavy traffic of Mexican citizens here into the United States. Also, the consulate, like most of Mexico's in the United States, is a center for their intelligence operations. Jordan knows from EPIC's intelligence that employees of this particular consulate are rumored to be part of the car theft ring in El Paso. Simple logistics creates this reality. In 1982, DEA stumbled on a major car theft ring in the San

Diego area that was shipping vehicles to the elite in Mexico City. A
Mexican general was nabbed in this sweep, but then cut loose when it
was discovered that he was an asset to U.S. intelligence. Still, the ring
was blown and had to move and there is only one other major U.S.
city that close to the Mexican border, El Paso. And a car theft ring filling exact orders for models needs a good supply of automobiles in
order to operate successfully.[35]

So Jordan enters the building with an awareness of who he is dealing with. The structure is modern with walls of glass flooding the
interior with light, potted plants here and there, marble floors, and
has the look of some strange cross between a doctor's office and an airport terminal. It is only a block from the jail where Miguel Angel
Flores sits and waits. Jordan runs his cards through his head and is
confident. It is too sweet a deal, it solves a problem for Mexico and the
United States, cleans up a messy and politically embarrassing murder—this time one of their citizens has killed the brother of the head
of DEA intelligence. Besides, Mexico is in crisis what with this new
president, the economic collapse, and the usual scandals suddenly
being revealed about the previous regime. The time is right for a gesture of cooperation.

The head of the consulate is effusive in his greeting and drips with
courtesy. Jordan can hear this my-house-is-your-house bullshit in the
air. He lays the offer out: Miguel Angel Flores walks free, his family is
brought to the U.S., made citizens, relocated, protected, and given a living. He has brought along two El Paso police detectives with him who
tell the consulate that the deal is real and they have no objection to it.

The head of the consulate beams at the offer, and says, this is great,
there will be no problem, no problem. They must, of course, consult
with the family but that will be almost a formality given the offer. Do
not worry, we will be back to you in a day or two.

Jordan sits there and thinks, against his better judgment, that this
is a done deal. Surely, the consulate can pound some sense into the head
of a thirteen-year-old boy and his family.

Two days later, the El Paso police call and tell Jordan the consulate
has turned down the offer and rejected it firmly and out of hand. The

consulate insists the boy is innocent and thus no deal can honorably be entertained.

It will be more than two years before an informant tells Jordan that at the time of the meeting, some officials in the consulate were meeting daily in Juárez in a cartel bar with key members of Amado Carrillo's organization.

The detective in the El Paso police department insists the things have to be seen in context. The Mexican car thieves that plague his city are very adept. They have schools in Juárez, he explains, to train them. Sometimes Mexican federal police will cross the bridge with some of these kids and cruise the large parking lots scattered about the University of Texas at El Paso. They have lists with them of models and makes to be acquired and when one is spotted, a kid is dropped off and goes to work. They busted one such kid and he agreed to be videotaped stealing a car. He went to work on a locked BMW with pliers and a screwdriver. Nine seconds later, he drove it away. The kid complained that the car had a defective hand brake and that this caused his slow time. The bridge to Juárez was less than a mile away from where the cops made the videotape.

All this troubles the detective. An organization with such skills hardly needs to try carjacking. Or violence.

Nothing connects. In May 1993, Cardinal Juan Jesús Posadas Ocampo is murdered at the Guadalajara airport. The killers calmly board a flight to Tijuana, an AeroMexico flight held at least twenty minutes so that they could make it. In the almost empty first-class section, they share the seats with Jorge Hank Rhon, the son of Carlos Hank Gonzáles. The son is never formally questioned.[36]

There is an investigation, arrests, an official government explanation that the cardinal perished accidentally in a shootout between drug dealers. No one believes the official explanation of the cardinal's murder. Leobardo Larios Guzmán, a state prosecutor, takes on the case. He moves very lightly. When one of the key suspects, Ramón "Spunky" Torres Méndez dies, he asks very few questions. Torres is strangled in his jail cell. Eventually, the investigation ends and Larios winds up teaching at the law school in Guadalajara. On May 10, 1995, he leaves his house for his classes. Nine rounds pass through his head. A backup guy waits with a hand grenade in case the bullets are not enough.[37]

The death remains unsolved.

Jordan is down to a final card, an end run around Miguel Angel Flores's lawyer and around the Mexican consulate. He will cross the bridge into Juárez and talk with Graciela, the mother of the boy. He does not tell his parents of this plan. He talks to his cousin Sal Martínez, who is always working in Juárez, and he asks for his help.

In a few days, Sal delivers a Mexican security detail for his cousin. Jordan gets in a car with three other DEA agents and crosses the bridge by his parents' home and goes to a parking lot deep in Juárez by a bunch of stores. Two federales await them. They proceed, with the DEA agents and the federales commingled in each car. They leave the central city and start climbing the rutted dirt lanes into the hills where the poor cluster. In Mexico, unlike the U.S., the house on the hill almost always belongs to the very poorest who are driven to barren ground where there are no water connections, no sewers, and little or no electricity. The rich live down below on the flats with all the services. A blur of shacks of cardboard or concrete block or wood scavenged from loading docks plays across Jordan's eyes. It all looks familiar to him and very normal.

They pull up to a house. The fence is constructed of pallets from loading docks, as is the house. One of the federales goes in and a woman comes out to the fence. The street is full of kids but they keep a distance. Two shiny recent model cars are enough to cause caution. Federales are enough to cause fear. Adults largely disappear from the street, or peer at a distance.

Jordan gets out alone and approaches the fence. The federale moves off and Jordan thinks he is probably out of hearing distance but he cannot be sure. Any more than he can be sure what the federale has told the woman before she came out of her shack.

The talk takes maybe ten minutes.

"I am not here as an adversary. I am here to help your son."

Graciela blurts out that her son had nothing to do with the crime, that it was this other person, El Chino.

Jordan nods and moves along.

"I know this is hard for you to believe but I do not want your son to go to prison."

And then he explains the offer, freedom for her son, sanctuary, new identities, and money for her and her family in the United States.

She nods and says she will talk to Miguel Angel.

Jordan asks how often does she see her son in the El Paso jail?

Two or three times a week, she replies. But she must take the bus and that requires money.

Jordan reaches into his wallet and gives her a $20 bill for the bus fare.

She nods.

It is going well, he thinks. She has all but admitted her son's involvement by bringing up María's ex-boyfriend.

Jordan looks at her and makes one more promise: "Señora, no one will get hurt."

She nods and says her son is not violent at all. He simply went to El Paso to work so that he could help feed the family.

Jordan returns to El Paso and waits for his answer.

It comes in a few days. The consulate calls and is outraged. How dare he go and intimidate the mother of Miguel Angel? The offer is firmly rejected. The child is innocent and this will be proven at the trial. Later, at the trial, the $20 will come up and be characterized as an attempted bribe.

Much later, Jordan learns that the federales who accompanied him to the home of Miguel Angel, the ones provided by his undercover cousin Sal, are both part of the organization of Amado Carrillo.

About the time of Miguel Angel Flores's trial, a convoy escorts a college student to his class at the university in Mexico City. Suddenly, the car with the student is cut off and four men leap out to rob it. The rest of the convoy comes up on the scene and arrests the men. The four

would-be robbers are off-duty policemen. The student being chauf-
feured in the car is the son of the president of Mexico.

Jordan has nothing now. The trial is coming up and a verdict of guilty
will be some comfort to the family. But not enough. They know the
boy charged with murder is simply some kind of instrument that has
brought death to their house. They know that someone had to be
behind him. And at that point their knowledge stops and they say
nothing more. Or they offer, like Tony, that it must have something to
do with Phil. Tony is around a lot now, flying in every week or two
since his brother's death to comfort his parents. To somehow replace
Bruno with his own presence. And he is always upbeat, smiling, making them laugh, singing a favorite song.

But it not enough. Tony, like the rest of the family, waits for Phil
Jordan to deliver. Not just answers. But justice, and justice means
blood for blood, justice means vengeance. Tony thinks back to his own
grandfather and he knows exactly what justice has to contain.

Jordan himself is at an end. He can hope, as he does at times, that
a verdict will shake some kind of sense into the kid, getting him talking. Just as he hopes the jailhouse snitches will hear some words that
will jump-start the case. But his hopes are limited. The rejection of
his deal by both the kid and the family tells him what he is up
against. Just as the fact that María can be reached five hundred miles
from El Paso and frightened into silence tells him what he is up
against.

He has limits and now these are becoming painfully self-evident to
him. DEA instills a black and white world, bad guys and good guys.
There is very little shading and no need for deep understanding. Catch
the guy dirty, bust him, extort more leads and busts from him with the
hammer of the harsh federal laws now on the books for drug dealing.
Then move on.

It is all tidy and there are a bunch of things this work does not
require. DEA does not ask its agents to understand their adversaries, to
crawl inside the minds of their targets. Nor does it require much
knowledge of Mexico for its work beyond some Spanish and some con-

tacts with crooked federal and state comandantes. For example, DEA has never created a profile of Amado Carrillo that probes his mind and quirks. It is not necessary. Case work means busts, a regular quota of busts. And weight, increasingly the busts don't really count unless they bring in a big pile of kilos. Snitches, of course, are essential, endless numbers of snitches feeding little tidbits to earn their money or cut a deal on their own busts.

So when Jordan realizes that Amado Carrillo and his cartel have checkmated his investigation at every turn, he has nothing to go to. Except DEA files that give names of associates, addresses of businesses operated as fronts, photographs of private homes. Footprints but no study of the mind behind the footprints.

Jordan can hear them laughing at him.

Medrano feels vindicated during jury selection. He sits there in late May and hears juror after juror express disbelief and outrage that a kid from Mexico has the right to a fair trial in the United States. And one by one such malcontents are struck from the pool. He can hardly believe that in a city that is 75 percent Mexican-American, it is still a novel notion that Mexicans are human and have equal rights in court under the U.S. Constitution. But he knows it is true and knows it is bedrock reality along the border where people on the U.S. side are called pochos, poached, by people on the other side, meaning they are seen as culture-less ghosts of real Mexicans. Naturally, the contempt is returned in kind.

But Medrano has real hopes for his case. He is sure he can throw dust in the jury's eyes by pointing out the contradictions in the eyewitnesses' testimony. And for over two days, he does just that, having the shooter come out as tall and short and this and that. The stolen truck magically changes color back and forth. His client never takes the stand. But he has the mother and her husband there and that helps. Besides, the kid in his buzz cut hair and small body looks like a harmless tyke. One by one, the cops and people in the parking lot that night parade through the room with their tale of a dark truck following another truck into the lot, with some person jumping out, that glint of something metallic, the sound of shots, the puff of smoke, and then a man going down on the pavement, the ambulance, the police coming back in a short while with his client and on and on. Israel Reyes, Bruno's friend following him in that beat-up old VW, is a problem. The guy is too close to the action, too emotional, and just too believable. But in time, his testimony gets smothered by all the other conflicting testimony. So Medrano, after he gives his summation, feels some hope for an acquittal, or at least a hung jury.

The Jordans have been a problem too, that's true, sitting there every damn day like a mourners' bench and staring at the jury. And Phil Jordan sitting there glaring with that cop look. Graciela, Miguel Angel's mother, has been a mixed bag. On the one hand, hell, she's Mom and that shows a human touch. On the other hand, she dresses like the rag woman she is and he fears the jury is looking at her like some creature from another planet.

No matter, after three days, the thing is off with the jury as evening comes down and Medrano thinks he may have pulled off a little miracle. The case has had saturation coverage in El Paso and he doesn't think there is a soul in the city who has not been poisoned by the media. And then, it seems half the city knew Bruno Jordan. The damn funeral had a turnout like a sporting event.

But now Medrano sits and waits for his verdict. Then, he gets word that the jury has asked to see the black-hooded sweatshirt the kid was wearing that night. What in the hell can that be about? he wonders.

And then around seven, the judge calls the court back into session. Medrano checks and finds out two things: one, the jury has taken one vote that came out seven to five to acquit his client and that sounds damn good; two, one of the jurors in handling the sweatshirt felt something odd, and fished the roach of a marijuana joint from the lining. How did the El Paso police manage to miss this after having the thing as evidence for months?

Well, that's not the issue at the moment. What is on the table is whether a mistrial should be declared because of the discovered joint. Medrano has to decide fast and he decides to gamble. He thinks, "I've got seven for acquittal and five for conviction. Fuck, people who vote acquittal are usually tougher and I've got seven of them. Ain't no way I'm gonna lose all of them. If there'd been only one or two, yeah, one or two could be beaten back and switch to conviction. But fucking seven? Shit, I could win this case, and at worst have a hung jury. I mean my client's charged with killing a twenty-seven-year-old American for a fucking car. And every fucking person in this town knows fucking Bruno Jordan. Ain't no way I'm gonna lose all seven."

He tells the court he has no desire to file for a mistrial.

The jury is sent back to its deliberations. Later, that night, they break off to resume again in the morning. Medrano sleeps well. The next morning at 10:20 A.M. they bring in their verdict. Guilty.

Medrano is reeling.

By one count, citizens of Juárez begin disappearing in 1994 and within three years at least thirty-eight have vanished. Alfredo Medrano Villareal, president of the Ciudad Juárez lawyer's bar, notes that the families of the vanished believe they were abducted by Mexican federales, or possibly drug traffickers posing as police. The key suspicion falls on the Mexican attorney general's office and its police agencies, particularly its national Institute for the Combat of Drugs. The vanished people are last seen arrested by police but never turn up in jail. Nor can any records ever be found of arrest warrants.[38]

They have been worried. The family had told Tony to stay in Las Vegas during the trial because they feared his temper might erupt in some scene in the courtroom. They have come each day and borne witness to their loss, made sure that the jury never forgot their presence. When the verdict arrives the family hardly knows what to feel. Beatrice, Antonio, and Virginia sit in the courtroom and hear the word guilty with relief. And yet it is unsatisfying. It leads nowhere for them emotionally. The conviction of a thirteen-year-old boy is insufficient to explain to them the murder of a twenty-seven-year-old man. In part, the verdict only covers one small part of some larger thing. It nails the person who fired a gun but stops far short of whomever sent the boy into the parking lot with the gun.

Phil Jordan has an even deeper sense of emptiness. He considers the verdict a technical step toward answers but discards it as any measure of justice. And after the verdict, he leaves his family in the courthouse for a private errand.

He drives down Alameda, through the barrio he was raised in, past the bridge leading into Juárez, and then goes down a small dirt lane and finally stops. He gets out of his car and walks over. He takes out one of his DEA business cards, and writes on the back: "Bruno, one down and two to go. Phil." Then he tapes it to his brother's headstone.

He stands there and talks and talks into the grave. He tells his brother of the state of the investigation, of every twist and turn in his efforts. He details his conversations with people, explains the visit to Miguel Angel Flores's mother in Juárez, honestly recounts his disappointing dealings with the El Paso police, his growing fear that the FBI and the Justice Department are literally doing nothing. He is alone in a cemetery, a middle-aged man talking to a mound of fresh-turned dirt. As he talks on and on, his brother's face stares at him from a small cameo portrait affixed to the headstone. Traffic rolls past on the bridge into Juárez. The city hums all around him, trains rumble through on the nearby tracks.

When he arrives at the home on Frutas Street, a gaggle of reporters awaits him. He stands outside and feeds sound bites to both the print and video press. Then he goes inside and has dinner with his family. It is an unsatisfying dinner. Somehow, they eat and yet remain hungry.

He is supposed to fix it. And he knows it is not yet fixed.

They walk six hundred miles from a coastal state called Tabasco to Mexico City. They are protesting an election stolen in November 1994. The peasants go the Mexican stock exchange, the Bolsa, and block its entrances with their bodies. The market opens two hours late this June day. At dawn on June 5, a vehicle pulls up next to the protesters, unloads boxes, and then roars away. The boxes hold the regime's financial records for its expenses in the contested Tabasco election. The government's party reported spending only $1.1 million in the governor's race. The receipts in the boxes note expenditures of $70 million. Tabasco has 500,000 voters.

In late June, Judge Abraham Polo Uscanga, age sixty, is dead in his Mexico City office with a bullet in his head. He has been dealing with the bankruptcy of a major urban bus line in the capital. Just three days before, the prosecutor involved in the case also was found with a bullet in his head. Earlier, in April, the city official who had closed down the line and broken the union was found dead. He had been shot twice in the chest. The authorities ruled this last death a suicide.[39]

During the sentencing phase of the trial, Phil Jordan testifies. He says one simple thing about the murder's effect on his family: "It killed all of us."

Miguel Angel Flores is sentenced to twenty years. Under Texas law, he will most likely serve twelve and a half years and gain his freedom when he is just about twenty-six years old.

Medrano begins piecing together an appeal based on relatively novel grounds: his own incompetence. This decision grates on him but it is the only thing he can think of now that might help his client.

Jorge Hank Rhon is unable to contain his love of wildlife. He lands in Mexico City in June after a long flight from Asia. Inside his twelve suitcases, Mexican inspectors find jewels, ocelot pelts, ivory tusks. He has declared the value of his imported goods at $1,000. He calls his father, Señor Hank González, for help over this small matter. His father has helped him before. In 1988, when a Tijuana gossip columnist named Hector Félix made fun of him in print, Jorge's bodyguards cut him down on his way to work. They went to prison, but Jorge was untouched. People of his position in the elite are called untouchables. He explained that the bodyguards, however mistaken, were just defending his honor. When Graciela de la Garza, an employee of the Mexican environmental protection agency, looked into his passion for collecting animals in the early 1990s, she was run off the road and received telephone threats. She was also beaten twice. After the cardinal was killed in Guadalajara in May 1993, and his killers boarded a waiting airliner, Jorge rode back to Tijuana with them in first class. All this is merely coincidence, a misunderstanding. As are the new charges this June day in the Mexico City airport. They will soon go away.[40]

Things tend to go away in the Hank family. A major drug figure, Juan Esparragozo Moreno, "El Azul," began working with them in trucking in 1982. The family shipping company, TMM, has had its mishaps. In October 1990, one of TMM's trucks entered California with nine thousand pounds of cocaine. Another one in 1997 is found with 2,517 pounds of coke down in Jalisco. In 1998, DEA is convinced a TMM boat offloaded a ton of coke in the Florida Keys. Amado Carrillo is a major investor in TMM. Colombian cartels are also believed by U.S. intelligence to be backers of the company.[41] The Hank family has consistently denied all such allegations.

Jordan is called to Washington as June winds down. He knows the trip is a signal. Ever since the Reno briefing he has been feeling these flutters in the wind. First, there is a certain tartness in Washington's reaction to the briefing because his analysts had been so free with names and facts and connections. The briefing had spoken the language of street agents who habitually weave together little shreds of information. And in the briefing, this fabric woven from shreds had led to the very top of the Mexican government. Part of the chill he has felt since the briefing, Jordan can easily dismiss as the rivalry between headquarters and the field, the internal tension that exists in every organization. EPIC is in an anomalous circumstance since it is the invention of headquarters and technically simply a branch of headquarters. But since Jordan's arrival in January, it has grown in a new way with the enlarged Mexico task force devouring raw data from the streets and weaving this endless fabric of analysis.

In many ways, this work of gnomes within the building has been Jordan's salvation, a place he can hide from his failure to solve his brother's murder. And so he resists all pressure to curtail this effort. Headquarters assigns new analysts to his group to keep an eye on it. Eventually, they send out one analyst who functions as nothing but a mole.

Now Jordan is back in D.C. reporting to his superior, Paul Daley. But he knows it is more than that. Daley is a longtime crony of the head of DEA, Thomas Constantine, one of his drinking buddies. And within the agency, Daley is widely perceived as Constantine's confidante.

The reason for Jordan's summons to headquarters is a new report his special task force on Mexico has put together, one on the corruption by the cartels of U.S. law enforcement along the border. The report holds fistfuls of intelligence on the penetration of U.S. Customs and of Immigration and Naturalization.

Daley flips through the report and asks, "Why are you putting this shit in a report?"

Daley explains he is concerned about the reaction from sister agencies.

"If you want me to delete this," Jordan says, "then you sign the report because it will no longer be a complete report."

Jordan is enraged. He wheels out of the office, grabs a phone, and calls his task force. He tells them to fax the raw intelligence reports on corrupt officials in U.S. law enforcement along all 1,800 miles of the border. Then he sits by the machine as the reports tumble out.

Finally, he gathers up the pile of papers and walks into Daley's office and flings them on his desk.

Jordan can sense his time running out. He gets a briefing at EPIC every Monday morning and these, to his surprise, and at times to his embarrassment, have been revelations. People he has indicted in the past now suddenly loom larger as the briefings outline their linkages to other people. People he has had done away with in the past now have a lingering force in the world of the cartels that he never imagined. He is unconsciously graduating from the world of the street agent into the textured world of the analyst. He is being forced to face what he always at some level knew: that operations against drug cartels play second fiddle to foreign policy and economic policy and domestic politics. His brother's ghost now figures into his new understanding. He knows that he has been called on the carpet about the report simply as a warning, a signal to pull back.

Since his brother's murder, his family has run advertisements in the newspapers offering tens of thousands of dollars in reward money for any tip leading to the perpetrators of the killing of Lionel Bruno Jordan. In such instances, particularly in two such low-income cities as Juárez and El Paso, the typical problem with such a posted reward is a flood of misinformation from cranks and from the greedy. But in this instance, such has not been the case.

To date there has not been a single call. Not even a call with just heavy breathing. Or a message left that is nothing but obscenities, possibly laughter.

blood

Dusk seeps along Frutas Street and smothers the row of houses lining the block along the railroad tracks. Phil Jordan is ten or fourteen or sixteen and it is always the same, the men—his uncles, his father, his grandfather—sitting out front on their porches until 10:30 visiting, the street quiet except for the voices of children playing. El Paso stretches along the river, a small city of a hundred thousand or so, the whole place sleepwalking. He is the second-oldest child of what will be five. Life is serene and there are no questions. His grandfather owns the block and the block across the street, and all the land behind the houses. It is a compound for people of the same blood.

Juárez, five or six blocks away, barely exists, a place with maybe 25,000 souls, and he never goes there alone and seldom goes there at all. He is not Phil Jordan but is Felipe and his last name is pronounced Hordan in keeping with Spanish. In his life, Spanish is the basic language.

The world is sports. His father is keen on baseball, one of his uncles owns a sporting goods store and sponsors teams. Felipe is the obedient child who returns promptly after school, does his homework, eats, and then goes to the park for a pickup game. He is always watched by hundreds of relatives and he knows it. He lives within a family empire. His grandfather systematically sets up each of his children in a business and plants each of them in a home along the block as they marry. So Felipe plays for one uncle's teams, and works at another uncle's feed store. This work begins long before he is legally of age for employment. Felipe debeaks thousands of chicks, tends to the loading and unloading of sacks. There is no time unaccounted for, not a minute. And time is absolute: being one minute late for a curfew is a

109

violation not to be contemplated. Once when he is fifteen, he takes a date to the nearby park where there is a small artificial lake. He is maybe a half hour late. His mother is racked with fear and rage when he returns, his father is icy in his silence. He never ventures to break the rules again. His father never strikes his children. His mother goes for the belt.

Sunday always means a family dinner at his grandfather's and the old man has a table large enough for all the children and all of their children. No one sits down until the old man sits down and he sits at the head of the table. Food is Italian and the women have toiled for hours making it. The wine is always some made by the old man. He is the center of the family and a man of unexplained but vast influence. He owns the El Paso Salvage Company and his junkyard surrounds his home along the tracks. He has a store filled with things old and new and the business boasts "The Only House That Buys and Sells Everything." In the back of the store, women manufacture his line of chile sauces and salsas ("Hot As Hell," on the label). He peddles a cure for baldness, and downtown owns a dance hall that is whispered to be a front for a brothel. He buys property, accumulates rentals. And every week, he files his column for the El Paso daily paper. His parties bring hundreds to Frutas Street and the leading politicians and officials make it a point to attend. His origins are vague to Felipe, something about coming from somewhere in Italy. He is very learned. The old man knows a fistful of languages: Latin, Italian, Spanish, English, French, Portuguese, and classical Greek. He keeps those secret notes in this last tongue.

No one asks the old man questions. His bearing precludes that. Felipe will work with him in his store, see people come in with problems, and watch his grandfather listen and then say, he will look into it. Sometimes an Italian will show up, and they will talk in their native language and if the visitor is special, the old man will send the person off with a bottle of his own wine. The old man keeps in touch with everything somehow, devours current events, notices little trends. When rock 'n' roll erupts in the mid-1950s, Felipe finds a hundred cases of one single stacked in a back room: Bill Haley's "Rock Around the Clock." And the store does not even sell records as a rule.

The dinners on Sunday are almost acts of state and they are the glue that holds the growing family together. No one is ever really totally relaxed around the old man what with his oceans of silence, his many opinions, his far-flung secretive interests, and his temper. He is not a man who answers questions, he is a man who delivers statements. He is the counselor, slowly, patiently explaining the way the world is and how a man deals with such a world. And such a man has no patience with trifles. Or with objections to his statements. Once, enraged, he grabs the tablecloth and a veritable banquet of plates and glasses and dishes crashes to the floor. And at such moments, nothing is said by anyone.

Eugene Forti, the old man, is called Nono, Italian for grandfather, by his children's children and, in time, somehow this becomes the family nickname for Felipe, who is the favored grandchild. After that, the old man becomes Papa Nono. Felipe lives in a border town totally sheltered from the famous vices that flow around him. Once, he secretly steals an uncle's cigar and puffs on it a few moments before getting ill. As a senior in high school, he ventures across the bridge to Juárez with friends and enters a saloon. But even there, he can feel family eyes on him and has only a Coca-Cola with a lime. He is afraid to smoke lest one of his aunts or uncles see him.

There is a bully in his neighborhood and Felipe is afraid of him. One day he is out in back of his parents' store when the other kid shoves him around. He flees into the store and his father asks him what is wrong. Felipe explains and his father says simply, "Push him back."

So he goes out again and beats the kid up. It is a lesson for him. Not about standing up to bullies but that he is permitted to respond to some situations. To strike back. Within his world of discipline, he learns there are moments of anger that are permitted.

He is fourteen or so and walking home in the evening with some friends after a game in the park. Two guys leaning against a wall say, hey, would you like a marijuana cigarette? Felipe and his friends hurry on. When he gets to Frutas Street, his grandfather and uncles and his father are on their porches. He tells them of the encounter. They leap up, throw Felipe into a car, and all go on the hunt. He sees the two guys, his uncles and father and grandfather stop. They beat the two to a bloody pulp.

There is no time to really think about things since all time is accounted for. Ambition is instilled in the Jordan children. Christina, the oldest, upsets the regime when she runs off as a teenager and marries and this rebellion only tightens the discipline. Felipe is an honors student, a baseball and basketball player, eventually student body president and a performer in school plays. He learns not to coast. Once he is benched by his coach for failing to play up to his potential. His father says nothing except that if he wants his position back on the team, he will have to win it back. And he does. But what he remembers is his father's silence and his lack of criticism. He receives neither sympathy nor a lecture. He is to do the right thing, period.

Only a few glimmers break through this tight little world. Once in a while, his family travels to the mountains about a hundred miles away and he marvels at the green forests. But that is the only journey. He never sees another city besides El Paso–Juárez. He barely knows that the world is round. A new horror movie, *The House of Wax,* hits El Paso and he rides the bus downtown to take it in. He leaves when it ends only to find out at home that he has left during the intermission. Felipe has never heard of a movie with an intermission and he scurries back downtown to take in the second half. In high school, the highlight of his week comes after a basketball game when his family in the stands will have left and gone home in the car, and he walks the streets back alone. He always stops in the drugstore and has a banana split alone, an adult occasion he cherishes decades later.

His brother and sister each carve out niches. Tony—the youngest then, with Bruno not even imagined as a possibility—has this talent for song and disappears into music. Virginia is the beauty entranced by clothes and the design of them and, eventually, she is the queen of the city's annual fiesta. Felipe has deeper ambitions, ones he can hardly admit even to himself. He fantasizes about being a pro basketball player. But more deeply, he catches a glimpse of the greater world when his team travels to other towns to play. And for one tournament they go all the way to Houston. He starts taking private tutoring in high school to erase his barrio accent.

He is going to be a lawyer. Everyone tells him that, especially his grandfather, who once dreamed of being a lawyer himself. He will go to college, absolutely. He will be a success.

His grandfather will capture songbirds in the backyard, kill them, and then roast them on a spit. He will appear and disappear on his various errands. He teaches business to his grandson, who watches him cut deals day after day. His grandfather will act neither surprised or superior. He will remain calm, revealing nothing of his inner feelings. Felipe watches and learns.

The old man lectures Felipe. Don't ever mess with the government. Don't lie under oath. Years later when Felipe has been long buried and only Phil Jordan exists, he will keep a complete collection of his grandfather's newspaper columns in his office as a touchstone. In the 1950s, his grandfather wrote one column denouncing the lynching of Emmett Till, a fourteen-year-old black boy vacationing in Mississippi from Chicago who was hanged from a bridge when he allegedly spoke inappropriately to a white woman. When Papa Nono went to his store after the column was published, he found a death threat on the door. He disregarded it. He explained that only cowards leave notes. The real killers give no warning.

Mexico spins on as a world ignored by Americans. In the late 1950s, there is a massive strike of railroad workers. It becomes a test of strength between the Mexican regime and the workers. And it is a test the government is determined not to fail. The military seizes the trains and arrests 10,000 to 25,000 railroad workers who vanish into stockades. The leadership of the unions go to prison for about a decade for the crime of "social dissolution." One leader dies under torture. His body is left on the railroad tracks, his nails painted red and lipstick glowing from his lips. He is a warning and labor essentially collapses as a force in Mexico.[1] The greatest living muralist in Mexico, David Alfaro Siqueiros, denounces the regime. He is imprisoned for years. This all happens under a president, Adolfo López Mateos, who is in the eyes of Americans the Mexican counterpart to John F. Kennedy, a handsome, womanizing man who loves literature and fast cars.

•   •   •

He is born in Guamuchilito, Sinaloa, in the early 1950s—no one outside of his family is sure of the year. He will live almost all of his life
before many outside of his family are even clear on the name of the
town. In the 1990s, secret DEA documents would state: "AKA Juan
Carlos Barron Ortiz, Amado Fuentes, Amado Carrillo, Alfonso Paredes,
Cuatro, El Cuatro, Zero Cuatro. DOB: October, 1950 or December 17,
1954 or December 17, 1955. Place of birth: Villa Angel Flores, Sinaloa
or according to INS records, Badiraguato, Sinaloa."

His father is a farmer with no money and many children—no one
outside the family is certain of their number. Sinaloa is a small state on
the west coast of Mexico that harbors a long tradition of banditry. It is
a place of legends and poverty. His father belongs to the poverty and
the boy becomes a herder at an early age. He loves to milk cows. He
loves to play soccer. Much later, he will be remembered as decent,
hardworking, and true to his church.

He comes up in a world rich in culture. In the late nineteenth century, Chinese immigrants bring opium to Sinaloa and it flourishes here
and there as another crop. The state is tropical and when World War II
deprives the United States of the Asian opium necessary for morphine,
Mexico is encouraged to replace the supply and Sinaloa booms. Even
Mexican soldiers tend the poppies and fortunes are made. When the
war ends, the United States ends its purchase of this licit production.
But in Sinaloa the culture of opium persists because of another rich
culture that swaddles the young Amado Carrillo. Crime. Sinaloa dotes
on its bandit heritage. In the capital of Culiacán is a major shrine, one
unacknowledged by the church, which tends to this culture.

On May 3, 1909, Jesús Malverde was hanged from a tree and left
to rot. Or so the story goes. There is no evidence that Malverde ever
lived and scholars wonder if he is a merger of two other renowned ban-
dits. In legend, he is born in 1870, and worked as a construction
worker or as a tailor or maybe on a railroad. But in the stories, somehow he is wronged and then he becomes a robber because his parents
died of hunger. Or he becomes a robber because the governor makes
some challenge to him and he steals inside his mansion, takes his
sword, and writes on the wall, "Jesus M. was here." He takes from the

rich, gives to the poor, on this there is agreement. He dies because he is shot. Or he dies because a friend cuts off his feet and then drags him to the authorities for a reward. Or he dies swinging from a limb on May 3, 1909. Or a cop shot him with a bow and arrow, he contracts gangrene, and has a friend take in his corpse for the reward and his cadaver is hanged from a tree. His betrayer is dead within three days. The governor perishes in thirty-three days from a cold he caught when he forgot to wear his slippers. Or none of this happened.

After the death of Malverde, a woman loses her cow, prays to him, and it is returned. Or a friend can't find his mule train laden with silver and gold, prays to the bones of Malverde hanging from the tree, and his treasure is restored. A small shrine comes into being, more people come, more people pray.[2] Malverde, who existed or never existed, exists absolutely as a source of succor for the people of Sinaloa. He is part of the culture Amado Carrillo sucks in like the air itself.

Carrillo becomes very educated, a lawyer. Or Carrillo is almost illiterate, speaks bad Spanish, has little schooling. He tends cows in Sinaloa. He is unknown. An uncle, Ernesto Fonseca Carrillo, takes an interest in him. He is part of the drug business of the state. In the 1950s, tough bars began to appear in Culiacán, the capital, bars frequented by country people deep into the drug business. There would be killings from time to time in these bars, but no one paid much attention to the ways of these lowlifes. Also, the traditional folk music of the area, corridos, began to tentatively offer a few tales of the drug business. Fonseca comes from this world. And he notices that his nephew Amado and his brothers could be useful in it.

Eventually, the state government grows uneasy about this new emerging life amid its licit economy of agriculture. The state trucks vegetables north to the U.S. and Canada in the winter, hosts big fields of wheat and soybeans. The opium is an embarrassment, as is Malverde, a criminal folk saint. The shrine is a pile of stones on what is believed to be Malverde's grave. The government decrees the site will be bulldozed and a new state office building erected on it. In the late 1970s, as the blade pushes the rocks aside they are said to explode and jump like popcorn. The entire city is said to have turned out for the occasion, or so goes the legend. Protests force the government to give land for a shrine just across the street. Malverde slowly becomes known as El Narcosantón, the Big Drug Saint.

Carrillo is beneath the surface of this world but woven into its fabric.

"He sure liked milking the cows," one local woman later remembers. "He did it very fast. And he liked to drink milk too. Sometimes he would drink milk right out of the udder."[3]

People in his hometown of Guamuchilito remember that when he leaves at age twelve or thirteen, he says, "I won't come back until I'm rich."[4]

They live in relative obscurity and they live off the traffic of the line. The family of Raúl Salinas Lozano hails from the tiny municipio of Agualeguas in Nuevo León, a border state facing Laredo and San Antonio, Texas. The name comes from an all but extinct Indian tribe (only one speaker is listed as left in the municipio) and the area has but five thousand people. The father is trained as an economist, publishes books in his field, and most important, rises in the ruling party, the PRI, Party of the Institutional Revolution. He helps write Mexico's tax laws in 1952 and makes the president's cabinet in 1958 in charge of commerce and industry. He has five children: Raúl, Jr., the eldest; then Carlos, the future president; Enrique, who becomes a business consultant; Sergio, an academic sociologist; and Adriana Margarita, who eventually marries power.

The children are raised in a culture where privileges bar one from any hard knowledge of one's own country and of any consequences for one's acts. The American rich, particularly of the political class, live almost as populists in comparison. Mexico has long had a secret habit of self-hatred among its rulers, who are generally European in descent, fair in skin color, and educated in Europe for generations, and then in the latter decades of the twentieth century, increasingly schooled at major U.S. institutions.

Thus, when Carlos and Raúl, Jr., execute their twelve-year-old Indian maid as children the episode is erased from public discussion. And they are raised in the family business, one that includes a ranch in

Agualeguas and a fine home in the capital. They are what are called "the juniors," the children of the ruling class, and this class is feared by average Mexicans because of their behavior and immunity from punishment. Years later, a drug cartel in Tijuana will begin recruiting killers from this class for these very reasons.

The family business, besides politics and ranching, is whispered for decades to be smuggling. Raúl Salinas, Sr., allegedly has, through political connections, control of Customs stations in his area of the northern frontier. This is hardly a small matter in Mexico, which for decades lives under a state-managed economy with large slabs owned by the government and Mexican enterprises sheltered by high tariffs. This wall of Customs agents in a nation with an inability to produce consumer goods leads naturally to smuggling. In the capital, a traditional thieves' market dating back to the Aztecs, Tepito, flourishes on contraband and the government winks at the practice in hopes of placating the nation's middle class. And the bulk of the middle class is in the capital where over 20 percent of the nation lives.

Raúl Salinas, Sr., becomes the successful, respectable man who is building a fortune and founding a dynasty. And like so many men in such work, he forms relationships that do not appear on his official vita. In the 1950s, he allegedly teams up with a man named Juan N. Guerra, a player in the region's smuggling network. Guerra is a border legend. Once he shot his wife dead and the case was dismissed as self-defense. He is also rumored to have murdered a son of Pancho Villa's and on another occasion to have killed someone for talking too loudly in a café. He explains to people, "I don't live by dreams but by realities."[5] He is the uncle of a youngster named Juan García Abrego, a man who will eventually head the Gulf cartel, have a fortune of billions or tens of billions, and become a friend of Raúl Salinas, Jr., and other family members.

The two oldest boys, Raúl and Carlos, form an intense bond that strikes others for decades. They are less brothers than best friends, intimates of the deepest kind. When they travel in France as young men, they compete with each other in bagging women. They are dedicated horsemen. They share a consciousness much like identical twins. Raúl is seen as the leading son for years, the one who will assume the mantle. But there is a willfulness in him that causes concern. As a student in the 1960s, he joins rebels plotting a revolt in Chiapas. Even at the peak of his career under his brother Carlos's presidency, he continues to spew forth volumes of poetry and books of short stories with titles like *Muerte Calculada,* Calculated Death.

Carlos becomes interested in economics. In the 1960s, he is a kind of grandee at school in Mexico City, and at one point he deputizes a fellow student, Eduardo Valle, to go to Cuba, attend a conference, and then return to Mexico City and report everything to Carlos. Valle is struck by the young Salinas. Years later he will serve as his drug investigator during the presidency. But he retains one strong impression from their student days, that Salinas is all but insane, living within a kind of power-obsessed psychosis in which he functions as a veritable emperor. Once when Salinas is president, I have dinner with a Mexican newspaper publisher in the north who knows Carlos Salinas. I offer that maybe he will be the Gorbachev of Mexico, the man whose reforms will alter the totalitarian regime. The man looks at me in amazement, and snaps, "Not Gorbachev. Stalin." Another student who hangs out at the family home in the 1970s once engages Carlos in a typical college argument about social justice. Carlos looks at the student coldly, and announces, "You do not live in the real world."

Carlos eventually attends Harvard as a graduate student and produces a thesis on the impact of the Mexican ruling party among the campesinos. He concludes that the more contact peasants have with the regime, the more they hate it.

But mainly, Carlos is being groomed for power. He misses the major event of his generation, the student revolt of 1968 and the subsequent massacre of the students by the regime. He is after power and that is found within the boundaries of the nation's single ruling party. He is lucky also. For decades, Mexico's rulers have come from a political class that works up a ladder of governorships and other posts that require participation in the staged elections. But as Salinas begins to rise, there is a shift toward administrative functionaries from the capital's elite being picked for the highest posts. This new breed of bureaucrats is called technocrats and Salinas is a leader of this new group. Since he is short, bald, and politically unskilled in speechmaking and handshaking, this is an unforeseen break in his quest for power.

Like Carrillo and Jordan, Carlos Salinas comes up in the nest of family and saturated in a culture that will be extinguished by the world he will eventually operate in. All three of them will come from an intense local world and rise in a world that obliterates the local. And all three will early on realize the potential of a new global economy in drugs.

When Felipe Jordan is a senior in high school, he begins to piece something together, to assemble a kind of understanding from family silences. He keeps hearing of other Fortis, of other families sharing his grandfather's last name, but never asks about these families and in those idle moments when he thinks about them, he decides maybe his grandfather had an earlier marriage that no one wishes to discuss. His grandfather is at the height of his powers, and he has decided that Felipe will go to college, no matter what. No one in the family has ever gone to college but the grandfather has made this decision. He has also decided that his grandson will be a lawyer. This last matter is a passion with him. And Felipe's father, Antonio, is equally adamant. Antonio, also an athlete, had won a college scholarship. But he could not accept it because he had to work to support his parents.

Felipe for the first time hears the whispers about his grandfather's past. The old man was born March 6, 1886, in the village of Bovo in Calabria, a criminal state south of Naples with an organization that rivals the Sicilian Mafia. Government records note that he entered the United States around January 1905 at New Orleans. On the record, he is Eugenio Levini Forti. The last name is a lie.

In Calabria, he was the bright young student learning classical tongues and training to be an attorney. Two of his brothers were local priests. When he was eighteen, a man came to the parish house, asked for money, and murdered one of his brothers. Or two men came. This part is unclear. The dead brother's name was Carlo Bruno. Eugene and another brother sought out the killer or killers. And slaughtered them.

In some stories, they slaughtered their families also. They fled the inevitable vendettas that would surely rain down upon them, and also, any possible charges by the police. They parted in New Orleans with one brother heading for Pennsylvania. At the port of entry they took the family name, Foti, added an *r* and became new men in a new world.

Eugene left New Orleans because of a fever outbreak and took a boat to Tampico, Mexico. He somehow crossed northern Mexico and appeared in Juárez. Then he entered El Paso and for years built a business out of rag picking and salvage. These years are lost and when he next enters family memory he is the father, the patriarch, with sons named Lionel, Victor, Felipe, and Mickey, and a daughter, Beatrice, out of Dante's *Inferno,* of course. He has his *Casa que Compra y Vende Todo,* his El Paso Salvage Company, and a slogan for all his enterprises, *Fortíquese con Forti,* Fortify Yourself with Forti. He has his hooks into local power and cuts a deal for scavenger rights to the city dump for a lump annual payment of $900. He also has at least one other family of children on the side, something Felipe Jordan and his siblings will not discover until the 1980s.

But then, the old man kept everything about his past so obscure that his son-in-law, Antonio, would eventually name his last son Lionel in honor of the old man's middle name, ignorant of the fact that his real middle name was Levini.

As Felipe graduates from high school and entertains a full scholarship offer from Texas A&M, the old man quietly shores up his destiny. Each summer, while he is in college, Felipe will return to El Paso and work at jobs—an oil refinery, a steelworks—arranged by the old man through his influence. Felipe will constantly talk with him, and listen to him. He will never ask him about what happened in Italy, simply feed off little scraps that slip from the adults in his family. The old man is setting his house in order. When Felipe gets what he thinks is a better offer from the University of New Mexico and leaves Texas A&M, the old man agrees and, after all, now the boy can come down to El Paso more easily from his new berth in Albuquerque. In 1962, Eugene Forti's wife dies, and, his businesses largely distributed among his children, he moves across the river to Juárez and takes up with a much younger

Mexican woman. He opens a junkyard there, a grocery store, and other ventures. He is a born capitalist. Felipe will come down and visit him and seek advice as his college years grind on. The old man will calmly explain things to him, tell him about foreign affairs, domestic politics, a whole grim world that he keeps tabs on. Everything but what to do when someone murders your brother.

It is a kind of harsh fantasy world. The old man lives surrounded by prosperous children from his various families. He will, by the time he eventually dies, have from his legitimate family twenty-seven grandchildren and twenty-eight great-grandchildren. And he has this legacy no one speaks of but that hangs in the air.

He has brought some of the ghost world of Calabria with him, a world where strange powers move and darkness can penetrate the blaze of day. Once, before he moves to Juárez, the old man is reading when something falls from the ceiling and splatters him but when he looks up there is nothing there. The old man shouts out his late wife's name and Tony and his mother, who are next door, race across the intervening patio and find the grandfather in shock, the ceiling black with flies leading from the kitchen to the bedroom where the old man had been reading.

After the old man moves to Juárez and his new woman, the house on Frutas Street where he ruled for so many years stays empty. None of his children living up and down the block knows quite what to do with it. They think it is haunted. While in high school, Virginia and Tony decide to spend the night there. In the dark hours, they hear sounds, strange winds, and then the solid floors begin to buckle and make waves. Closets open and close. They flee in panic. After that, the house becomes a place to store things and no one enters it very often or spends time there. Once, one of the family dogs refuses to enter and flees in panic. The house sits right across the patio from the Jordan family home in El Paso, well painted and kept up and avoided. When the old man finally dies, another thing is noticed: the buckled floors go suddenly level and stay that way.

The old man would come over to El Paso every week or two to buy things. In the 1960s, he takes young Tony along on his shopping trips, expeditions the grandson grows to dread. The old man has opinions and is not shy about voicing them. He objects to women wearing pants because such garments give away their shapes and destroy anticipation. He also has little sympathy with males wearing long hair. Tony and his grandfather, who is moving up on eighty, will be in a checkout line and a guy with long hair is ahead and the old man taps the guy on the shoulder and says, "Excuse me, miss, excuse me, lady." Then Tony has to calm everyone down. The old man, he thinks to himself, doesn't give a fuck about anything.

Years later when Tony is on the road singing, he calls his mother from St. Louis. He has just been to a movie, *The Amityville Horror*, about a house possessed by demons. The film has shaken him and taken him back to the memories of the night he and his sister tried to stay in the old man's house on Frutas Street.

He asks his mother, "Papa Nono really did kill that family in Italy, didn't he?"

His mother says, "Yes."

Amado Carrillo lives in a world where there are laws but these laws are not for everyone. The Sinaloa that formed him is a slippery environment even by Mexican standards. From 1945 to 1950, it was ruled by General Pablo Macías Valenzuela, who took up the governorship after serving as secretary of war and defense. He was accused of running an opium ring by Mexico City newspapers. A brief meeting with the president of Mexico ended such press reports.[6] This was the first time there was any public mention of the link between the drug trade and the government. In the 1930s, it was widely known that a woman called Lola la Chata was the queen of dope in Mexico City and protected by the anti-narcotics police. Of course, the narcotics police of that era were paid with part of the drugs they seized.

In Sinaloa, this soft policing and official acceptance of the trade reached a new level. By the 1950s, Culiacán, the capital, was described in the Mexican press as a "new Chicago with gangsters in sandals." At that time, the local press sought a United Nations sanction of the state's opium crop. The editor leading this campaign became the attorney general of Sinaloa in the early 1950s. At the same time, the federal government would wage campaigns against the opium growers to placate the United States. In 1953, the federal government announced the closing of an aviation school in Culiacán as part of this gesture of compliance. Beneath the gestures, business continued. By the late 1960s, at least six hundred secret airfields operated in the Mexican north. At the same time, federal police officers dreamed of being assigned to Sinaloa because of the money to be made in the drug trade. The local press referred to the federal police as "Attila's hordes."

A curious climate slowly rises in the tropical state. The drug business is blinked at by a government feeding off its profits. There is never a war between the drug business and government in Mexico, simply moments of friction caused either by the state's desire to assert its power or by the government's need to mollify the United States. It resolves conflict with a hard hand. After the student revolt in Mexico City in 1968, there are sweeps into the Sierra Madre of Sinaloa to crush growers lest they finance rebellion. This is part of a general clampdown by the central government on all forms of dissent. Dozens, possibly hundreds, of students are slaughtered by the military on the night of October 2, 1968, in a plaza in Mexico City. The bodies vanish, presumably burned. The living are hauled off to prison and military stockades and tortured. Then, they face the courts. The judges issue and publish sentences for 113 students before they hold the trials. One defendant, Gilberto Rincón Gallardo, is charged with tossing grenades and burning twelve buses. Rincón was born with both arms short and malformed.[7] A week after the slaughter of the students, Mexico City hosts the Olympics and the memory of the massacre is erased from public discussion. Two years later, the man in charge of the slaughter becomes the president of Mexico.

Amado Carrillo is formed by these events and by this sense of law and order. For Amado, born into the business thanks to his Uncle Fonseca Carrillo, the path is clear. He becomes typical of his drug culture: intensely patriotic, deeply distrustful of his corrupt government, absolutely enmeshed in family.

•   •   •

Phil Jordan emerges in Albuquerque as the sixth man on the varsity team. He knows he will never make the pros, that he is good, that he is all hustle, but that he is not gifted. The head coach who recruits him leaves, the new coach sees him as someone else's idea. The trainer, Tow Diehm, becomes his mentor and he sizes Jordan up as a fair basketball player but someone with world-class work habits. Jordan graduates in June 1964 and that fall marries his college sweetheart, Mary. She is an anglo from South Dakota, a wife for Phillip, rather than Felipe. Soon she is pregnant and Jordan is scrambling with marriage, studies, and odd jobs such as coaching the university's junior varsity team. He is about to enter law school.

In May of 1965, the college placement office sends him a postcard about a possible job opening with the Bureau of Dangerous Drugs, the forerunner to DEA. Jordan looks at the card in amazement: he did not even know there was a federal narcotics agency. So he goes to the interview on a lark and meets agent Jack Kelly. Kelly is the son of a tough New Jersey cop and has spent his career chasing small-time marijuana, heroin, and opium dealers. The United States at the time has a midget drug market and BDD has about three hundred agents. Kelly heads the Albuquerque office. He sells Jordan an attractive bill of goods: a safe federal salary, great benefits, retirement after thirty years, the fun of the chase, and, best of all, sure advancement for any Spanish-speaking agent because there is a growing flow of drugs from Mexico. Diehm, the trainer, tells Jordan it is a great opportunity.

Jordan takes the job and abandons his law school dreams. He goes for the sure thing. He reports that summer and Kelly reaches into his drawer and hauls out a gun and a badge, number 207. That is the training.

Within two days, Jordan is undercover and makes a heroin buy. He works out of a two-man office, himself and Kelly. And he is essential because he is the only one who can speak Spanish. His son is born soon after he starts the job. He loves it and is full of self-righteous feelings as he takes down dopers. After a few months, he is sent to Washington for some training: classes on the law, time on the shooting range, some physical workouts. That is it. Nothing on how to work undercover.

Nothing much at all. He lives in a quiet backwater of the federal government, a tiny facet of the government with only 397 agents. The agency was created during the marijuana panic of the 1930s, the fabled reefer madness, and now lingers on mainly tormenting ethnic Chinese who use opium, the tiny colonies of big-city heroin users, and the new Mexican networks that are bringing north some marijuana and heroin from Sinaloa.

Within six months, he is transferred to Phoenix, a move he loves. He often visited Arizona for games during his college basketball years and he has fond memories of the desert and of the more open and booming society than the one he knew in El Paso. He enters a world where analysis is not valued and where the big picture is that there is no big picture. There is this thing, the drug problem, and it is made manifest by drug dealers. These are small-time operators, peddling a few ounces here and there. A bust of a kilo of heroin is major-league and something that might not occur during an entire career spent with BDD.

Think small, think finite. Depend on snitches, make a buy, then slap on the cuffs. One of the curiosities of the drug business is that the police forces form networks and systematic outlooks more slowly than the dealers. Jordan stationed in Phoenix has a viewpoint that barely covers Arizona. The people he tries to arrest have connections that at a minimum go deep into Mexico and at times reach over into Asia. And this tendency toward operating with blinders on is increased by police pressure and police habits. For cops, informants are assets not to be shared with other cops. They are the source of career advancement. Few DEA agents trust other agents with their informants. Arrests are essential to individual careers and, thus, information about drug dealers tends to become a kind of private property within the agency.

People in the drug business are forced by circumstance into alliances that make them have a broader perspective. The grower must buy protection from government. The drug dealer moving goods north also must work with government and, hopefully, bribe and form alliances with American officials to facilitate the smuggling. Then there is the need for further contacts and alliances to enable distribution of the goods. Money must be laundered, creating yet more networks. And, through trial and error, these associations must be kept isolated from each other, like cells if possible, so that one breakdown, one arrest, does not threaten the organization. Over time, as each tendency is heightened by the needs of each culture, the drug business slowly pulls away from the police business and leaves it in the dust with its lack of sophistication.

An early arrest of Jordan's in Phoenix captures the chasm between the two realities. He gets a tip that a man named Jesús Aviles, an operator of a restaurant and owner of a fine home, is dealing heroin. He starts meeting with him in dives like the Peek-a-Boo bar. In time, he makes the buy and takes him down. But he never understands who Aviles is and what he represents. He is from Sinaloa and related to Pedro Pérez Aviles, a cutthroat who has been active in the drug business since the 1940s. The treasurer of Pérez Aviles's organization is one Ernesto Fonseca Carrillo, Amado Carrillo's uncle. And Pérez, a name Jordan does not know when he takes down Aviles in the 1960s, is forging a new kind of thing in Sinaloa and Sonora, a cartel to blend and make harmonious the interests of various drug groups in Sinaloa. He is doing this because the pressure of paying off the Mexican government and dealing with U.S. police agencies is forcing him into some new form of organization. He is inventing order almost unconsciously amid the natural disorder of an outlaw culture.

Pérez moves multiton loads of marijuana to Southern California and Arizona. Then he fashions South American connections for cocaine. He handles the local Sinaloan heroin. He is the center of a growing marketing organization.[8] Jordan is part of a three-man office in Phoenix. He is making arrests, getting good reports and promotions. He realizes that there is a network supplying the small-time dealers he busts but he has no idea of its scope or members.

Then he meets his guide in this new world, a man named Fernando Terrazas.

When he is about forty, Fernando dreams of owning a bar. One day he visits a friend's saloon and in the parking lot he notices a man put a bag in the back seat of his friend's car and then vanish. He tells his friend and they check and find a bag of marijuana planted to cause him trouble. They throw it into the river. Fernando thinks this over and goes to the state police and says, "You know, I could help you catch some drug guys if you help me get a liquor license." They turn him down, so he tries federal agents. They are interested but can't be of any help in getting a state liquor license.

And then a year later, the federal agents call him and say they will pay if he can help. So he does. That is how he begins. His first case is a very old man, a man who has been selling heroin for decades and whom no one can catch. To make a deal with the old man, you must walk alone eight miles into the hills and pick up what you have purchased under a tree. The old man himself never gets near his product, the cardinal rule of survivors in the drug business. Fernando starts cultivating the old man and soon the guy is quite taken and wants to make Fernando his partner. Fernando walks the eight miles into the hills, gets the heroin, makes the case, and so his first deal results in a man in his late seventies going away forever.

Fernando discovers something special: he is a natural and he loves the work. He also discovers that the federal agents are fools, a bunch of damned gringos who are an embarrassment to be around. And they cannot speak Spanish. Then he meets this young guy just assigned to the Phoenix bureau, a kid from El Paso called Phil Jordan.

Fernando hails from Chihuahua. He is raised on a small rancho and, eventually, he comes north, works in the fields, and winds up with a job running heavy equipment in a mine. He marries, has children, builds his own house. Jordan instantly knows who and what Fernando is from a thousand childhood conversations in the barrio. And there is a deeper bond: he recognizes a mentor. Normally, agents run their confidential informants like cattle. But Fernando hardly fits this mold. He is not a felon forced to cooperate, he is an independent. His large frame carries a silence and distance that say he refuses to be simply a tool or gofer for federal agents. He is a man you can never order, simply ask. He sizes up Jordan and adopts him as a son. Then the lessons begin.

"All you gotta be," he calmly explains, "is be quiet. Don't tell. It's not the business of anyone else. My children don't know. My wife knows, I have no secrets from my wife. To do this kind of job you have to be a liar and don't forget what you say. It's easy, it's easy. Don't tell.

"The only way you can do the cases is I'm the dumb one. I don't know anything about drugs. I buy, you sell, we make money. That's it. Never be smarter than the other guy, even if you're just selling a truck. When you talk, don't tell them anything you don't know or anything they don't need to know. Don't open your mouth if you're not supposed to. Be nice, buy drinks, go out to eat. Never lose control."

Jordan listens. For the work, Fernando favors an $1,800 gold bracelet, a gold watch with the face surrounded by diamond chips, $400 cowboy boots, a fine cowboy shirt, gold rings with rubies, a $350 Stetson. Jordan becomes the man in the suit, the middle-level business guy in a large distribution network who employs Fernando as a contact for transactions. Fernando avoids drink in his work and he despises drunkards. He hates all weakness, all loose talk. He is an accomplished liar.

Once on a case, a dealer tells Fernando to get in a car in the driver's seat and then the man climbs into the passenger seat and thrusts a gun into Fernando's ribs and says, "I'm going to find out if you're for fucking real." Fernando, as is his custom, carries no gun. He is of the belief that guns cause trouble. Besides, he knows, "Assholes never kill you. Anybody who shows you a gun won't kill you because he is a coward."

As he feels the cold metal of the pistol against his side, Fernando makes a decision. He gets out of the car and sits on the ground. He then tells the stranger, "Shoot me and I'll keep my fucking money and you keep your fucking shit."

The man thinks, and then does the deal.

And goes down.

Fernando is formed by an iron life. When he was a fourteen-year-old in Chihuahua, he planted, tilled with horses, and harvested an eighty-three-ton crop of pinto beans, alone. When someone crosses him at fifteen, he shoots him. He is a dead shot with a .45. He lives within compartments. No one at the mine knows he works undercover on cases. His children do not question his absences. Once, he comes home from a case in his Cadillac and his young son finds bullet holes in the door. He never asks.

Jordan finds in Fernando a gold mine of cases. He never fails. Jordan can send him in anywhere and Fernando makes a deal. Soon promotions are raining down on Jordan. The two families become close and visit back and forth. Fernando is a new father for Jordan. And he is a stern father. When his two sons balk toward the end of high school at the idea of college, Fernando scoops them up and drives to the great central valley of California where stoop labor brings in the crops. He drops them off in a field with a tent.

He says, "You'd better get use to this because you are going to be doing it the rest of your life."

When he comes back at the end of the summer, his sons have decided to go to college.

As Fernando teaches the young agent the ropes of the drug business, Jordan's marriage disintegrates. There are now two children, Sean and Brigitte. A house in the suburbs of Phoenix, a steady check but it is not enough. In part, it may be the hours, the nights prowling joints doing deals. In part, it is the fate of college romances, people change and realize they married young and now they are someone else. But in good part, it is because Phil Jordan lands in a world where the lessons taught Felipe Jordan go by the boards.

He has power, an office, a secretary. He is out of the discipline of Frutas Street and the basketball squads. Like most successful narcs, he begins to live the hours of the drug business, the velvet hours of bars and drinks and stancing and deals. Narcs and drug merchants have a lot in common. Neither group hails from the traditional elites or the schools that groom the promising to join the elites. And then suddenly, due to the realities of the trade, they are presented with possibilities of money and power alien to their backgrounds. And women. They change without changing. The drug merchants tend toward religious devotions amid their occupational mayhem. The narcs discover saloons and women who are available.

In the fall of 1969, he divorces and does not remarry for ten years. He cannot bear the failure, the inability to do what his grandfather and father achieved seemingly without effort. And as Jordan wheels and deals in Phoenix, his family is never far. He calls his mother every day.

And in 1967, he learns he has a new brother, one named Lionel Bruno Jordan. His parents redesign their life around raising this late child.

Phil's sister Virginia falls in love and marries. Her husband is a man on the rise. In the early 1960s, he is a dishwasher at a joint in Juárez. Then suddenly, he owns his own club. Virginia meets him in 1970 and he is the perfect gentleman, a man in his late thirties who wears glasses and extends every courtesy. And his club is impressive: a bar, restaurant, stage, mezzanine, a class place. No one asks about his sudden rise in the world.

The entire Jordan family is not prone to asking questions. The grandfather has created a climate and it is an unquestioning climate. In this world, Mexico is a reality but an unexamined one.

When Bruno is born, Tony is about fourteen and he becomes the one who must keep an eye on the new child. Phil's children, Brigitte and Sean, spend the summers on Frutas Street when Phil has them because of the custody settlement. But he is a failure as a parent, a man consumed by his work. Tony becomes like a god to them. Tony is outgoing, the sunny son, and Bruno becomes the brother Tony knows best. He goes to high school, parties, and works on his singing.

In 1972 when Tony is nineteen, he leaves El Paso and goes to Mexico City to try his fortune as a singer. He is broke, hungry, and in a huge city. He knocks on doors and finally gets an audience with Capitol Records. He wants to be a star singing in Spanish.

One night he walks the city to shake off depression. He comes on a club named after Roberto Cantoral, at the time about the biggest songwriter in Mexico. He looks in and walks on. About an hour later, he returns, shells out the money to go in, and sits through the show. He can't even afford a drink while he listens to the performance. He screws up his courage and approaches the singer, saying, "I came to see you."

Cantoral starts to blow him off but then changes his mind and gives him a phone number and says call. Tony is desperate. He has this audition coming up he arranged with Capitol Records. But he does not know what to do at the audition. Finally, he nails Cantoral between shows at his club and sings "The Flower Has Died," a song that begins softly and ends strongly. Cantoral is impressed. He takes Tony under his wing and arranges a deal with another record company, Polydor. Soon Tony records the Spanish language cover of "The Most Beautiful Girl in the World," and it is a hit. He is now Tony Solo, singing star. He travels to Colombia, Spain, anyplace he can get a gig.

Virginia and her husband come down and they see the city together. Tony is impressed with his brother-in-law, who speaks excellent Spanish, has such a fine club, and a wonderful sense of humor. Everything is working out. Virginia has made an excellent marriage. Phil is rising as a federal agent. And Tony is on his way to a career in show business.

In Mexico City, Tony meets some important people. Manuel "Chapo" Ibarra, secretary of the gobierno, has him sing at parties at his ranch. He personally signs visas for Tony. Then there is this guy named Carlos Hank González. He grew up with Cantoral and Ibarra, and Tony becomes friends with him also. Once, Tony is at a party at the palace when President Luis Echeverría gives his *Informe,* the Mexican State of the Union message, and Hank González sits there with Tony.

Hank González, orphaned at three, became a youth leader in the ruling party at age seventeen and in 1955 became mayor of Toluca, a city just outside Mexico City. He swiftly amassed a fortune based on cronyism and skimming contracts and feeding state money to his own trucking firm. He is famous for his cordial nature and his iron fist. In the 1960s, he moved up in the federal government and snared large portions of the shipping for his company. He is the essence of power in Mexico: wealth based on pillaging the federal treasury through graft. For decades he will be a rumored link between the business of drugs and the business of the state.

Tony is in tight: these guys tell him of a coming devaluation in the late 1970s three months before the peso tumbles. He travels back and forth to El Paso, jets to other countries, cuts records. Life is a lark.

For Phil the deals he makes keep getting larger. He is in a two-man office, then it expands to three men. Things are offhanded. Once he gets shorted on a buy and his superior hauls sugar out of a desk drawer and suggests they use it in order to make up the weight for the records. Jordan is stunned by this act. He can never get enough flash money from the agency and is reduced to wrapping a hundred around a wad of singles and praying no one ever demands a closer look.

He is in the middle of a boom. In 1969, the federal government drops $65 million in policing narcotics. By 1974, the budget is $719 million. In 1973, a new entity is forged and called the Drug Enforcement Administration. The staff keeps expanding. And yet it is still a provincial place. Federal drug policy is based on political considerations, not drug use. It is a charade to placate voters about a problem that barely exists. For example, in 1975, DEA has 111 agents in Chicago handling only 138 cases in a year and 119 of these cases are for weights less than a pound. At the same time, the federal snitch budget for DEA nationwide zooms from $750,000 in 1969 to $10 million in 1976.[9]

Jordan, working out of a now eight-man bureau in Phoenix, is accidentally in one part of this new industry that is experiencing a real increase in traffic. He keeps working on his buys and busts with Fernando and they slowly follow a trail back to Mexico. The deals keep growing in size and they encounter a new name, Pedro Pérez Aviles. He is the spider at the center of the web they are brushing up against. Jordan meets with Pérez in Mexico and talks a deal. He finds a man who is very calm and collected and all business. Pérez is fair-skinned, of medium height, and has a .45 stuffed in his waistband. He is surrounded by pistoleros. They continue to negotiate over the phone and talk in code. Jordan makes small buys and goes deeper.

Fernando is in a cantina just across the line in Mexico in San Luis Río Colorado, Sonora, a town owned by Pedro Pérez Aviles. He is wearing fine things. He is speaking with a man, a stranger, and he says, "I need something good."

The man says okay, and gets him some kilos. Fernando never buys small amounts, that is beneath him. When he begins working with Jordan, he would negotiate small buys but after he hit his stride, he would only stir from his home for real weight. So the kilos of heroin, samples to determine the seller's quality, are delivered on the U.S. side and then tested. They are low-grade.

Fernando goes back to the man, the stranger, and says, "You give me shit. You embarrass me before my people."

The man apologizes. The next shipment, much larger, is high-grade. And then he goes down.

These busts keep chipping away at the business of Pedro Pérez Aviles and eventually he notices this gnat, Phil Jordan, causing problems for his organization.

As Jordan and Fernando slowly probe Pérez's organization, money becomes a problem. Jordan is pretending to be the buyer for an organization that sells in Arizona, New Mexico, California, and Colorado. He is scrambling for money. DEA can't ever seem to come up with the kind of wad he needs to flash to dealers. At one point, he's been fronted a couple of kilos by the Pérez organization as a good-faith gesture and now he can't pay them. So he tries a ruse. He signs a personal promissory note at a big bank in Phoenix for $500,000. He takes the money to his next meeting. He tells Pérez's people that the kilos they have fronted have been sold back east but that the money has not yet reached him. However, he would like to enter into a new deal, a much bigger deal. He shows them the half million in cash. They are very interested.

Jordan is on a roll, building his private war machine. He's young, hot, and hungry to make some bones. Florentino Ventura, a big federale, comes up from Mexico City with a team and Jordan plops them in a nice hotel and treats them night after night to sessions in the Phoenix Playboy Club. The Mexican federales love this part of work. One of them is a nothing named Guillermo González Calderoni. He is half Italian and from an upper-class family. His father is an executive with the nationalized oil industry, Pemex, and Calderoni has had private schooling and speaks French, Spanish, and English. He is a crack shot and will turn out to be almost a ghost in Jordan's career for twenty years.

On February 20, 1973, Jordan and Fernando are ready for their next move. They gather with DEA agents and Mexican federales in

Yuma, Arizona, just across the line from San Luis Río Colorado. The Mexican federales do not give the local Mexican police any warning that they are coming lest they be betrayed. In San Luis, the group of American and Mexican law enforcement seize a semi-truck with ten tons of pot. Calderoni alerts the army of the next phase, and then they proceed to Pérez Aviles's rancho. They can see dust rising in the distance where a convoy of vehicles is fleeing. Coffee is hot on the stove. Guns, heroin, and a safe have been left behind. The Mexicans look around and find nothing more. The DEA contingent sniffs a bit more and finds fifteen tons of marijuana is hidden in holes under bales of hay. Jordan thinks this is a stroke of good luck. It will be years before he understands some things were not supposed to be found. But Pérez Aviles and his men are gone, apparently warned by someone. They take pictures, Jordan beaming with the huge stash in the background. The seized drugs are hauled off by the Mexicans.

Pérez puts a contract out on Jordan's life for $10,000.

Jordan tells reporters that his death should be worth at least $20,000.

The world is young, this is a sport. Newspapers dub the raid the work of Jordan's Raiders. It has the look and feel of everything Americans have failed to do in the recent debacle of Vietnam. This time they have found the enemy and struck back. Each time Jordan gets deep into a case he does the same thing: he calls his mother in El Paso and asks her to light a candle.

The operation continues until midsummer with various buys and busts by Jordan. It is the dream song of DEA in the early 1970s: March 17, twenty-seven ounces of heroin, seven and half of cocaine; March 19, four ounces of heroin; April 9, a half pound of coke, an ounce of heroin; May 23, a pound of heroin; June 12, twenty-five ounces of heroin. He has scored big against the source, he thinks. But the flow of drugs into his sector does not drop at all. It is as if the day at the ranch never happened. And Jordan has no clear idea just who or what Pérez Aviles is. It will be years before DEA starts to understand the drug structure across the line.

•   •   •

The old man acts indestructible. He is ninety and still filing his weekly column, running his various enterprises from Juárez, and dominating his children and grandchildren and great-grandchildren. Sean and Bruno are four or five and six and they love going to Juárez and playing in the old man's junkyard. Tony and Phil regularly report in to the old man and listen to his advice.

In 1976, Tony is singing at a club in Mexico City and has two weeks more to run on his engagement when suddenly he is overpowered by a feeling that he has to get home to Juárez–El Paso. He walks out on his contract. He is married now with his wife living in El Paso. He catches a flight to Juárez and she picks him up. They drive immediately to his grandfather's home in the junkyard where he lives with his Mexican common-law wife. The old man is lying in bed and when Tony bends over to kiss him he can feel that his forehead is sweaty though his skin feels cool. He is, as always, completely lucid.

Tony is wearing a jumpsuit, then a new fashion. The old man looks at him and says, "So you're wearing your sister's clothes now."

Tony senses that the old man is on his deathbed and yet still he retains the will to give his grandson one more shot. When Tony is leaving, his grandfather says, "Tell your mother to come and see me."

Tony crosses the bridge to El Paso, tells his mother, and then goes shopping with his wife. When he returns to Frutas Street it is lined with cars. The old man has just died on the El Paso–Juárez bridge with his woman. She gets the body through by telling U.S. Customs agents that the old man is asleep. When they demand some identification, she pulls one of his newspaper columns from his suit pocket. They glance at the well-known byline and wave the car through.

The funeral cortege is hundreds of cars, many of them police.

In the 1970s, DEA suffers a kind of mission creep. Set up principally to handle addictive drugs, it goes increasingly into stopping marijuana when the plant becomes a favorite in the American market. At the same time, Mexico has honed an internal secret police, the Federal Security Directorate, DFS, and is increasingly concerned that guerrillas might tap into the growing drug industry as a source of money for guns.

The key thing about the War on Drugs is that the war never occurs, there are simply skirmishes dictated from time to time by political needs within the United States and Mexico. The second thing is that drugs threaten power more than people. The money, whatever its amounts, goes to feed the basic hungers we call capitalism. The violence, whatever its oscillations, mainly kills people in the business, either drug merchants or the police who feed off them. The only matter seriously altered is power because the new source of money creates new men with money. And this, like DEA itself, is subject to a kind of mission creep. First in the 1960s, a growing U.S. appetite for illegal drugs stokes this flow of money. Later, shifts in U.S. policies will, in the case of Mexico, almost exponentially increase this amount of money—for both police agencies and drug merchants—and other policies, such as the hazards of global trade, will make drug dollars more and more important in maintaining the health of the licit economy. And almost none of these matters will be discussed in public or became part of political discourse. But they will make the world of Phil Jordan and Amado Carrillo and that of Carlos Salinas de Gortari.

Operation Condor is a Mexican sweep of mountain drug fields in the 1970s, a sweep supported by American aircraft and aided surreptitiously by DEA agents. It will have unintended results and endless reverberations. Ten thousand Mexican soldiers destroy or depopulate two thousand villages and hamlets in Sinaloa alone.[10] The Mexican general in charge is the same commander who led the slaughter of the students in 1968. The president who signs off on the operation was the head of security for the nation in 1968 and ordered that slaughter.

When Condor wreaked temporary havoc in Sinaloa, many traffickers left the state and settled in Guadalajara to the south. This migration was the origin of what became the Guadalajara cartel. Others scattered to Sonora, Chihuahua, Durango, Zacatecas. From this operation comes the curious fact that Mexico in the 1980s and 1990s creates a national drug industry and almost everywhere in the nation this industry is headed by Sinaloans. Amado Carrillo is sent by his Uncle Fonseca Carrillo to Durango and then Zacatecas—the exact chronology is unknown—to learn how to manage marijuana plantations. And to master the intricacies of heroin production and distribution. Fonseca himself settles in Guadalajara and within a few years is one of four men in power there in a new cartel. Pedro Pérez Aviles is not so lucky. His operation in Sinaloa has flourished and in fact most of the coming drug leaders in Mexico are his students. Rafael Caro Quintero begins with him as a boy of thirteen. But Pérez is allegedly stopped at a federale roadblock in September 1978 in Sinaloa after leaving a fiesta at a ranch. He is cut down by federales, quite likely as a result of DEA pressure. Another theory has him killed at the instigation of his partner, Fonseca Carrillo. Such matters seldom get sorted out for any clear historical record.

A new era has begun with the trained Sinaloans dispersed for safety and forming new national networks, and with the government temporarily showing compliance with American demands and yet not threatening the cash flow of the drug business at all.

Tony loves song. He is the man dedicated to the classic nightclub ballads and when he sings his voice booms. As the 1970s roll along, he moves in a world of music, clubs, and drugs. In Mexico, as in the United States, the world of night has both music and criminals. But nothing really matters to Tony except the music. He meets powerful people and yet barely knows who they are. He is that pure thing, a man who has found his passion, music, and this passion supplants everything else.

Virginia and her husband prosper. Her husband takes a job in the mid-1970s with Mexican Customs and is assigned to Matamoros. Customs is notoriously corrupt, a place where goods move because of bribes. In this new job, Virginia's husband does not wear a uniform. In fact, to Tony it is not clear exactly what he does do.

The husband is working a sector that has allegedly been controlled for years by a prominent Mexican politician and former cabinet member, Raúl Salinas, Sr., father of Carlos and Raúl, Jr. In 1977, Virginia and her husband are suddenly back in Juárez. And have money. Her husband has rich friends, like a guy who supplies all the food for AeroMexico, the major airline for the nation. The couple has apartments in Juárez and El Paso, plus a nice townhouse. The marriage is dying but it is dying amid plenty. Tony does not ask but he can tell "they're not earning little bucks." Then, her husband's nightclub burns. He sells out to people in the drug business. No one asks any questions about the fire or the sale since asking questions can be a dangerous habit. The husband is drinking hard now and the marriage ends.

Virginia finds a new boyfriend, a man named Pedro Zaragosa. His family is enormously wealthy with deep holdings in natural gas. In fact, they supply by some estimates almost half the natural gas in the entire nation. This wealth has been created in a few short decades. They are intertwined by marriage with the drug leader of Juárez at the time.

Then at about this time something happens that is a shock to Tony. He is singing in a club in Juárez and after his show, he is brought to a customer's table. A man is sitting there with a woman much younger than he is. He introduces himself as David Forti and says that he is Tony's uncle. They sit and talk and Tony finds out there is this entire other family of Fortis fathered by his grandfather and that it is also in El Paso and Juárez. He falls into a new universe. David owns a restaurant, Forti's, and soon Tony and his siblings try to knit the two families back together. He learns from his mother that she knew of the other family but in a whispered way. Phil himself is enamored of finding a new universe of kin left by his grandfather and throws himself into some kind of healing between the two branches.

Tony senses something amiss. He instantly loves his newly discovered uncle but his younger wife, Consuelo, seems somehow off. He discovers that she does not come from what he considers a good family and that her brother has a bad coke habit. And she seems, he thinks, to know the wrong people.

Well, no matter. This is a detail compared to this reunion with lost flesh. Besides, coke is not a big thing. Tony can hardly have a drink in the bars in Juárez without pals shoving some into his pocket. This is always awkward, of course, what with his brother being a narc, but none of his friends seem to even care about this fact. When Tony walks back over the bridge to El Paso, he always pitches the stuff away. None of it touches the real things, like music, his family, his blood ties. And now Phil is getting married again after ten years of running around. An anglo girl named Debbie.

Jordan is in Nogales, Sonora, doing a drug deal with some scumbag named Pegleg. Things go bad suddenly and he hears the bullets skittering across the pavement around his feet.

He and Fernando are down in Chihuahua. They've got this good lead on a major heroin lab, got the patron in charge on a string ready to be reeled in and gutted. Fernando is hot for the deal. He can taste it. To be sure, he gets paid off with part of the take and so a big deal is a good deal for him. But it is more than that, it is the joy of the kill. The love of the deception.

There is an erotic quality to the work of DEA. First you meet someone, then you seduce them, win their trust, eat with them, drink with them, share memories. You cannot do business with strangers, señor, you must know the person. You must earn the trust of the person. And then you betray the person. Or you are betrayed. That is the rub all along the line: you can only do business with people you trust and you can only be betrayed by someone you trust. And so you trust no one, but you must trust someone. And so, in the end, you are always betrayed. It is simply a matter of time.

Fernando relishes this part of the work, the high-wire nature of earning trust and betraying it. It fits his code of honor, which is fierce. He is a man who will brook no lying from those close to him, just as he holds drunks and other weaklings in contempt. Or those who sell their souls in order to get drugs. Once he does a deal so huge, DEA balks at paying him his percentage and when Phil finally gets a check out of them it is for a piddling amount. Fernando rejects the money out of hand: "Give it back to them and tell them to shove it up their ass." It offends his sense of honor and worth. He is not to be trifled with. Still he continues working with Phil. In his mind, he tells himself: "I will work with Phil for nothing."

He becomes almost an architect of Phil's career, making cases that propel his rise in the agency. Sometimes Phil loans him out for other cases, but this is delicate because Fernando will not work with people he does not respect or who he feels fail to respect him. He maintains his usual role: the friendly man who keeps his reserve. The man who is cordial but all business. The man who asks questions but does not answer them. He trains Phil up and Phil is always the man in a suit, the man who does not drink, who rejects offers of women, the man who is here to do business not foolishness. The man who represents a large organization that can buy very large amounts if the quality is good and the service dependable. But a man who has no time for punks and no taste for flashy cars and ridiculous gold chains.

Phil lives this life of late hours, drug negotiations. He is going to make it, his government rating keeps climbing. He is the husband who cannot explain to his wife where he has been. DEA is the bristling exponent of values that consistently asks agents to live other values. The agent is supposed to be an exemplar of family, home, and hearth and yet, if ambitious or worth his or her salt, spends long hours in saloons, late hours in dives, and constantly shifts schedules for meets and negotiations. And beyond that tension, one known to any cop, there is the rush, something akin to drugs, the adrenaline hit of doing the deal and making the sale.

The job is not nine-to-five and the rush, the real addiction of successful agents, becomes a yearning that runs seven days a week and twenty-four hours a day. This hunger hides behind rhetoric of jailing bad guys, keeping pushers out of schoolyards, making America safe for Americans. But this hunger rules. No one ever leaves the drug business easily, no dealer, no informant, no narc, because of this rush.

The person is across the table, a cocktail waitress leans to serve the drinks, her breasts almost spilling out of her costume, it is around midnight, and only one thought exists, nudging the person to act, to do the deal, to come across with money or dope, to supply that element necessary for the handcuffs, and this hunger rises in the gorge, this sense that it is so close, so very near, and that it can be done, the thing can be had, it is there, right on the table, the victory is near, and beneath the calm voice, the businesslike demeanor, the studied use of language and gesture there is this screaming hunger to crush the other person, take them down and show them who really is in command. But of course, this is not to be discussed, there are so few who even can comprehend this hunger. There you are riding on a shoeshine and a smile and a 9mm tucked away on your person and you can't get enough of it. Ever.

Contrary to normal agency custom, Jordan befriends reporters and uses his press connections to publicize cases. He becomes a figure, the young guy with hustle and style. He is on a roll. He will be out of all this in his early fifties with a fat pension and a lifetime of lucrative consulting fees. He can feel it. He maintains order at all costs. He tries to keep an eye on his children from his first marriage, who live with their mother, the children whom he carefully ships to Frutas Street each summer where he trusts his mother and father and aunts and uncles to instill discipline and family. He calls his mother every day. He keeps things under control. Keeps up with his brothers and sisters on the phone and, like everyone in the family, dotes on Bruno, who is now almost a teenager.

So, now he wants to go into Chihuahua and get this big heroin lab. He can almost taste it. And DEA won't front the money for the trip. Too risky, too expensive, too something. Jordan can't figure it out but in a way knows. DEA is a bureaucracy and designed for anything except action. Like every agency designed to solve a problem, DEA becomes wedded to the problem and this marriage means stats and regular collars, not big schemes that could go bad and cause trouble. Jordan decides simply to go with Fernando on his own money. And so they do.

In Chihuahua, on that green belt against the Sierra Madre, Fernando is a fish returned to native water. He knows every gesture cold, every idiom, all the body language, the easy stance, the constant grabbing of the crotch while talking, the low almost monotone voice, the elaborate courtesy of speech, the lack of hurry or anxiety, the folk world of Chihuahua. He is back in the world where as a teenager he shot a man. He is home. Jordan keeps pulling off into little towns, hunts up a pay phone, and calls the office to report their progress. Fernando stands off and smiles at this routine since he, by his very nature, has chosen a life where he reports to no one but his inner self.

There is no backup since this is not supposed to be happening. So Fernando will stand there with amusement as Phil reports in to his hopeless agency. Fernando is above such nonsense. He is on the hunt and he can smell the prey.

They have entered a zone that has nothing to do with the War on Drugs or with dope or with anything but themselves. They are past fear. This is the delicious part. Being so deep into making a deal, into ferreting out the world behind the mask of the scenery, that every thought is on the operation and fear is squeezed out because of lack of space, that slow-motion sense that comes when peril is so vast and can no longer be grasped and so, however briefly, it fades from consciousness. It is the drug of the combat zone.

Fernando has this constant thought that keeps recurring to him in this work. Eventually, someone he has betrayed and taken down in a bust will come for him to kill him. They will find out where he lives and slaughter him in his home. So the man who does not carry a gun on drug deals, practices regularly at home with a .45 in preparation for such a moment. In his mind, he sees it clearly: "When they come, there will be only two of us. And one will be dead."

They reach the isolated ranch. The lab is protected by large black dogs and pistoleros. The patron can deliver anything that is desired. A deal is struck for a very large shipment. The big bust is moving into reach. There is the joy of touching the place things come from, the pleasure of penetrating into the factory floor behind all the drinks in dives in Phoenix. They cut a deal for tons of drugs, tons. The shipment will be delivered to the United States. The money? No problem, señor, the money is not a problem. There will be an exchange on the other side, the money for the drugs. And let there be no foolishness, no shorting of weight, no cutdown of purity. The big black dogs mill about, the gunmen watch, the deal is struck. It is a clean thing between men who know the real world.

But the deal never goes through. DEA balks at the millions required for front money, a gesture of cash necessary to close the deal. The clerks that are any agency cluck their tongues. The whole trip is a waste. Phil and Fernando have gone too far and hit a gold mine too rich. All they have accomplished is this: they have caught a glimpse of a bigger world than they imagined and it is not a world of punks and lowlifes. It is a big business, over there, just across that river. And it has hardly begun to really grow.

Phil marries Debbie, his second wife, in the fall of 1979, and then is reassigned to Dallas, where he heads the bureau. He and his new wife find a house in the new booming northern suburb of Plano. Soon a child is on the way. Phil disappears, as usual, into his work. He throws himself also into coaching basketball, a way to keep kids clean, he thinks. He starts making powerful friends. Politicians and the rich have a need to know someone in DEA. There is always a relative caught with something who needs consideration. He, of course, keeps using Fernando. Fernando is transportable and can succeed in any room. He is always the man willing to do a deal, tell a little joke, and then get down to business. He never once fails to complete a transaction. The place hardly matters. Dallas, Chicago, Los Angeles, San Francisco, it is all the same to Fernando.

He keeps his job in the mines. He keeps building his house and builds a lot of it out of stone. He is the man raised on family and honor and hard values.

Once, one of his sons gets suspicious of his strange trips, the flashy clothes kept in a closet, and of course the memory of those bullet holes in the car. He asks if his father is in the drug business.

"No son," Fernando says. "It is not like that."

Amado Carrillo lives in a kind of prehistory. He is raising marijuana somewhere against the Sierra Madre. His brother Cipriano is with him and they work damned hard, and they party hard, drinking, doing some coke, running through women. It is around 1980 in the vagaries of the records. There is a rub in tracking the path of Amado Carrillo. He is keenly aware that he can only be betrayed by someone he trusts and so he trusts few, if any, outside his blood family. This will make life difficult for DEA when they finally discover that Amado Carrillo actually exists. They will backtrack, try to piece together his background, and they will find almost nothing. In part, because they investigate his beginnings years after the fact and many of those who knew the early days had already perished in the carnage of the business. And in part, they will fail because as time goes on anyone who knows anything about Amado Carrillo learns to stay silent.

So little glimpses float up.

She is seventeen and has run off with some boys from the drug business. She is hot and she is smart. She winds up in Juárez with some punks who wait outside the clubs and roll the drunks. And then she finds better work. She will go to Coahuila, the state just south and east of Chihuahua, and there in Saltillo, the capital, she will pick up a car from a Mexican general and drive it to Juárez and deliver it to another Mexican general. The general will keep the car. The two hundred kilos of cocaine in the trunk are delivered elsewhere. She gets $100 a trip but the work is easy. This is the way she meets him. His Spanish is poor, his education worse. In the clubs just across the bridge from El Paso, he is sitting there surrounded by fifteen-year-old girls whom he paws. She notes his behavior is very vulgar. He is Amado Carrillo. He is using a lot of cocaine. She goes to work for him. Her contacts are a man and a woman but then they get too deeply into using cocaine and so Carrillo has them killed for security reasons. But she stays with him. He pays very well, he makes a point of that. He expects perfection but at least he pays. After coming back from one trip, she finds his face is swollen and bruised. He has just had plastic surgery, this in those early years, 1978–80. The operation is not to improve his appearance, though he is not a handsome man. It is to change his appearance. His people begin to call him the man with a million faces. Or El Señor.[11] She says he has sixty to eighty people working for him at that time.

He is whoring and boozing and doing coke against the Sierra Madre as he tends to the marijuana harvest. He marries in 1980 or 1981. At his wedding, something upsets him. He murders one of the guests, a relative. Or so it is said, very softly.

Within a culture of graft and central control, Mexico had kept one faith for decades: the peso. Beginning in 1940, the nation's presidents had been slaves to business and worshippers of the central bank.

When Adolfo Ruiz Cortines left office in 1958, the national debt stood at a piddling $64 million and the peso was rock hard and becoming a favored global currency. For the next twelve years, the nation was functionally run by one man, Gustavo Díaz Ordaz, first as key minister to the president of Mexico and then as president himself. He despised personal liberty, worshiped state power above all, and kept a tight rein on spending. His successor, Luis Echeverría, broke this mold and in an erratic six years hammered the economy and escalated the debt. He in turn picked an economic illiterate, José López Portillo, who based his six years on a promised bonanza in the Mexican oil fields, which radically increased government income and spending. And graft. When Portillo left office in 1982, the CIA estimated he'd personally stolen between $1.5 and $3 billion. But that was not the problem. A man subject to delusions—he seemed to think he was the reincarnation of the ancient Aztec god Quetzalcóatl and published a pamphlet to that effect[12]—he is noted for adding the first woman to the cabinet of a Mexican president, in this instance, his mistress. He also broke the economy. The peso, steady for decades, collapsed from twelve and a half to the dollar to suddenly seventy. The national debt blossomed to $91 billion. In response, Portillo nationalized every bank in the country. By August 1982, the nation was functionally bankrupt.[13]

Portillo's handpicked successor, Miguel de la Madrid, came from a different background. He was the first wave of what would be called the technocrats, men trained in economics, not politics. And in his circle as he came to power, de la Madrid brought a key aide, Carlos Salinas de Gortari. During de la Madrid's six-year term, Mexico would experience slow death. His achievement was simply to slow the death. Salaries, in real pesos, shrank. The national debt climbed to $102 billion and the peso kept sinking over the six years until it traded at 925 to the dollar. Mexicans call the 1980s the lost decade because of economic stagnation and the shrinkage of personal income.[14]

De la Madrid also allegedly did two things in the matter of the drug problem: officially cooperate with the U.S. government and unofficially cut a deal with the drug business. The terms of the deal would float as a rumor over Mexico for years. Simply put, the major drug merchants would be unmolested if they kept their money in Mexican banks. Drug dollars would provide the floor for the collapsing economic system. One member of de la Madrid's cabinet, Manuel Bartlett Díaz, was the alleged go-between who struck this deal.[15]

Like most actions, it had unanticipated consequences. In 1982, the Mexican drug business was prosperous but largely limited to marijuana and heroin. During de la Madrid's six years in office, this changed. American pressure on Colombian routes for cocaine into Florida caused a shift in transport to and through Mexico. This increased drug income exponentially. Second, the Reagan administration's support of the contra war in Nicaragua led to CIA complicity in narcotics sales to help finance the contras after Congress in the Boland Amendments cut off funding. Third, DEA agent Enrique Camarena was kidnapped and murdered in Guadalajara in February 1985 and Bartlett Díaz, the man assumed to be picked to be the next president, was implicated by DEA and thus barred for political reasons from the job. In his stead, an unknown would eventually be selected, a baldheaded bureaucrat, only forty years old, a man named Carlos Salinas de Gortari.

Ronald Reagan signs National Security Decision Directive Number 17 in November 1981, a federal plan for overthrowing the Sandinista government, and seeks $19.5 million from Congress for funds. When the press wonders if this means the CIA is financing a contra army, the former CIA deputy director, Admiral Bobby Inman, allays these fears by saying, "I would suggest to you that $19 million isn't going to buy you much of any kind [of an army] these days, and certainly not that kind of military force."[16]

About sixty days after President Reagan signs his secret finding, which authorizes the secret U.S. support of the contra war, Attorney General William French Smith writes to the CIA head, William Casey. It has been the custom of the American government for federal agencies to report when their various hirelings are involved in crimes. The attorney general is happy to tell the head of the CIA, in that wooden language that all governments prefer, that, "I have been advised that a question arose regarding the need to add narcotics violations [to] the list of reportable non-employee crimes . . . no formal requirement regarding the reporting of narcotics violations has been included in these procedures."

On March 2, Casey replies, "I am pleased with these procedures which I believe strike the proper balance between enforcement of the law and protection of intelligence sources and methods will now be forwarded to other agencies covered by them for signing by the heads of those agencies."

In plain English, this means that now deals between the CIA and figures in the drug industry need not be reported.

Manuel Buendía is on top of the world in May 1984. His column, "Private Network," is the most widely read in Mexico. He is famous for having great sources, for example the previous president of Mexico, López Portillo, a friend who liked to leak him little facts about CIA operations in the country. Buendía had just written a whole book on the CIA in Mexico. Also, he is deeply into stories on the connections he senses between the current Mexican government and the drug business. He can smell something and he does not like the smell.

He is a rare kind of reporter. In Mexico, the press lives on bribes from officials and publications are controlled by a neat bureaucratic fact: the government has a monopoly on newsprint. Buendía tends to live independent of these conditions and writes what he chooses. Besides, he is apparently without fear.

On May 30 he is walking in the parking lot of his newspaper, *Excelsior,* near the Zona Rosa, the area of chic shops and restaurants in the heart of Mexico City. He is at ease. When his book on the CIA came out, a colleague asked him if he feared a reprisal. He dismissed such a notion out of hand by saying it was "an occupational hazard." Besides, Buendía is a crack shot and everyone knows this fact. A motorcycle comes down the street. The four shots that kill Buendía all enter from the back.

After his body is removed, agents of DFS, the internal security agency revitalized by then president Luis Echeverría in the 1970s, ransack his office and take his files. DFS is an evolving force. Recently, it had been a terror squad sent out to kill guerrillas and disappear dissidents. But lately its commanders, generally trained by the CIA in suppressing leftist radicals, have ventured into a new area: being drug merchants.

When he dies, Buendía is rumored to be looking at the links between the drug business, the CIA, and the contra war in Nicaragua.

Enrique "Kiki" Camarena is a gung-ho agent. Born in Mexico, he exhibits a patriotic feeling for his adopted country, the United States, that has the fire of the converted. A high school football star, he then serves in the Marines, becomes a cop along the border in California, is recruited into DEA, and now is stationed in Guadalajara, the second-largest city of the nation and since the flight caused by Operation Condor in Sinaloa, the very heart of the Mexican drug cartels. Camarena is frustrated. He keeps finding links between the drug business and the government and he is never allowed to really pursue these links. He deals with corrupt Mexican officials, can trust no one, and is about to transfer back to the United States before he dies or his wife and children are murdered. That is what he thinks.

In May 1984, he picks up Phil Jordan at the airport in Mexico City. Jordan has been sent down from the Dallas bureau to do a routine inspection of the Mexico City and Guadalajara stations. And he's specifically requested Kiki as his escort. In part, because they've known each other for years and feel a bond from being raised on the border. But mainly because Jordan thinks Kiki can get him out of any kind of jam and is the man he wants watching his back when trouble arrives. They are both armed in violation of the diplomatic agreement between the United States and Mexico for stationing DEA agents inside the country. In Mexico City, Jordan notices that they are tailed everywhere by DFS agents. He thinks, What's going on? DFS is supposed to be snuffing radicals, not interested in narcotics.

Camarena brushes off Jordan's alarm by noting that DFS is trained by the CIA and is functionally a unit in their mysterious work. And he says they are also functionally "the eyes and ears of the cartels." Jordan is stunned at his complacency about the surveillance.

Jordan asks idly, "Goddamnit, aren't we all on the same side against the bad guys?"

Kiki answers softly, "They have a different mission."

Wherever the two go in Mexico City, a car tails them in an obvious manner so that they will know they are watched. Jordan finds it unnerving in a subtle way. Like anyone in DEA, he knows that drug investigations always come in second to concerns of foreign policy and to the appetites of trade. DEA is a bastard agency fathered by politicians seeking to respond to the soft and easy target of something called the drug problem. It has been rapidly expanded by bringing in people from the FBI, Customs, and other narc groups. It lacks a core identity and a kind of group morale. And in the United States it is widely detested by local police agencies as a bunch of showboats hogging busts and running roughshod over rules.

As they sit in a café, Jordan notices the other tables are filled with pistoleros who glare at them. Kiki says don't worry, those are just more DFS agents. As he feasts on red snapper in the style of Veracruz, Jordan senses the Mexico he once wandered with Fernando has undergone a sea change. Suddenly, he feels he is not the hunter but the hunted. And he is struck by the casual way Camarena links the DFS and the CIA and the cartels together in some loose kind of package. He senses Kiki knows a lot more and he thinks this kind of knowing can be risky.

Camarena tells Jordan that if DFS discovers the identities of informants working with DEA, they kill them.

Recently, Camarena and others in DEA have gotten wind of something strange even within the realm of the normal abnormal experience. There was reportedly a kind of marijuana plantation up in Chihuahua, a place called Rancho Búfalo. The rancho covered twelve square kilometers. Twelve thousand campesinos work the marijuana fields. Agents of DFS supervise the operation. Allegedly, Rafael Caro Quintero is backing the project. But some doubt this claim and see Caro as a kind of front. The thing is just too big for one guy. Too big to be independent of government. Twelve square kilometers is about four and a half square miles. When complaints about this place are made to the Mexican authorities, they are finally forced to raid it at the end of

November 1984 and photographs appear in the press of huge fields going up in smoke. Thousands of peasants flee the army assault on the rancho. The guards and other regular personnel had been warned a day before of the coming raid.

The plantation is one of several or possibly of many: reports vary on this point. The marijuana is all high-grade sinsemilla. DEA estimates disagree by the billion on the value of the crop.

For Camarena, Búfalo and its sister plantations are an insult because their obvious nature points to what is at the heart of his interests: the linkage between the Mexican government and the cartels. After all, Búfalo itself was guarded by men carrying DFS credentials and commanded by a DFS leader, a Rafael Aguilar Guajardo, stationed out of Juárez across from El Paso. No one, not even Camerena's colleagues, know exactly what Kiki has learned or is learning. They know his anger and sense of frustration, know that he is looking forward to going back to the United States and escaping the pressure of his work. But not exactly what he is up to. This is normal for DEA, where agents guard their informants from the agency and the agency tries to create a wall between the sources of its information and the government officials it briefs. They do know he is focused on a man named Félix Gallardo, a Sinaloan generally viewed as the leading figure in the Guadalajara cartel, a man whose key aide is Ernesto Fonseca Carrillo.

The U.S. remains largely silent about Búfalo. This has to irk its agents. No one can seriously think that a four-and-a-half-square-mile marijuana patch with twelve thousand field hands is a clandestine operation. It can only function with the consent of the government. And at this scale, the consent would have to come from very high up. Also, there is the problem of American spy satellites such as those that feed constant images to CIA analysts. Just how could such overviews miss a four-and-half-square-mile green blob suddenly erupting in the brown desert of Chihuahua?

As Jordan and Camarena have lunch they are focused on their thing, all the narcotraficantes running wild in Guadalajara. They are cops and cops are about cases. The big picture is the bust. Less than a year before, an amendment had cleared the House of Representatives in

Washington after being thrashed about for close to a year. It was called the Boland Amendment and cut off military aid by the federal government to forces seeking to overthrow the Sandinista government of Nicaragua. The amendment legally kicked in in the closing days of 1983. Enforcement of the Boland Amendment and evasion of it would eventually lead to a scandal that almost toppled Ronald Reagan's presidency, a thing that came to be called Iran-contra. The Boland Amendment passage almost appears like a signal for planting time at Búfalo.

But it hardly matters, just as all this talk about DFS tailing U.S. agents, about some weird connection between the Mexican government at its highest levels and the drug cartels hardly matters. Street agents in DEA are seen by the CIA as kind of jerks, cowboys kept on the payroll to make gestures toward drug enforcement. What would they ever know about the big picture and matters of state? And no one really bothers to calculate how long it takes to set up a billion-dollar marijuana plantation, or why it suddenly springs into being on the dry dust of Chihuahua.

On February 7, 1985, in Guadalajara, Kiki Camarena leaves the consulate for a lunch date. There is an air of violence hanging over the city. Six Americans have recently disappeared. The U.S. and Mexican governments have both downplayed this fact and no travel advisory has been issued by the State Department warning Americans of any particular risk in the city. Four of the disappeared Americans are Jehovah's Witnesses on missionary work. The two others are a disabled Vietnam vet and a dental student on a kind of holiday. In addition, one of Camarena's fellow agents has had his car shot up.

Camarena keeps his truck parked across from the consulate in the parking lot of the Camelot bar, a place where he and fellow agents have a beer after work. Five men approach him and he gets in a car with them. He is never seen alive again.

When Jordan and other DEA agents learn of his disappearance they can only think of one explanation for him going off with strange Mexicans: they had to have had police credentials. A few hours later, Camarena's Mexican pilot, Alfredo Zavala Avelar, who worked with him on various flights to discover drug plantations, is snatched at the Guadalajara airport in front of witnesses. And then nothing happens. The federales search for the two men in a desultory way, that's it. The head of DEA slowly grows angry. On February 15, he talks to William Von Rabb, the head of U.S. Customs, and asks for help. Von Rabb obliges and at six o'clock Eastern Time Operation Camarena begins. Every vehicle entering the U.S. from Mexico is searched, every person is questioned. The border grinds to a halt, the waits grow into hours. Television shows long lines of cars and trucks and the faces of enraged drivers. A wall has temporarily gone up between the two nations.

Camarena and Zavala next come into view by a roadside in the neighboring state of Michoacán on March 5, 1985, a month after their disappearance. The bodies are rotted beyond identification and only later will dental and other records prove they are the missing agent and pilot. An autopsy performed by U.S. doctors (after serious pressure on the Mexican government) can find no bullets in the men. They were tortured and beaten to death. Camarena has broken ribs and bones. Both men had been sodomized by some unknown object. The doctors conclude that Camarena finally died from a tire iron slammed through his skull. Much of the physical evidence vanishes because a Mexican judge orders it burned. This decision is explained by the vile odor hanging over the clothing and bags found with the dead men. There is an endless series of unseemly details brushed aside by the Mexican authorities. And one finding that comes out of the blue for the Mexican government: FBI forensic experts determine by examining soil samples that the bodies were not buried where they were found. They have been killed, buried, dug up, and moved. This last finding stuns the Mexicans, who until that moment were not aware of the science of soil types used by American police. In the future, there will be growing numbers of instances of bodies being burned in drug killings.

The investigation of the murder will never end. Or more accurately, the various investigations will start and probe and always be stopped—by the Mexican government but also by the U.S. One DEA investigation in the 1990s will be shut down when it concludes: Camarena and Zavala were tortured in a house in Guadalajara for thirty hours after the kidnapping; almost everyone at this interrogation was at one time trained by the CIA; seven tapes were made of the torture and questions, and DEA eventually obtains versions of three tapes and a transcript of a fourth; the full set of tapes resides within the CIA; Manuel Bartlett Díaz, minister of the interior in the government of then President Miguel de la Madrid, was at the house for part of the torture session; DFS was the instrument of the kidnappings. Bartlett Díaz has consistently denied these allegations or his involvement in any other wrongdoing.

This knowledge will come years later and be smothered by the U.S. government. What is known or suspected almost immediately is that Rafael Caro Quintero is behind the kidnappings and the murders. He is apprehended in Costa Rica on April 4, 1985, after flying out of Mexico with police help, and four years later is sentenced to a ninety-two-year sentence. Félix Gallardo is captured on April 8, 1989, and five years later sentenced to forty years. Ernesto Fonseca Carrillo is also arrested; oddly enough he allegedly is carrying one tape of the torture sessions with him, a fact that baffles American authorities since it would link him to the crime. This is supposed to close the case. By the late 1980s, Mexican media and the former head of Interpol in Mexico were hinting that Camarena had really been a dope dealer himself and was hardly dead but allegedly living in California, or maybe Colorado.[17]

As for the inmates, they endure. Caro Quintero tells the press, "I am sure of myself. I feel content with the time I have lived and that I am living still. I have no enemies. There is no one who wants to kill me. My heart is for all the world."

He attests to his love of women and gold, his disgust with drugs, and his retirement from the business. He lives in a suite in prison with videos, fine food, Scotch, women, and parties complete with mariachi bands. He pays handsomely for bodyguards while in prison since he is said to fear a DEA hit on himself.[18] Gallardo, when finally incarcerated, lives much the same and continues his business of moving multiton loads from prison. When he was being hunted after the Camarena killing, he stayed for a while with the governor of Sinaloa.

In Mexico, Caro Quintero becomes the subject of movies and many songs. Years later, I will sit with an open-air audience of one such film at a fiesta where thousands of campesinos gather against the Sierra Madre, many of them in the drug business. While an old projector clatters and the film dances across a sheet hung for the occasion, the audience is enraptured. He is the hero who refused to bend his knee to the United States. For years, DEA will get reports of both Caro Quintero and Gallardo, although technically imprisoned, showing up in Sinaloa at fiestas and family occasions.

Songs celebrating narcotraficantes began appearing in Sinaloa in the 1950s but with the Camarena case they become a new national melody.

> *The Americans over there in their lairs*
> *They take him to make our souls sweat.*[19]

He arrives in Ojinaga, Chihuahua, and few notice. Sometime late in 1984 or early in 1985, Amado Carrillo moves to this small isolated border town across from Presidio, Texas. Ojinaga, like most border communities, has been a smuggling center for generations. Traditionally, it has moved marijuana, both locally grown and from Sinaloa, and the black tar heroin from Sinaloa and Durango. The business was always small and then with the growing U.S. appetite for drugs in the 1960s, it began to expand. With the 1970s, it expanded again and now in the early 1980s it has reached a new level of volume. And of violence. The boss of Ojinaga is Pablo Acosta, a bright man who has lived in the U.S. and is now a fugitive from an American warrant. He is in control of the plaza, that slippery but simple Mexican concept that means he is allowed criminal activities so long as he causes no trouble for the authorities and he pays them off. When Carrillo arrives, Acosta is paying at least $100,000 a month to government officials. Anyone who moves drugs in his zone, which reaches along the Rio Grande for about 250 miles with Ojinaga roughly in the center of his dominance, must pay him a fee. Acosta carries various police credentials. One of his key companions, Marco de Haro, has just returned from about a year in Mexico City working for DFS and possibly he was part of the detail

trailing Jordan and Camarena. The Ojinaga organization has been in a
turf battle with a rival group and dozens of bodies have littered the
area in settling this matter.

Carrillo slips almost silently into this dusty town of twenty thousand. He first comes to American notice when he is stopped entering
Mexico with an AR-15 automatic rifle. He is photographed, released,
and the gun seized. The incident goes into the files and sleeps there for
years.

Quickly, Carrillo grows close to Acosta and parties with him,
drinking brandy and freebasing cocaine. That is the second part of
Carrillo's presence. He has come with cocaine connections and presumably these are through his Uncle Fonseca Carrillo, who is bound to
Gallardo in Guadalajara and through him connected to the Colombian
cartels. This speculation will never be verified. All that is known is
that Carrillo arrives, has the small incident with the rifle on the bridge
linking Presidio and Ojinaga, and then vanishes from U.S. notice or
concern. In 1985, DEA documents will list two hundred members of
Acosta's organization. Carrillo is not on the list.

Two things happen in the first few months that Carrillo settles in
Ojinaga and DEA knows nothing of them. First, Acosta gets an order
from New Mexico for seven hundred pounds of marijuana. All his
mules are already out on deliveries, so he uses two young campesinos
for the trip. A truck is packed with the cargo and this is topped with a
load of ripe cantaloupes. They cross several hours upstream from
Ojinaga at an isolated desert spot and then take a back road twenty
miles through the mountains to Van Horn, Texas, where they can hook
up with the interstate. It is one of many traditional smuggling routes
in the area.

The load never arrives. Acosta worries that the two young men
have ripped him off. Finally, they return to Ojinaga on foot claiming
the truck slipped off the back road in the dark and lurched into a ditch.
As a lark, Acosta, Carrillo, and others decide to take the two peasants
back to where they claim the incident occurred. If they are lying, they
will, of course, be murdered. When they get to the Rio Grande and are
about to cross into the United States, Carrillo balks.

"This idea sucks," he says. "We don't know what's up the road. Those two jerks could have been caught and then worked out a deal to get us across. Or the truck could really be in a ditch, but it's been found and they're waiting for someone to come for it."

They all stand on the river and assess the situation with the aid of some cigarettes stoked with crack.

Acosta decides and says, "Screw it. We all go. If they're out there waiting for us, we're going to take a bunch of them with us."

They cross, find the truck, discover the peasants have told the truth, get it back on the dirt road, and send it and the campesinos on their way. It is a tiny event, one of thousands of mishaps in the saga of border smuggling. Nothing about the moment will be known for years and then it will gain an unusual importance. It will be one of the very few moments that Amado Carrillo officially exists in American records and can be heard to actually speak.

The second feature of Carrillo's arrival is not noticed in the United States at all. Sometime in late 1984 or early in 1985, a twin-engine plane lands at an Ojinaga airfield. Acosta and his people unload 1,800 pounds of cocaine. The drugs are stored. When later they must be moved, the Mexican army provides security. The connection that has brought them on a flight from Colombia is later concluded to be the handiwork of Carrillo. This first flight is a small beginning. Within months, sixty tons of coke a year, about 30 percent of the estimated U.S. consumption at that time, will begin to flow through Ojinaga and cross the rickety bridge into Presidio.[20] Acosta begins to make trips to Colombia and furthers his connections in the coke world.

This will not be noticed for some time. Presidio, Texas, is over two hundred miles from El Paso. Ojinaga is a long day's drive from Ciudad Chihuahua, the capital of the state. The small dusty town is physically the gateway to that section of the river called Big Bend. Acosta is getting maybe $1,000 or $1,500 from the Colombians for each kilo he stores in his town, this as part of his fee for controlling the plaza. He is running the warehouse on the line and supplying organizations at Matamoros, down by the Gulf of Mexico, and at Tijuana on the Pacific Coast. He is a short, brooding man with a very limited education. He is beneath notice, but then everything is. Carlos Lehder of the Medellín cartel makes visits to little Ojinaga.

Carrillo takes a house on a hill outside Ojinaga where he has a fine view of the river and of Presidio, Texas.

DEA absorbs the slaughter of Kiki Camarena as a test of family. They have killed one of our own, we must act. When Caro Quintero is nabbed in Costa Rica there is muttering within the agency that DEA took him alive instead of killing him. This is part of the culture, the cowboy attitude that is the agency's pride and key asset. And it is also part of the effort to finally build a culture. For DEA Camarena's body becomes the flesh consumed at their first communion. His murder underscores the value of the work and the risks. It is the making of the agency. And Camarena becomes the patron saint of the agents, eventually having his name attached to the new building of EPIC. But then that naming of that building is indicative of the problem. Camarena's case is also a sign of weakness. True, various cartel leaders have their lives disrupted and wind up in Mexican prisons. Various Mexicans are arrested and convicted. The links between the cartels and the police agencies are briefly exposed and there are mass firings, eventually DFS itself is gutted as a gesture of concern by the Mexican government.

But the case goes nowhere and everyone in DEA knows this fact. The links between the various police minions who are either disgraced or jailed is never pursued. For some in DEA, the War on Drugs begins the day Kiki Camarena is kidnapped. This belief is based on the assumption that his murder and its aftermath finally illustrate how deeply entrenched the drug business is in Mexican society and how dangerous this mutual connection is for U.S. foreign policy. This belief is grounded in faith, not facts.

Never again will the United States government, however briefly, ever seriously pursue the connection between the leaders of Mexican government and society and the drug business. Never again will this connection be as tenuous as it is on February 7, 1985. Camarena and his slaughter belong to an age of innocence in the drug business before the serious violence and the serious money arrived. At the very

moment Camarena is being tortured and beaten to death in the bedroom of a villa in Guadalajara while a host of CIA-trained people listen
to his answers to questions, new things are coming into flower.

In Florida, the pressure of the U.S. efforts at interdicting Colombian cocaine is bad for the business and leading to a movement to shift
the routes to Mexico. Initially, this has various results. Mexican traffickers get paid a set fee for moving each kilo of coke and this is a welcome
bonus for them. The Colombians make an effort to move into Mexico
themselves but are promptly killed. What they face is not simple greed
but something more striking, Mexican patriotism. The narcotraficantes
may be rough and ill-educated but they are intensely bound to the
Mexico they know. And they resent outsiders. The drug dealers are far
more patriotic than the elites that rule Mexico since they neither know
nor desire a world greater than the campo that created them. Another
factor influencing the change in the Mexican drug business is the
American support of the contras in Nicaragua. DEA agents in Mexico
begin to get reports of new airfields and plantations, of flights that go
apparently without a hitch or without records. Instances are noted of
planes apparently full of coke landing at U.S. military airfields. This
information is buried and never pursued. But it does lead to comic
moments when drug dealers will make baffling comments about aiding
the United States. It also leads to an explosion of money and the dimen-
sions of that money will never be known. But what is interesting about
the Camarena case is that it pivots on huge marijuana plantations, a
product soon to become as quaint as near beer in the drug business.
Coke and heroin are the coming thing and they will change all the
numbers.

But no solid numbers will ever exist, except for the growing number of American convicts. More than a decade after Camarena's death, a
U.S. commission on drug policy will throw up its hands and say there
is no real database that meets even the minimum standards of science
or sound social policy.[21]

Of course, in Mexico solid numbers are far more difficult to come
by than in the United States. It will be the end of the millennium
before Mexicans even get a clue as to the salary of their own president.

Nor does anyone in Mexico know the actual population—the census is not only difficult to administer to a nation of people who fear their government, but also notoriously manipulated at a federal level to limit the return of federal pesos to local governments on any per capita basis. Unemployment figures are skewed by a quirk of policy: any Mexican who works in any capacity for one hour a week is counted as employed, even if this employment means standing on a traffic island for sixty minutes with a box of Chiclets. Commonly, 40 to 50 percent of the population is assumed to live outside the economy, meaning God only knows how they survive. Crime statistics are notoriously inaccurate since many Mexicans are reluctant to call the police under any circumstances.

And of course, Jordan lives in his own shadow land of numbers and information, a fact he knows and yet denies. On a personal level, Camarena's murder is almost a high since Jordan sees his agency pull together to avenge the death of a brother agent. He feels part of a unit. And he feels a relief. Camarena is almost a twin, a Mexican-American from the same border culture with the same intense patriotism and gung-ho attitude. For a brief while, Jordan and his colleagues can sort out the slaughter of Camarena and Zavala and yet at the same time feel the world is finally making sense.

Bartlett Díaz, who controls DFS, fires hundreds of agents en masse. He is fighting to save his political career, his shot at being the next president of Mexico. U.S. agents do notice that when they are allowed to sit in on interrogations of Mexicans involved in the Camarena case, any statements made by the Mexicans about bribes to officials are never recorded by the interrogators. Nor are any of the fired DFS agents ever charged with any crime.

It will be years later before Jordan even gets close to the reality he is actually living in. He will discover in time that some of his fellow DEA agents are actually working for the CIA and using his agency as a cover. And he will slowly face the fact that things are known by the CIA but kept from him. He will never be able to exactly pinpoint when this sensation of being kept in the dark becomes a reality for him. Maybe, he will think later, it begins when they nab a Mexican connected to the Camarena case and the Mexican gets into some things he knows and suddenly the guy is taken away by a fellow agent and delivered to the CIA before he can tell what he knows.

There is one point nine years after Kiki's murder that does stick in his mind. He is in Washington at a windowless CIA briefing room getting their dog-and-pony show on the Mexican drug business. One little part of the briefing is a series of satellite images showing all the airfields being used by the Juárez cartel. Jordan is hungry for those images and approaches the analyst afterward. The CIA briefer is very cordial and says certainly, you can have those images, they will be on your desk tomorrow morning. They never arrive.

But these moments are brushed aside, or mainly surface in talk with other agents. The drug business is set up with compartments for security. On the cartel side there is the desire to keep people sealed from each other lest an arrest threaten an entire organization. On the law enforcement side, a similar tendency occurs for other reasons. Agents protect their informants, agencies protect their information as part of their capital. And government segregates information about the drug business between various agencies. There is no big picture, nor is there any market for such an image.

In 1986, a trafficker tells a federal grand jury sitting in El Paso, Texas, that until quite recently Mexico had two mafias, the drug merchants and the secretive federal force in charge of national security, the DFS. Because of the scandal over the murder of Kiki Camarena, the DFS has been disbanded. He continues on about the good old days: "The commander from the DFS [in Juárez], Rafael Aguilar had Gilberto Ontiveros [El Greñas] working under him, Rafael Quintero and Don Neto [Ernesto Fonseca Carrillo]. . . . DFS had a ranch specially built just to grow marijuana, and it was called Búfalo." The witness went on to explain how payments were made to the officials in Mexico City. But none of this information ever leads anywhere. It might as well not exist.[22]

Facts crumble at a touch. Caro Quintero is serving forty years in a Mexican prison. In January 1986, he complains that prison officials have stolen $700,000 in cash that he was keeping in his cell. And suddenly, DEA finds the volume of cocaine moving across the line in the American Southwest is doubling, then doubling again.[23] The U.S. experiences a drug panic that prompts politicians to pump additional billions into something called the War on Drugs. DEA grows like a weed, adding five hundred more agents immediately. In Mexico, a visit to Félix Gallardo's cell finds him in a silk dressing gown and making do with a live-in cook and other accoutrements. When the DEA agents stumble upon Caro Quintero, he warns them that he will sodomize them with a stick if they do not leave his quarters.

They hold a meeting. On February 14, 1986, a batch of federal agents from Customs, DEA, the FBI, and other groups create a task force focused on Pablo Acosta and his work. It is part of the logic of the times, one that believes the way to crush the drug business is to take out the leaders of cartels. Phil Jordan, head of the DEA in Dallas, controls DEA in El Paso and West Texas. This is his baby in part. And after the torture and murder of Camarena, DEA feels a kind of rush, a sense that the federal government is finally willing to give them operational freedom.

The group in the meeting settles on a five-page memo of understanding that reads in part:

> The tentacles of this organization reach throughout the Mexican states of Chihuahua and Sonora, and into the United States in West Texas, northern Texas, southern and eastern New Mexico, and into areas of Kansas, California, Colorado, Oklahoma, Missouri, New York, New Jersey, Nevada, Idaho, North Carolina and Michigan. The current assessment, by an analyst of the El Paso Intelligence Center, depicts the Acosta organization as a multi-faceted group of family members and well established associates of over 500 individuals.[24]

The document also notes that various parts of U.S. law enforcement in West Texas—cops, prosecutors, and elected officials—will also be investigated.

Two months later, Phil Jordan goes to the press with information about the task force's target, Pablo Acosta. He describes Acosta as a "vicious, extremely dangerous person with little regard for human life." Suddenly, stories appear in American newspapers about Acosta's alleged penchant for atrocities such as dragging corpses behind his vehicle until they are shredded into nothingness. Acosta had not made the American press since a bust back in 1964. Now he is a headline. Amado Carrillo is not mentioned.

Acosta operates on coke and booze and instincts that will not be seen again in the Mexican drug business. He is a merchant who tosses money at the poor and they become his eyes and ears for a hundred miles in any direction. He also talks to American law enforcement from time to time and feeds them tidbits that can lead to arrests. One Customs investigator, David Regela, has an ongoing relationship and visits Acosta repeatedly in Ojinaga. He is dickering with Acosta over delivering up some of the Colombians who have apparently started to crowd Acosta's fiefdom and threaten his power.

Because of these ongoing negotiations there is one tiny glimpse of Amado Carrillo that will be the closest look into his mind the various agencies ever see. It is 1986, and Acosta takes Regela to breakfast in Ojinaga. In the restaurant they run into Carrillo and his pistoleros and Carrillo is formal and correct in his greetings. Regela can sense a coldness between Carrillo and his gunmen and Acosta and his entourage of thugs. As they leave, Acosta goes over to Carrillo's table and there ensues a flurry of Spanish that Regela cannot manage. Later, an informant who is also there explains the conversation.

Carrillo and Acosta have had a coke storage place leaked somehow to DEA. Carrillo has rounded up the six men who handled that storage unit, systematically tortured and then killed them. All this, apparently, without Acosta's foreknowledge.

"What have you done?" Acosta exclaims. "You've killed six people and what have you accomplished by it?"

Carrillo answers, "It is better for six innocent men to die than for one guilty man to go unpunished."[25]

As Acosta speaks he wears a $4,000 gold watch and a gold bar formed in the image of a small ingot from Credit Suisse on a chain around his neck. Both are gifts from his partner in freebasing binges, Amado Carrillo.

In 1986, the U.S. Congress adds twenty-six new mandatory sentences for federal drug offenses. It is argued that this will result in a deterrent effect. There are no hearings. On August 9, Ronald Reagan, then president of the United States, submits to a urine test to prove that he is pure and free from drugs. The climate is frenzied in the United States. When polled, 75 percent of Americans argue drugs are a major national problem. Curiously, in the same poll only a third of the people think drugs are a major problem in the community where they live.[26]

For drug agents, business booms with expanding budgets and more personnel. Phil Jordan, who joined an agency he had never heard of back in 1965, now is the division head in Dallas of an economic engine building an empire.

Acosta continues his curious path. He talks to Terrence Poppa, a reporter from the El Paso newspaper, who visits him in Ojinaga. Poppa prints the story on December 3, 1986, and it receives a wide national press, complete with photographs of Acosta. In the story, Acosta tells of his arrangement with Mexican federal police and the army, of his payments to government in order to continue with his business. When the story is reprinted in Mexican newspapers these references are deleted. Two days later an FBI agent is in Comandante Calderoni's office in Juárez when Calderoni takes a call from Mexico City ordering him to get Acosta. Calderoni has risen since his days as a nondescript federale on Jordan's raid against Pérez Aviles in San Luis Río Colorado.

Calderoni has been assigned recently to Juárez from Matamoros, where American law enforcement concluded he was a different kind of federale because he sometimes gave them real information. The comandante basks in an image where he is a kind of real cop functioning in a frontier setting that has not yet evolved into modern law enforcement practices and ethics. He immediately sends people to Ojinaga to get Acosta, but his target has vanished.

On December 13, 1986, the comandante has a long talk with a fellow federale and some other Mexicans. In the talk, Calderoni tells of his contempt for American cops and calls DEA agents sons of bitches. He feels the same way about the FBI. He explains how he smuggles cocaine into El Paso. And then he wanders into questions about Juan García Abrego, the head of the Gulf cartel in Matamoros, his old posting. He is told García wants to give him a gift. Calderoni notes that he will be in neighboring Reynosa in three days and such a gift can be delivered to him then.

The comandante continues on about what a mess he found in Juárez, how the federal police were incompetent and corrupt and how he had reorganized things on a more efficient basis. He emphasizes his close ties to his boss, the head of the federales, and that this relationship was very solid. His boss is the same man Phil Jordan hosted for days at the Phoenix Playboy Club while preparing the raid against Pérez Aviles. As for DEA, he says once again, they are a bunch of assholes.

The hunt for Acosta stalls because he has a talent for vanishing into Mexico and not leaving a trace. At times in the past, when his drug business seemed overwhelming, Acosta would go to Cancún and work as a waiter. It seemed to amuse him to carry trays for vacationing Americans. Or he would disappear into secret journeys to Colombia.

This time he holes up in Torreón with a brother. The brother, a heroin addict, consumes his supply and one night secretly drives to Ojinaga, fueled by cocaine, to get some more. Calderoni's men seize him. He is tortured. The official record says he dies from a heart attack. Rumors float that his interrogation involved the severing of his digits with a bolt cutter, a charge denied by his immediate family, who viewed the corpse.

By April of 1987, Acosta is in the village of his birth, Santa Elena, a hamlet on the Rio Grande facing Big Bend National Park. Huge cliffs back the village on the Mexican side and no land approach is feasible because of the rough terrain, bad roads, and campesinos who will instantly alert their patron, Pablo Acosta. This leaves the U.S. side. Calderoni contacts the FBI and cuts a deal. A joint group of Mexican federales and FBI agents will chopper in and land at Big Bend, where the Americans will form a perimeter on the river blocking the possibility of Acosta fleeing north into the United States. The Mexicans will then proceed in their own choppers to Santa Elena just across the narrow river and apprehend Acosta. A handcuffed informant flies with Calderoni. The man knows the village and can point out Acosta's house. He has been advised that if he balks, he will be pitched from the chopper.

The federales hit the village at the last hour of light when a fiesta is just beginning to celebrate the birthday of Acosta's half-brother. A fierce firefight roars on for a while. Acosta dies. His body is flown out in a bag at the feet of Comandante Calderoni.

Carrillo is not caught. In fact, several days before the raid, he vanishes. He leaves behind a large church he has had built in Ojinaga. The FBI and Calderoni get massive publicity in both nations for a triumph against the drug business.

It will be some time before the agencies learn a detail, and years before this detail leaks from the agencies: Comandante Calderoni has earned a million-dollar fee for killing Acosta. His paymaster for the work is Amado Carrillo.

Carrillo moves to Torreón, Coahuila, after the death of Acosta. He works with the Herrera organization, a family business based out of Durango that provides heroin, marijuana, and cocaine and has deep Colombian connections. The Herreras have a lock on drugs in Chicago and Buffalo. The organization totals over three thousand members (at the time a force greater than all of DEA) and almost everyone in the outfit is kin. The Herreras are deep into opium growing and heroin production, have a village bearing their name in the Sierra, and constitute the civil and criminal government of the state of Durango.

DEA has agents in Torreón trailing the local Herrera, Jaime, and they observe this other guy hanging out with him in the bars. They dismiss the stranger, who they notice speaks Spanish well and who is clearly a nothing. They ask themselves, Who is this shit, this fat fucker? He lives in a one-story house that is also a warehouse for drugs. But he is seen as a loser. They're after Herrera because they are convinced he is the man with the connections to the Colombians and their endless cocaine. For two and a half weeks they watch and sometimes they keep an eye on the stash house also. They are teamed up with Comandante Calderoni, who is now seen in American eyes as Mr. Mission: Impossible in Mexican law enforcement. He has taken out Gilberto Ontiveros in Juárez. He has killed Acosta. He is clearly different from the average crooked federale. He is a personal friend of the head of the federales.

They all decide to take down Herrera. They watch the stash house. Three women come out with some kids, get in a car, and drive away. Then the fat pointless guy comes out and drives away, but who cares. Finally, some real-looking guys leave and get in a pickup truck and they follow them with the comandante and his men.

The truck is pulled over and a federale walks up to the driver's side. He is immediately killed by a blast from the driver's AK-47. Another federale creeps up undetected on the other side of the truck. He shoots two of the occupants with a .45 by putting the gun to their skulls and blowing their brains out. The DEA agents watch this with admiration. The third man in the truck takes off running. Calderoni motions to his assistant, El Negro, who gets out, goes into a shooting crouch, and drops the man with a .45. When they roll him over, they discover he is the local army commander there for his payment. Then they all go for Jaime Herrera, a custodian of Colombian connections in the Mexican drug business, and bust him.

The fat man, the worthless punk, escapes. His name is Amado Carrillo, a fact one of the DEA agents will idly tell me years later. At the time, of course, Carrillo was seen as a nothing by U.S. law enforcement.

Comandante Calderoni becomes a fond image for the DEA agents, a man of fair skin and civilized demeanor who always wears custom clothing—shirts, pants, coats, boots, all handmade. The comandante is almost a role model for agents—"helluva shot with a .45," one DEA agent offers, "the only man I've ever shot with that was as good as me." Each year he takes a holiday in Germany and brings back new breeding stock for his hobby, raising rottweilers.

There are some messy edges, such as this talk of the comandante practicing interrogations with a bolt cutter. But this is easily handled with the thought that "they all do that."

She travels, she says, and does little things for Raúl Salinas Lozano, the father of Raúl and Carlos. Her name is Magdalena Ruiz Pelayo. Years later, when she speaks up, the father will say he never employed her, never even met her. Later still, he will remember that yes, he did in fact know her but not very well.

Pelayo remembers meeting in 1982 a new son-in-law in the Salinas clan, a man named José Ruiz Massieu. He has just married the sister, Adriana, and was being positioned to rise in power in the state of Guerrero, the fiefdom on the Pacific Coast that features the tourist mecca of Acapulco. She would be sent as a courier to Massieu to deliver money gathered from Juan N. Guerra, the godfather of the Gulf cartel and his rising nephew, Juan García Abrego. Sometimes the payments back then would be $300,000 or $400,000, one time she remembers it was $1 million. Then at other times, she would fly to the U.S. and give money to José's brother, Mario. Once, she took a couple of hundred thousand to Austin, Texas, and gave it to Mario there. Later, when U.S. Customs tried to check out her story, all the hotel reservations and airline flights proved accurate. She would also be at family gatherings with Raúl, Sr., and others when there were open discussions of the business, of loading planes with cocaine and the like. Raúl, Jr., would be there, the Ruiz brothers, Adriana, Juan García Abrego.[27]

There are also reports of fund-raising events at the Salinas family ranch, meetings held to bankroll Carlos's successful run for the presidency in 1988. And at the same time, Mexican authorities are alleged to have sanctioned three planes a week that landed at Matamoros, the heart of the zone controlled by García Abrego and the Salinas family. Each plane carries six tons of cocaine.[28]

•   •   •

Bruno, just out of high school, gets a job busing tables at his Uncle David's restaurant, Forti's. He is a bright, pleasant kid and soon rises to be the manager of the place. By this time, David and Consuelo's marriage has ceased to function in all but name and she has carved out an independent life. David runs the place during the day. She takes over for the night shift. Bruno works with Consuelo.

She becomes an intimate of Heidi Slauquet, a fashionable woman who once swam through high society in Mexico City and arrived in Juárez just about the same time as Amado Carrillo began his moves toward power there.

But this hardly touches the Jordan family. Anyone on the border develops a kind of divided consciousness and this state of mind protects one from problems by teaching one not to inquire deeply into the work of other people. If they say they are in import-export, for example, one does not push the point but accepts it and moves on. So it is natural that Bruno either notices nothing amiss at the restaurant or dismisses what he does notice. And it is even more normal for him not to mention what he notices to his family.

Just as when his sister Virginia becomes involved with Pedro Zaragosa after her first marriage fails, Bruno blinks at that family's rumored drug connections—allegations which the family has consistently denied. Eventually, Virginia redecorates a mansion in El Paso for Zaragosa and then he defaults on paying her. They go to trial, and she eventually wins.

Before Calderoni swept into Torreón to take out Jaime Herrera, Carrillo had gotten deep into projects. He and Herrera had a deal going to move fourteen thousand kilos of marijuana from Colombia to Mexico. He had forged routes through Juárez and penetrated banking in Los Angeles. And he'd increased his connections in Colombia.

He has also moved into Sonora and sets up a base in Nacozari, a town just south of the American line. He stores weapons there with the help of the Mexican military, has stash houses. His brother Cipriano runs a coke laboratory for him. On September 21, 1988, his brother allegedly commits suicide. DEA reports cast some doubt on this when they conclude he was shot numerous times in the head.

Amado Carrillo takes his brother's body home and buries him in the floor of the family chapel next to their father. Like almost everything about Carrillo, there is no record of what he thought of his brother's death or why he thought his brother died. Simply, this journey home with his corpse to Sinaloa.

In 1989, Fernando enters the El Camino Real, the fine hotel in El Paso six blocks from the bridge to Juárez. The streets outside are alive with Spanish as Mexicans flood central El Paso to buy cheap goods. Fernando is here to meet two men from the Herrera family. The family is a legend to Fernando. Starting right after World War II, the founder, Don Jaime Herrera Nevares, set up heroin labs. They are untouchables. No one can penetrate deeply into their organization except by marriage. And no one can cross them without facing those three thousand blood-related enemies scattered from Mexico to the American heartland. Fernando is eager to teach them a lesson. DEA itself has been able to do almost nothing with the family save their cooperative venture with Calderoni back in Torreón. Now they see the chance to entice a key family member onto U.S. soil and bust him.

The Herreras live in their own universe and it is one not lightly trifled with by either law enforcement or other cartels. They often carry badges of various Mexican police agencies, a commonplace in the drug business. They spend money on parks, streetlights, and other Robin Hood touches to buy the complicity of the poor. They do not simply bribe the authorities. They *are* the authorities. A DEA internal document from the 1980s whined: "Herreras are and have been chiefs of police at the town and municipal levels, directors of state police, mayors and police agents in every law-enforcement agency. Those who reportedly respond to the Herreras have been [high officials in the state of Durango]. Jaime Herrera himself is said to encourage bright young men to pursue political careers."[29] Of course, the memo is out of date. The Herreras are better organized now.

At the hotel, a father and son, one sixty-three, the other thirty-four, await Fernando. This is a coup in itself, this wooing of the Herreras to cross the line and talk a deal in the United States. DEA has gotten the deal this far but can go no further without Fernando. Jordan, running Dallas, has had to call for Fernando in order to close this transaction. The Herreras and Fernando go to the coffee shop and they talk for three hours.

The older Herrera is very bright and he asks many questions of Fernando.

What do you do?

Oh, I buy things and then sell things.

Where do you live?

Oh, that hardly matters. I am here to buy something good, not to talk about my house.

The older Herrera keeps trying to get Fernando off balance. Pancho, the older Herrera will say, or Arturo, or Paco, or Chuy. He keeps talking and then tossing out these different names to see if Fernando will react, to see if he can catch him off guard.

Fernando is at ease. This is the part he loves, the reeling in of the stranger. Fernando talks of horses, blooded horses, of how he loves to race his horses in Baltimore. The old man listens, the Herreras with their millions are into blooded stock.

And then suddenly, yet another name pops out and Fernando does not flinch and continues to ignore the probe. Fernando is feeling better and better. The older Herrera is the smartest stranger he has ever met.

They get into real matters, money. Fernando says he is looking at say a $2 million deal. He represents some very large people and they do not wish to do little things.

Ah, that is no problem, the Herrera replies, we can get any amount of goods and deliver it. Where do you live? We will fly it to you, our planes will go right under the American radar, it is no problem.

No, no, Fernando says, my people prefer to handle their own shipments.

No, señor, the older man replies, let us. It is easy. We have tons warehoused right here, just across the river in Juárez.

That is very kind, Fernando says, but we handle our own deliveries. You just get it to El Paso.

But the money, the Herrera says, we want you to bring the money to Juárez.

No, señor, Fernando smiles, I am not going into Juárez with my money. That would not be the act of a wise man.

Okay.

This goes on for hours, this probing, this testing.

And they agree to talk some more later.

The Herreras try to find him, they call a dummy number he has given them, a line controlled by DEA, but they cannot reach him. When he comes to the second meeting at the El Camino Real, they sit in the bar, a place legend claims was once visited by Pancho Villa. The bar has a Tiffany-style glass dome, a circular black marble top. Splashes of green and blue play across the faces as the sun streams through the fine stained glass overhead. The room is full of soft chairs and sofas. This is a bar where deals are made and nothing is ever rushed. They sit there for hours.

Where were you, the older Herrera asks. We called and you were not there.

Oh, I had some business in Las Vegas.

How did it go?

Very well, señor.

Fernando can feel him relaxing, feel it getting closer. He tells jokes. A man's wife says, get me some *huevos*, some eggs, from your compadre. In Mexican Spanish, huevos also means balls, so the man goes to his compadre and says my wife wants your huevos. The man looks startled and asks, what does she want with them? Oh, his friend says, she wants to fry them and eat them.

He tells jokes, many jokes, and the older Herrera never laughs, but Fernando can sense he is rising to the bait, he can feel it in his bones. The older Herrera says, look, why don't you come to Mexico with me, we will go to Durango, to my village, Las Herreras. We have just built a public park there for the people, everyone there works for us. It will be easy. We will send a plane for you.

No, señor, I cannot do that. This is business and I do not mix pleasure with business. Surely you understand.

Hours of this, hours. And then the older Herrera says, we will do a deal. For over two million. No problem. And they go into the fine restaurant of the hotel and eat thick steaks.

"He was ready to go. It was already made," Fernando says.

The third meeting is in the hotel coffee shop. Here is the arrangement: the older Herrera sits with Fernando and they talk. Across the street is a parking lot, and the car with the kilos of heroin is to be delivered there right before their eyes. Then one of Fernando's men will take the car away and test the load for quality. At the same moment, the younger Herrera will be in a nearby bar where he will be paid for the load. It is a pretty good plan, no? Fernando and the older Herrera will not get near the load.

So they sit and drink coffee and wait.

They look out the window and see a man approach the car and then drive it away. *Perfecto.* Fernando, full of coffee, tells the older Herrera that he must use the bathroom. As he leaves, the agents move in and take the older man down. When Fernando comes back from the bathroom, the waiter comes over and says, "What is going on? The police came and took your friend away."

Fernando shakes his head and says, "I don't know, I hardly know the guy."

And then the police come and handcuff Fernando to give him cover. They take him to the DEA office, and then he goes to the airport and home. The best part is over, the completion of the deal.

The Herreras get twelve to twenty years, and this time Fernando testifies. He likes it when he testifies, when they see his face. Normally, a deal is structured so that no one can be certain who was the traitor. This matter is clouded by bringing in several agents toward the end to give cover to the Fernandos of the world. So usually, Fernando remains an anonymous and unknown wizard at his work. But when he testifies, then they know, they know who did them.

Tony is busy singing in Juárez and El Paso. He is living the good life. He knows a world where a murder can be bought for an ounce of coke or a gram of heroin. He'll be in a club and go in the bathroom, and all these guys will be washing up with their guns on the counter. They are dark and from further south and he senses killing is nothing to them.

He knows a dealer, a woman called La Señora, and sometimes he is over at her house. In 1989, he hears her say on the phone, "Carrillo! No! They can't have arrested Carrillo."

Tony has never heard of the guy before and he is struck by how upset La Señora becomes.

In 1989, Amado Carrillo has a mansion in Guadalajara valued at $1.5 million when he is arrested there. He spends some months in custody and then his case is dismissed by a judge. DEA never discovers what, if anything, he tells Mexican authorities. He is barely known even to American drug agencies.

bones

song

The dark red floor is dirty, the coffee steaming and black. I hold a
fresh June 1995 copy of *La Jornada,* a left-of-center Mexico City
daily, and bumble through stories with my few scraps of Spanish. In *La
Jornada* at that time articles printed in italics are reputed to be paid
plants by the regime and knowing readers are supposed to use this
typeface as a sign of government lies.

Somewhere around page thirty, I hit a small item in the center of a
left-hand page about a killing and trial in El Paso. My eye catches the
initials EPIC and I pick up because I've noticed a fresh and surly voice
in the press from some guy running EPIC. Here it is: a kid killed the
brother of the head of EPIC and has just been convicted. The article
suggests the kid is innocent, and that he is being railroaded by the
widely mistrusted DEA. The alleged killer is called Miguel Angel
Flores. Great name, I think.

I think, why not cold-call EPIC and ask for this guy and find out
why he thinks his brother was cut down in some parking lot. DEA
intrigues me. Local cops have told me one thing: Never trust DEA.
Never deal with DEA. Never turn your back on DEA. They're outlaws.
They say this warning with the same stern voice they use for caution-
ing me about the Mexican federales.

Six weeks or so earlier, a call came from Mexico and I learned that
Ramón Salazar Salazar had been killed and that everyone was upset and
that I should do something. In my mind, I could see his face, smiling
with a flash of teeth, hear him speaking, see him flirting, feel his laughter and bright spirits.

Ramón Salazar Salazar went by the handle of El Güero. He was a
fair-skinned man, hence his nickname, which means Blondie or Whitey,

around forty. I met him at one of his weddings, a five-day drunk attended by narcotraficantes and federales. I remember standing on the roof of the hotel and looking down at the throng in the patio—hundreds of drunks with guns and women, a band playing Sinaloa music about the life. I was up there making notes when someone saw me, the federales grew alarmed at the note taking, and people started reaching for guns. Güero calmed them, said that I was okay, that I was his historian, and so the days rolled on and on. The wedding never really came off. The bride, a niece of Hector Palma, a drug guy with a good-sized operation, looked virginal and beautiful and frustrated. This was the third or fourth attempt at a wedding Güero had staged and somehow he never made it to those few moments with the priest. But that was his trademark: fucking things up and yet tending to business. He had some kind of head for figures, and some kind of soul for fiestas. He'd just been in Mexico City for a meeting, and the meeting was run by a guy I'd never heard of before, someone called Amado Carrillo. The guy at the party who told me this name whispered it when we are alone, and then paused and said, "Never repeat this name."

A federale major gave me his card. At that time, all the federales in the area are under the command of Amado Carrillo's cousin, whose headquarters was about thirty miles from the wedding itself. Right after the party broke up, Cardinal Juan Jesús Posadas Ocampo was gunned down at the Guadalajara airport and suddenly an oppressive stillness descended on this part of Mexico, the state of Sonora, and I could taste it and feel it and I got the hell out.

And then, about two years later, the call came that Güero was dead. I went down, stood where he was murdered in a coastal resort town named San Carlos. He was on the beach with his wife and baby and mother and brother. He came out to the car, two federal cops, ones called madrinas, bridesmaids, who are off the payroll but on the force for special assignments, shot him as he stood there in his swimming shorts. He died, blood ran out onto the pavement where I now stood, the blood a faint rusty stain on the surface. There was a brief clamor in the Mexican press in which Güero was described as a local businessman, and then nothing.

Güero was killed at the orders of Amado Carrillo. A local politician drank with me and lamented that Güero owed him about fifteen grand in rental expenses for private aircraft and now he was never going to get his money, dammit. I talked to Güero's brother and he was still angry about the time up around Tijuana when he and Güero shared a room and he didn't like the accommodations. There was a corrido, the ballad style of the Mexican north, written about Güero and the killing. There was a funeral with stories of pistols fired in the air. But Güero was being erased. After Güero's earlier botched effort at a wedding, I took the card of the federale major at the fiesta and checked it out with the government in the state capital. According to their records, no such person existed in the federal police. But then Güero carried credentials issued from the federal police and now he never existed at all.

I went to the campo santo where they'd buried Güero. Two kids haunted the graveyard. I asked them where I might find the grave. One said, "You mean the guy who took all the bullets? Over there." That was the last note of Güero's existence.

I kept thinking about a drug dealer I knew from Culiacán, Sinaloa, a cousin as it happened of Rafael Caro Quintero, the man serving time for the murder of DEA agent Enrique Camarena. I remembered his quiet but insistent claim that he worked for the government. He would sit in my backyard with a beer, surrounded by his pistoleros and calmly say this as if it were a fact of nature rather than something to debate.

I sip more black coffee, keep hesitating. Two years earlier I'd been drinking with a Mexican newspaper publisher and I mentioned the War on Drugs. He looked at me with pity and said, "The war is over. You lost."

I dialed and talked to the receptionist at EPIC and she put me right through and suddenly I'm talking to Phil Jordan.

He says, "I won't talk over the phone. If you come here, I'll talk."

On June 23, 1995, a Learjet faces landing problems on the west coast of Mexico. The passengers are left injured but alive. They have all spent time celebrating in Culiacán, where much of a hotel was rented for their pleasure. The owner of the plane is Hector Palma, the uncle of the would-be bride at Ramón Salazar's botched wedding. He and his banged-up entourage drive to Guadalajara and move into a mansion where he is hosted by a senior judicial official. Palma is guarded by thirty-three federal policeman, all on his payroll.

Palma is a family man. And a man of ambition. Earlier, he had decided to carve a piece out of the empire called the Guadalajara cartel. Félix Gallardo, the head of the empire, dispatched a Venezuelan named Rafael Clavel to infiltrate Palma's operation. He wooed Palma's woman and ran off with her and the two small children. She cooperated by withdrawing $7 million from a bank account her husband had in San Francisco. One day a package came to Palma's house and he opened it. Inside was the severed head of a woman with long black tresses. His wife. He learned his two young children had been pitched headlong from a bridge.[1] He erected a headstone with their faces beaming over a row of scenes of angels and the Holy Family, all this carved in stone. He also paid a federal police chief to murder four people in revenge.

As I drive to meet Jordan at EPIC, Palma is in for another rough patch. True, sometimes he is lucky. He has been cleared by the courts of murdering six people in a Puerto Vallarta disco. And he will soon be cleared of murdering the cardinal at the Guadalajara airport. Just as he has been cleared of killing nine people in the state of Guerrero three years earlier. He will be eventually cleared of having the thirty-three federales as bodyguards on the grounds that no proof existed that they were being paid to specifically protect the body of Hector Palma. When Palma is questioned by the authorities, he explains that he is a simple rancher with an income of about $8,000 a month.

Palma is also noted for his care in the case of Norma Corona. She was a young woman active in Culiacán in handling human rights cases. This is a peculiar field of law to take up in such a place. Culiacán has a murder or two a day. A few years earlier, I sat in the best hotel downtown and listened during the night as gunshots barked through the open window as a local drug dealer did lines of coke off the top of my television and sang the praises of his city. The dealer gives me a photograph of himself as a keepsake: he is squatting in camouflage clothing, clutching a Lite beer in the darkness, and cradling an Uzi as he awaits a load crossing the line into the U.S. In the case of Norma Corona, who was mucking about in some drug murders, Hector Palma's private world, she received clues about what could happen to her. A box of black roses arrived for her with a note explaining a murder, her own. A state police officer was eventually imprisoned for her death.[2] President Carlos Salinas responded to the public outcry by creating a National Human Rights Commission. She did not die alone but as part of a cavalcade of death. In the 1990s, at least forty lawyers are murdered in the state of Sinaloa. As the head of the local bar explained, "There are no threats. There are executions."

Palma carries a semiautomatic pistol with a palm tree fashioned of diamonds and emeralds on the handle. He is arrested to great press acclaim by a Mexican general, Jesús Gutiérrez Rebollo. The military is also detailed to guard the attorney general's office in Guadalajara to protect the lawyers from the federal police. The attorney general of Mexico speaks of a problem of "contamination" in the region's police forces. The general becomes a kind of hero in the U.S. narc community. He is on the payroll of the Mexican army and that of a man named Amado Carrillo.

Palma is a fair-skinned man and for this reason carries the same nickname as the late Ramón Salazar, that of El Güero. His arrest causes a brief stir and then vanishes. Not simply from the Mexican press or the American press but from consciousness. The flicker of fact about the $40 million-a-month bribery budget also vanishes. To pay attention to such a report would suggest that a person most readers had never heard of and who never is mentioned in matters of state could afford almost half a billion a year as a simple business expense. At that time, the U.S. government was spending about $150 million a year to transport the president around the nation and world.

When Bill Clinton assumes office in early 1993, he cuts the White House drug czar's office from a staff of 146 to twenty-five. His National Security Council moves drugs from third in priority on a list of twenty-nine to twenty-ninth. But at the same time, the drugs budget for state, federal, and local cops keeps creeping up and is at this moment about to bump $30 billion a year.

When I visited Culiacán, I drank with drug dealers, went out to the ranches that function as stash houses. Listened to the small-arms fire in the night. In front of the fine hotel was a hot dog stand with cars lined up to place orders. It was a simple curbside affair, a crude stall hunkered on a chunk of sidewalk. The customers would order the dogs and many would insist on mayonnaise on the side. Such an order immediately jacked the bill up to twenty or thirty dollars American. The condiment was in a tinfoil packet and was cocaine. A short walk away was the state capitol and government complex. A young fire eater spat out flames at the stoplight and then begged for coins. The air at night had a tropical lushness and at dawn exotic-looking birds streamed down the river toward the sea. Everything was green and tasted of paradise.

The first time I see Sam Medrano's law office, it has an air of camping out about it, as if he were simply here for a few brief moments before he finds a permanent residence. His name is not on the door, and his few personal items, the bottle of scotch, a few knickknacks about golf, have the temporary feel of suitcases plopped down on the carpet of a room at a Holiday Inn. He is short, heavy, and sweating. He tells of his planned appeal for Miguel Angel Flores, one that will call his own competence into question. The room is windowless and he fills it with his anxiety and anger. He runs through the murder, the case, the icy silence of his client, the interference from the Mexican consulate. All these things are tossed out like pebbles and they are never linked, they simply are. Juárez is mentioned but it is a matter of no concern. The case is in a U.S. court and what lies across the river four or five blocks from his office is a matter of no official concern to Medrano. He does not follow his case across the river, he has no reason to do so, he explains.

But something is bothering Medrano. He talks on and on. Finally, he flips out a mug shot of María's ex-boyfriend. He says, "Don't say where you got this."

And then, he adds, "Why don't you ask Phil Jordan about it?"

I say I will. I sense the comfort for Medrano in trying the case on the fallibility of eyewitnesses, and trying the appeal on the prejudice introduced by the discovering of the marijuana roach in the sweatshirt and by his own failure to demand a mistrial at that point. Talk of such matters keeps everything on this side of the river and spinning on points of law. It is an absolute habit of mind all along the border.

I leave and walk downtown El Paso. The local banks bring in deposits of over $700 million a year that cannot be accounted for in the local economy. San Antonio, five hundred miles to the east, is running $3 billion in deposits over the legal economy. A few blocks from Medrano's temporary office is a U.S. bank owned by Amado Carrillo. On a main drag of El Paso, a Jaguar dealership flourishes.

The attorney general of Chihuahua has fired a third of the state's 950-man police force in three years. In Juárez itself, half the city's nine-hundred-man force has been fired in the same period. The police chief of Juárez announces that he recently turned down a $1.3 million bribe. He says he was asked simply to leave the drug business alone for a three-month period.[3]

I call Jordan at EPIC.

His office faxes a map to lead me to the bunker nestled inside the military base.

People disappear in El Paso and Juárez. It is explained by saying many of them are young lovers who have run off. A group is formed in El Paso to track the missing. It announces it must keep its offices in El Paso for safety reasons. But generally, the group and its claims are ignored. Just as in Juárez the bodies of raped and murdered young girls are given scant attention by the authorities. If mentioned at all, it is dismissed and seen by the government as an effort to smear their modern and growing city.

The economy is collapsing. Mexico in June 1995 has an economy pegged around $200 billion GDP. It manages to export about $20 billion (this is everything, including oil) but has a foreign debt service of $25 to $35 billion a year. Against this stands a shadow industry, drugs, humming along at $30 billion a year.[4]

Jordan feels his grip slipping. He is still in charge but he is essentially told not to leave town. And to shut up about Mexico. New people are assigned to his Mexico unit at EPIC without his consent. Two come from Washington as analysts but seem to be mainly monitoring the analysis for the DEA shop back in the capital. He has been trained up in DEA and is an old hand at its culture of backbiting and suspicion. He has played the minority game in seeking promotions but knows this is a double-edged sword in DEA, where Spanish speakers who can pass in Mexico are at a premium but also, because of this fact, are not trusted and looked upon as possible traitors who will sell out to the cartels.

Still, as June dribbles away after the trial of Miguel Angel Flores, he has some hopes. His shop is cooking up a master plan to seize tens of millions of dollars of assets and bust dozens of individuals tied to the Juárez cartel and others along the line. Jordan buries himself in this work, a place where he can actually strike out at something. In the case of his brother's murder, he is impotent, striking at shadows to no effect. And he knows it and it eats at him.

The black guy at the gate is bored and after a phone call inside, waves me into the parking lot. The rows of cars face a low light-brick building on Fort Bliss. Cyclone fencing topped with concertina wire circles the installation. The lobby sleeps and a receptionist sits behind a bulletproof window. No one is waiting. Now and then employees with ID tags dangling from their clothing silently cross the lobby. Each door has a numeric pad demanding code. The employees say nothing but glance furtively at me. The men have the trim mustaches that cops favor as a claim of personal identity within a life of rules and regulations. A glass case holds memorabilia, caps, coffee cups, and the like saying EPIC. A plaque memorializes Kiki Camarena, for whom the building is named.

A floor below, an array of computers take up about a football field of space. The entire building is an organism to protect and foster these machines, to create the proper temperature and moisture so that they can thrive. Just a few feet past the door by the receptionist is a gallery view of the action below, a raft of analysts sitting before screens and pawing through the huge memory of the machines. EPIC loves numbers: 75,000 requests a week, thousands of other communications about flights now arcing over Mexico or the Caribbean, car plates run instantly that alert some cop by a roadside to bust someone or let them continue their journey because they are coded as part of an ongoing investigation. Ships at sea also flow into this room, as do fleets of trucks. This warehouse of information is supposed to mutate into actions. When EPIC was pasted together in the 1980s from the analysts of various federal agencies and cop shops, it handled a couple of hundred requests a week. Now it has grown and by this act made the work grow. It watches more and more traffic and thus creates more and more traffic of its own.

If there is a characteristic to EPIC with its bland government walls, regulation linoleum floors, and color-murdering fluorescent lighting, it is a passive air. Not simply the somnolence that dominates all government offices, but a deeper core trait. EPIC can react but cannot act. It can notice an odd flight from the wrong airfield in Colombia but it is inert until someone else initiates a flight. For several years, the Juárez cartel simply ran cars through U.S. Customs at the bridge by accelerating, storming past the inspectors, and then disappearing into the traffic of El Paso. Finally, the government installed concrete barriers that curved the lines and made such tactics difficult. But they noticed an unnerving thing: before they could even get their defense in place, the blockade running had ceased. The cartel had adopted different tactics. While I wait in the lobby, the drug merchants have their crews on the bridge, beggars peddling things to travelers trapped in the wait at Customs, and these beggars have cell phones stuffed in their pockets and call in which inspector is on which lane, which one checks diligently and which blows off his job, a constant flow of information that shifts the car with the load from lane to lane seeking the soft point in the U.S. armor.

On a business level, it hardly matters. The U.S. claims it glances at about 10 percent of the vehicles but it is unlikely that even 5 percent get a real look. Which means with no plan, a smuggler will get through between 90 and 95 percent of the loads. One group ran nine hundred loads across this bridge and never lost a single gram of

cocaine. Which, of course, led some analysts to yet another dark conclusion: no one could statistically pull that off. They had to have
bought U.S. officials. But this latter matter is never discussed, it is
unmentionable. Just as the impregnability of EPIC is a given and not
to be questioned as it squats bunkered on a military base. But as I
watch the pale faces cross the lobby in their wrinkle-free shirts and
slacks, and there are over three hundred staff in the building, I wonder
which one is on the pad. Because that is another part of the game: you
just need to buy a few. One or two inspectors on a bridge. A few eyes
within EPIC. And what I think is that no one really cares what EPIC
does, simply what it knows. Any route or structure can be changed if it
is blown. The initiative always lies with the person moving goods,
never with the cop looking for the goods.

I wait fifteen or twenty minutes, just enough to put me in my
place. It is a ritual I've learned with government, one always pushed a
little further by cops. I'm wearing Levi's, a wrinkled shirt, running
shoes, and need a haircut. I sit there and think of El Güero, Ramón
Salazar, and how this building is fixated on people just like him. I
remember once driving past his boyhood home in the Sierra Madre, a
low-slung mud building on a rutted trail. The privy was out back, the
water pulled up by the bucket from a hand-dug well. A brilliant
bougainvillea bloomed by the door and a mountain stream purred
nearby while parrots screamed from the trees. Güero had long ago left
the place for his work in the cities and his dinners with people like
Amado Carrillo. A Mexican had told me Güero came from wealthy
people, that they always had all the tortillas they wanted.

Someone comes through the door, approaches me, and I follow into
the labyrinth. The next phase is a small conference room. A secretary
fetches me some weak coffee in a Styrofoam cup. The door to the room
is left open, the secretary sits with a clear view of me. I get up and
begin to walk around the table, leave her view, and instantly she is up
with a manic need to do some filing that brings me back within her
gaze. I notice plaques on the wall from cooperating narcotics intelligence forces around the world—even Finland. I make some notes to
kill time and whenever I move, she moves in the other room. There is

no plaque from Mexico and when one of Jordan's aides finally comes to get me, I mention this absence to thin-lipped silence.

Down the hall I enter a big room, Jordan's office, designed for the kind of pointless scale that an executive post demands with a desk on one side like an aircraft carrier and then, across the room, the conference table. The room is government-issue and adamantly bland. Jordan turns out to be over six feet with a bluff manner and easy movements; the echo of a former athlete rings from his frame. He wears glasses, a suit and tie, and takes up space, more space than his body requires. He keeps moving, both his body and his eyes, constantly moving. He wears a distracted air, stumbles around in his statements, yet moving like a fighter in the ring always dancing to maintain a physical center. His face is beyond bland, it is a blank. There is nothing in the face, some features, lips, eyes, a nose, but beyond that nothing. I think he would be a perfect killer, that no witness could recall anything about him. He has two aides with him and they become mute after a handshake and a hello. One aide is thin, the analyst I assume. One is shorter and more solid, a street agent I speculate who is now doing a tour in EPIC.

The voice is soft and yet has these spikes in it, almost a breaking sound. It is not the voice of authority in some booming bass way, but it is the sound of command.

The voice says things that sound odd to my ear: "These drug people are cowardly killers."

What does he think this is all about, some joust between knights?

He goes right into the case: look, he says, the kid was the shooter, the powder burns on his hand show this. And we know who drove the truck, some local guy with a straight job. His ex-girlfriend, Jordan lies in a slightly softer voice, is cooperating with us. We know the guy is part of a car theft ring operating out of Juárez. The Mexican side of the ring is this lawyer and he calls and orders the cars. They also move dope. Been doing it for years. Look, the kid admitted the killing to the cops when he was first picked up, there is no question about the kid. And now the kid is bragging about the shooting in the joint—we've got him surrounded by informants.

"I want," Jordan says, "the individuals who are behind the murder. The kid was talking, he was talking to the police. And then he was told harm would come to his family."

He shrugs and says he went over to see the kid's mom and she told him that her boy liked to play with toy cars but could not drive a real one. He made her a good offer but she blew him off. And then when he left he gave her twenty bucks or so for bus fare so that she could visit her son in jail in El Paso and the damned Mexican newspapers claimed he was trying to bribe her. He shrugs again as if to say, what else is new?

Look, he tells, me, on June 21 he finished thirty years as a narc in DEA. He's seen everything. He was twenty-five years old and working for DEA when Bruno was born. He knows his brother was clean. And he knows dirt, and suddenly, Jordan is riffing off his history in the drug wars, dropping names I either do not know or barely know, talking faster now as if all these back pages were a bore but he'd better make sure I know whom I am dealing with. Years ago, he nailed Pedro Pérez Aviles, the godfather that created all the cartels running wild today, the guy who trained up the pioneers like Rafael Caro Quintero, Félix Angel Gallardo, Hector Palma, Amado Carrillo, you name anybody and Pérez trained them. Once, he notes, Pérez Aviles put a $10,000 contract on Jordan's head. And he knew Kiki Camarena, had lunch with him in Guadalajara shortly before he was kidnapped. He knows these cartel guys, knows they are cowards. And his kid brother Bruno had nothing to do with any of this. Clean, absolutely clean. Nothing in the autopsy either.

I listen. His two aides say nothing. Everything is written in some pre-agreed-upon script and I know if I wait I will get to my part. I also notice one other thing. I have come here on a phone call, I have no credentials. I am freelancing, self-employed, a nobody. No one asks that I prove I am who I claim to be. No one asks anything. I sit there for two hours and there is never a question directed to my past. They've run me through their machines.

Now, Jordan's speaking again, he's saying, "My brother was the apple of my family's eye. He was our counselor, our advisor."

And then he stops as if there is nothing more to be said on the matter or nothing more he is going to say to me.

As I ask questions, Jordan gets up and moves around, comes back and sits. I never get answers. He always turns my question into one of his own. And when I accidentally seem to strike too close or hit some nerve, he gets up and goes across the room to his desk, rustles through piles of papers, and comes back with a newspaper clip or some other piece of public knowledge. But not with an answer. He is running me. He is giving me names, the lawyer in Juárez, the ex-boyfriend of his relative's wife, giving me addresses and places, tossing out things he wants me to look into. At one point, his aide magically produces a map that will lead me to the ex-boyfriend's house. I am to be the decoy sent into places where Jordan and his colleagues have worn out their welcome. Or can't go. This is okay with me because no one ever really deals with me except to use me. Even Güero's kinfolk down in Sonora wanted me to make the gringos aware of his death. And even though they knew this would accomplish nothing, at least it would be notice, something that they could not get in the Mexican press with its fears and restrictions. So being used is normal for me. But being used by DEA is something else, since they have a reputation for burning informants, for letting them dangle and be murdered in pursuit of a case.

But I'm hungry for names and addresses. All I have is a news clip from Mexico City and a long conversation with Sam Medrano. I think: this could be a decent magazine story, maybe a few thousand words about border violence crossing a forbidden line and entering the white-bread world of a federal agency. And that is a mild bone of contention as we talk in Jordan's office. When I say it looks like a hit to me, his two aides in unison say that they wouldn't dare, not after the crackdown following Camarena's murder ten years before. I'm taken aback, they really seem to think they are safe. That they are the big men and these lesser brown beings would not dare to touch them or theirs.

There is a problem in reaching certain answers to Bruno's death. If he was killed on orders from Juárez, then the crime crosses the river into Mexico. This makes it more difficult to solve. But even worse, this means federal badges and a U.S. passport no longer protect one. It would mean that a new world had emerged across the river with new powers and new arrogance. There is a point in this small debate that rings like a bell in my mind. One of the aides mentions the two sisters in El Paso who sheltered Miguel Angel when he was hustling the streets for some money for his family in Juárez. The aide ridicules one sister's testimony in court because she had said Miguel Angel was a good boy and gave as proof the fact that he sometimes bought food and milk for her family and because he never stole her food stamps. The tone of the aide suggests who can believe such trash? But I realize that I can, that I can understand the honesty of not stealing from your second family and that I can taste the meaning of the sister's words.

"In my mind," Jordan offers out of the blue, "this kid has stolen cars before." The standard cop view: there are no first-time offenders, just first-time busts for offenders. They're all repeaters, all dirty, all of them.

We are at a standstill. Jordan in two hours has surrendered molecules of information and sought to suck a few tons of details out of me. It is a habit of mind, along with the blank face, the constant movement. He is DEA and DEA is trust, deception, and finally, betrayal. It is the pattern of the work. The analyst has never been far from a desk. The other aide is resting up from some stint in Mexico. And this case, I can sense, has nothing to do with them, just something on the table that concerns the boss. And I am less than nothing. It is not simply the normal rational distrust by cops of the press. Cops live off secrets, the press lives by leaking secrets and blowing operations. This time it is something deeper: we know and you don't. We listen in, we open the mail, we track the bank accounts, we have snitches in every room. We know. I can sense almost a feeling in their faces that they are among the elect. The ones who know how the world actually works while the rest of us are ignorant.

But they never see it coming. As I sit there in EPIC with the machines peering into so many lives a floor below, I realize they never saw a kid enter the parking lot, never saw the truck and gun disappear. Never saw the El Paso police stop on a dime that night with the arrest of a thirteen-year-old. And never foresaw that a kid could stand up to their pressure, take the fall, be sentenced to prison, and never say a single word.

I look down at the chart they have shown me of the Federation with its hierarchy of bosses and cartels. With its leaders and mid-level guys and the border specialists who have been named gatekeepers, the technicians of smuggling. It is all so orderly. A similar chart must have comforted American generals in the dark of night in Vietnam. Once, El Güero was expecting a load on the edge of the Sierra in southern Sonora, a load coming just outside the small town where I attended his failed wedding. And he had a hangover or something, and suddenly realized a damn shipment was coming and raced down to a local hotel where he knew the staff, borrowed some bedsheets, and stormed off into the campo, found the dirt strip, and he and his cohorts stood there waving sheets in the sun to beckon the load down. I remember at the wedding the manager of the hotel panicked over all the guns in plain view and called the police and the police chief told him he couldn't come because Güero and his guys had more firepower. And then, the head of the local army base came and talked and some money changed hands and the wedding went on, the wedding where there was never enough time carved out for the priest and a ceremony. One morning I got up and wandered the patio and found thirty-eight empty scotch bottles littering the party scene. And the affair went on for two more days. I look down at the EPIC chart and think, this is anglo and will be buried under a mounting wave of brown mud. Or cut down by a thirteen-year-old who is not even five feet tall.

Jordan stands. The meeting is over. I have been given my instructions, tasks coded as tips with names and addresses, mainly in Juárez. I will be sent out as the reporter to see what happens to me.

I again tell Jordan as we stand that the thing looks like a hit to me, that the gun is wrong for a carjacking, a 9mm, that the silence is wrong for a punk, that the interest of the Mexican consulate makes no sense. I say that Amado Carrillo could do this hit and he would arrange it so that it looked like a carjacking and so that the only one to be found, if anyone, would be a thirteen-year-old kid who didn't know anything beyond the handle of whoever drove him into the K-Mart lot.

And this crime could not happen to the brother of the head of EPIC without the consent of the Juárez cartel since it could cause problems at the very crossing where they made their money. And that it had to be very satisfying to someone to sit in Juárez and know what had happened and know that no one else could know. Except for him, Phil Jordan. That this had to be very sweet and satisfying.

Jordan says, "Umm, that's interesting."

On July 2, 1995, a body is fished out of the river. The Mexican officials report it is an adolescent, a Mexican citizen, who has drowned in the high water of summer when large flows are released for the fields downstream. The boy, sixteen, is named Juan Alfredo Flores, the older brother of Miguel Angel.

In early July, a tiger suddenly appears in Juárez and roams the streets. The police are called and capture the animal. No one knows quite what to say—Juárez lacks a zoo to explain such an escaped tiger. Eventually, the animal is transported to the zoo in the state capital. No one says much about the tiger but it is general knowledge that it has broken free of the menagerie of Amado Carrillo. After that some executions take a peculiar twist. As usual the bodies are found with the hands and sometimes the feet bound with duct tape. Signs of torture are evident. Several rounds have been fired into the head. And some now are draped with cheap tapestries bought in the public market, tapestries with tigers on them.

At the toll bridge connecting the downtowns of El Paso and Juárez, the dying Mexican mayor is in the middle of a hunger strike. He is a man in his late sixties and his body is racked with lymphatic cancer and heart disease. To this he has added starvation. He is a member of the opposition PAN and his rule over Juárez is an embarrassment to the government. Nothing seems to bother the mayor. Cancer may kill him before hunger. He is protesting the fact that the tolls from the bridge to El Paso, a sum of some $5 million a year, go to Mexico City and never return. The federal government uses the money to subsidize the famous modern subway in the capital. This underground transportation system causes constant complaint in the north where it symbolizes the real fact of Mexico: the nation is bled to finance the center in Mexico City. One hundred thousand citizens of Juárez have signed petitions supporting him. And hundreds throng around his trailer late at night in a vigil of solidarity.

Mexico has thirty-one states and they get 80 percent of their revenue from the central government. The new president, Zedillo, in response to the general economic collapse, has reduced this money by 14 percent. Now he must figure out a $2.9 billion bailout of the state governments lest they collapse completely.

Manuel Hernández, of the Mexican consulate in El Paso, is thirty-three and he looks like diplomats are supposed to look: thin wire-rimmed glasses, close-cropped hair, conservative tie, white shirt, spotless office, and a gift for serene and meaningless patter. He is cordially explaining to me why I cannot talk with Miguel Angel Flores. You see, he says, we are his guardians since his incarceration in the United States and we must consider not merely his legal rights but since he is only thirteen, his moral development and protection. Questions, even if simply about his life, he continues, could lead to painful, and for such a young child, morally damaging thoughts. Hernández has long supple fingers and as he tells me these concerns they splay out in a pattern of total relaxation upon his desk. He is the press officer of the Mexican consulate in El Paso. He tells me that Miguel Angel is very confused in his juvenile prison and does not understand why all these bad things are happening to him. Also, the appeal is soon to be filed and the consulate must consider this legal movement and the child's interests.

The press officer nods politely as I tick off a list of problems with the case. He listens with pursed lips. Ah, yes, he sighs. The consulate general has given repeated interviews that Miguel Angel is a scapegoat in some evil Yanqui scheme and he and Manuel Hernández hint darkly at the machinations of EPIC, about the sinister force of the DEA, and how those employees try to please the boss of EPIC, Phil Jordan, the older brother of Bruno.

Hernández continues his diplomatic drone, "We see that the boy's mother, Graciela, is facilitated in her visits with her son whenever she wishes to cross and see him and sometimes she does this two or three times a week." As I sip black coffee, I am numbed by the order and peace of the glass-walled office, the blond parquet floor, and the spotless computer station. Hernández gives me a copy of the Mexican autopsy report lest I think the consulate is not being cooperative with the press. On this paper Juan Alfredo Flores dies at 10:00 A.M., July 2, 1995, from *Asfixia por inmersión,* basically suffocation by being underwater in the Río Bravo, he is sixteen years old, and under *ocupacíon habitual* is listed *limpia vidrios,* windshield washer. I thank the consulate press officer and note the family address: 2065 Calle Calchaquies, Colonia Azteca, Ciudad Juárez. And he notes my identity and the name of a New York magazine I toss out for him.

Fernando de la Sota has suddenly become an embarrassment. He has worked hard for years. In the 1970s and 1980s, he toiled for the federal internal security agency, an outfit now officially abolished because of problems. Then in 1985, he signed on with the security force at the Mexico City airport. He also spent a year in jail for misusing his authority. After that he worked on the president's military staff, and was a deputy of the nation's attorney general. In 1992, he became a federale comandante. Somehow he became chief of security for Luis Donaldo Colosio, the regime's presidential candidate, in early 1994 and was standing near the candidate when he was murdered in Tijuana on March 23, 1994. He could not see too well, he admits, because the gunfire unfortunately set off a diabetic attack. He is six feet tall, weighs 280 pounds, and is known as El Gordo.

Also, it is noted in passing, from 1990 to 1992 he was on the payroll of the Mexico City station of the CIA. But the agency insists he was cut loose from them in 1992.[5]

There are hundreds of street gangs in Juárez. Many do tasks for the cartel. Many sell drugs. Many murder. Every square foot of the city has been carved up and divided by the gangs. In July a man is found dead with twenty-three rounds in his head. He is reputed to have been in charge of Juárez street gangs for the cartel. First the boys with Miguel Angel in the K-Mart parking lot on January 20 disappear. Then Juan Alfredo drowns in the river. Then the cartel's contact with the city's criminal youth dies.

The river brushes the shore, faintly stirring the reeds as I look south into Mexico on the outskirts of Juárez and from this caress a soft sound rises up from the slick waters. I am on the spot where officially Juan Alfredo drowned. They fetched him out very near here. The July air is heavy with the promise of rain and the river runs big as dams let loose a heavy flow for fields downstream. There is a bladed dirt track on a dike right behind me where the U.S. Border Patrol squats every few hundred yards in trucks waiting for them to try to come north. Here and there are huge, portable floodlights borrowed from the military to aid in the night work. The Mexican newspapers say El Paso firemen towed the body to shore and that the local county coroner examined it and declared the boy dead.

I drive to the main fire station. The staff gives me pages of printout itemizing every call in that sector of the river on the day the body rose up from the dark bottom of mud. The dead boy is not on the list. I visit the coroner, and he says that he did some floaters in July, but not this one, not a sixteen-year-old boy.

"Why do you want to know?" he asks.

The first two analysts who are transferred into EPIC without Jordan's request catch his eye but do not surprise him. After thirty years in DEA, he is a good bureaucrat and understands the ire of the main office in D.C. over his briefing of Attorney General Janet Reno. In part, the briefing told her things she had never heard before and this embarrassed the main office. And then there is a cultural rub to the briefing since it was based extensively on the intelligence of street agents, the grubby facts gathered in cantinas and parties. Street agents and desk analysts live at odds with each other. So when the two analysts descend onto this Mexican unit, he accepts the matter and pushes on.

The mole is a greater problem. She arrives in June and through his contacts in D.C., Jordan instantly knows what she is. Besides, he monitors her, pores over her phone logs, and sees she is spending hours and hours calling his enemies at headquarters. He's been a cop too long to be surprised by this. He's been investigated, benched, and threatened at times with transfers to nowhere. And he's always won.

He has other problems. He can sense that with the completion of the trial the investigation of his brother's murder is closed. And he can tell that the FBI is really doing nothing. His own investigations have failed. He has turned up nothing on the car theft ring and the ex-boyfriend of María's. He has learned nothing since the first week after the murder. Still, he can feel the pressure of his family and their demand for justice. His marriage is getting rockier also, what with the money he is pouring into the case, money he is silently taking from their savings account. And with his absences from Plano because of his new job in El Paso.

There is one more tension. His wife cannot fathom his continuing involvement in the case. The jury decided, they voted guilty, let it go. You have a family in Dallas to think about. Your brother is dead, there is nothing more to be done about the matter. Jordan cannot explain his feelings to her. He cannot even comprehend why an explanation is needed.

He'll get up, leave the family home on Frutas Street in El Paso, and go to a diner for breakfast. He will order poached eggs. The waitress brings them and he looks at the eggs in the cup with a pool of water and he says in a mild voice, "I'm really sorry to be a bother, but could you take them back and drain a little of the water off? I know it's crazy, but it's a thing with me, I guess."

And she'll smile, and do as he asks. Sometimes, this requires two trips, as he homes in on getting his poached eggs just right. All the while, as he is accomplishing this mission, he will look distracted. But he will get what he wants.

He does this all day long. Gently guiding and prodding, appearing here but not here, starting sentences he never finishes, moving about while he is talking, listening to questions and never delivering answers.

Controlling. And yet at the same time not even projecting a presence, all but becoming invisible.

Getting his poached eggs just right while looking blankly out on the world is essential to maintaining his sense of the world. Often he thinks of his grandfather and how he accomplished things. And every day he thinks of what his grandfather would do if his own brother were murdered.

In Juárez, I talk to a reporter for a Mexico City daily. Ah, he tells me, as if it hardly matters, yes, I saw the body of Juan Alfredo Flores, the brother of Miguel Angel. He describes a body in the Mexican morgue that was bound hand and foot, black from torture, and with a cord around the neck. I point out that according to the Mexican press the body was found on the U.S. shore and the autopsy performed there. He shrugs at this detail. Later, I am drinking with a newspaper photographer who says he photographed the body coming out of the river. Yes, he says, he has a negative of the body and it was bound, tortured, and strangled. He will see if he can find the negative. But these two claims lead nowhere. The negative never turns up. The reporter's recollection remains in the café and never appears in the Mexican press. The negative of the body, ah, that the photographer tells me must be in a box right by his bed. He will look for it, there is no problem. We drink many times, he teaches me much about Juárez. He is thirty-two years old and has photographed five hundred murders. But the negative, it stays out of reach.

Sometimes, I think he is being cautious about the negative as self-protection. Sometimes, I think the negative does not exist. It will take me years to realize that the negative, whether it exists or not, can never really matter here, that facts as I know them have become slippery and some other kind of reality dominates this place.

There is a corrido that becomes popular. It details the life of Pablo Acosta, the man who once helped train Amado Carrillo when he was coming up in the drug business. The song follows the traditional form of a loose chronology tracking a man's life. But it has one stanza that escapes the normal language of such songs and ventures into a new country.

Overconfidence and power
are the weakness of brave men.[6]

Jordan needs to assert power. His analysts and agents have concocted a plan that will seize, he thinks, at least $100 million worth of cartel assets. And arrest dozens of individuals. The plan will cost $10 million to operate and pay back at least ten to one. Jordan knows that nothing he does can really stop the drugs from coming north. Nor can the murder or arrest of any cartel leader slow the traffic. Such an action will merely create a job opening at the top. Of course, he does not admit this in agency discussions but still he knows.

There is this other thing that drives him: he wants to make them hurt. He wants to cost them money and he wants to cause them pain. It will be an act of vengeance and it will be a secret act, an agency action that in a huge sweep all along the border from the Gulf of Mexico to the Pacific Ocean will cast dozens of people into American prisons. His analysts and agents produce organizational charts of the Federation, schedules for the operation. It is almost an automatic thing based on intelligence of cells of traffickers and their various fronts and assets. And it will cause a splash with this massive takedown of people and objects in a corridor almost two thousand miles long. Implicitly it will reveal the new dimension of the cartels and snuff in one swift move all talk of local drug gangs and petty smuggling. With any luck, the busts will shine a light on a power structure that reaches far beyond the border and leads to the biggest political names in Mexico. And of course, it will send a message across the river, a message to at least one person sitting in a mansion in Juárez.

In July, he and key staff members fly to the Phoenix area for a briefing to Justice Department officials on the plan. Federal attorneys from jurisdictions all along the border gather. One of Janet Reno's key aides is there to hear out the plan.

The Justice Department turns it down. They question spending $10 million. Jordan is caught off guard, he never sees this rejection coming. He has deluded himself and he knows it. He has succumbed temporarily to the fantasy called the War on Drugs. He complains afterward and is bitter but in his moments alone, he knows rejection was inevitable. For years, he has seen operations constrained by an unspoken barrier: not causing problems for the regime in Mexico. Drug policy is low on the list of priorities, a stable trading partner in Mexico is at the top of the list.

Jordan has been a fool and humored himself with a fool's dreams. He knows this. He is bitter, but still he knows this. He has thought of staying at EPIC two or three years. At first, he was simply going to pull a one-year tour and finish out his career and put the fine touches on his résumé for a life of consulting after retirement. But the briefings by his Mexico unit excited him. He's been fascinated by how much they know, how deeply they have penetrated into the bonds between the drug business and the government. And he thought that he could sit in El Paso in his bunker on a military base and make an end run around U.S. foreign policy.

On the plane flying back from Phoenix to El Paso, he is empty. This delusion is now over. He knows he is a stooge running a face-saving intelligence center. He does not say this out loud. He mentions this to no one, naturally. He tells his staff things will be okay, that it will work out. He thinks of all the basketball games he has coached and how no matter how hopeless the game is going, the coach always lies. But he knows.

He tries to put this cold reality out of his mind. He continues to probe his brother's murder. He drives the Mexico unit to more research. He is intoxicated by the wiretaps, by the mutterings of informants that cross his desk, that lifelong savoring of secrets the public does not know. He eats dinner at the family house on Frutas Street and enjoys their sense of his power and status. His parents keep clippings of his career. But he knows.

Helen and Flori have apartments in the project and each lives with a fistful of children. When Miguel Angel was picked up the night of

January 20, he was a block or two from their place and most likely heading home. They became home for him somewhere back in 1992 or 1993 when he was nine or ten years old. Their children found him on the streets and brought him back. The sisters live on little, some food stamps and random income that is never explained. Their project is coated with graffiti and has an aura of gangs and drugs. They live in the world the Jordan family left a generation or two ago, and the world Miguel Angel struggled to enter. The apartment is dark and sad in the late afternoon. A television drones on in one room, the kitchen table is cluttered with spent meals, dirty dishes, and crumbs. The housekeeping feels casual and children are underfoot everywhere.

Helen and Flori are uncomfortable talking to a stranger. They live in a world of the projects where people with questions always mean trouble. Miguel Angel fit into their world and he would stay with them for a week or two at a time when he was working the street corners of El Paso. Sometimes he wiped windshields, more often he juggled, his face painted white like a mime's. He is convicted now as July draws to a close and since the arrest they have not spoken with him. It is not permitted by the consulate. But they have gotten some letters, though replies have not been written since they hate to write letters.

They know a happy kid who would sit and watch Mexican soap operas, laugh often, and in a pinch, dig into his own earnings to buy their families food. Sometimes they would drive over to Juárez and go to his house. He was small, and in some ways timid. Once they tried to teach him to drive but he was too frightened to even attempt it. He was also, they explain, afraid of guns and knives. He would shift from one sister's apartment to the other's, "so," he told them, "you will not get tired of me." They remember visiting Miguel Angel in Juárez that time he got hurt on the bridge. He was about nine, sneaking across by clinging to the bridge supports out of sight, and it was snowy that day. He fell twenty feet to the concrete embankment along the river and injured his hip. The sisters from time to time taught him English so that he could pass more easily in El Paso.

When he wrote Helen from jail, he instructed her to tell her children to stay free from the law because jail was a bad place and very hard. The dusk falls down, the television drones on, the sisters and their children sit in the growing darkness with only the glow coming off the screen and remember Miguel Angel, the small child who was laughter and help. They know nothing of these other matters. He is just a little kid.

He lives in the house where he was raised. It is almost dusk when he arrives home and finds me waiting in the street. He drives a dark pickup and is at first mildly taken aback by having a stranger staking out his home but almost instantly assumes an air of command and calm. He is the ex-boyfriend that is alleged to be some kind of key to a car theft ring.

He is young and he insists on his innocence. The night of the killing, he says, he was at a party with his new girlfriend, went to bed at eleven, and got back up at 1:30 A.M. to go to work. No question appears to bother him, including the question are you the person called El Chino? Of course not, he says. Nor did he know Miguel Angel. Nor is he part of car theft drug ring. Nor did he drive the truck that night into the K-Mart parking lot. Nor is he part of the murder of Bruno Jordan. And no, he says, he has never been arrested or had his mug shot taken. Sure, the cops talked to him once within a week of the murder but all they were interested in was his truck and they never asked him to account for his whereabouts on the night of the murder. As he speaks, I have his mug shot in my pocket. I am impressed by the ease of his lie, the fact that his eyes and facial muscles betray no tension as he denies the existence of the mug shot. His body language is that of command, leaning toward me, standing erect, arms hanging casually, legs apart but with a definite air of being centered. I instantly like him because of his sureness of purpose.

I lean against his dark truck, and it is in perfect condition, obviously a cherished object for a guy who lives with his mother and sister. I can sense that he has survived the first wave of police suspicions, the wave that allegedly caused him to seek out a lawyer the day after the murder. And he has gotten through the second wave, the trial, and come out unscathed and unmentioned. And now I am here, and I am a very small wave compared to what he has already faced.

He can't figure out who is trying to frame him. Jordan, he's got something to do with it, he says. He's never met Jordan but he knows he has so much power.

What about his former girlfriend, the wife of Phil Jordan's relative?

"She," he explains, "is almost a perfect person."

There is tenderness in his voice as he speaks of her. They were a couple from their mid-teens until just a year or so ago.

Did he make a service call to the Jordan family home after the murder?

Sure, it's part of the job.

"Bruno was a good friend of mine," he goes on, "we'd go out drinking. He was an educated man, you could talk to him about anything.

"This is really getting to me," he goes on, "to the point where I can't be at peace with myself. They're trying to pin something on me. It really hurts me. I try to take care of my household. I take care of my mother, my nieces, my truck payments. I've got a good job . . . I've no enemies I can think of . . . They've got this poor kid and now they're trying to hit on someone else."

He is a handsome, well-built man with almost hooded eyes. When he speaks he is absolutely reasonable and even-tempered regardless of the question. He wears a wristwatch and on the clock's face is a trademark: Guess.

Jordan's boss, Thomas Constantine, the head of DEA, enters the meeting room of the Senate Foreign Relations Committee on August 8, 1995. He is a former head of the New York state troopers and within the agency is disliked. At one point, he sought to get the agents into uniforms, a bizarre thought to the undercover narcs. Constantine is at odds with the street agents, a group of cowboys in his eyes who go off half-cocked and do not follow regulations and protocols. He is increasingly upset by leaks to the press about Mexico. And yet, at the same time, he sometimes gets exasperated with what he sees as the wide-open corruption in Mexico and launches a few grenades into the press himself. This August day is such a moment.

He tells the senators in a matter-of-fact voice, "[Amado] Carrillo Fuentes owns several airline companies, which enable him to fly 727s from Colombia into Juárez, where he runs his organization from his ranch headquarters. Increasingly, murders in Juárez have been associated with Carrillo Fuentes."

His testimony is barely noticed in the American press.

The dog knows something. When Bruno was alive, the family would play a trick on his dog, Brownie. They'd ask, "Where's Bruno? Where's Bruno?" and the dog would race all over the house looking for him. After Bruno died, they noticed the dog refused to play the game and would not look.

One night Beatrice and Antonio were awakened with a start by Brownie whining. They listened for a possible intruder that might have disturbed the dog and then heard nothing and Beatrice fell back asleep.

Antonio remained awake. He heard his Bruno's voice clearly from the living room. The voice said, "Mom, I'm okay."

In the morning, he told his wife of the message.

The reporter heads a bureau in Mexico City for an American daily. He begins to suspect his phone is bugged and checks into the matter and has it traced down. He is right. So then he gets a security firm to do a sweep of his office. He finds the place is wired.

But he never writes about this. He figures if he kicks up any kind of a fuss, things will just get worse for him. He has enough problems already. Take his motorcycle. As the crime rate explodes in Mexico City, he finds no one will insure it. The car is trouble also. He never drives the car down the streets unless his massive dog is in the front seat with him.

I meet with Jordan at a businessmen's hotel along the freeway. He grabs a banana from the free breakfast buffet and we sit down to talk. I ask a question, and he unconsciously stands, walks out the door, and leads me to the edge of the parking lot. Then he answers. This happens repeatedly when I meet with him. Not at EPIC, he does not want me coming to EPIC. Nor does he want me to call at EPIC. Jordan will hardly use a telephone in El Paso. Or e-mail. One of the agents I deal with on the sly won't use a fax machine either. The city is a wired thing with the FBI, DEA, CIA, Customs, Border Patrol, and INS all listening in on someone. Plus, the cartel.

Jordan never speaks freely if a third party is present. Including any of the agents under his command.

Initially, theories flourish. The hit on Bruno is about Phil since Phil is too dangerous and public to kill, so his brother will serve as a warning shot across the bow to the new head of EPIC, or the hit on Bruno is about Bruno, about some tangled web he has entered into in El Paso–Juárez. Or the hit on Bruno is not a hit at all, just a carjacking that got botched because the kid panicked. The witnesses at the K-Mart see the hit as almost instantaneous. Bruno makes no move to protest the car theft, in fact acts as if unaware of the kid until the slugs tear into him. And the gun costs too much, the caliber is 9mm and quite possibly the make is an Uzi. Not a cheap scare gun, like a Saturday night special. Who would give a kid such a gun for a car theft? And why were three people, at a minimum, involved in stealing a car, something American boys have done solo for generations without the need of accomplices? And how did the Silverado and the gun disappear so swiftly and absolutely, lost to permanent view within minutes of the shooting? And how come the kid never talks, never takes a deal, regardless of his guilt or innocence?

After a while, the theories float away and then the facts erode and become hard to recall. If María and her ex-boyfriend are involved, how does one explain that nothing turns up to link them and that they never make a misstep?

By the summer of 1995, the carjacking only exists for a few souls. The Jordan family. The Mexican consulate. Whoever is supplying the Mexican consulate with money for Miguel Angel's mother and for his legal expenses. And for Miguel Angel, who lives surrounded by snitches and who says nothing.

And Phil Jordan knows, at some level he keeps hidden from himself, he knows it was not simply a botched carjacking. But his knowledge earns him nothing. You can know what happened and yet never know why it happened. Because you never know why it happened, you can never be certain what did happen in the K-Mart parking lot.

Across the river, a world is coming apart. In Mexico City reported car theft of parked vehicles has gone up 78 percent, violence in car theft has grown 40 percent. The U.S. embassy announces that its staff is averaging eighteen attacks a week. They plan to build a compound of housing for the staff and guard it with U.S. Marines. A Mexico City doctor tracks crime as a hobby. He notes the current rates are $5,000 for a professional murder, $2,500 for a rape, and $500 for a robbery. Of course, prices are lower outside the capital.[7]

Tony sits in Las Vegas and tries to forget Juárez and tries to remember everything about Juárez. He keeps making vows to himself: he will not rest until someone answers in blood for his brother's death; he will fly to El Paso every August on his brother's birth date and take part in a memorial mass, an upbeat one that remembers his birth not his slaughter. And he will write a song about it all, he will make it into music.

Still, Juárez floats into his mind at odd hours. He remembers sitting down by the river and these poor kids in Juárez would have these $500 remote-controlled toy planes and they'd zip them across the river and then bring them down in El Paso. Hour after hour, kids playing with planes. Someone in El Paso would unload the planes, and then they'd take off and return to Juárez. He'd watch this and the Border Patrol would be parked along the bank every hundred yards or so guarding the line. They never seemed to notice the toy planes overhead, coming and going like gnats.

Tony smiles. God, he thinks, I love Mexico.

Nobody tries too hard to keep the names straight. They flit into the news suddenly like swallows and then flit away and never reappear. The names simply do not connect and if they do once in a while connect, it is so fleeting that it hardly registers. And there is another factor: hardly any Mexican name means anything to the U.S. press.

Suddenly, a wiretap surfaces in Mexico of a conversation recorded in 1992.

"Hello," a woman says.

"Hey, baby. What's up," a man replies.

"I miss you, my love," she responds, "José, my love!"

The man is José Córdoba Montoya, chief of staff to then President Carlos Salinas and also the head of Mexican internal intelligence. The woman, his lover, is a television personality named Marcela Bodenstedt. Once she was a federale. She is viewed by U.S. intelligence as a courier and link for the Medellín cartel in Colombia. Córdoba is a vital man in Washington. During the first Bush administration Under Secretary of State Bernard Aronson recalls, "to talk to Córdoba was almost the same as talking to Salinas."

Córdoba advances when the Salinas presidency ends in 1994 and for the next two years works in Washington, D.C., for the Inter-American Development Bank and for the World Bank.

The wiretap is not unusual. At any given moment in Mexico, 200,000 phones are bugged by the Mexican government.[8] The tape achieves almost no notice in the United States.

Sal Martínez is out on the street day after day, month after month, gathering little tidbits. He listens in on cell phone wiretaps, he hears the purr of intercepted police communications in Juárez. But he does not look into his cousin's murder. For him it is as reported in the newspapers, a carjacking gone bad. DEA in El Paso is supposed to stay on the American side of the river. But the action is in Juárez, at that moment the biggest drug city on earth with tons of coke, heroin, and marijuana warehoused, and Sal and his partners dive in with the joy of young guys making their bones. There is no official paperwork recording these jaunts. Everything is verbal, the assignments, the reports.

Bruno has been dead eight months, the case settled with the kid now in prison. Sal has closed the books on this one and gotten over his shakes about dying.

Shit, he enters a bar and sees an informant of his sitting at a table with some cartel guys. He takes the kid aside, warns him. The kid says, ah, don't worry. The next morning his body is on the street, an overdose. The kid didn't use drugs. Keep moving, don't think about it, do the deal.

Rolling and tumbling, the blues ringing in his head—he always loves the blues—that steady bass and then the harmonica riffing, and then over the bridge into Juárez, where the music in his head changes. Life now becomes heavy metal, full of electric moans. Into the cartel, into a city of one to two million, into the dives, his hair long, that fucking earring, a 9mm tucked in at the waist under this shirt. Now he is the drug dealer, at your service, sir, park, keep the submachine in the car, walk the walk, walk alone, without backup, go inside, they call the joint the Electric Q, walk in, yes, a double on the rocks, hey, they're here, all the assholes with their fine threads and chains, all the guys packing, part of a machine that earns $200 million a week, moving those loads and the killing, shit, bodies in the *calles* each dawn, hands tied, duct tape across the mouth, a single slug in the skull, those are the lucky bastards, not like the ones buried alive, or taken apart piece by piece, that fine bone tickling with an ice pick scraping along on the arm while the questions ring in the head and it is so fucking hard to talk after they knocked the teeth out with the butt of the AK-47, talking the talk, hey, *cómo estás?*, he glides over the bridge and into the backbeat coming off the drums of gunfire, shuffling and jiving and one mistake and . . .

There is no paperwork. What happens, never happens.

Back to the ranch, debrief, tell the boss, a few drinks with the guys, and home, and how was your day, honey? Classes go all right? Me? Naw, nothing much, just checked on some things, same-old-same-old. Huh? Sure, let's go get some ribs, you look beat, honey.

He'll flip on the evening news, nurse a beer while the noise of a day in El Paso is reported. He hears nothing. A major murder, one splashed for months in both newspapers, and in his time in the bars shuffling and jiving, his boozing it up with comandantes, never a word. It is as if the word Bruno is forbidden.

No matter. He loves his work.

• • •

We meet by accident. The house, a few blocks from the line, has a fence, a stout gate, and an outraged rottweiler. Carlos Vigueras is a stringer for several dailies in Mexico City. I need a guide into Juárez and a translator.

He holds citizenship in both nations, lives in El Paso, and curses the United States. This is not unusual. The fabric of law in the U.S. is attractive to many educated Mexicans. The coolness of the culture is repellent. Carlos maintains an office in an ancient three-story house. Portraits of Pancho Villa and Emiliano Zapata decorate the walls. The gas has been cut off. The bills pile up.

He believes Miguel Angel Flores has been framed by DEA. He is mildly horrified by my visits to EPIC, the heart of darkness for a Mexican. We plunge into Juárez day after day.

We go to a Juárez hotel once owned by a local cartel leader. Across the room three men sit at a table. One is fat, the owner. The second is laughing, the supplicant. The third talks on a cell phone and stares at me with hard eyes, the cop. Of course, he is not in uniform, such frills are unnecessary. At another table I can see a beautiful woman with dyed red hair and a fine-boned haughty face. Her breasts ride high and cleavage shines into the room like an amiable neon. A fat man at her table reads a newspaper and ignores her. The mistress. Juárez is an oven, and everyone complains of the heat.

I look over at the rich mistress with her glowing cleavage and she does not smile. Carlos is still speaking, talking about how it is intricate, never simple, many layers, things connected but the connections are unseen, patterns, plots, conspiracies, mysteries.

Suddenly, he beckons the waiter and asks, "Who owns this hotel?" The waiter gestures toward the fat man at the table in the corner. Then, the waiter scurries over to that table and whispers something to the owner, who slowly nods his head.

About fifteen minutes later the waiter comes and tells Carlos that he has just heard on the six o'clock news that the ex-president of Mexico and his former chief of staff have been so-to-speak indicted by the nation's attorney general and an order issued for their prompt return to Mexico. Carlos is excited by the news.

The waiter lied. It is a prank by the owner and his cronies. In the hotel is a room for torture, a chamber created by the late cartel owner for his amusement. Once, he showed it to Carlos.

We begin to hunt for the mother of Miguel Angel Flores. August settles on the city, the air crackles with heat and yet almost collapses with dust.

As Carlos and I wander deeper into the byways of Juárez, he faces a limit: he is a fair-skinned Mexican and there are sectors of the city where he is both a stranger and an alien. We hook up with a factory worker named Mike, a dark-skinned man born to poverty.

The neighbor's wash line sags with wet T-shirts as she busies herself sweeping her dirt yard. Carlos leans over the fence and talks to her and soon the woman's eight-year-old daughter sidles up, shy but curious, and Carlos learns that she has just scored very high in her school tests and he turns to Mike and borrows thirty pesos from him and hands them to the child. The mother looks on with faint amazement and then the child hands the money over to the mother.

This barrio is shacks of cardboard and building pallets. Here and there a house built of concrete blocks stands like a gleaming tooth on the dirt lanes. The woman explains that her neighbor Graciela Flores, Miguel Angel's mother, is not at home at the moment. She has hardly been seen, it turns out, since her husband tried to murder her two days ago. The dust in the rutted lane is an inch deep. The barrio nestles on a hill and looks down at the river and I can see the El Paso jail where Miguel Angel spent months awaiting trial

The family home itself is a small shack built of scrap lumber with a plastic sheet held down by blocks functioning as waterproofing for the roof. The fence is made from old loading dock pallets and the gate fashioned from two rotting pieces of quarter-inch plywood. Over the doorway is a family plaque with two metal owls. Some pots and pans are stacked up next to the tank of propane and a pirate electric line snakes from the pole in the street. There is no source of water except for a green hose that roams next door to a neighbor's faucet. The privy tilts and the sheet at the door has blown askew. Back against the fence a small pink bicycle tilts without tires next to a broken chaise lounge. Three small trees struggle in the yard and two look to be dying. There is not a hint of grass and the air is dust. Halfway down the block someone has painted a six-foot image of the Virgin of Guadalupe on a wall. A skinny eight-year-old girl smiles her way by wearing a T-shirt that says GONE FISHING.

There's been a domestic problem for Graciela: her husband attacked her. Between 1990 and 1995 the number of women telling a facility in Mexico City that they had been beaten rose 1,900 percent.[9]

When the neighbors arrived, the younger children were attacking the man and trying to save their mother. The neighbors took the mother and children away. Later, when he left, Graciela returned and got some clothing. Her drunken husband had gone to the police to file a report that she had attacked him and to demand the custody of the three children. Graciela was afraid to respond to this matter with the police and fled the barrio with her children.

The rutted road follows the railroad tracks past the nice well-lit maquiladora. Outside the plant, men and boys are playing at the volleyball court and shooting baskets as dusk approaches. A hundred yards past the factory is a barrio, one of the possible hiding places of Graciela. We turn off the rutted road into a rutted lane. The shacks are one-room, tarpaper–scrap lumber construction, and more bootleg lines run to them from a big power pole down by the tracks. The men sit outside this Friday evening staring with blank faces. Up ahead, the lane is blocked by a barrio meeting, one of mainly women sitting with babes in arms on inverted buckets in front of the tiny tienda.

The children are all dirty because of the lack of water and the people are all short and dark—immigrants from the Indian south. The men here either work in the maquiladoras or make adobe bricks and as the meeting moves softly along in the dusty air of the *calle,* a black cloud boils out of the nearby arroyo where burning tires are used to fire the adobes. There is not a single tree, and homes look like they were thrown up temporarily in the last few weeks. This barrio of five hundred souls is fifteen years old. A light breeze plays with the growing dusk and a stone-faced man walks by with his liter of beer.

Graciela has obviously slid down the social pole to the point where the next stop is sleeping under a bridge or on the sidewalk. She has entered deep into a world that economic charts and reports prefer to ignore.

She has four mouths to feed—her three children's and her own—and no one to find food for her. The two boys who begged and hustled to feed the family are gone. Her husband is trying to find her and kill her. She has no roof over her head. She is thirty-four years old. Recent studies by the Mexican government show that at least 60 percent of the children of the poor suffer from serious malnutrition and 80 million Mexicans qualify as poor.

As the night falls down, tiny electric lights throw a pale yellow inside the shacks. There is little furniture—a few cots, busted old chairs, a drawing of a red rose tacked bravely on a bare wall—and the hovels are jammed together. Small color televisions begin to glow like flowers in the shacks and the families huddle around them looking at a world of light-skinned people, of blond women with large breasts, of new cars, spacious homes, swimming pools, jet planes, shiny bicycles, clean clothes, fine meats, special chemicals to alter one's scent, undergarments to artfully arrange one's body, toys, liquor, machines, computers, entertainment centers, satellite dishes, smiling faces, perfect teeth, and always, absolutely always, very light skin. The light from the picture tube shines off dark faces that look like hard wood. The expressions on the faces are blank, they are in a trance staring into a world of magic. The black smoke comes off the burning tires, the dust hangs everywhere in the air.

Graciela has a few things left: a stash of letters from her son Miguel Angel written from his prison. Her children. And maybe God. Each day, her neighbors explained, Graciela went to the church in her barrio to prepare one of her children for first communion.

The black plume of smoke from the tires soars against the failing of the light.

Simple questions, such has how many people perished in the great Mexico City earthquake of 1985, are never answered.

Homero Aridjis is a leading intellectual in Mexico City. He fights for the environment. Sometimes his books are printed in Mexico but usually no one will even risk selling them within the country. In the 1990s, he researches pollution and wound up in 1997 with death threats and government bodyguards.

"It's a Soviet mentality of denial, with an Aztec ritual of secrecy," he explains. "The files mysteriously disappear, they get lost, the official you need to speak with is never in. Only the tlatoanis [bosses] are allowed to see the important information."[10]

One day he tells an American reporter, "Murder in Mexico is committed by insinuation. Bosses do not say, 'Kill this fellow.' They say, 'This fellow is bothering me,' and their subordinates are expected to understand."[11]

Pregnant women line up outside the factory trying to catch their men with a week's pay before they disappear into the cantinas and drink it up. The women glow with the life growing in their bellies as the afternoon light plays against their skin. They are very young, as are the workers ending the shift.

Mike finally comes out. He says he can find out nothing about Graciela. The people in the barrio, he can sense, are very afraid and they will no longer talk of her or her fate.

The National Institute for Statistics, Geography, and Information has issued a study, "Statistical Profile of the Mexican Population, an Approximation of Socioeconomic, Regional, and Gender Unrest." The study finds many Mexicans work for less than $1.40 a day. About 15 million people depend on the earnings of girls fifteen years old or younger.[12] Another study finds that eighty-two children a day die from malnutrition, a piece of an estimated thirty thousand deaths due to malnutrition.[13]

You are a natural entrepreneur so you leave school to get a part of the action. You realize there is a greater market for your product abroad than at home and so you leave your nation and your culture and your language and become a pioneer of free trade and open markets. You understand the fierceness of markets and competition so you go into partnership with several others of a similar bent. After looking at various opportunities, you pick two businesses that are easy to enter and reward innovation and hard work. One is the cleaning industry, a service industry to be sure, but one that can be entered with low capital. The second is the entertainment world, a constantly growing sector of the global economy as the slightest glance at any business publication would tell you. You are dedicated and leave your home at seven or eight in the morning and do not return usually until dark. You are aggressive in your marketing.

You leap out from the curbside at intersections and busily begin washing the windshields of motorists. You allow the customers to set their own fees. That is your cleaning business. Your entertainment venture requires more preparation. You apply makeup to your face until you have the classic visage of a clown. Then when the light turns red at an intersection you leap out and begin to juggle. Motorists give you various fees for your work. If you work very hard and very long, you make $6, $7, or $8 a day. This you return to your family in the home country. When you begin your work, you are nine years old. When you take mandatory retirement, you are thirteen. Your name is Miguel Angel Flores—Michael the Archangel of the Flowers. You are every thing societies endorse—independent, characterized by initiative, open to new experiences, comfortable with the idea of changing jobs, technologies, and futures, centered on family values.

When they arrest you, you tell the consular officials of your nation that you feel very confused. You thought you had been doing the right thing.

Under pressure from the American government, particularly DEA, the Mexican attorney general's office now and then raids narcotraficantes and winds up with some of their baubles. They have pendants dangling off men's necklaces shaped like AK-47s, each with a tiny compartment for storing a line of coke. A gold horseshoe pendant with a horse's head is encrusted with rubies. One pistol had 203 grams of 18 karat gold in the handle and is smeared with diamonds. Then there are gold figurines of crucified naked women that serve as coke spoons.[14]

Carrillo travels to Las Vegas, Dallas, Houston, Los Angeles. Though DEA has gotten two indictments against him, U.S. officials never seem to catch him in his journeys.[15] One agent tells the press in August 1995 that Carrillo "handles $60 million the way you and I handle $5." A narcotics official in the Chihuahua government says the Juárez cartel moves thirty tons of drugs a week across the river to El Paso.[16] But no one in Mexico can find Carrillo either. Out at EPIC the computers hum along logically finding what they seek and logically missing all the thirteen-year-olds in parking lots and billionaire drug dealers partying in Las Vegas.

In Washington, D.C., Paul B. Stares toils away on his drug report for the Brookings Institution, one finally issued in 1996 with the title *Global Habit*. He notes that people in the United States and in Europe drop about $122 billion a year on heroin, cocaine, and marijuana. Then he calculates that after being laundered, $85 billion of this boodle is invested in businesses. This last number means that the outlawed drug trade is greater than the straight economies of about three fourths of the world's 207 nations. Cops seem hardly to make a dent in his numbers regardless of how much stuff they seize. No matter how he fine-tunes his numbers the dope trade comes out as "one of the biggest commercial activities in the world."[17]

Juárez is one of the world centers of this vigorous business. It is a model of the New Economy, stateless, borderless, global. It rewards merit, ignores class origins, hires and fires at will. It despises regulations and ducks tariffs. It is color-blind and judges the work, not skin color.

Two thirds of the streets in Juárez are unpaved.

We find her eventually in Colonia Tierra y Libertad, land and freedom. Once this was the battle cry of Emiliano Zapata. The government killed him in 1919. They killed Pancho Villa in 1923. North Americans tend to forget the blood price that is Mexico. During the revolution from 1910 to 1920, one in eight or one in twelve Mexicans died. The economy did not regain its 1910 general air of poverty until 1940. We have been hunting Graciela since Thursday night, seeking her in the bad barrios where the police refuse to enter and where the people live off making adobe bricks, selling dope and guns, and stealing whatever is not nailed down. Mike explains that in the neighborhood where Graciela had lived with Miguel Angel and Juan Alfredo and the other kids, some friends of his once had their car break down. When they came to retrieve it in the morning, there wasn't much left but the frame.

While we hunt her, the city does not sleep. It is alive with sounds and squeals. Between sundown Friday and sunrise Monday, the police report eighteen murders.

The minimum wage is shrinking minute by minute as 1995 rolls along. The year begins with a minimum wage of $5.25 a day and ends with a figure of $2.59.[18] Mexico's GDP shrinks 6.9 percent on the year. Livestock production falls 81 percent, forestry goes down 67 percent, and out in the fields the harvest of basic foodstuffs declines 31 percent.[19] President Bill Clinton declares as the year slides by, "The Mexican economy has turned the corner and the markets have taken notice." President Ernesto Zedillo on a visit to Washington takes the opportunity to deny that he got $40 million from the Cali cartel for his 1994 campaign. DEA, the source of the allegation, now denies the allegation.[20]

At dusk we pull over where an old man with a white beard sits in front of his shack. An aluminum walker is perched in front of him and the man himself is dark as mahogany and looks to be a thousand years old. Carlos asks him if he knows where a certain street is and the old guy cocks a hand around his ear as he strains to make out the words. He turns and calls out and suddenly a twelve-year-old boy appears. Yes, yes, he tells Carlos, he knows the street, two blocks down, then go left and then right and so forth. As an afterthought, Carlos shows him a photograph of Graciela, and the boy says, oh, she's living two doors down.

The narrow lot is crowded with an L-shaped building. Up front in one small room is the family business, an arcade full of outdated video games from the U.S. Kids from the barrio come and go to the room, which is dark except for the glow of the screens. Their faces ride like moons in the darkness.

The yard is bare dirt, there are no trees. People sit on buckets and old electric spools under a ramada made of scrap lumber. The house itself is made of concrete blocks. The night air sags with scents of sewage, cookfires, auto exhaust, and dust.

A bunch of young boys sit in a row across the dirt *calle* and when girls walk past they make clucking sounds and plaintive yowls. A man clutches a liter of beer as he pisses against the house. Graciela sits in the back bedroom. Her face is smooth and unlined, her hair jet-black and brilliant. There is a scar on her chin. She is stocky, maybe five feet, her arms powerful, her eyes very dark and quick. A native of Juárez, she has spent every day of her life in barrios such as this one. The United States is as distant as the North Star for her, and reporters are as strange as a visit from God. She is now living in a world where the boss of DEA intelligence drops into her life, where the Mexican consulate keeps tabs on her, and where the police watch her.

As I look at her perched on the edge of her chair, I can see caution all over her face. She is wearing a white T-shirt from a Las Vegas casino, lavender shorts, and on her feet thongs. She wears no jewelry, not a bracelet, a ring, or an earring. There is no makeup on her face either.

She says the consulate has been helpful in comforting her and giving her a little money. How much is she living on with her three children? Eighty pesos a week, she says, at the current rate of exchange $13.33, less than $2 a day. Her husband of thirteen years is a drunk. She washes clothes for a few pesos. Or she walks the streets selling used clothing. In El Paso, near the bridge, old warehouses offer thousand-pound bales of clothing brought from the bad neighborhoods of New York City. Mexican women claw at these piles seeking things to peddle back in Juárez. They pay so much a pound. The warehouses are all but silent as the women hunt with predator eyes for the right garments.

"Miguel Angel," she begins, "went to school, he was a good boy.

He would bring home twenty to twenty-five pesos a day. But then he didn't pass the fifth grade. Both he and Juan Alfredo had trouble in the school because they had to work. Miguel Angel was eleven when he began to cross the river. Then Juan Alfredo began to cross."

Odd, I think, the sisters in El Paso where he stayed say he was nine when he began to cross. Such a small thing to change in order to protect the sense of motherhood and care. Her voice stays flat, her eyes often stare down at the floor.

But she explains the boys did not do this often and would always come back the same day.

"Miguel Angel," she says with a warm smile, "loved to play with toy cars and to watch television. He loved to sing also."

She used to work in a café but for the last two years she has had no regular job. The day begins at 6:30 A.M. She always makes breakfast for her children, she is very insistent on this point. When her children go to school she does the washing. The seam on her T-shirt has given way and been crudely resewn with a cross stitch. She makes her children study in the afternoon, she continues, and helps them with their lessons. In the evening, they gather and watch television. She always cooks a meal late in the day, usually beans and taquitos.

She lived with the father of Miguel Angel and Juan Alfredo for four years and then he left when she was pregnant with Miguel Angel. He was a macho, she says. Then after a year she met her next husband and by him she had Nataly, eleven; Guadalupe, ten; and José Alberto, nine.

She explains, "I don't demand anything from a man when I live with him. The men never accept responsibility. My second husband ignored Miguel Angel and Juan Alfredo."

The door gapes open into the night, the men sitting under the ramada steal glances from time to time. She ticks off her life note by note and molds it into some kind of sense. A harsh overhead light plays across her face as she speaks.

Last Wednesday, her husband came home. It was evening and he demanded food. But since he had drunk up all the money, she had no food. So he beat her and then tried to strangle her. She screamed for help and her young children began to fight him. Neighbors heard and came and pulled the man off. When Miguel Angel and Juan Alfredo lived with her they would protect her from her husband, she says softly. They were good boys. After her husband tried to kill her she fled with the children to a neighbor. She took only two bags of clothes. Then she went to her mother's, but she had no room and no money, so she came here. Her husband demanded to keep the two girls but she refused. Then he went to the police and tried to file charges against her for attacking him. The neighbors wanted to go with her to the police station and tell them the truth. But she did not want to do this—she did not want to get involved with the police. And so she fled.

The room she is temporarily living in with her three children is a big step up from her former home in Colonia Los Aztecas. There are two beds and the headboards are white with gold trim. On the wall are portraits of Christ and the Virgin, and a dresser is covered with cheap figurines, the kind you win at carnivals. There are two ceramic German shepherds, a doe with her fawn, and a big red valentine heart full of helium floats in the dead air. The floor is cement, not dirt. And there are photographs of her host's children.

The police and consulate have been very kind and helpful. When Miguel Angel was arrested, the police came and told her. Then later she was harassed by some undercover agents but they were Americans. They tried to scare her and refused to show any identification. They wanted her to talk with Miguel Angel and get him to admit to a crime he did not do. Then Señor Phil Jordan came with the Mexican police. He also wanted her to talk to her son but she refused to force her boy to admit to a murder when he was innocent. Señor Jordan offered her and her family safety in the United States but she prefers to live in Mexico. He gave her money so she could ride the bus and see her son.

She is uncomfortable as she rolls off this account. She is moving into the world of officials and documents where people such as herself get hurt without warning.

Earlier, her neighbors in her old barrio had told us that two weeks before Juan Alfredo drowned, the Mexican police came to the house and took him away for hours. They made him look at photographs of the kids who were in the K-Mart the night Bruno died and asked him to identify those kids. They worked him over also. And when they brought him home they told his mother that if she talked too much they would kill her. After Juan Alfredo died, the Mexican consulate paid for his funeral. This is very unusual—the government of Mexico does not have a history of showing such tender concern for its citizens.

Oh, she now recalls, about two weeks before Juan Alfredo died, the Mexican police came and wanted him to look at some photographs of kids who may have hung around Miguel Angel. They took him away for a few hours but did not harm him. So you see, there is no problem. And the consulate helps her see her son and with money and with emotional support. Yes, she sees her son once a week but she has not visited him for forty-five days because he is no longer in El Paso.

Suddenly, Graciela changes her voice. She drops down to a place where she is whispering confidential matters. A light breeze plays through the open doorway and she explains she was not allowed to see his body and that the Mexican consulate would not let her open the coffin. Her sister did identify the body and a doctor told her that Juan Alfredo had a serious blow to the top of his head, to his forehead, and to the left side of his face. His hands and feet were also crushed.

"My first impression," she says, "is that somebody killed him. But I am not sure. I do not have evidence. I am desperate. I cry, I think of the problems. I think about what happened to my sons. Also, I think about my husband trying to strangle me. Two ladies defended me from the attack.

"I have integrity. I am strong. But sometimes I am lonely. But my husband hit me with his belt and then tried to strangle me in my bed. This was last Wednesday, August 1.

"Juan Alfredo was a very serious boy," she adds. "He did not have a girlfriend."

She says she is Catholic. She thinks maybe God has taken her two sons from her to punish her for the way she once treated her mother.

"Miguel Angel is okay," she offers. "He helps the staff in the detention center. He is a good boy, a quiet boy. He is safe.

"I am honest, señor," Graciela begins. "Señor Jordan wanted Miguel Angel to say he is guilty and he is not guilty. I did not want to lie. When I was young, I was taught not to lie.

"My life is hard. I have my family, my mother who is sixty-one, my five brothers and four sisters. But they don't help me. They are poor too, they have their own problems."

Helen, she recalls, with pleasure. She is the lady with whom Miguel Angel would stay when he was in El Paso. Suddenly, her son is not coming home every night. We have been talking for an hour and now the talk shifts. Yes, she says, he would stay with Helen and her children for a week or two at a time. Graciela met this family a few years ago. You see, Miguel fell when he was crossing the bridge and hurt himself. So Helen and her children came over to make sure he was okay.

She says Juan Alfredo was with seven boys when he tried to swim the Río Bravo. Only three of the boys came to see her afterward. They told her they saw him swim across the river and that he almost was to the other shore when he suddenly called for help. One boy, Manuel, tried to help but could not get to him and then the water took him away. The boys told her the Border Patrol were on the other shore watching and they watched Juan Alfredo drown and did nothing. Her voice is very animated now, her hands move with a flourish, her arm suddenly extends as she speaks of her son calling for help and reaching out.

"I believe in God," she says. "If He decides this should happen, that is okay. Maybe He decides this because I was not good to my mother. So I am punished.

"My first husband came to Juan Alfredo's funeral. That is all. He is macho. He has no sense of responsibility."

Yes, but what about the night Bruno Jordan was murdered, señora?

"Juan Alfredo," she says, "and three other boys were all together on the day of the crime. When they see the police lights, they go over and see Bruno lying on the ground. Juan Alfredo said to Miguel Angel, 'Let's go.' You see, fifteen days before Miguel Angel and Juan Alfredo were picked up by the American police. The police took them to Sierra Blanca, an hour and a half away out in the desert. They beat them up and left them there in the desert. Juan Alfredo was worried the police might do this to them again. So Juan Alfredo and Miguel Angel were desperate when they saw the body on the ground. They separated. Miguel Angel went to stay with Helen and then he is picked up. He does not run. Juan Alfredo and El Kala went to see a movie. The next day the Mexican police came to my home and told me to call the chief of the Juárez police. And that is how I find out.

"But Miguel Angel is innocent. He does not know how to drive. When they pick him up he doesn't have the truck or the gun. When they test his hand for powder burns, the test is negative."

She is frightened, and this she admits. Do I have any credentials, she suddenly asks. I hand her my Arizona driver's license. It has a color photograph of me. She looks at it closely and mouths my name.

It is eleven o'clock on Monday night, August 7. Carlos and I give her sixty bucks so she can feed her kids—enough for a month or more. Her nine-year-old boy, José Alberto, stands in the doorway wearing a straw sombrero. He is anxious for them to be off, and she quietly tells him to wait. But he is persistent. They must go out before the tiendas close. The children are hungry, they have not eaten. The children want two things: a quart of milk and a box of Froot Loops. The television softly purrs in the next room.

At 9:00 A.M. Tuesday, August 8, the Mexican consulate phones Carlos and says they must have lunch at a very fancy restaurant in downtown El Paso. It is very important that they meet and talk. The man from the consulate tells Carlos that Graciela said we were very nice and only asked her about how she lived and what her children were like. She said it was very pleasant and we did not say hard things.

Carlos slowly exhales smoke as he waves his Benson & Hedges like a wand. It is a day after our talk with Graciela and he is busy spinning yet more intricate webs from the evidence. Everything is possible for Carlos. He suspects Phil Jordan had his own brother murdered. Why not, he says, maybe they did not like each other.

On Friday, August 11, *El Norte*, one of two dailies in Juárez, runs a story about a reporter from Tucson, Arizona, who has been asking questions in Juárez for days about the murder of Bruno Jordan and about the drowning of Juan Alfredo Flores. This reporter is doing a piece for *Esquire* magazine and he has gone to the El Paso police and told them that Juan Alfredo didn't drown, he was murdered. I'm the reporter and I have not talked to anyone with the El Paso police department and I have never spoken to the Mexican reporter who writes about me in *El Norte.*

A man publishes a book in Mexico City. He sees it like this: "It is not inconceivable that the regime of Carlos Salinas should have reached an agreement with Mexico's drug traffickers at the beginning of his term, assuring three goals indispensable to both sides and of benefit both to them and (why not say it?) the country as a whole. The first goal of this speculative agreement was to encourage the drug lords to bring at least part of their money to Mexico, so as to ease the balance of payments. . . .

"The second goal would have consisted in ensuring that drug-related activities stop interfering with U.S.-Mexico relations. The profile of the trafficking . . . would not expose or embarrass either the Mexican government (as did, for instance, the murder of DEA agent Enrique Camarena in 1985) or that of the United States. . . .

"The third objective of this hypothetical tacit (or perhaps not even tacit) agreement would have been to allow the traffickers—or at least their most modern factions—to proceed with their activities if the first two objectives were met."[21]

It all sounds too pat. Six years later the writer, Jorge Castañeda, will become the foreign minister of Mexico in the administration of the reform candidate, President Vicente Fox.

I sit in a room with a U.S. government analyst who has spent eighteen years devouring everything about the Mexican drug business. The guy has tired, hooded eyes and skin that appears never to have tasted the sun. Jordan has arranged this briefing. The guy is slight and ill at ease. His voice is a drone.

He talks of buying up industries, of shopping for cheap steel mills or the like in the fire-sale atmosphere of Eastern Europe, of the penetration and purchase of legitimate corporations in Mexico. The analyst scatters information on the table between us like bread crumbs. He mentions a Mexican financier who has bought a big chunk of Del Monte Corporation and is negotiating for the rest when he disappears in August 1994. He is widely believed by U.S. intelligence to have been a front for drug money. The voice drones on. Banks in El Paso and Laredo, airlines in Mexico, maquiladoras in Juárez. Amado Carrillo falls from his lips now and then, but never becomes flesh.

I offer that guys like Carrillo now move in the highest circles, visit the president in his palace, have dinner with industrialists.

The analyst bristles at this thought.

"Look," he chastens me, "these guys may deal with the Carrillos but they will never have them in their homes."

There is a window in the room where we speak at EPIC but the curtain is closed. The man who buys Del Monte steals $700 million from his own bank. On the day the regime's candidate for president is murdered in Tijuana, the drug-front banker is meeting with the candidate's campaign manager. And the campaign manager is now the president of Mexico. The bank embezzler is a fugitive at the moment and no one admits to being able to find him. The analyst takes me back to this trail of bread crumbs.

The analyst falls silent when the murder of Bruno Jordan comes up. He insists they would not dare.

I say, Carrillo is known for big binges on cocaine. How can you know what a man will do who binges on coke for months?

This thought is wiped off the table like dust.

The room Bruno wanted for watching football games is being built. That is a small step. Now they think of a birthday mass, a way to remember the good and ignore the killing on January 20 in the K-Mart parking lot.

The candle still burns in Bruno's bedroom, the water glass goes down. When Beatrice takes an afternoon nap, she can feel someone come and sit on the bed. She will open her eyes and there will be no one there. Her Bruno is with her.

Tony Jordan fills St. Pius with song at the celebration of life on August 24. There are flowers before the altar and a football balloon floats emblazoned with the name of Bruno's favorite team, the Redskins. One stained glass window, the Christ that watched over

Bruno's funeral eight months before, still stares down as a Latino on the cross wearing a white shirt, tie, and business suit. Our Savior is wrapped in bandoliers of huge red chiles.

Patricia had planned to marry Bruno thirty-two days before this mass. She was going to keep working, he was going to become a lawyer. She met Bruno on June 19, 1994, fell in love with him on June 20, and by July they had a joint account and were saving for their wedding. Now she says, "One minute you think you're going to live a happy life, then someone just takes it all."

Tony's song goes:

> *If he hadn't shot you*
> *If he hadn't killed you*
> *Where would you be right now?*

After the service everyone goes to the home on Frutas Street.

Tony is talking about how Bruno loved Vegas, and always had a system for roulette. He has stopped by the cemetery with Phil after the service and poured a can of Bud Light on the grave for his brother. He's in a warm mood, working hard to remember the good times. A television runs silently in a corner of the room and he glances at it and says how he used to see these terrible things on the news and thought he cared and felt bad about them but until something like this happens to you, you just don't know, you just don't know.

> *Why did you have to die my son?*
> *Why did you have to die?*
> *I'm not complaining*
> *I just need explaining*
> *Somebody tell me why*

Patricia tries to maintain. She still works at a store a few doors down from where Bruno worked. She is not by nature a gambler but now she buys lottery tickets for Bruno.

"When I was with Bruno," she explains, "I would see my husband,

the father of my children. I want to see him, hear him, feel him. I go
visit him at the cemetery and I can't believe I am doing this, that I was
going to be married this summer."

Patricia wonders if her seven months with Bruno were a way to
give him happiness before his murder.

There is an endless amount of food—frijoles, tamales, chicken,
salsa, potato salad, nachos, and cans of cold Budweiser. All the rooms
in the house are packed—Phil says with mild surprise, "I can't remember the names of all my relatives." At the mass some wept. Now everyone laughs and the words come as often in Spanish as in English.

> *I want to stop crying*
> *I feel like dying*

Patricia is trying not to cry. She says softly, "I know Bruno and I
had a conversation about what we'd do if something happened to one
of us. And I can't remember, I can't remember what he said."

She has had a visitation. She is riding a horse, looks back in the
desert, and Bruno is standing there.

The celebration continues until 1:30 in the morning. Many stand
out in front of the house talking and laughing and drinking beer. Tony
is relaxed, he has celebrated Bruno properly. At the end of the mass, he
sang Frank Sinatra's signature song, "My Way," to a large photograph
of his brother. When he finished, his brother Phil embraced him.

> *I want to be with you now*
> *And I know I'm gonna miss you a lot my son*
> *'Cause the times we had together had just begun*
> *But I know I'll never see you alive anymore.*[22]

In September, Jordan gets a call from an old friend in DEA, one who is
now above him in rank and works out of the Washington headquarters.
The call is brief and to the point. Jordan is to use no personnel or any
investigations by DEA in pursuing his brother's murder. Period.

The mole has done the job. Jordan puts down the phone and realizes his career is over. He has just lost his final reason for staying in
command of EPIC.

In September of 1995, when Ross Perot finishes a narcotics briefing at the DEA intelligence center buried in the bowels of El Paso's
Fort Bliss, Phil Jordan takes Perot out into the installation's parking
lot and points out Carrillo's house, just a mile or two away hunkered
near the bank of the Rio Grande. Perot says in disbelief, "You mean
he's right there and we can't do anything?"

Raúl Salinas, Jr., the brother of the ex-president, served during his
administration with a maximum salary of $192,000 a year. He was
wise with his money. Suddenly, the authorities discover he has $84
million in a Swiss account, forty-five bank accounts scattered about
Mexico, twenty parcels of land, six mansions, and thirteen apartments.
A Mexican official cautions that "what we have found is just the tip of
the iceberg."[23]

The afternoon wanes through the Tiffany dome over the bar in the old
hotel near the bridge in El Paso. It is November and Bruno Jordan's
case is now as cold as his grave. I'm about to give up on the case and
DEA and Phil Jordan and Mexico and the border. Carlos Vigueras has
dropped in to talk me down. I see this baldheaded guy in the almost
empty bar swilling triple shots and leaning across the marbletop to
chat with the barkeep. Carlos follows my eyes and suddenly leaves his
chair, goes over and returns with the guy, who says simply that his
name is Memo.

He is of medium height, fair-skinned, bald, and with a gut.

He announces his name to me and then drunkenly says, "You don't
believe me? Okay, don't believe me."

Then he downs his drink and laughs as he slips a leg over the
padded arm of the red leather chair. The beginning is easy, all about
this franchise he has bought for a million dollars in Portland, Oregon,
and how he will put alfalfa in bags and do some voodoo and two years
later the alfalfa will have all its protein and other nutrients and the cat-

tle will eat and grow fat and all over South America and Central America he will sell his own franchises to the process and grow rich and the steers will grow huge. He is especially keen on the market potential for alfalfa nuggets in Costa Rica and Paraguay. But not in Mexico. No, never. He is out of there. The wife and family have been left behind like worn-out luggage.

"Okay, don't believe me."

He crossed the bridge an hour ago, he explains. He has the air of a successful man, the gold watch, good clothes, arrogance. He cannot sit still and squirms in his chair, his arms thrash about, now his leg is over the arm, now it is back on the floor, the foot nervously tapping. He has a need to talk, one he cannot seem to control. He announces that he had a big job in the attorney general's office in Mexico—"Okay, don't believe me"—and then things got bad and here he is. I eye him with curiosity. There is only one solid fact to him: he is very frightened.

He gets this job when Carlos Salinas de Gortari becomes president in 1988 in the PGR, the attorney general's office of Mexico. And then six months later they call him in and say you will be in charge of every federal attorney in Mexico.

He replies, "Well, I don't know, but okay."

Next, he is in the president's office and the president says you will do this and this and this or I will have you killed. And he says, okay.

Memo is on a roll, he is going to explain all the mysteries. The assassination of the regime's presidential candidate in March of 1994, the killing of Luis Donaldo Colosio, no problem.

"Colosio. He comes to me two months before he died and I say, they are going to kill you, be careful, watch what you say. And he does not pay any attention to me. He goes around saying how this is going to be a new day, he tells Salinas how he is going to make a new start for Mexico, a democracy, a republic, something, that the past is over. And Salinas says okay, and then he is killed. And, naturally, he has him killed in Baja Norte, the PAN [the leading opposition party] territory, so that it is their problem."

The killing of José Massieu, the head of the regime's official party, the PRI, in September 1994? That is no problem.

"Massieu says he knows everything, he will tell everything if he wants to or is bothered or . . . it does not matter. So he is hit too, by the president, Carlos Salinas. Carlos, he's not as smart as his brother, Raúl, Jr. The father, Raúl, Sr., he is the brains of them all, the godfather, like in Sicily, you know?"

Of course, Carlos Salinas has denied any involvement in murder or in any other wrongdoing.

Memo goes through napkin after napkin. He will outline the various lines of power, then turn the napkin so that I can clearly read his design. And then he crumples it, every time, and puts it in his pocket. There are patterns, these can be drawn on napkins, the world is a conspiracy. The image in my head is always the same and hardly original since it is an image that in some variation comes to visitors who seek facts in Mexico: there is an onion, you keep peeling it to get to the center and when you get to the center there is nothing there, nothing at all, and you are left with this disorderly heap of peelings that now denies even the idea that it was once an onion.

"What about Amado Carrillo?" I toss out. "Did you have any dealings with him? What can you tell me about him?"

Amado? Memo grows excited at the very sound of his name. He leans forward, drink in hand. Twice, in his presence, Amado came to Los Pinos, the Mexican White House. Raúl brought him and they met with Carlos Salinas, the president. Twice. He is certain. No, he was not in the meetings. But he saw, he knows. For certain.

I try to imagine Carrillo strolling into Los Pinos and I cannot. I am resistant. It is not simply a failure of imagination, although certainly there is that failure, it is also a reluctance to open the floodgates and let all these napkins into my life and mind. I want a log of presidential visitors, a memo signed and dated at that time mentioning the visit, a record buried in CIA and DEA files that will eventually belch up and confirm the visits, or note an informant in a bar a thousand miles away who tells of the visits.

I ask, "What about the murder of Bruno Jordan?"

"Jordan? Okay, you want to know. It is simple. Amado Carrillo. Bruno was fucking this woman, or spoke to this woman, or looked at this woman, how does it matter? It was Carrillo's woman, that is all that matters. Amado, he's doing so much shit, all this coke, he is crazy. If he were sitting here drinking, I would kill him before he killed me. He's crazy. He shoots everyone. So he has Bruno popped. They know this, they know everything, the DEA, the FBI, the CIA, they all know, they are more corrupt than Mexico. I'm out of this, next Europe, then Costa Rica, then . . . I'm sitting in the presidential palace, for real, and Raúl arrives with Amado, this shit is in Los Pinos. I'm out of Mexico. Raúl, those guys you read about in Colombia, they work for him. You don't believe me? Okay. After tonight, you never see me."

He excuses himself. I wait a moment and go the restroom. He is in the vestibule, where there is a pay phone. He sees me coming through the door and panic sweeps his face. He holds his arm up to shield his face and crouches down, still holding the phone. It takes me a few seconds to realize that he thinks I've come to kill him. I smile and laugh and throw my hands up in the air, and relief comes to his face and he slowly comes out of his crouch and goes back to standing.

The next day I tell Jordan and his people. They demand to know which phone he used. I draw a sketch. They say they'll check the calls. They never report their results to me. But what strikes me is their interest when I mention Memo and I realize that this kind of thing is part of the database of EPIC.

Months before, when I was writing about El Güero, Ramón Salazar Salazar, and I was growing frustrated with the various versions of his death paraded before me by newspapers and witnesses, I sketched out a theory of the life of truth in Mexico. I decided it went through three phases: what happened; then, the fantastic tales that erupt to deal with what happened; and then, always, this final phase in which it never happened at all.

One night, I am sitting at the table at Frutas Street having tacos and conversation. Virginia is there, and Beatrice and Antonio. The talk is light and the food good. I drink a beer. Bruno drifts into the conversation. And somehow Virginia says that even with her strong feelings about her brother's murder, she would not exact personal justice, not kill the killer. She would abide by the slow but sure system of justice, the rule of law.

Antonio listens carefully.

Then he says, he would kill the killer without a qualm. He is an old man and it is of no concern to him what the authorities might do to him for such a murder. He says this in a very calm voice and speaks almost softly. His tone is very matter-of-fact. And somehow by gesture or inflection, he makes clear that his killing would cross the river five blocks from the house on Frutas Street, go over there into Mexico. He never mentions the name Amado Carrillo. But then he is a man of few words. But his tone has nothing of the hypothetical in it.

On November 29, 1995, Heidi Slauquet calls a cab. She lives in a fine townhouse in Juárez and is known for running a nightclub favored by narcotraficantes. She is a woman who has lived by her looks but her younger face has slipped away and now she can no longer live off such assets. She is Dutch in origin and has wound up in Juárez after a life-time of self-invention. Once she was a lover of Amado Carrillo, now she procures women for him. She has very fair skin.

She is a close friend of Phil Jordan's aunt, Consuelo, the one who runs a restaurant in El Paso, the same restaurant that catered the food at the house on Frutas Street after Bruno Jordan's funeral.

Heidi is taking a trip. As the cab approaches the entrance to Juárez International Airport, people see what looks to be federal police stop it. That is all. A day or so later the body of the cabbie is found. Heidi never turns up.

Everyone who is anyone is there. All the leading politicians, all the socialites, all the community leaders of Juárez. The new club is called La Serata and is near the university and not that far from the river. The exterior is fine marble, the fittings all polished brass. It is early December.

Inside the club, a huge wall holds a fresco that replicates part of Michelangelo's Sistine Chapel. In the panel, God reaches out to Adam and his finger offers the touch that gives life itself. The Juárez paper gives a full page or more of photos and words to the opening. The attorney that allegedly fronts the car theft ring is in the photos as the owner of this new club. So is his wife, quite young and very fair-skinned. Everyone in the photographs is fair-skinned and many of the woman have blond hair.

One person is not in the photographs, Amado Carrillo. He is said to be the real owner of the club and he is there opening night sitting at a table doing cocaine. At the time, there are two U.S. indictments hanging over his head, but the Mexican authorities say they cannot find him. I know he is there because the photographers who cover the event say he is there. Just as almost everyone in Juárez knows who really owns La Serata.

But no one mentions this fact in print on either side of the border. Nor does DEA make any announcement. EPIC is as silent as a tomb over the opening. They are busy keeping track of things and then filing what they find. They track Amado Carrillo on one trip as he wanders without a seeming care from Cuernavaca, the town of the very rich just south of Mexico City, to Hermosillo, the capital of the border state of Sonora, to Juárez just across the river from their headquarters. Carrillo moves with human waves marking his progress, a team ahead of him testing the waters, checking out the communications systems, making sure of security. He has an armored and bombproof vehicle at his service wherever he alights. His communications systems are the very best, highly encrypted and absolutely secure. He employs wizards, some of them American, to keep him technologically at the cutting edge. His organization eavesdrops on hundreds of phone calls at once, and his ears are everywhere listening for the slightest whisper. He is part of a network of Mexican cartels, the chief among chiefs, and now DEA figures these organizations employ about 200,000 people moving the drugs and guarding the operations.

But even DEA sitting in the bunker of EPIC can hardly retain a sense of the scale. They take down a guy crossing the bridge in El Paso. He tells them his story. He has crossed the bridge in a van, he says, about two hundred times a year. Each time he carries three hundred to five hundred kilos of cocaine, or in U.S. measurements six hundred to one thousand pounds, a haul. They sit down and figure out the numbers: even at a low-ball figure like $10,000 a kilo, about $600 million worth in twelve months.

They take down a courier at an airport. The woman is carrying $250,000 that she is supposed to deliver to Juárez. Normally, she explains, she lands in El Paso, grabs a cab, and crosses the bridge and makes her delivery. She averages about a hundred trips a year, she continues. That adds up to $25 million. She does not know the scale of the operation, she admits. But she does know of twenty other couriers.

Then there is the detail of a federal indictment in Miami against Amado Carrillo. He is charged with making a single airplane shipment from Cali, Colombia. The plane, a Boeing 727, carried six tons of cargo. The goods were a single thing: cash in the form of U.S. currency. DEA cannot determine how much money was on the plane. They sit down and think: what if it is in $20 bills? That would bring the load to $225 million. Make it $100 bills and suddenly the number is $1 billion.[24]

Phil Jordan says, "I don't believe anyone in La Cosa Nostra could order a murder two thousand miles away and expect it to be carried out. Carrillo Fuentes can do that and much, much more."[25]

In Culiacán, the capital of Sinaloa, a reporter asks a federale how he manages to own a new Jeep Cherokee on his $500-a-month salary.

He explains, "I save a lot."

When the federal comandante, José Barragan, is asked about Amado Carrillo, he says, "I'm not aware of any problems with Mr. Carrillo. There are no major trafficking organizations in this state."[26]

At the moment, one estimate has Carrillo paying $500 million a year in Mexico for protection. He is said to rarely see his family. Or spend two nights running under the same roof.[27]

Tony Jordan flies to Plano, Texas, for his brother Phil's retirement party. Tony has never been there before and instantly hates the white-faced, smug suburb of Dallas. But this is Phil's world and his people and Tony has written a song especially for the occasion. He is surrounded by cops, herds of narcs from DEA, and he smiles and is the good brother. Plano is one of the wealthiest communities in the nation, a fortress. Ross Perot is headquartered in Plano, the television series *Dallas* was filmed in part at a ranch just east of the town. Jordan settled here years ago as a safe and sound place to raise a family. Basically, any Mexicans in Plano are bent over working as gardeners and Tony knows this at a glance.

At the party, he finally sings his new song.

> *Saw a brother fall to gunfire*
> *Comrade Kiki who died*
> *Well, I've been through the heartaches*
> *And I near lost my mind*

dreamtime

A report floats in the intelligence community. In this story, Amado Carrillo is in the rich section of Havana where distinguished foreigners are lodged. He is walking down the street one day when he spies a jogger paddling past him. The jogger is the former president of Mexico, Carlos Salinas de Gortari. The image hangs there, and then melts away like the curl of smoke off a cigar. It connects with nothing.

She has a small pension of $109 a month. In 1988, when she was sixty-nine years old, Celia Reyes placed about $24,000 in a savings account at Banco del Atlántico in Mexico. She got an interest rate of 149.35 percent. The money came from a lifetime of scrimping. She is the mother of nineteen children, fifteen of whom survived. This simple deposit is beneath notice in the flurry of activity that year. The presidential election puts Carlos Salinas de Gortari in office for six years.[1]

Salinas promises a new Mexico with a new economy, a new order that will make Mexico a First World nation. He is Harvard-educated, young, barely forty, and surrounded by similar men with U.S. educations. He is seen by North Americans as clean and promising.

Salinas will leave office in 1994. After NAFTA unfolds, after Amado Carrillo rises to full power, after Salinas becomes an international figure, Celia Reyes will technically own more than all of them. She is the skeleton key to dreamtime, a state of being where things never are exactly the way they seem.

On July 6, 1988, the early election results stream into the office of the Interior Ministry on Avenida Burcareli. They show the ruling party, the PRI, losing to Cuauhtémoc Cárdenas, son of a former president, a longtime PRI stalwart now suddenly refashioned as the head of an insurgent party called the PRD. Suddenly, the count stops. The PRI had elected a president in the 1950s with 90 percent of the vote, hurled José López Portillo into office in 1976 with close to a hundred percent of the vote. Then in 1982, this show of fraud declined to 72 percent, and now, in 1988, the impossible is happening, the actual defeat of the ruling PRI. But then, those computers counting the vote suddenly go out of commission. When they finally come back up, Carlos Salinas de Gortari is elected by a razor-thin 50 percent of the vote.

When he is sworn in as president, 143 members of Congress walk out rather than witness the ceremony. One hundred and one members of the opposition party hold signs that declare of outgoing president Miguel de la Madrid, "Six-Year Term of Fraud." Under de la Madrid real wages had declined 50 percent. Salinas says in his inaugural address, "The most urgent political guarantee is electoral transparency. I share this popular concern." In the basement, which is directly under his feet as he speaks, are the sealed ballots from the contested election. They are guarded twenty-four hours a day. Eventually, they will be burned.[2]

Soon Salinas appoints Manuel Bartlett Díaz, a man held by DEA to be deeply involved in the torture and murder of Kiki Camarena, as his secretary of education. He makes Fernando Gutiérrez Barrios his secretary of government, the man to be in charge of all police and intelligence functions. Barrios has been in the secret agencies for decades and was in charge of the internal security police (DFS) at the time of the student massacre in 1968. Barrios was also one of the architects of the White Brigade, a secret police unit that kidnapped thousands of Mexicans between 1972 and 1980. At least five hundred of the disappeared never reappeared. Barrios's successor at DFS, Javier García Paniagua, is put in charge of the Mexico City police. And García Paniagua's successor at DFS, Miguel Nazar Haro, gets a job as director of intelligence services. A former member of the White Brigade is made head of yet another Mexico City police agency. Four days before the election that resulted in Salinas's presidency, two leaders of the opposition party were executed in the center of Mexico City. By the time of Salinas's inaugural, the same opposition party, the PRD, had had thirty-four of its workers murdered. Haro will soon have to resign when he is indicted in the United States on drug charges.[3]

In 1981, in a series of four articles in a major Mexico City daily, *Excelsior,* a younger Salinas had lambasted free trade by noting, "History has proven that the social cost of the free market and the extreme individualism that [is proposed] has been exploitation, neo-colonialism and the loss of the national independence."[4]

As president, Salinas sees things differently.

Juan Manuel Gómez Gutiérrez feels his work pace increase. He is an accountant based in Mexico City, and suddenly one of his clients has great need of his services. The man has holdings and they are growing and the man has many bank accounts and they are fattening. He trusts Gómez completely, in fact some of the man's accounts are in Gómez's name. His client is Raúl Salinas de Gortari, the brother of the new president. The brothers are famously close. Carlos Salinas dedicated his Harvard thesis to "Raúl, companion of a hundred battles." Raúl now has a job in the administration but one that pays less than $200,000 a year. Nevertheless, he needs his accountant. Needs him to tend to what will eventually be at least 289 bank accounts scattered in Mexico, the U.S., and Switzerland and holding at a minimum $250 million. Then there is the problem of keeping track of the real estate, houses, apartments, ranches, other chunks of earth, at least 123 such properties.

The accountant is thus very busy. He operates mainly in Mexico City. But oddly enough, he also has a base in a distant border city, Juárez.

Another accountant is busy also. Luz Estela Salazar keeps books for the Medellín cartel in Colombia. Now, suddenly, she must attend meetings in Mexico City with cartel members as they meet and discuss business propositions with Raúl Salinas. This is not really new. One cartel member earlier had pumped $200,000 into Carlos Salinas's campaign. At the meetings a reasonable deal is struck. The Colombians will pay a fee of $300,000 for each planeload of cocaine they ship through Mexico. Eventually, these fees and others will pile up to at least $80 million.

Raúl earns a nickname because of his fees. He is called El Chupasangre, the Bloodsucker. Besides the Colombians, one other man tithes him, an obscure figure in that distant border city called Ciudad Juárez. This man is named Amado Carrillo.[5]

In April 1994 a full-bodied cargo jet flies from Cali, Colombia, to Mexico. Another similar-sized plane duplicates the flight in June of that year. Each carries $20 million cash for the election year needs of the ruling party of Mexico—an election the American government later called the cleanest ever.[6]

His voice is even, his words exact. He says, "We're like a deer paralyzed in the headlights. Mexico is our biggest foreign policy problem but no one has a solution to it. It begins with a political problem: the last three presidents of the U.S. have sold us on the proposition that Mexico is a developed, stable country and the way we should relate to it is by opening our borders and developing trade. Now they find it difficult to come back and describe the reality. The reality of the moment is: serious questions as to whether democracy even exists in Mexico, the question of corruption going to the very top of the government, that we have a next-door neighbor whose principal export is narcotics. Once you accept the problem, you wind up saying you can't do anything about it, you can't solve it."

His name is Jack Blum.[7] For thirty years, he has, off and on, been a man of the Hill. He worked with the Senate Judiciary Committee from 1965 to 1976, with William Fulbright at the Senate Foreign Relations Committee from 1972 to 1976, and then returned for another bout at Foreign Relations from 1987 to 1989 to run hearings on Drug Law Enforcement and Foreign Policy, which meant Noriega, the contra war, and the flood of dope coursing through both. Since then he's had a private Washington law practice specializing in money laundering and has been a consultant on the problem of money laundering for various clients, including the government of Colombia.

The drug economy, he explains, is untouchable because it runs $30 billion a year ("conservatively," he notes) in a cash-short nation. Intervening in Mexican politics by demanding action against the drug organizations blows up in our faces and fuels Mexican nationalism. Money laundering cannot really be contained because the same avenues used by criminal cartels are used and protected by U.S. corporations for tax evasion. We now live in a world where the fifth-largest nation in booking bank loans is the Cayman Islands, population 30,000.[8]

"We are married to Mexico," he finally explains, "you can't sever a head from a body."

"All the options are bad," he states flatly. "Everything you want to do doesn't work. How do you live in a world like that?"

Sean grows and gets out and suddenly Phil Jordan notices that his son is beyond his simple control.

For Sean it is clear: "My parents divorced when I was five. A lot of people want to say it affected me but I can't say why or how because my family's close. My father was always around, he was always there. The only negative thing I remember was hearing my mother argue with my dad for the 350 bucks a month. I missed my father very much, I wanted to live with him. I think it affected my sister more than me. And they'd ship us off to El Paso—there'd be a three-day vacation from school, like Easter or whatever—we're there in El Paso. Every Christmas, every summer. It was my father's preference because of security. My mother was a free-spirited hippie chick, you're talking early 1970s, she was kind of happy not to have the responsibility of dealing with the kids, she was teaching art in the public schools. Everything was art. We grew up in a very artistic environment, we had our own little artwork stations.

"It was a sense of security for my father knowing his kids were in very good hands with his parents in El Paso. He was so busy doing the whole drug thing. I thank God very much that he did that because El Paso was a very essential part of my upbringing. My earliest memories are of hanging out with Bruno, he was probably two or three years old. I'm three, and there's the train in the back, and at three in the morning, Tony would be wiped out from partying or being with his girlfriend, and I'd wake him up and make him take me out back to see the train and he'd be half asleep. We'd do this two or three times a night."

He remembers his great-grandfather catching birds in the yard on Frutas Street and then roasting them on a spit.

Between 1988 and 1990, Raúl Salinas heads the government agency, CONASUPO, that delivers subsidized food to the poor. This part of the government paws through $1.2 billion a year in contracts and other expenses as it seeks to deliver rice, corn, and beans to the poor. It is the last place one would look for the New Economy or any of the fetishes of new global networks. But then Raúl Salinas is not a natural businessman, or an experienced one. His entry in the 1989 biographical dictionary of the Mexican government lists only one job that is not government in his work history: from 1970 to 1972 he was a "helper" at an engineering firm.[9] Years later he will be accused of buying 39,000 tons of powdered milk contaminated by the nuclear release at Chernobyl. Of taking bribes. Of faking the price paid for corn and taking a $20 million cut for himself. Of selling U.S. corn given through foreign aid back into the United States.[10]

Sean is young, hitting the good times of his early twenties, and so he ducks questions. His father is running the Dallas bureau of DEA. Sean is carving out a different life, one not based on regulations.

He finds a life that throbs with his father's work and yet he remains oblivious of this link. While his father connects to a larger world based on narcotics, Sean finds his own world that is incidentally saturated with drugs.

He says, "Then I met this girl in Tempe and I was nineteen and I moved out of my mother's home and in with her for three years. I come home one night, and she split, took everything in the apartment and I never saw her again. It crushed me. She went into the military. She meant the world to me. Bruno flies out and helps me pack up my Monte Carlo and we split to El Paso. That's where all the interesting things started going on in my life. We both enrolled in the University of Texas at El Paso.

"We were living at the family house on Frutas Street. We were into music, Bruno loved making tapes, R&B, dance. I had some women and I met one at the Good Luck bar, a trashy little place. Bruno was working at Forti's restaurant. He had his separate life. I had my clique. I wanted to go party and he had a different set of friends. We'd play basketball together, intramural, city leagues. I joined a fraternity and I thought, what am I doing in El Paso? I hate this town, nothing is going on here, I was going through hell. And I met this woman at the bar and everything went nuts. I dropped out of school, I would just stay at hotels all the time so I could be with this woman. She was older. She became my life. I was twenty-two and she was twenty-nine. That completely alienated me from the whole family. I took off, I just left Frutas Street. It got to the point where my grandmother wouldn't take it anymore because I'd come home at 5:00 A.M. They hated the woman. I wasn't going to school. I'd get fired from jobs. And we'd go across the border. She always had money. I don't know how she got it. My father started investigating her. She was always seeing men, lawyers you know. I'd ask, 'Where do you get all this money all the time?' She'd say, 'This old man left me a hundred thousand dollars.' She lived right in a raw barrio, right in the war zone, off of Estrella and Rivera Streets. She was Mexican-American, born in El Paso, beautiful thing and a partyer. I loved to drink, get wasted, and screw all night. That's all we did. She helped me grow up real quick.

"She'd take me to Juárez all the time. We'd just go and do crazy things. We'd hitchhike even though we had a car. We'd give'm two bucks. We'd walk around everywhere, the worst places in Juárez to be. Or we'd ride buses over there. I went through the whole town. We were bored. Her kid would go to school, and we'd take off early in the morning. We'd end up being wasted. This went on in a way for three years.

"Once I disappeared, I said, shit, I need to get some money. I came back to Tempe and sold service manuals for gas stations, coupons, I'd make a hundred an evening between four and nine. I'd wake up drinking beer. I was flying in and out, Tempe and El Paso. My father thought I was living in El Paso. But I was AWOL. I never called my mother or my father, and absolutely disappeared for almost a year. This was 1987 or '88. I called and left a message for my father, told him I loved him, called him from a pay phone 'cause I knew he could track from wherever I was. I said, see ya, I'm having a good life. And that put the family in hell.

"Bruno would see me but he'd keep it to himself. He was always trying to pull me out of this relationship and the more they tried to pull me away from this woman, the deeper I fell. I was rebelling. So what happens is they find out I've been living with this woman, very close, a mile or half mile from Frutas Street. Now my dad comes into the picture. My father would constantly call that house, he would have agents call the house, he would have agents out in front, he would come to the house. He put so much pressure on her to get rid of me, he ran plates, found out about warrants. I don't know what she was into. She'd always leave me at a bar and say I'll be back in a couple of hours. I never saw a transaction. I've been to every raunchy bar. I was so blind. She was off with other dudes. So my father puts on this crazy pressure. And now I move to Dallas.

"I finally get this thing in my mind, I'm doin' wrong, I want a new life, I can't stand this woman. I'm twenty-four. I've talked to my father a couple of times on the phone, I'd be wasted and call him."

He works on cars. He helps out at the restaurant run by his wife. He is in his forties, beard grizzled, hair a shock gone mainly white. He smiles easily, is friendly and relaxed. From 1976 to 1993, he was a federale, mainly stationed in Mexico City but also working Aguascalientes, Querétaro, Guadalajara, Oaxaca, and Hermosillo, Sonora. He was a friend of Comandante Calderoni. In 1993, he was reported to Mexico's human rights agency, an organization created by Salinas after the slaughter of a lawyer, Norma Corona, in Sinaloa, and he became hunted. He knew he was quite possibly doomed, that he was being offered up for sacrifice. He hid for months and eventually fled north. He says he was framed, that he didn't really do much in the way of torture, but then, he adds, he was not a saint.

But now as we sit on under the soft sky of early evening, he wishes to talk about those good years. When he entered the federales, narco-traficantes dealt with the commanders or below. In the mid-1980s, in about 1985, they suddenly leap-frog their connections to the top. Things then changed.

That is how he made his big mistake. He remembers it all very clearly as we sip our drinks and swat at mosquitoes. He laughs now at the mistake. In 1989, he spots three men in a car on a Mexico City street. Something catches his eye, he does not explain this bit of cop instinct, but something definitely makes him look twice at them. He pulls them over and finds that they are from Juárez.

They say, "Hey, let us go, we're here for Amado."

But the name didn't ring a bell with the federale. He finds $650,000 in the car. They explain they are bringing it to Amado from Juárez. Fuck this, he thinks, who the hell is Amado?

He books them. They are upset and keep saying, Amado, Amado. The federale begins to wonder about what he has just done. He goes to his comandante's house at 3:00 A.M. and tells him.

His boss says, "What? Release them! Tear up the paperwork."

So he returns to the station and does as he is told. The next day, the three men from Juárez come to the office to thank the comandante.

But for the federale, the mistake is not yet over. He goes with his comandante to a street corner in Mexico City. Carrillo walks up surrounded by bodyguards. He is not physically impressive, he does not look like much of anything really. Félix Gallardo is very impressive, the federale thinks, what with his laserlike eyes. He thinks back to being around him and recalls his high intelligence. Caro Quintero carried with him an air of menace. But Carrillo is just a stocky nobody.

They talk, the incident is papered over, the federale is relieved. Now he knows the name and will not make the same mistake again.

Later, the federale hears that Carrillo meets in Los Pinos with Salinas. He is adamant on this point as we sit out in the evening and drink. And even though he is now a fugitive from Mexico, he is not exactly living in the dark. He is still friends with Comandante Calderoni; in fact, Calderoni has given him a puppy.[11]

•   •   •

Phil Jordan is caught off guard when his son suddenly drops every-thing and moves in with this woman.

Sean says, "I made this lie to her, I packed up, I said I'm starting college. Something broke and my father gave me one more chance to get off the street. My father said, 'Come to Dallas, and I will take care of you.' He hooked me up with a great job with Ross Perot at EDS, and I got my car and then I got my apartment. I was making bucks. So here's this woman calling me, I'd given her my number, and I'd say, 'Oh, babe, you gotta come up here,' and she would and now starts the hell all over again. I drop out of college, I end up not showing up for work, I end up getting fired from my job. And during one of these times, she put capsules of phenobarbital in my drinks and laid me out, man. We were in the bathtub together. Here's a woman you love and she pours this down my throat. She tells me what it is. My body goes numb, I'm throwing up. She said she was getting even with me because I left her. I say, no problem, I love you, baby.

"A couple of days go by, and it was mostly sex and drinking all the time, E. J. Gallo brandy, we'd just go through bottles of that shit. A few days later she drops me off at a bar in Dallas, a nice place, and says I'll be back, I'm gonna go buy a bedspread for us at the mall, and I say okay. She leaves me there six hours. She's gone back to the apartment, taken all the money I have, all my musical instruments, taken every-thing, stuck it in my car and split back to El Paso.

"They find my car way out there, she'd just left it at a truck stop. She must have picked up a ride. The car was empty. My father tracked it down. I'm crushed. I got to be with her. I saved up $800, bought a plane ticket to El Paso, locked up my apartment and split. My father's still thinking that I'm on this routine, he'd call me every day and the next thing he sees these notices on my door and he says, where's my son? Now Bruno plays a great part.

"Bruno is very disappointed in me. He's going to college, and I don't want nothing to do with my family. I'm back in El Paso for three or four months. I call my mother in Phoenix, and she says, Sean, I'm having this family reunion and it's so important, please come, she bought the plane ticket and return date, please, I'll give you money. I said, okay, I'll go. It was October 1988. I'm there a couple of days and having a beer and my mom says, Sean, could you go with me to the doctor. I need your help, it's a counselor, it's for me but I need you to be in the room. So I go there, it's at Summit Hospital. I walk into this room and there's my father, Bruno, Tony, Virginia, a cousin from New York, everyone, all these people. I was tricked into an intervention. I completely shut off. They'd all been going through this thing all day long, this class on how to get through to me so I would just kick off my shoes and go upstairs and check in for thirty days. And I didn't say a word, I was stone-faced, everybody was crying, there is an intervention asshole there. But it was the most important thing that ever happened to me in my life.

"I absolutely resisted. They would ask me questions and I would not talk, I won't say anything. They had these lists, these things they'd written up, a whole list of how my drinking or absence had affected people. Bruno had a list of ten things . . . the drinking, we're not close anymore and like that. My mom's was a fucking long list, thirty minutes on how I'd destroyed her life. Tony's was emotional, tears the whole time. My dad was very hard. He's the most incredible human being on the face of the earth now that I look back. He's my idol. I felt betrayed for the very first time by Bruno and Tony and my cousin. I'm twenty-four or twenty-five. The thing was, I wasn't drinking that much, I didn't have the money to drink. If I had two quarts, Pabst Blue Ribbon, 69 cents a quart, I was set.

"The story gets better. The intervention doesn't work. The tough love thing kicks in. This lady gives me a ride to my mom's house, I get just my bags and my clothes, and they say you better be out of that house or we'll call the police, and don't call any of the people in this room, they are not going to respond. You are now on your own. I'm like, fine, so what. It's getting late, the cops come and tell me to leave. I walk down and try to call my woman in El Paso to get some money to fly back to El Paso. Turns out she's been talking with my father and she's now in on this thing. And she wants me out of the picture because my father's now applying a lot of heat on her and her family. That night I come back and pass out on the lawn at my mom's house. Two cops bust me for trespassing in Tempe and put me jail. The next morning the prosecutor tells me you got thirty days in jail or thirty days at Summit. I pick Summit.

"Here we go. It changes my life. They deprogrammed me, flushed me out of denial. My life turned around. They taught me how to react and act. I don't know how it helped me, but it helped me. It taught me responsibility. I was running away from responsibility. The other addicts, some serious fucking people, meant a lot. I was at AA meetings three times a day. I got out and two days later I smoked a joint and drank a beer. A week later I borrowed a hundred bucks from a doctor who'd been in therapy with me and I flew back to the woman in El Paso. That lasted about three months. I begged my mom for one more chance, that was June 21, 1989. My liberation day. I left the woman for good and went back to Tempe.

"Never called her again. It was done. I met up with a girl a week later and moved in with her. She found me a job at the music store. I have a very addictive personality, period. I hook on to something, whatever it is, and stay hooked, playing video games, whatever."

Adrian Carrera Fuentes directed the federal police for a while during the Salinas administration. Sometimes he ran the prison system also. His superior in 1993 and 1994 is one Mario Ruiz Massieu, whose own brother, José Francisco Massieu, once was married into the Salinas family and continues to be a major power in the government. Carrera hands over about $2 million in bribes to Ruiz Massieu, money he says he gets from drug dealers.

Early in the Salinas administration when Carrera is running the prisons, a former inmate invites him to drop by his fine home in Mexico City. The man asks for protection in order to pursue his business. Carrera dispatches police agents to guard the man and promises him his enterprises will not be disturbed. The man's name is Amado Carrillo. At one point in their dealings over the years, Carrillo hands Carrera an attaché case with $300,000 inside and then shouts to one of his men to buy Carrera a Cadillac, "the most luxurious one there was."

Soon Carrera is earning $1,500 for each kilo of cocaine that crosses

Mexico from Colombia on its way to the United States. Carrillo's take is $10,000 a kilo. Carrera is helpful. He appoints federale comandantes to work with various cartel leaders. He visits Carrillo from time to time to keep up relations with his former convict.

Both Mario and José Francisco Ruiz Massieu helped Carrera get his job in law enforcement. But Carrera has many friends. In 1994, he attends the Super Bowl in Atlanta with Carlos Salinas's private secretary, Justo Ceja.[12] Ceja will vanish after 1994 when reports surface that he accumulated a $3 million fortune (later revised to $7 million) during the last ten months of the Salinas administration. His government pay was about $100,000 a year.[13] Also, a photo will appear showing him having drinks with one of the leaders of the Tijuana cartel, the group generally credited with the murder of Cardinal Posadas in May of 1993. He will be described by one Mexican commentator as "closest to the president."[14]

By 1991, Raúl Salinas's appetite for business matters attracts unwanted attention. DEA tracks $6 million of his money to a Swiss account assigned to a phony name. Friends of the president privately advise him that his brother is getting out of control and this is not an easy thing to do given Mexican tolerance for looting of the treasury by members of a president's family. Also, the ruling party finds that knowledge of Raúl's activities is registering in public polls. So a solution is devised. In 1992, Raúl spends the year at the University of California Center for United States–Mexico Studies in San Diego. Wealthy businessmen kindly kick in to pay for this academic sojourn. He pens a forty-two-page paper on "Rural Reform in Mexico." Inside Mexico, he is now called Mr. Ten Percent for his acute business talents. Raúl, an amateur poet, addresses this penchant of his in some verse from 1990:

> *If you rob from the many 100 percent*
> *There could be a moral offense.*
> *A few points more, a few points less*
> *Morality is a question of percent.*[15]

· · ·

The plane is tracked by U.S. radar and tailed by a U.S. plane before it puts down in Veracruz. Mexican federales fly the plane, which is coming up from Colombia. They are murdered by a Mexican army unit, the entire episode captured on film taken by the U.S. aircraft circling above. The U.S. ambassador to Mexico brushes aside this slaughter of what are supposed to be fellow drug warriors by calling the killing "a regrettable accident."[16]

In the early 1990s, certainly by 1993, Amado Carrillo begins holding regular meetings with the leaders of other drug cartels in Mexico. These meetings occur about every three months and settle business disagreements. The drug business is divided into zones of influence that cover suppliers in South America and Mexico, connections within Mexico for transport, entry points to the United States, and of course, retail markets in the U.S.

Carrillo is, like most capitalists, against competition and in favor of cartels. He brokers loads through his growing Colombian connections, he shares ports of entry for a fee, and he tries to avoid wars over any retail market. Silently, over a few years, he revolutionizes the drug business until his only real enemy of any stature is the Tijuana cartel, a band of brothers hell-bent on killing him. He pays the Mexican government to try to kill them.

He alters the Mexican drug business from isolated groups of thugs into real organizations. Killing still continues—it is inevitable in a business lacking access to courts and contract law. Without death, the business simply cannot function. And in a business rife with problems of industrial espionage—the constant danger of snitches—murder and torture are inescapable business expenses. As is bribery, the only accepted form of taxation in the drug business. But given these realities, Carrillo brings a new harmony and cost-effectiveness to the business.

This is coupled with a decision made by the Mexicans in the early 1990s to take as payment for moving Colombian cocaine half the load rather than simply a flat fee of so much money per kilo. This radically increases profits because once the load moves into the United States a multiplier takes place at a factor of at least four in profit. A final stroke by Carrillo rounds out his business. He makes forays into Peru and Bolivia so that he has sources of cocaine besides Colombia. This enables him to drive down the price.

The Wilson Quarterly, an American intellectual journal, credits Carlos Salinas for allowing Mexico to "shed much of the debilitating ideological baggage of the past." In *American Enterprise,* Mark Falcoff notes that "Mexico is ceasing to be 'Mexico.' That is, Mexico has begun to discard an entire set of civic values and practices that for more than seventy years defined its national identity."

Glyn Robert Chambers works out of Alpine, Texas, a small town an hour or so north of the border. His partner is the local sheriff, Rick Thompson. They are arrested in December 1991 for moving thirty tons of cocaine and twenty tons of marijuana, loads worth an estimated $700 million. They work for Amado Carrillo and are a piece of his larger schemes. He is building his own air force and DEA will eventually discover that in this aviation business Carrillo loses at least thirteen full-sized jets in seizures. And that this loss means nothing to him.

"They say the loss of the plane is just part of the overhead," Phil Jordan tells the press. "They're saying their drug money affords them the luxury of jets that are as disposable as Kleenex."[17]

On June 11, 1993, a lawyer publishes an article in a major Mexico City daily, *La Jornada.* The lawyer is Luis Javier Garrido, and the article is entitled "The Narco System." He details the Faustian bargain made by President Miguel de la Madrid with the drug cartels in the 1980s in an effort to shore up a bankrupt Mexico. He connects Kiki Camarena's murder to the worry that he was penetrating the collusion between drug merchants and the government. He notes the links to the current Salinas administration.

He concludes, "The production and sale of narcotics has been, as we know and as many studies have shown, a 'lifesaver' for the Mexican economy. As a result, the most recent governments have tolerated and even sponsored it, thus turning it into a major political factor. . . .

Given the shortcomings of the Mexican economy, drugs have furthered the agenda of the [PRI] technocrats by creating jobs, raising the income and living standards of poor peasants, contributing to local causes among low-income earners, building schools, clinics, or roads, and thus gaining support of entire communities."

Garrido's article is ignored by the U.S. press. It is translated by the CIA and circulated among U.S. agencies.

About the same time, President Salinas in an interview pegged the flow of illegal drugs in Mexico at about $100 billion a year.[18]

Imagine you are Amado Carrillo. You have no face, no one is sure when you were born, your family tree is a puzzle also. No one is even certain just who is your sibling and who is not. Yet you exist, fly in planes, handle billions. When you see that headline about the Lord of the Skies, you grow worried because you know that fame in the drug business is a death warrant, just look at what is happening in Colombia. Just look at what happened to your old partner, Pablo Acosta.

The press talks of presidents but you buy presidents. It talks of global trade but your portion of this flow of merchandise is hardly ever mentioned on the business pages. You deal with major financial institutions and major political figures. But you must live in the shadows.

I sit in a room and watch a home movie of Carrillo at a family gathering and see him move through the crowd celebrating a birthday. But even this tape is a U.S. government secret and not publicly shown at the time.

Eduardo Valle has survived. He lived through the student massacre of '68, through torture, through prison, and then for years worked on newspapers. In 1992, he is appointed by his old classmate, Carlos Salinas, to head part of the War on Drugs. So he plunges into the work.

The bribes get his attention. The first time they offer him $2 million to intervene when Juan García Abrego's brother-in-law is arrested. The second time really strikes him: $400,000 and "This was for a little, little, little man. For a nothing."

He turns them down. He does not yet understand.

He turns his attention to the Gulf cartel because he keeps hearing of its links to the government, including Carlos Salinas.

The thirty big ones arrive at about 8:30 P.M. on February 23, 1993, for their meal at the mansion in Mexico City. They expect to discuss ways to prop up the ruling party, the PRI, and they have been invited to the sit-down by President Carlos Salinas. They are all men and they are all very rich and they have either become very rich or become yet richer because of the selling of state industries and privileges by the current administration. Salinas has sold off over three hundred government industries, including the banking industry and the telephone company. Telmex, the phone company, then raised its rates 247 percent. Wages only went up 18 percent. The phone company remained as before, a monopoly. From this seedbed rose the sudden crop of Mexican billionaires. The men dining that night tended to count their money by the billions.

They eat smoked salmon and steak.

Salinas says that he favors the changes that will end the government's financial support of the ruling party. For years, the government has forked over about a billion dollars annually to the party, the money disguised as funds for public works. Mexico is riddled with ghost projects, bridges paid for on the books but never built, phantom highways, hotels, hospitals, airfields, waterworks. He wants the private sector to pay the party's expenses. The ruling party, some guests say, will need $500 million for the 1994 presidential election.

Roberto Hernández, a banker who has come out of nowhere and whose name is dogged for years with rumors that his money is drug money (a charge he denies), pledges $25 million. Emilio Azcarraga, owner of the nation's largest television network, one famed for only reporting what the government approves, pledges $50 million. The dinner ends at midnight with $750 million pledged by the guests. Mexico, with an economy of about 5 percent that of the United States, had managed to raise for its ruling party over dinner five times what the Democratic Party spent to elect Bill Clinton in 1992.

Reports of the dinner hit the Mexico City newspapers on March 1 and then appear in the U.S. press. Within a week, Salinas has suggested a $600,000 limit on individual campaign contributions and issued a public statement advocating reform. Reform proved a tonic. Soon the ruling party has put together a campaign fund of $700 million from unexplained sources. The two major opposition parties make do with $5 million and $3 million respectively.[19]

Beginning in 1993 and at the direction of President Salinas, fifty secret bank trusts were allegedly set up around Mexico. The accounts were slush funds for the candidates of the ruling party. The fifty secret bank accounts were fed and nourished by cartels in Colombia and Mexico and when the election ended in late August of 1994 probably three quarters of a billion dollars had cascaded through these slush funds. At that same moment, the man who had set up the accounts, a banker, disappeared; his two banks collapsed and were taken over by the government. In 1996, Alvaro Cepeda Neri, a Mexican lawyer and human rights advocate, published an account of the buying of the election. In May of 1996, he was severely beaten and left hospitalized.

People in the small town of Tetecala, Morelos, begin to notice things in the early and mid-1990s. The nearby hacienda has very wealthy visitors and now and then police helicopters fly in and out of the estate. It has fifty gardeners, masons, guards, and maids making around $65 a month, eight video cameras staring out for security, and a Doberman ranging freely. The governor of the state is the former head of narcotics intelligence, but he notices nothing amiss, not even when Amado Carrillo buys a mansion two blocks from his official residence. Nor does anyone sense anything odd when Carrillo begins landing his jets at the main airport. Nor does anyone notice when he befriends the senior state police commander. Or surrounds his properties with armies of gunmen.[20]

In 1993, Amy Elliot of Citibank's private banking section in New York receives an $80 million deposit from Raúl Salinas. The money is forwarded to Swiss accounts. Ms. Elliot admits later to investigators that she did receive a phone call about Raúl Salinas's banking with Citibank. Carlos Salinas, the president of Mexico, wished to chat about how the money was being managed.

Elliot has been handling Raúl Salinas's banking needs since 1988 or 1992 or 1993, the dates vary in reports—but most likely since 1992. For the bank he is never Raúl Salinas but rather always referred to as Confidential Client Number 2 and his initial deposit is $2 million.[21] Citibank has been the favored foreign bank in Mexico for most of the twentieth century, a special funnel used by the rich to secretly ship their cash abroad. Under President Salinas when a huge number of state-owned businesses were privatized the number of billionaires rose from two to twenty-four (between 1991 and 1994), this without any appreciable increase in the nation's gross domestic product, an achievement almost without precedent in economic history. Elliot is an employee in good standing and is drilled in the bank's rule on private customers, which is: "Know your customer." In the case of Raúl Salinas, she did no investigation, filed no standard financial profile, made no standard financial background check. Nor did she ask for a waiver from these bank requirements. What she did is simply take the money. And handle the transfer of money from Citibank in New York to Swiss accounts. Ms. Elliot helps Raúl Salinas and his wife, Paulina Castanón, work out a system wherein Raúl's wife would pick up cashier checks at Mexico City banks, usually one named Banco Cremi, then hand-carry them to the local Citibank branch and deposit them under an alias. These little deposits ran $3 to $5 million every few weeks. After that they would be wired to New York as dollars. Sometimes, of course, they then went on their way to Switzerland. Sometimes they traveled to shell corporations in the Cayman Islands that were secretly controlled by Raúl Salinas.[22]

Raúl has a thing for Switzerland. Both he and his wife studied there, and he has been in equestrian competitions there, sent his daughters to school there. As it happens, Amado Carrillo is rumored to also have children at school in Switzerland.

Early in the Salinas administration, Carlos Peralta Quintero obtains a cell phone concession from the government. In 1993, he sells a 42 percent share of it to Bell Atlantic for $1.04 billion. In April 1994, he puts $50 million in Raúl Salinas's account in New York. He keeps no record of this deal and later denies that it is linked to any government favors or to anything like a payoff. And no, he can't seem to remember just which New York bank he wired the money to. According to Raúl Salinas, they decided on the sum while having dinner at a nice New York restaurant. Carlos Hank Rhon, the son of Hank González, gives Raúl $9 million for his little fund and also sees no need for any paperwork on the deal. Nor is he bothered that his millions flow into an account that has a fictitious name rather than Raúl's. He has known Raúl, and his brother Carlos, since they were in high school together. He is the man who introduced Raúl to private banking at Citibank.[23]

During the first year of Carlos Salinas's administration about $4 billion left Mexico. During the final year, 1994, the number reaches $20 billion. That same year a secret DEA document finds $100 million in Raúl Salinas's Swiss accounts.[24] Meanwhile, things went differently for the average Mexican: private savings constituted 21 percent of gross domestic product in 1989 and only 11 percent in 1994.[25]

In these same years, Raúl Salinas starts making investments in major Mexican businesses, $29 million to a television network that is partly owned by General Electric, $15 million to a glass company, and so forth. No one is sure just where the money came from or why it was invested in certain things.

One recipient of a Salinas investment, Adrian Sada González, a prominent businessman from a distinguished family, suggests, "Those that are involved in business are human beings and therefore imperfect. What we should do is look for good examples, and not bad ones, and support our more noble principles and values."

A good example involves a bankrupt bus company that the government privatized in 1988, and that Raúl Salinas and others pounced on in 1989. The $4.4 million deal was worth $36 million four years later. The bus company thrived because of deregulation rulings by President Carlos Salinas.[26]

At the same moment, DEA finds trails of investments by Amado

Carrillo into the major infrastructure of Mexico. These trails will go nowhere as agent after agent learns not to pursue matters.[27]

Amado Carrillo also has an account at Citibank in the name of a wealthy Chilean businessman.[28]

Manuel Bitar Tafich is a friend and business associate of Amado Carrillo. Or he is not.[29]

Later, he recounts a conversation with Carrillo.

"The people who steal money from Mexico," Carrillo tells him, "and take it out of the country to Switzerland are more of a disgrace than I am. I bring money here to stimulate the economy."[30]

Rafael Aguilar Guajardo is a very successful man. For years, he worked for DFS, the key internal security agency in Mexico. In that capacity, he helped create and nurture Rancho Búfalo, the massive marijuana plantation that caught the eye of Kiki Camarena before his death. Aguilar is a fair-skinned man and marries into the upper crust of Juárez. Eventually, he has many holdings, including a hotel named after his wife, a place containing a torture room for his interrogations, and a place where I wind up drinking in the 1990s.

Aguilar stumbles now and then. In September 1986, he is arrested by the federales for illegal drugs and guns but this charge is dismissed. The U.S. attorney in El Paso seizes about a million dollars of his property in 1988. But these are small matters. DEA grows frustrated with Aguilar and his immunity and one agent complains that the problem is Aguilar gets confused and actually thinks he is legitimate.

In April 1993, he takes a holiday in Cancún. One day, his driver does not show up and Aguilar is murdered. Within a week, the driver who missed work is in Juárez in the employ of Amado Carrillo. Aguilar had been known as the man in control of the plaza, the boss of trafficking in Juárez. New hands takes over.

They rendezvous near the federal building in Dallas to dicker over a $750,000 cocaine deal. When they are arrested in the fall of 1993, the indictment spins out to name one Amado Carrillo. This is the second federal notice of Carrillo, the first in five years since his earlier indict-

ment in Miami. Of course, Carrillo remains free in Mexico. The
Mexican government says it cannot find him. And of course, the sum
involved, three quarters of a million, is barely a detail in his operation.

Phil Jordan, working out of the Dallas bureau of DEA, is behind
the bust and indictment.

The Ochoa Bali Hai restaurant feels open to the air. Huge sheets of glass
bring in the light, green plants break up the interior, and a rough stone
wall gives an air of coolness. It stands on a busy avenue in Mexico City.
On November 24, 1993, Amado Carrillo arrives around 10:00 P.M. with
his wife, six children, and pistoleros for dinner. Ramón Salazar Salazar,
the man I know as El Güero and whose murder I will cover, is there also.
Things are going fine until about a dozen men enter with briefcases.
They machine-gun the diners. Carrillo dives under the table and survives. One of his key assistants is cut down, quite possibly because the
killers thought he was Amado Carrillo. Legend has it that the killers
shot the wrong man because they were working from an old photograph
of Carrillo.

Carrillo flees in a car. Some accounts have him running over a
policeman, then backing up and shooting him for good measure. No
one is sure who sent the killers and DEA buzzes with different theories.

On New Year's Eve, as his guests wait to ring in 1994, President Carlos
Salinas is feeling very good. He has picked his protégé, Luis Donaldo
Colosio, to be his successor. He has successfully achieved the NAFTA
treaty, which locks Mexico into a common trade market with the
United States and Canada. He is spending $11 million a year in the
United States on public relations. Around 10:00 P.M., the president
and his wife join the party. His father and brothers and sister are there.
Everyone dances and they toast with champagne at midnight.

Around 2:00 A.M. a message is whispered in the president's ear. In
the southern state of Chiapas, rebels have seized at least one city. They
claim they are Zapatistas, in honor of the famous revolutionary
Emiliano Zapata, a man murdered in 1919 by the elements that went
on to forge the ruling party of Carlos Salinas. For the president this is a

blow. After all, he has named the presidential jet *Zapata*. And for three years, he has known of this guerrilla movement. In the summer of 1993, two major Mexico City publications had done extensive reporting on the guerrillas. But the problem had been largely ignored lest publicity mar Mexico's new image as a modern nation and interfere with the recent passage of NAFTA in the U.S. Congress.[31] At 2:10 A.M., the president leaves his party and never comes back.

For months to come, the world press will be full of statements from a masked figure who calls himself Subcomandante Marcos, a pipe-smoking man who is adept at fighting a war with a fax machine and over the Internet. He will become a hero to the Mexican people and celebrated by the nation's intellectuals.

In 1994 with NAFTA a reality, U.S. Customs streamlines its border inspection policy and initiates a line release program. This means it increasingly waves through trucks. The result is stunning. In a twelve-month period, three busy ports of entry, Laredo and El Paso, Texas, and Nogales, Arizona, have two million trucks cross. Customs fails to find a single pound of cocaine.

Rumors of corruption in U.S. Customs are rife on the border. Investigations begin and then falter and go nowhere. I have a drink with a drug dealer in Culiacán, Sinaloa, and he tells me in an offhanded way of the port of entry he owns. I track a sixty-kilo U.S. seizure of a load of cocaine and then discover I can find no announcement of this seizure. Mexicans, of course, continue to be indignant at the official U.S. position that corruption stops at the fence separating the two nations.[32]

On March 23, 1994, Luis Donaldo Colosio, the ruling party's presidential candidate and the handpicked choice of Carlos Salinas, visits a slum in Tijuana and is shot dead. Earlier in the month, on March 6, he had given a speech suggesting reform, one studded with phrases such as "excessive concentration of power" and "to end any vestiges of authoritarianism." This speech was said to irritate party bosses. He had also recently bowed out of a dinner party with select supporters such as members of the Gulf cartel. There were rumors he was distancing himself from the president. A lone gunman was arrested for his murder and eventually sentenced to forty-five years. No one in Mexico believed this explanation. Within days of his murder, his campaign manager, Ernesto Zedillo, was picked as the new candidate. Zedillo, a native of the state Colosio was visiting when he was murdered, had failed to travel with him that day. Instead, he was meeting with someone in Mexico City.

The man who picks Zedillo to be the new standard-bearer is rumored to be one Carlos Hank González, the bulwark of all the presidents and of their power since the late 1970s. Hank is the very symbol of every anti-democratic element in the ruling party, a group called the dinosaurs. He even signs Zedillo's nomination papers.[33] His son in Tijuana, Jorge Hank Rhon, the same man who rode with the killers of Cardinal Posadas Ocampo after the slaughter in the Guadalajara airport, is noted in DEA files as a major money launderer for the Tijuana cartel.

Carlos Salinas has his future sketched out as he approaches the end of his six-year term. He is a top candidate to head the new World Trade Organization. He is going on the board of the Dow Jones. He is celebrated in the world press. Britain's *The Economist* concludes, "Mr. Salinas has a claim to be hailed as one of the great men of the twentieth century." In 1992, *Time* magazine almost made him Man of the Year. Henry Kissinger in 1993 offered that Salinas had "quelled corruption and brought into office an extraordinary group of young, highly trained technocrats. I know of no government anywhere that is more competent." A former secretary of state, Lawrence Eagleburger, added, "Mexican President Carlos Salinas de Gortari sees in NAFTA a way to lock in the sweeping economic and political reforms he has had the courage to initiate."[34]

On May 24, 1994, Saúl Sánchez, Jr., and his wife, Abigail, cross over to Juárez from El Paso to attend a theatrical event. A snitch for the Chihuahua state police has gotten the tickets for them and promised to wait for them. They are never seen again. Sánchez, a navy veteran and U.S. citizen, has been doing a job in Juárez, helping police agencies with devices that intercept cell and satellite phones.

The organization based in El Paso that is dedicated to missing persons keeps adding names. Many are last seen in the company of police or the army. No one will ever know their true number. And it is likely no one will ever list many of the missing. Rumors of secret graveyards circulate. There is talk of a giant oven where bodies are cremated. And of course, there is the matter of the executions on city streets and of bodies found poking out of the ground in the dunes just outside Juárez. DEA creates a list of secret graveyards. But little or nothing will be said out loud for years and years. During the 1990s, the entire matter will exist outside the talk of governments.[35]

In Ojinaga, Amado Carrillo builds a church. In Sinaloa near his mother's house, he builds another church. Drug merchants have been at this work for years. Caro Quintero, who tortured and murdered Kiki Camarena, builds a pink-and-white church on a hill in his hometown.

The Reverend José Raúl Soto Vázquez, a priest at Mexico's most important shrine, the Basilica of Guadalupe in Mexico City, eventually explains, "Such as Caro Quintero—we'd like to do the kind of charity he did. People like Amado Carrillo, who at times gave money to do great works, and people didn't care if he was just a drug trafficker. . . . If sinners do good things, how much more should we, who aren't sinners?"

The Reverend Benjamin Olivas, the Carrillo family priest in Sinaloa, speaks of Amado Carrillo as a friend "very attached to God," and adds, "If you build it, I thank you very much, and God will also take it into account."

In the spring of 1994 or 1995, the dates never quite get sorted out, Amado Carrillo is in the Holy Land for Easter week. He comes with a church group and accompanies his mother. He walks the path of Christ's suffering dragging a giant wooden cross on his shoulders.[36]

On September 28, 1994, José Francisco Ruiz Massieu, the head of the PRI, has a meeting in downtown Mexico City. He is a longtime partner of the Salinas family, though his divorce from the president's sister has clouded this relationship. Across the street from the hotel, a guy waits in jeans, a black shirt, and tennis shoes. He holds a newspaper.

Finally, Ruiz ends his meeting, cracks a joke, and walks out. He climbs into his Buick to drive, his bodyguards in cars behind him. The man with the newspaper fires a 9mm and the bullet enters Massieu's neck and goes to his heart. The shooter flees but trips, drops his gun, and is subdued. His name is Daniel Aguilar, and he is twenty-eight years old. He hails from the state of Tamaulipas and is described in the press as a semi-literate farm hand. Tamaulipas is the bailiwick of the Gulf cartel and allegedly part of the fiefdom of Raúl Salinas, Sr.

At first Aguilar implicates Raúl Salinas, Jr., in the killing, then recants. Later, he claims his wavering was based on threats to his family. The only thing that is clear is that he is not a bumpkin from the hinterlands. In the turmoil of the violent economy that characterized the Salinas presidency, Daniel Aguilar has tried to better himself.

Aguilar studies under experts and becomes accomplished in martial arts, flying single-engine aircraft, and the use of helicopters. He learns weapons also. His group kidnaps people on a contract basis. For the Massieu project, he explains, his end was to be a $15,000 fee for a kidnapping to get Massieu's attention. Later, this contract was upgraded to murder. He says his group was hired by Raúl Salinas, Jr.[37] One key witness will have his ribs broken as Mexican detectives dissuade him from mentioning Raúl Salinas, Jr., in connection with the murder.[38]

Within hours, President Carlos Salinas appoints Mario Ruiz Massieu to investigate the murder of his brother. He has been serving the administration in its War on Drugs, and, in fact, has written a book entitled *The Legal Framework for the Combat of Drug Trafficking*. Within days, he arrests thirteen people, almost all of whom are tortured. Massieu apparently does very sound work because in November President Salinas calls him into his office and hands him a $220,000 cash bonus, or at least that is Ruiz Massieu's account.[39] But his investigation falters and on November 2 he publicly announces his failure and resigns. In early 1995, he flees Mexico, and is stopped at the Newark airport for failing to declare the amount of cash he is carrying. More than $9 million is found in his U.S. bank account, money deposited during his brief months as one of Mexico's drug fighters. There is also a $700,000 mansion he had acquired. He is placed in detention. Soon, with new President Zedillo in office, authorities focus on Raúl Salinas, Jr., as the main suspect. Mario Ruiz Massieu drops out of the picture as he fights extradition back to Mexico, eventually committing suicide in 1999. He leaves a note blaming President Zedillo for his own death and for that of his brother.[40]

On December 3, 1994, Subcomandante Marcos sends a letter to Ernesto Zedillo, the newly inaugurated president of Mexico. The letter goes on for pages lambasting the government as illegitimate. It gains notice, though, for its opening sentence: "Welcome to the nightmare." And a few thousand words later, Marcos signs off: "Vale. Health and a parachute for the cliff which exists in your tomorrow."[41]

On February 28, 1995, Raúl Salinas, Jr., is staying at his sister's house in Mexico City. Unbeknownst to him, the place is secretly surrounded by seventy troops of the presidential guard wearing bulletproof vests. At 11:00 A.M. on February 28, 1995, a packet of material is delivered to former president Carlos Salinas at his Mexico City home. The material ties his brother to the murder of José Ruiz Massieu the previous September. Salinas had just returned from a trip abroad to push his candidacy for heading the World Trade Organization. Three hours later, he goes on the air of a Mexican television network denouncing the charges and connection between the murder and himself. His brother is arrested.

The next day a flurry of phone calls occurs between Citibank's private banking office in New York and its branches in London and Switzerland. The thrust of the calls, a later inquiry by a U.S. Senate committee will decide, is about which Salinas accounts should be hustled off to Switzerland where privacy is easier to maintain. Months later, on November 17, 1995, Citibank does file a criminal referral form naming Raúl Salinas with the U.S. government but this referral mentions only $200,000 in the New York account and neglects to mention the hundreds of millions of dollars already shipped to Swiss banks.[42]

In early March, Carlos Salinas takes a private jet to Monterrey, the capital of the border state of Nuevo León. He begins a hunger strike in a working-class house and holds court for the press. Such gestures are part of the lexicon of protest in Mexico. On March 3, he returns to Mexico City for a secret meeting with President Zedillo. Rumors would circulate following the meeting that Salinas agreed to end his hunger strike and the government agreed to stop making statements linking him to the murder of Colosio, the former PRI presidential candidate, and to the collapse of the Mexican economy. Zedillo has denied such a deal was struck. On March 10, Carlos Salinas leaves Mexico and his brother remains in prison.

In 1995, Amado Carrillo buys an interest in a small banking group, Grupo Financiero Anáhuac. He pays cash for his share of the bank and begins using the bank to wash money, which is then sent on to the Cayman Islands. His son uses one of the bank's cars. The son of former President de la Madrid is vice president of the bank.[43]

Former President Carlos Salinas enters his own dreamtime now. The press bubbles with little reports: he is seen in New York and Boston between March and June of 1995, then he pops up in Montreal between June and December of 1995, he is rumored to be in Costa Rica, Cuba, various Caribbean islands. On April 18, 1996, he appears in a navy blue trench coat on a New York sidewalk as he arrives for the annual meeting of the Dow Jones board, of which he is a director. Dow Jones refuses to comment on his attendance or nonattendance. Then, he vanishes again.[44]

In August 1995, Guillermo Pallomari decides to leave his job when his life is threatened. He is a Chilean computer expert working for Miguel Rodríguez Orejuela of the Cali cartel in Colombia. American drug agents interview him in the United States for three months. Apparently, they never bother to ask him exactly how the Colombians move massive amounts of cocaine through Mexico. Later, when the Swiss investigators become interested in Raúl Salinas's huge bank deposits, they visit Pallomari and he tells them of the connections made through Amado Carrillo and notes that his bosses in Cali even created a kind of corruption manual and sent Carrillo a copy. He also says they shipped $80 million in bribe money to Mexico, half going through Raúl Salinas. Once, he notes, Raúl Salinas intervened to get back a five-ton load seized in Acapulco by cops working with American agents. Raúl Salinas has repeatedly denied all such allegations.

Pallomari becomes a kind of clue for American agents investigating Carrillo and the Salinas brothers. The Chilean has helped launder at least $400 million while working as the accountant for the cartel. His wife and his best friend are dead, his children are in the U.S. witness protection program. He helps make at least forty-four cases concerning Colombia. But no one appears eager for his knowledge of Mexico. Federal prosecutors are reluctant to let him talk to U.S. drug agents. The Swiss themselves are puzzled by the U.S. government's seeming lack of interest in the matter. At one point the key Swiss prosecutor sends an angry letter to Attorney General Janet Reno.[45]

The Swiss keep blundering on, while the U.S. intelligence agencies simulate paralysis. Finally, they conclude Raúl Salinas used Mexican government railroad cars and trucks to move cocaine north and took at least $500 million in fees for this help. They learn that he held what he called "green light days" when he made known that loads could cross Mexico without being pestered by the army, coast guard, or police. The Swiss also conclude that the Salinas brothers were introduced to the drug business in the late 1970s by Raúl Salinas Lozano, their father.

There is no explanation offered to explain how a small group of Swiss investigators could stumble into Mexican corruption and the drug trade in 1995 with no background and no connections and figure all this out while U.S. agencies remained stymied.[46]

Early in 1996, the National Security Agency notices that $6 billion has been laundered by drug traffickers in Mexico over the period of a few weeks. This report causes alarm. Then disbelief. The amount is almost as great as all foreign investment in Mexico that year. How could such numbers be true and yet not be noticed in the economy? So, it must not be true.[47]

They buy their own public notice in the El Paso newspaper. It measures two inches by six inches and has a smiling photograph of Lionel Bruno Jordan, 8/24/67 to 1/20/95.

> Ever since you were so cowardly taken away from us last January 20th, it has been a very lonely and sad year without you for your family and friends. Our only consolation is that, thanks to witnesses coming forward, your killers will soon be brought to justice. Then, and only then can you truly rest in peace.
>
> To everyone who has been sympathetic, supportive and cooperative this past year, thank you.
>
> *The Jordan Family*

In May 1996, Declan Kiberd, professor of literature at the University of Dublin, met with students who lined up outside his door. One man comes into his office wearing a wool cap and a scuffed suede coat. He tells the professor that he has a background in political science and he wishes to discuss books, especially a volume the professor had published, a seven-hundred-page work on Irish literature. In the book, Kiberd linked Ireland and Latin America in the realm of the imagination, noted the similarities between the inventions of, say, James Joyce and the magical realism of Gabriel García Márquez. They talk for forty minutes. The visitor believes the Irish and Mexicans share common values, that both are emotional, traditional, and not very materialistic.

Later, the professor sees a newspaper photograph and realizes that his visitor was Carlos Salinas. He learns he lives in a $1.8 million house on the same street as singers Sinéad O'Connor, Bono, and Van Morrison.[48]

• • •

In early May, Phil Jordan talks to the Washington, D.C., correspondent of *El Financiero,* Mexico's major financial newspaper, and tentatively but firmly brings up the name of Amado Carrillo as the new big power in Mexico. The mention of Carrillo is ignored in the American press.

After this interview with Jordan, a mechanic in a chop shop in Juárez is burned alive.

In the spring of 1996 DEA shares the names of some of its informants with Mexican authorities. The list evidently makes it to Carrillo. For months, executions clog the streets of Juárez and by August somewhere between forty and sixty people have been dispatched.

Edgar Eduardo García Larralde is twenty-two and his family sells used cars. Cristian Mauricio Rodríques Tarín, eighteen, is his friend. Together, they are known as Los Bimbos, after a popular trade name of Mexican bread. They disappear on May 3, 1996, and then reappear on May 5 in the Juárez cemetery. Their faces are covered with bandages, their mouths stuffed with toilet paper and sealed with gray duct tape. They are covered with cheap tapestries such as can be found in the public market, tapestries of tigers. There are signs of torture—hemorrhaging of the intestines and of the rectum. Rumor has it that all this mayhem is about love.

Rocío Agüero Miranda is a businesswoman and when Los Bimbos disappear one of them is said to be the father of the child she has been carrying for seven months. She is a local kind of celebrity. In December of 1995, she opened a flashy club and called it Top Capos, with a big outside illustration of an old 1930s car with two gangsters driving and a good-looking woman staring out from the trunk and hoisting a glass of champagne. The club would run all night and she would bring in entertainers from out of town and pay them $20,000 or $30,000 a night. Rich kids flocked to the place because it was a club where they could do cocaine. People who sold drugs tended to celebrate in her club.

But after the murders of Los Bimbos, she loses heart for the business. She eats very little. She closes Top Capos. Twice, she comes back with a chauffeur-bodyguard who stays in the car while she supervises the cleaning of the empty club. She sits inside smoking and drinking coffee and seemingly lost in her own thoughts.

Her current lover is a narcotraficante, head of a car theft ring, and a contract killer. His brother is a famous car thief in an El Paso gang and is now in jail in El Paso. But the police say that in the weeks before the murders of Los Bimbos, 567 kilos of cocaine were seized and, thus, the killings represent an adjustment of accounts between different gangs of narcotraficantes.

Rocío gives premature birth to a girl a week after the bodies are found draped with tiger tapestries. And then she takes off for Cancún for two weeks of relaxation, finally returning to Juárez and moving in with her nineteen-year-old daughter. After her return, she lives very, very quietly; in fact, she hardly ever leaves the house.

In the summer of 1996, Adolfo Aguilar Zinser, a Mexican congressman, feels kind of overwhelmed. He's long been a dissident in Mexican politics and now with the end of the Salinas years and with the collapse of the economy there is this tiny window he can crawl through, a window that opens up to view how the government of Mexico actually operates. For decades, in fact almost all of the twentieth century, this simply has not been done.

Aguilar is on a committee looking at four thousand boxes of documents left by CONASUPO, the government agency for feeding the poor, from the years Raúl Salinas ran it. He discovers lots of trips for Raúl and his friends, jaunts to those hot spots of the world of rice, beans, and corn like Madrid, Paris, and London. Aguilar tells the press, "Every time I go to the files, I find something [illegal]—quantities of money you can't believe."

His committee is too small to do much and most of the committee members are committed to not doing anything at all. He discovers that he is not looking for some needle in a haystack but that everything in the boxes smacks of corruption, every trip, contract, deal is rife with fraud and favors. He finds the hand of the current president, Ernesto Zedillo, in some of the deals. Zedillo denies this allegation, as he has consistently denied any wrongdoing. Aguilar thinks, "They're not crooks who sneak around in the middle of the night. They do it institutionally."[49]

In the fall of 1996, one U.S. attorney estimates that no more than 30 percent of U.S. Customs officials are on the take.[50]

In Juárez, many of the satellite communities are the inventions of squatters. One, Anapra, sits right on the line staring at the western fringe of El Paso. The community of ten or twenty thousand souls clings to sand dunes and is rife with drug smugglers and struggling workers who toil in the border factories. The Americans are busy building a huge metal wall to keep Anapra in its place. The colonia has responded by erecting a metal sign that reads, "The ten thousand residents of the pueblo of Anapra protest against this Berlin Wall. We solicit the governments of the United States and of Mexico to make an international crossing at this place." This policy statement is followed by a few lines of verse:

> *I had a dream*
> *I saw people holding hands together*
> *with no iron walls but*
> *bridges of freedom.*

Richard Cordero Ontiveros is a drug warrior and in 1995 he was sent to Tijuana as the head of an intelligence unit to clean up the mess there. He discovered his colleagues were preoccupied with escorting drug shipments and serving as bodyguards for drug merchants. In November of 1995, he quit his post and began writing letters to Mexican officials outlining the problem as he saw it. At first, he only received death threats. He noted, "In this country, you talk about corruption and people kill you."

When he arrived in Tijuana to ramrod his unit of seventeen agents, he found them boozing in two rented houses, both paid for by DEA. They also watched a lot of television.

When Cordero took them out on the streets to do a little work things just seemed to get worse. Once he spots a bunch of police lights and goes over and finds some federales protecting a drug dealer from local cops. Then, he gets a tip from DEA about a drug shipment, pounces on it, and finds federales protecting the load. He concludes he has been sent to Tijuana to command the unit because his superiors realized "I was a fool." When he jumps on a multi-ton coke shipment and cooperates with DEA and the FBI, he is reprimanded from Mexico City. Then in late October he stumbles on a five-ton coke shipment in a small border town, one guarded by a Mexican anti-drug agent. He is commanded by his bosses in Mexico City "to leave the city immediately." Also, there are four attempts on his life.

So in July 1996, he decides to go public with his experiences. At the moment, the U.S. government and the Mexican government are deeply involved in promoting an image of the new Zedillo administration making giant strides against corruption. Cordero's claims are not compatible with this goal. So he is promptly arrested for filching funds while working in Tijuana the year before. His arrest comes immediately after a U.S. congressional committee invites him to come to Washington to testify.[51]

On July 24 at about 4:30 A.M. Rocío Agüero Miranda finally leaves the house. She is escorted by fifteen men carrying AK-47s. Some witnesses say she is wearing blue shorts. Others see her in simply a bra and silk panties. The maid, who flees into the bathroom of the house with the baby, says the men sounded like they were from Mexico City, and acted like federales. But then, she also says they looked like the guys she always saw hanging around the Top Capos nightclub when it was still open. She does recall that the visitors surrounded the house, sprayed the big dog in the backyard with something, then jumped the wall and entered the house through the back door. Rocío was taken by force. She may have felt suddenly confused since she was, among other things, a former lover of Amado Carrillo. On the other hand, she and her boyfriend have ripped off five hundred kilos of cocaine from Carrillo's cartel, plus a Jeep Cherokee and some jewelry. Such actions are not likely to be ignored.[52]

Rocío's family does not call the police. They simply wait for a ransom message. The phone does ring and a voice says instructions will be delivered later.

The police doubt the whole event. They say that a year earlier, Rocío had faked a kidnapping in order to get some ransom money. Besides, she is seen as a little foolish, a mother of thirty-six who dresses in the provocative and loud clothing of a younger woman. Also, they continue, she herself is a known drug smuggler.

Rocío turns up on July 31 in Juárez. Two guys walking along a canal see a barrel floating. They decide to retrieve it and then sell it for salvage. When they pry it open, they see what looks like parts of a body. Rocío has been floating in two hundred liters of acid. She has retained two feet, some internal organs, some brown hair, and part of her head, which displays a fracture at its base. She is identified by her breast implants, ones she had imported from France and that have small but now useful registration numbers.

In the summer of 1996, the investigation of the assassination of Luis Donaldo Colosio continues to creep along. But the attorney general of Mexico finds he has one little problem: no one wants to head the investigation. One day in August, he fires seven hundred federales for corruption. Then a few days later, someone shoots up the house of his key aide and puts three rounds through a bodyguard's chest. Then, *El Financiero,* the *Wall Street Journal* of Mexico, notes that seventeen cops and others with close ties to the Colosio case have been murdered. By then at least eleven potential suspects, witnesses, and prosecutors connected to the 1993 murder of Cardinal Juan Jesús Posadas Ocampo have been murdered. The medical examiner in that case lives under permanent protection because, in a case where the official explanation of the murder is that it resulted from mistaken identity, he found powder burns on the cardinal's chin.[53] The attorney general of Mexico continues his hunt for a special prosecutor to look into the Colosio murder. So far, there have been three.[54]

In early August 1996, Sonia Yvette Ramírez of Juárez, a thirteen-year-old girl, is raped and then beaten violently to death. Her body is left in

front of the state judicial police office. On August 14, Ramiro Covar-
rubias Martínez, forty-six, is murdered in his house. He is the former
comandante of car theft for state judiciales stationed in Juárez. He
resigned after claims of corruption in June 1993. On Friday, August
15, Soledad Beltran, twenty-six, is found in a sewage ditch on the edge
of the city. She worked in a nightclub. She has been shot in the head,
execution style, and been dead three or four days. Police say that they
think the killing is about some romance. She worked in an area near
the bridge that is notorious for chop shops.

On August 17, Hector Lechuga Avila, is shot four times, and left
on the road to the Lote Bravo. He is twenty-six and until recently he
investigated crimes in Juárez for the government. That same day,
Leticia Palafox, sixteen or seventeen, is shot three times in the head.
Then someone uses broken glass to cut her up. Her body is covered
with a tapestry of white and yellow flowers. She is left near the bull
ring in Juárez, a few blocks from the Zona Rosa. As of August 20, *El
Norte* reports for the year 158 murders (one third women).

The Jordan family gathers for the second annual memorial mass to celebrate Bruno's birthday at the end of August. Attendance, maybe fifty
people, is vastly reduced from the year before. Phil Jordan is now
retired from DEA and the host of co-workers that came when he ran
EPIC is now absent. Members of the extended Jordan family in El Paso
attend but in much smaller numbers. There is a stillness at the mass, a
sense of futility. In part, it is the belief by some relatives that the thing
must be put in perspective, that life goes on and the loss of Bruno
should be absorbed rather than dwelt upon. Just as in DEA ranks there
are murmurs that Phil Jordan has lost his judgment in this matter, that
his brother's death is a carjacking and there is no point in making more
of it. The brothers and sisters gather and so do some of their children,
and of course, Bruno's parents, Antonio and Beatrice.

By the altar are two portraits of Bruno, one taken when he was
about twenty and wearing a red, gold, and blue University of Texas at
El Paso velour shirt, another when he is older, wearing glasses, suit,
overcoat, scarf, and white shirt—the image of a young banker or stock-

broker. A Redskins balloon floats in the air. This year Tony is in a dark suit, white shirt, red tie, red pocket kerchief. He sings and at the line, "The sun shines less brightly," he breaks down and weeps. The priest comforts him. Tony continues with the song he wrote for Bruno and also "You Were Always My Hero."

Afterward, the grave is visited, kinsmen make the ritual pouring on of beer, food, and drink appear at a gathering on Frutas Street. Nothing is enough. Sean, Phil's older son, fetches a photo from the house of him and Tony and Bruno as little kids playing in the street out front.

Tony looks and says, "One's missing."

Sean says, "No, he isn't."

I arrive at La Serata, said to be the private club of Amado Carrillo in Juárez.[55] Across the river in El Paso is a big bank and, according to DEA, he owns it. No one mentions this. He owns factories in this city. No one mentions this either. I'm stuffed with the lore of my government's research. U.S. agents love to gather evidence of assets, addresses, favorite aliases, kinship ties, and color photographs of Carrillo's various mansions. There are hundreds of pages of files on Carrillo but they still leave him a ghostly presence.

The doorman says the club is closed. I point out there are loud and merry voices coming from within. The doorman says, yes, but this is a special club, a very refined place, and I've failed to measure up to the dress code. My shirt, he explains, has pockets and this is a violation of the standards.

Carrillo's organization has, according to numbers compiled by DEA, killed six hundred people in Juárez in the last twenty-four months. The Arrellano boys in Tijuana have executed in that city 130 people between January 1, 1996, and late August 1996.

On October 6, 1996, Mayor Galindo of Juárez says he can do nothing about crime because criminal organizations run the city. On October 9, Mayor Galindo of Juárez says that crime is down in the city and that it is peaceful.

•   •   •

On October 9, 1996, at 1:30 P.M., the Texas Eighth Court of Appeals meets on the twelfth floor of the courthouse a half dozen blocks from the Rio Grande. A detective who handled Bruno's murder is there in a gray suit and a Bugs Bunny–Daffy Duck necktie. So is Virginia Jordan. The appeal will decide whether or not Miguel Angel Flores gets a new trial and the issue will be the jury's finding of a marijuana roach in the lining of his jacket during their deliberations. Phil Jordan arrives after the hearing is rolling. Teresa García presents the prosecution case, essentially an argument that the judges (all three of them) can hardly understand what happened since they were not there in the heat of the moment. The three jurists, Anne McClure, a former defense attorney, David Chew, a former councilman and defense attorney, and Chief Justice Richard Barajas, seem hardly taken with this claim of their inadequacy. Barajas had a brother murdered in Albuquerque during a drive-by shooting, a fact Virginia, wearing a dark blue dress, gold earrings, and bracelet, hopes will make him sensitive to the horror of her brother Bruno's murder.

Charlie Roberts handles the defense. The rumor is he has been paid ten or twenty thousand by the Mexican consulate, an action without known precedent in El Paso. He begins by saying, "This is a very, very difficult case . . ." and then steps free of the podium and nails the attention of the judges. His hands move in dramatic gestures and his argument is simple and blunt: "Let's say you're [the former defense lawyer, Sam Medrano] absolutely crazy and don't think that marijuana is prejudicial to your client . . ." As Roberts rolls on his voice rises and falls, here and there he cuts loose with a boom of oratory, and stays relentlessly on track about his point that inadmissible evidence, the roach, decided the case. Medrano "doomed his client." Roberts, whatever his preparation, consistently refers to Miguel Angel as sixteen, when in fact he was barely thirteen at the time of the murders. This hardly matters, so forceful is his language and so feeble has been the state's argument. As they sit there, Phil and Virginia know the defense is winning and only some crazed thinking by the judges can deny Flores a new trial. All through the hearing a power drill periodically fires up as some kind of work goes on in the courthouse. In the midst of all this, the chief justice blurts out, "We have in this community such an anti-immigrant feeling," a thought that enrages Phil and Virginia, who feel the issue is cold-blooded murder and not immigration policy or debate.

Teresa García stands nervously with the Jordans outside the court-room and rehashes the hearing. Once she told me her office kept no record of Miguel Angel's two confessions because she was afraid the defense would get them through discovery. After the hearing, I go to the Jordan home on Frutas Street. It is a sunny, warm day, and we have lunch in the new dining room, the memorial to Bruno. Phil and Virginia have already arrived earlier and it is obvious they have not told their mother, Beatrice, the truth about the hearing. When I do, telling her the kid's lawyer probably won and that there will probably be a new trial, she is broken.

Francisca Zetina Chávez brings comfort. She says that she is a witch and met Raúl Salinas during his brother's presidential campaign. Soon she was rearranging things in his office to ensure good luck, talking with him about the meaning of life. She sensed he felt empty inside despite his money and power.

And then after José Francisco Massieu was murdered on a Mexico City street and Raúl Salinas was later arrested for the crime, Zetina sensed blood on Raúl's life and turned away from him.

Which, as she explains, may be why on October 7, 1996, a boy brought her an envelope as she sat at home. Inside was an account of a murder at one of Raúl's ranches, where he was alleged to have beaten a missing congressman, Manuel Muñoz Rocha, to death with a baseball bat. Muñoz had long been accused of being part of a plot with Salinas to kill Massieu. The letter also revealed the place where the body was buried. So, being a white witch, Zetina turned the letter over to the government.

Attorney General Antonio Lozano García dug up the corpse and on October 9 publicly stated he felt it was Muñoz. The corpse lacked fin-gers and the lower jaw. Also, the top of the skull had been neatly sliced off. Salinas hired a U.S. expert in DNA (William Maples of the University of Florida at Gainesville, who did the 1991 work on the body of President Zachary Taylor) to study and identify the body. Also, a key witness against Raúl Salinas in the murder of José Ruiz Massieu, a former Muñoz Rocha aide named Fernando Rodríguez González, loses some credibility when a videotape surfaces that shows the top prosecutor coaching him.[56]

Later, it was learned that someone, possibly Zetina, had had the body dug up and moved to the ranch. It was not Muñoz's cadaver, that much was certain, but that of a relative of Zetina.

Later on October 9, after the witch has weighed in, after Miguel Angel Flores has had his case presented to the appeals court, after Beatrice has wept at the possibility that the early conviction may now be undone, I go to a bar and meet with a man. The man says, "He's their money man, he can guarantee loads. He's into everything now, wholesale, retail, growing the stuff. He's a ghost. A lot of people say they see him whether they do or not."

He is speaking of Amado Carrillo and he is a DEA agent who has returned after a long tour in Mexico.

What's the key thing I should know about Carrillo, I ask.

The man pauses and thinks and finally says, "I don't know."

When I ask Phil Jordan the same question, he offers, "There's no rhyme or reason to the way they operate."

The agents in the War on Drugs do not think in terms of victory. That is not important to the warrior culture. Only war is essential and proper tools to wage this war. It is all about the hunt, the plans, the ploys, the little skirmishes. Drugs cannot be stopped from entering the country any more than people can be stopped from consuming them. But drug traffickers can be arrested, jailed, beaten, and killed. Their loads can be seized, their homes and chattel confiscated, their money transfers tracked, their public appearances infused with terror. The war can be taken into their world.

The man explains that it is important to avoid prison in the U.S. because it is hard to do business in our installations. Not impossible but inconvenient. In Mexico, prison actually has some advantages over freedom and he ticks them off:

1. You become an official scapegoat in the drug problem and thus your profile is lowered.
2. You have a secure base with almost unlimited access to phones and faxes.
3. You can come and go as you like.
4. The media in the U.S. tend to forget you since they assume you are doing time and are locked up. Your case becomes closed.

Then he offers out of the blue, "Amado is in over his head."

On November 5, 1996, I knock on a door as night is falling over the small town in Texas. I look up and see a woman peering through a slat of the upstairs blinds she has delicately raised with a finger. The door itself has a lock, two dead bolts, and then the chain. A man finally opens it. He is shirtless, a generous beer gut spilling over his belt, and he has a gun in his hand. Inside, a red sign with a circle and slash is fastened to the door of the downstairs bathroom: NO FIREARMS PERMITTED IN THIS ESTABLISHMENT. Eduardo Valle has kept his sense of humor. He looks to be in his late forties, has a heavily grizzled three-day beard, a black shock of hair, and the trademark glasses that as a boy earned him the nickname El Búho, the Owl.

The television is roaring with a bad picture heavily rashed with the white sleet of interference. He has almost finished a bottle of Jack Daniel's. Valle is a wanted man. Until a month ago, he had no money and then the check came for his book—*The Second Shot,* which sold 65,000 copies in Mexico, a phenomenal number for a country of great poverty and illiteracy—and now the apartment has new furniture and a small black stereo system. Over the fireplace are three ceramic masks of fine-boned women, a variation on the traditional faces of the commedia dell'arte. The dining room table gleams with a fine rosewood sheen, the buffet matches, the couches in the living room are white leather. A large print of the Virgin of Guadalupe hangs on one wall. On the buffet rests a black cap that says DESPERADO.

Valle nurses a shot and talks through the television noise as if it were a fact of nature.

"I must tell you," he rumbles, "I do not trust gringos. They are liars." He drifts off into a dissection of a recent movie about Geronimo in which the warrior surrenders to the U.S. army only to be betrayed and shipped to a dank cell in Florida.

Suddenly, he blurts out, "My house is your house." He moves his hands constantly with great flourishes and they underscore his words. He prefers announcements such as, "Drugs are a problem of the whole world, not just Mexico." His face is plastic, a brow arched, a tilt of the head, the eyes narrowed, then wide, the lips a sneer, then a smile and an open volcano. I find him impossible not to like. He is the rebel of 1968 who did two and half years in prison, and became the scandal in 1994 when he fled Mexico with documents incriminating the regime, and now in November 1996 he is the intensely homesick Mexican living a few minutes from the border.

On the night the Mexican government machine-gunned hundreds of students in the public square in Mexico City in 1968, El Búho survived and then disappeared into the secret jails of the rulers. His mother found him two weeks later stumbling down a staircase "like a mole," she later recalled. El Búho had been beaten almost to death and his glasses had perished. So he blindly staggered toward his mother guided only by her voice and she looked into a face she could hardly recognize and only believed he was her son when she heard his voice.

At the moment, he is living only twenty-five minutes from former Comandante Calderoni. He dismisses any possible menace from that quarter. "Calderoni," he snorts, "that fucking whore, if he comes here, *he* will have the problem. I refuse to live in fear." Like many drunken men, Valle feels the need to praise his woman, who remains at the moment out of sight upstairs. He sweeps the room with one hand and says with great pride and relish that all this beauty is the result of her good taste. She is seven months pregnant with his child.

El Búho explains that his woman is very nervous. She is always watching, always waiting for them to come and close in for the kill. He is rambling now from subject to subject. Los Pinos? "Los Pinos is in the shadows."

I shift the talk to the matter at hand and bring up the meeting with the strange, frightened man called Memo in the El Paso saloon, the man who purported to be a high official in the Mexican attorney general's office and who was fleeing Mexico in fear of his life because he had participated in the Colosio investigation and as he had noted, everyone who looked into that matter was going to die. El Búho listens intently and then I get to the real issue: Memo said that on at least two occasions he was in Los Pinos for meetings with President Carlos Salinas and Raúl Salinas and Amado Carrillo. Valle nods and says he too heard of these meetings when he headed the attorney general's anti-narcotic force between 1992 and 1994, but he has no proof of them. However, he tosses out another story.

He knows a pilot, the kind of private pilot who flies the rich around in Learjets, and this pilot met Amado Carrillo when both happened to be jailed in Guadalajara back in 1989. They were there for separate matters and were shortly released. A few months later, in November 1990, he landed in Monterrey and walked into the terminal and there in the VIP lounge he saw Amado Carrillo in a deep conversation with President Carlos Salinas. And yes, El Búho continues on, he believes this story.

El Búho lived in Washington, D.C., between the summers of 1994 and 1995. He found the city impossibly expensive and the politicians cowardly and useless. He failed to find any major official who would tangle with his documents. Suddenly, in the midst of one outburst, he goes upstairs and returns with a fat wad of pages that he tosses at me and says, "This is a gift. It is very important. See if you can study it and understand its importance." I flip through the document and see it is a pen register of the phone of Oscar Malherbe, the second in command of the Gulf cartel. The register runs for one month in late 1993 and is a series of names, addresses, and phone numbers, a small part of the footprints left by the cartel's operation.

His sentences are punctuated with various forms of the verb *chingar,* to fuck. His deep, booming, and raspy voice dominates the room like a relic of his former station in life. He smokes Camel filters, sips his whiskey, and favors a Zippo lighter. When he talks, he often casts his head downward to the table as if his words were revelations to be whispered, and then tilts his head so that his black-framed glasses dramatically set off his eyes as he peers up at you seemingly searching your face for evidence of comprehension.

His first book will be followed in two or three months by a second volume, *The First Shot.* The implication is that he is this time delivering up some kind of primal cause and history for the calamity of Mexico today. The whiskey is long gone and we have been steadily draining a half gallon of white wine. He walks me to the door and gives me an abrazo.

About a week after the appeals court hearing, Phil Jordan for the first time tells a newspaper reporter that he thinks his brother was murdered because of his own work with DEA. When I ask him about this comment, he hedges and acts flustered and tries to suggest that somehow the story said more than he meant to say. No, it's not exactly a misquote and, well, he didn't quite say it that way and we need proof and yet in the end, his statement still hangs there.

I can sense some deep disturbance going on beneath his calm, placid exterior. He is now retired from DEA, yet money is to be a problem. He is married, yet there is a feeling of unease about the marriage. He flies in and out of El Paso, stays at the family home, and yet he is slipping away from Frutas Street. His brother has now been dead for eighteen months and he knows nothing more about the killing.

El Búho still has his typewriter, and at its mention his face brightens and he flies upstairs returning with a maroon-colored Olympic portable, his faithful companion during those two and half long years in prison following the student revolt of 1968.

"I don't have any protection provided," he says, "by the U.S. government nor have I taken any money from them. I work on my book. I have a fast car, a pistol, and a sensibility."

He is obsessed with the murder of Luis Donaldo Colosio on March 23, 1994, at Lomas Taurino in Tijuana, Baja Norte. El Búho has watched the thirty-second videotape of the assassination over two hundred times. He reenacts the hit, killing Colosio over and over again and he demonstrates the flaws in the official version. All this research will boil over in his new book.

The hit, he says, was done by elements of Amado Carrillo's cartel and Juan García Abrego's cartel for Carlos Salinas. Salinas, who everyone knows has run Mexico since 1985 when he became the power behind the throne midway through the presidency of de la Madrid, intended for Colosio to be a stand-in for himself so that he could rule another six years and escape the constitutional bar against a president succeeding himself. On March 6 Colosio gave that speech declaring his independence of the Salinases and of the conservative elements in the PRI. For Valle, that is the moment Colosio became doomed. Valle was a friend of Colosio's and as early as January of 1994 he sent him warnings about the people surrounding Salinas and their ties to narcotraficantes, especially those attached to Juan García Abrego. And then in March following the speech of the sixth, everyone in the ruling circles heard stories of an impending hit on Colosio. Valle became alarmed and made an appointment to meet with Colosio on March 25. He was going to replace the candidate's bodyguards with men of his own team.

Mexico attorney general Antonio Lozano García is fired by President Zedillo on December 2, 1996. There has been some embarrassment over the planted body dug up with such a flourish on one of Raúl Salinas's estates. Also, Lozano has made little or no headway in the murders of Colosio and Ruiz Massieu. He has had people try to kill him. And he has said that 80 percent of his police and prosecutors were corrupt. But still, he lasted two years in this sensitive post.

A former employee of Lozano's makes the press a few days later. He was currently the subject of two warrants—one for rape, one for extortion—and he had apparently been eluding arrest by living in his own home in Mexico City with his wife and three children and by publishing a magazine and helping his wife get out a recent book—*The Boss of the Gulf,* about Juan García Abrego. Fernando Balderas, his wife, Yolanda, their daughter, Patricia, eighteen, sons, Paul and Fernando, thirteen and eight, were found beaten to death in the family home.

Police note that robbery was not a motive but they are, officially, at a loss to explain the slaughter of the family.[57]

El Búho begins his estimate of Carlos Salinas by noting he is an Olympic-level equestrian and karate expert. He is a man obsessed with winning. He comes from a good background and is well educated. He is a man . . . well, he looks like a Marxist intellectual but he thinks in economic terms like the United States.

"Politically," El Búho offers, "he reads Mao Zedong, he reads the Germans, particularly the Germans behind the idea of the European Community. So you have a sophisticated Marxist studying the United States and the European Union. He also has a tendency toward criminal behavior. Salinas is always a man with a dark face. First, because of the murder of the maid as a child. Also he had a strong relationship with General Humberto Morelos, who was apprehended in France in 1984 for cocaine associations. The general was murdered in a Paris jail in 1985.

"Another example of this dark side is Raúl, Sr., who had several brothers, and one of them, Carlos, was a friend of Juan N. Guerra, the godfather of the Gulf cartel.

"Salinas's plan was to leave the presidency and take over the World Trade Organization and then have the constitution reformed so that he could return for another term as president of Mexico. Colosio said no to this scheme in his speech of March 6 when he criticized Salinas calling the president 'authoritarian.'

"For many years I was a newspaper columnist and knew Salinas. I first met him around 1966. In 1987, I was the first in the press to say he would be the next president. When he became president, I was the head of the journalists' union and I would talk to him about a minimum wage for reporters.

"But going back to 1966, Salinas and I were in the same school studying economics. I knew then he was a killer.

"Salinas behaves in this secretive way very often and his tendency to violate the law is very clear. This is the dark face of Salinas and too many times he wins. Carlos Salinas always stays behind the scenes, he

is never in front. He is not important at this time, but his father is secretary of industry and commerce and rich. I see him again in 1985. He
is the head of the budget and I am the president of the union of journalists and then I ask Salinas for an increase in the minimum wage.

"When Jorge Carpizo took power in the attorney general's office,
he asked me to be his personal assistant. I ask him if he has asked
Salinas and he says yes, that Salinas said this is a wonderful idea but to
tell El Búho we don't want any more adventures. I don't know why
Salinas gave me this job because clearly he misunderstood what I could
do. By June of 1993, I'm tracking the head of the Gulf cartel and by
October of that year I have everything located and I ask Salinas for two
helicopters and some soldiers. Salinas consents to one helicopter. It was
impossible to apprehend García Abrego with one chopper. If I'd tried
that forty or fifty people would have died. To me this decision means
Salinas doesn't want Abrego in jail. So I decide to work this way: I target the people in the Gulf cartel and apprehend sixty lower capos and
associates. On the other hand I secretly investigate Salinas himself.

"I learn of the relationship of the Salinas family with the narcos. I
give the most important information to Colosio in July and October
1993 and for the last time on January 6, 1994. The last message is very
important because I tell Colosio, 'Be careful.' This is an indication for
Colosio to go against Salinas. I did not talk to Colosio, I sent him a
report, an *aviso*.

"But my principal work was the Cartel del Golfo. This is in my
first book, which no one has asked to translate in the U.S. The criminals, you know, are transnational and have immense power. People in
the U.S. are more timid than in Mexico. In the U.S., oh, maybe the
sheriff is corrupt and so forth, they think. This naïveté is incredible.

"Anyway, Colosio starts his campaign. I don't tell Colosio directly
that Carlos Salinas is in the drug business. I tell him that the people
around Salinas are. Salinas absolutely had to know what I was doing,
except for the fact that I was investigating his family. It is a trick. If
you know 99 percent about me, you think you know 100 percent. But
the one percent is the most important part. And it worked. You don't
directly investigate the president of Mexico because you will die. After

Colosio was murdered, I asked for a passport the next day. I need also a receipt for my drug archives, proof that I had turned them in intact. I had made copies of everything but without the receipt I would be called crazy or a CIA agent. On June 2, I drove to the border and crossed at Brownsville. For a month, I had fought to get the signature needed for my files. I brought copies of the files out with me. I felt always in danger and I went directly to Washington, D.C.

"During the two months after Colosio's murder, I had to walk without fear because if they saw fear I would not get out. I took precautions. I stayed home at night and I carried a Colt .38 pistol with nine shots, a semiautomatic. I had a fast car, a Ford Victoria. But a common car that did not stand out. I called friends in U.S. Customs and told them I was coming. I drove during the day and made it to the border in eleven hours.

"In Washington, I sent Senator Jesse Helms important materials but he never used them. The Republicans are not serious. The government of Clinton just begins to understand the dangers of criminal corporations. Clinton, four years ago, did not understand. He didn't want to fight the criminal organizations because that could affect U.S., Mexico, and Canada relationships. I also talked with friends in U.S. Customs. DEA is the most corrupt agency in the U.S. EPIC has a bad foreign policy against Mexico. Fortunately, the DEA has less power each day because they make so many mistakes. The DEA is old and corrupt. They don't live in the moment.

"The big problem is not in the DEA, FBI, or CIA, it is in the politics of the National Security Council. They don't think about what is happening in the U.S. The big money is in New York, Boston, Chicago, Los Angeles, and Wall Street. Mexican narcos earn $30 billion a year. The U.S. criminals earn $120 billion a year in narcotics.

"A week or ten days before I crossed the border, a high official of the Salinas government tells me to come to Los Pinos. I go and he asks, 'Búho, what's happening with your life?'

"I say, 'I have my notes.'

"He replies, 'Well, take this book, *Crónicas que Matan* [Chronicles of the Murdered].'

"I say, 'Thank you.' Because I know he has warned me that I would be dead in a few days. I began to move fast then, rapidly, rapidly, rapidly.

"If I had anticipated that they would have murdered Colosio so swiftly, I would have moved faster earlier. We all knew it could come—it was announced, in the air—in a month or so. If many people like me knew, then Zedillo had to hear the same stories. When Zedillo came to the United States as president, I met him and shook his hand as a journalist. I asked him about the narcotraficantes and he said the attorney general would investigate this question."

After the killing of Pablo Acosta in the late 1980s, Comandante Guillermo González Calderoni became a hero of American law enforcement, being the honored guest at meetings and getting written commendations from both the FBI and the DEA. He became the national director of drug interdiction during the presidency of Carlos Salinas. Then suddenly, in December 1992, he fled Mexico to the United States when the Salinas administration accused him of taking bribes from drug merchants. DEA hid him for a while at a golf resort in Palm Springs, California. Eventually, he surfaced in McAllen, Texas, where he suddenly owned a trucking company. For a while, the Mexicans sought to extradite him but during one courthouse meeting Calderoni allowed that if were pressured, he might suddenly start remembering things. He was left alone in the United States.

In December 1996, he starts talking publicly. He had spoken to agencies in 1993 while Salinas was still president, but these debriefings were essentially buried by the U.S. government, which was busy promoting the passage of NAFTA and had little use for bad talk about the Salinas administration. Now, his words briefly flutter across American and Mexican newspaper pages.

He was a boyhood friend of the García Abrego brothers and continued this relationship after they became heads of the multibillion-dollar Gulf cartel and Calderoni himself became the national official in charge of drug interdiction. During the 1988 presidential campaign, he tapped the phone of the opposition candidate at the orders of Raúl

Salinas, Jr. Soon after Carlos Salinas assumed office he sent Calderoni to arrest the head of the oil workers union, a notoriously corrupt and powerful figure. After fourteen hours of interrogation, Calderoni persuaded the man to sign a confession.

Next he was sent by the deputy attorney general to arrest Miguel Angel Félix Gallardo, the prime force behind the Guadalajara cartel.

At first Calderoni balked and asks, "Why do you want me to catch him now, when you didn't want me to arrest him before?"

The deputy attorney general explained, "The certification is coming," a reference to the annual U.S. review of Mexico's help in fighting drugs.

Calderoni tracked down Gallardo and "I put the AK-47 in his mouth and made him stand up slowly."

Gallardo offered the comandante $5 or $6 million for his freedom but he was refused. Gallardo explained, "You know that if you turn me in, you are a dead man, you are going to die very soon." But Calderoni countered that he had tapes of Gallardo ordering the murders of his own men and he might make these public if he was threatened.

The capture was celebrated by the Bush administration and Calderoni was invited to Carlos Salinas's office and handed a $100,000 bonus. In 1991, Calderoni learned that the Gulf cartel was dickering with Raúl Salinas to buy two major Mexican seaports for their commerce. He said he told the deputy attorney general to warn the president of what was up. Perhaps, but at the same time, Calderoni himself was on the payroll of the Gulf cartel according to U.S. intelligence.

He insists as he talks to the newspaper that he told the U.S. about Raúl Salinas, Jr.'s drug connections in 1993 and cable evidence from the U.S. embassy in Mexico City shows that this was reported to Washington by July 1993. Government documents of the time only identify Calderoni as "a personal friend of Juan García Abrego," the then head of the Gulf cartel.

In the story, one source used to verify Calderoni's claims is Phil Jordan, the former director of DEA's EPIC. Jordan says, "He has nothing to gain by saying this if it is not true. And I can tell you that much of what he says fits with the intelligence we had."

Calderoni himself has neither been charged with a crime in the United States nor bothered to answer the whispers that he had ties with the Gulf cartel. He is in a real sense the perfect soldier of the War on Drugs and like all such soldiers a figure compromised by the very theater of the battle.

"I believe," El Búho says in a hard voice, "and this is important, that the government intelligence in the U.S. reveals that criminal corporations operate like normal corporations. The Latin mafias are not really on the streets in the U.S. but the money from this illegal activity is in the U.S. banks. Mexico has bad guys, Colombia has bad guys, but the U.S. banks are not bad guys? That's beautiful. The men from U.S. law enforcement think the bad guys are across the border. This is a big mistake. The drug question now has a simple answer: this is a crime. It is dangerous to the international community. The big business is in the U.S. It goes: I have coke, you have dollars, let's trade. The level of understanding of this question in the U.S. is like that of a child. It is a problem of the penetration of the drug money into U.S. politics and the economy. In Mexico the corruption is in the streets and we fight it. In the U.S., everyone is like a child. Well, Yanqui, go home, fucking gringos, that's what Latinos say. This is stupid. The drug business is being protected by a kind of narco-nationalism.

"It's a nightmare. The new role of the drug organizations is very frightening for your country and my country. They are too big. The criminal enterprises contaminate the industrial and the speculative economies. And they penetrate the legitimate economy in the U.S."

El Búho has been talking for hours and yet he is full of energy. The pen register he gave me yesterday is a solid artifact testifying to his frustration. For eight years, he says, the U.S. knew about Abrego and did nothing. Abrego would come and go in the U.S. unmolested—a fact I have verified from DEA. "This is very, very strange," El Búho notes. "Abrego comes and goes between the U.S. and Mexico like a butterfly or a beautiful bird. After '89, he is a fugitive from U.S. justice and yet they knew all about him—just look at the 1993 pen register. Meanwhile, Juan García Abrego is in Chicago drinking coffee and investing money in the U.S. The big people in U.S. law enforcement are like blind people. It is not simply a question of bribery."

Dust blows across Juárez, then the wind dies and the winter deaths begin, the people sleeping in shacks with gas heaters who die from carbon monoxide poisoning in their sleep. It comes with the weather, comes every year, and is hardly noticed. Bruno Jordan's grave is harsh in winter, the grass dry and brown, the air cool, the sounds not of life but of machines grunting over the bridge linking two nations. I stop by from time to time.

Carlos Salinas lives in Ireland, which lacks an extradition treaty with Mexico. Salinas himself travels. He pops up in the Caribbean and does lunch with former President Bush.[58] He stays at times in Cuba, rendezvous with his siblings at various island resorts.

Sometimes I drive to downtown El Paso and park and walk over and stare at the bank DEA claims Amado Carrillo owns. Or at a Mexican airport, I will watch a jet land from the airline he is reputed to own. Or I stay at hotels in Mexico where he is said to be the secret owner. Once I stay at such a hotel in Mexico City, stare out from the rooftop bar at a huge towering bank owned by the drug cartels. The U.S. embassy is a short walk away.

During his time at the helm of the Mexican drug wars, El Búho focused on the big fish of the moment, Juan García Abrego, but now he realizes that Carrillo was of course even then lurking in the background. He kind of sighs about overlooking Carrillo.

"I hope," he intones, "the civil society will respond to the drug world because the drug world is destroying their communities. The government has to react because what is happening is against the intelligence of the American people. They must stop the criminal invasion of their economy."

I ask El Búho about the November 1994 meeting, he says yes, yes, but you must note the earlier meeting. In June 1994 Carrillo called a meeting of all the top capos in Puerto Morales, Oaxaca, and created what the gringos now call the Federation, that loose assemblage of thugs that commit to certain rules and divisions of territory and the spoils in the interest of better business. The second meeting called by Carrillo in Cuernavaca in November of 1994 is clearly a follow-up meeting.

We wander back into the fabled deal cut by de la Madrid with the narcotraficantes in order to bail out the Mexican economy after its collapse under López Portillo in 1982.

"De la Madrid," El Búho says, "took the drug money for his country. Salinas took the drug money for himself."

Neither of the targets of El Búho's anger have ever been charged. Carlos Salinas has always denied any criminal activity, as has former president De la Madrid.

We touch on a former in-law of the Jordan family and El Búho instantly knows who he is. He says he is a middle-level money launderer and by this he means he handles big sums but he is not a capo. He worked for Carrillo and Abrego. Earlier when he was in Customs in Matamoros and on that section of the border, he ran contraband for Raúl Salinas, Sr.

Then he pauses and offers, "It's a dirty world. I'm sorry."

"The shit," El Búho suddenly roars, "is not only in Mexico, the shit is in the U.S. too. We need respect from the U.S. We need, both of us, for the shit to be in the light. If you don't clean the shit, you eat the shit."

In one Juárez warehouse sits a small part of the fleet. An armored-plated yellow Corvette. A bulletproof dump truck with slits for firing machine guns. A black pickup truck decked out with gold-plated door handles and a system for creating clouds of smoke, or tossing out nails, or oozing oil slicks when pursued. This is a small part of the fleet in just one city.[59]

Amado Carrillo is rumored to visit classic car shows in the United States from time to time.

Sometimes he comes home to his village in Sinaloa. Then steers are slaughtered, bands hired, and the party roars for two or three days. He likes to hand out gifts on those occasions to the locals—farm equipment, money, sometimes pigs.[60]

Back in 1992, he built the two-story church.

Guadalupe García, a resident, says, "He's a good man, not at all like you say he is. If it weren't for him, we wouldn't have our church."

Over one weekend in November 1996, Carrillo is reported to fly in twenty tons of coke from Colombia to Mexico.[61]

The general is esteemed, and in December 1996 he is made the drug czar of Mexico. For six years, General Jesús Gutiérrez Rebollo has commanded the army in charge of Guadalajara and the surrounding region—this despite the custom of having military commanders only pull two years of duty in any one zone. Guadalajara is of course a drug center for Mexico—in 1990 alone there were ninety executions—and the general served while Cardinal Juan Jesús Posadas Ocampo was murdered at the airport, while Hector Palma was arrested, and while many other drug businessmen were seized, all of them, as it happened, competitors of the Juárez cartel. But the general has a clean reputation and has worked with DEA on cases. He tends to ferociously pursue the Tijuana cartel. He ignores Amado Carrillo's operation. By January 1997, he is being feted by Washington and U.S. drug czar Barry McCaffrey calls him "an honest man and a no-nonsense field commander."[62]

There is the matter of shadows. In the house on Frutas Street, Antonio often stays up late watching a movie. His wife, Beatrice, will go to bed on the other side of the house. She will awaken and see a shadow moving in the room. At first, when this happens, she thought it was her husband entering. But she got up and found him at the other end of the house. Then she understood. It was Bruno coming to her.

In early January 1997, Amado Carrillo is in Sinaloa for his sister's wedding. The guests arrive in three Learjets—many of them are members of the federal police. President Zedillo of Mexico has recently fired his top law enforcement official and appointed a new one. The United States is making rumbles of punishing Mexico if it does not do something about the drug business. The wedding is raided by three hundred soldiers of the Mexican army, troops commanded by General

Rebollo, and the new attorney general of Mexico says, "This is a big step forward, we are attacking the country's top cartel." Twenty-five or twenty-seven people are arrested and charged with misdemeanors. At least half of them are cops. Three Learjets are said to be seized. Amado Carrillo escapes, according to official reports. DEA announces it has made twenty-eight investigations of Amado Carrillo to date. The Mexican press reports that three thousand police are now searching for Amado Carrillo in Sinaloa. An American expert on the Mexican drug business says of the raid, "He probably will not be too happy about that. We'll see who dies."[63] The *New York Times* account offers: "He [Carrillo] was arrested and released in 1989, but since then news of his whereabouts has rarely surfaced."[64] Several days later, the press reports that no one arrested at the party was connected to the Juárez cartel, no jet planes were seized, and that Amado Carrillo escaped because of a "timely warning."[65] On that same January day in Tijuana, the top prosecutor for that area had 120 rounds from four AK-47s pumped into his body. Then his killers ran over his body several times with a car. He becomes the eighth Mexican official connected to drug enforcement slaughtered in Tijuana in the past year.[66]

The U.S. government offers the Mexican military help in tracking Carrillo, who is referred to in the files as Pedro. They consider satellite observation of Carrillo's residence, of his children's school, and so forth.[67]

Very expensive cars with dark, bulletproof windows wheel in and out of Amado Carrillo's estate in Cuernavaca. People who manage to get as far as the front door are greeted by men wearing cowboy boots and dark glasses and lots of flashy jewelry. These facts are published in the Mexican press a few days after the thwarted raid on the wedding in Sinaloa. The National Institute for the Combat of Drugs [INCD], confronted with these reports, made a simple response: "we cannot accept or deny the report."

At one point, before he became the man in charge of the drug war, General Rebollo was considered for the governorship of Morelos, the state where Amado Carrillo lived on his estate outside Cuernavaca.[68]

•　　•　　•

Amado Carrillo is in Cuba with his wife and a daughter. Or so the Mexican press later reports. He is said to have a bank account of $10 million for trips. Besides Cuba, he is said to be in Argentina, Chile, Costa Rica, Brazil, Turkey, Ecuador, Europe, and Russia.[69]

General Rebollo, meanwhile, in some reports, meets with five other generals and Eduardo González Quirarte of the Juárez cartel. An offer is made of $60 million for some peace of mind, with $6 million on the table as a good-faith gesture. Conversations also take place between Carrillo and the general over his bribe schedule.[70] Carrillo offers a deal: he will end the violence and "act like a businessman, not like a criminal." He will keep half his fortune and give up half in exchange for having the government leave him and his family alone. Some accounts say there were three meetings: two in December, and one on January 14. Notes from the meetings have a humdrum sound: "A.C. does intend to surrender. A.C. wants to negotiate with the government, make a pact."

He also offers to not peddle drugs in Mexico, but rather sell them in the United States and Europe. To help crush other drug dealers. And to invest his money in Mexico. The notes conclude, "If the pact is not accepted, he will take his offer, with its 'benefits,' to another country."[71]

Some accounts have the offer being made directly to President Zedillo in a letter.

About the same time, Carrillo allegedly tells an associate that he can't really leave the drug business because "it's the only thing I know how to do. And besides, the people who steal money from Mexico and take it out of the country to send it to Switzerland are more disgraceful than I am. Apart from not selling a single gram here in Mexico, whatever comes my way, I keep here. I bring my money here to stimulate the economy. In the same planes that I send [the drugs] comes back the money."[72]

On January 7, 1997, a twenty-three-year-old photographer for a Juárez daily snaps photographs in a wealthy enclave of that city. He comes from a very poor family with a half dozen brothers and sisters and an ailing mother. Amado Carrillo, who does not exist, is said to own five or six houses in the neighborhood, including the one Ross Perot stared at from the EPIC parking lot, including the one I stared at in a government aerial photograph. The photographer vanishes that day on his assignment to get images of lovely houses. He disappears within two or three days of the Mexican government's raid or nonraid on the wedding of Amado Carrillo's sister or non-sister. Several days later, the photographer's family reports him missing to the Juárez police, and then after about a week, the local press complains to the governor of Chihuahua, who in turn assigns four cops to the case. Then after ten days, the photographer magically appears. He gives two stories to the authorities. In one he was kidnapped and beaten. Then, perhaps sensing this story is not popular, he offers them another version: that he sold all his photographic gear and took a nice vacation on the beach in Sinaloa.

In early February 1997, the Mexican government announces that it has discovered that drug czar Rebollo is really on the payroll of Amado Carrillo. His apartment, it turns out, is a gift from Carrillo, the very same apartment Carrillo was living in at the time of his near escape from assassination at a Mexico City restaurant in November 1993. Eduardo Quirarte had handed over the keys to Rebollo. The general is arrested and hustled off to prison. Within a year, ten key witnesses against him, some under the protection of Mexico's attorney general, either die or vanish.[73]

I fly south and go to Mexico City while the general enjoys his first days of imprisonment. The capital flutters with talk of scandal. Carrillo has mansions in Mexico City. There is the fine rancho in nearby Morelos. There are other places. I have seen photographs. And maps carefully prepared by DEA.

The American embassy on La Reforma has the look of a fort with big wire screens shielding it from the street, the fangs of concrete posts blocking car bombers, and Mexican guards.

I walk a block or two from the embassy and stare at the apartment of Heidi Slauquet, the woman who vanished at the Juárez airport. She survived World War II as a Dutch refugee in the smugglers' enclave of

Andorra, wound up in Mexico in the mid-1960s as the lover of famous bullfighters and politicians. After the massacre of the students in October of 1968, Heidi was jailed. The police frightened her. She was blond, sweet, funny, and lived day by day. Her goal was to meet significant people, not get mixed up in politics or dark thoughts. She came to Juárez in the 1980s where she was the pretty face of the drug cartel and then, in November 1995, she disappeared on the way to Juárez International Airport and became an incident. When I look up to the third-floor window of her former Mexico City flat all I see is a glass wall and a forest of potted plants. Across the street is a native arts store that was a front for a prostitution ring that was part of Heidi's ventures.

I continue to stay four blocks away in a hotel owned by a drug cartel. I walk a few blocks from the apartment and drink in a fine new hotel also owned by a drug cartel. Inside is soft jazz, cool marble.

I meet with a reporter in a fine restaurant in Texcoco. He is one of the key investigative reporters in Mexico, a man with the searing column, the evening radio program, the constantly ringing telephone. He tells me Amado Carrillo is now buying up army units. Not just the commanders, entire units, and regiment by regiment forging his own army. In this work, he is duplicating his purchase of the police in the 1980s and early 1990s. Carrillo is a big a topic this week because the drug czar of Mexico has been revealed as his employee. The czar himself, a general, has disappeared from sight. The government has announced that he has been hospitalized, since he suffered a "physical alteration." Outside the window of the fine café, guards with walkie-talkies constantly patrol. The windows themselves are stoutly barred.

I go to Tepito, the traditional thieves' market of Mexico City. There is a large glass-enclosed shrine to the Virgin of Guadalupe in the Casa Blanca, a tenement just off Tepito. It is a sensitive piece of ground because the American anthropologist Oscar Lewis spun a book out of its poverty that educated Mexicans hated. He called the book *The Children of Sánchez*. Corridos roll across the dirty air from the radios of the apartments and laundry wilts on the lines off the balconies. A nearby tower has a black paint message, "Guns N' Roses."

I find Luis, who in Lewis's book goes by the name of Manuel. He is old now and his father is dead. He has worked in the States but has always come back to Tepito. He has a small stall but almost nothing to sell. He tells me things are very bad. We go into his small unit in Casa Blanca. He says that Tepito is controlled and then he leans forward and whispers the name, Salinas. He says it softly even though we are in the privacy of his tiny apartment. Luis sketches out the history of the Salinas family's hold on Tepito, a history going back to the father, Raúl Salinas, Sr. The conduits for contraband are the border states under the family's power, Nuevo León and Tamaulipas. The story sounds like a fable as Luis softly intones it. The Salinas family has denied such allegations.

Outside, when I leave, the city roars around me. Later, I will learn through sources that while I putter around Mexico City and drink and walk the markets, there is a contract out on me. Of course, I never really learn much about this contract. Maybe it never existed at all.

DEA circulates a secret report on Carrillo in April 1997. He is born in October 1950. Or he is born December 17, 1954. Or December 17, 1955. He is called Juan Carlos Barron Ortiz, Amado Carrillo Fuentes, Armando Carrillo Fuentes, Amado Carrillo, El Cuatro, Cero Cuatro (Zero Four), Alfonso Paredes, José Luis Patino, El Niño de Oro (the Child of Gold), or El Señor de los Cielos (the Lord of the Skies). He is five foot ten, or six feet, he weighs 180 pounds, has brown hair and hazel eyes. Lately, he is not seen around Juárez much, the report notes, nor are his key people. Since the arrest of Juan García Abrego in January 1996, he has swallowed much of his operation. Sorting out his family is not easy and DEA is not always certain if someone is a brother or a cousin.

After the murder of the cardinal in 1993, Carrillo hid both Chapo Guzmán and Hector Palma, two leading drug figures, at his place in Juárez. The report lists numerous other acts over the years to forge alliances. Carrillo is said to own a Juárez racehorse, one named Silence.

He goes home to visit his mother Christmas, New Year's Day, and Mother's Day. He arrives by helicopter.

•   •   •

In late April 1997, Mexico decides to improve its anti-drug force by junking it and starting over. Over a thousand new officers will be hired after being screened for drug use and given polygraphs. The move is possibly motivated by the visit in a few days of President Bill Clinton. Also, another new agency, the Organized Crime Unit, is announced. Two of this newly minted agents almost immediately disappear. They are eventually found dead in the trunk of a car in Mexico City. They had been pursuing Amado Carrillo, officials say.[74]

Amado Carrillo is in Chile from March through June, according to some reports. He enters through Argentina on March 3 using the name Juan Antonio Arriaga Rangel. Eduardo González Quirarte is with him. So is Carrillo's wife, Sonia Barragan Pérez, his three young children, a twenty-year-old son by another woman, and various associates. Also, a big businessman from northern Mexico, Manuel Bitar Tafich. For money, Carrillo draws on his accounts at Citibank. He buys or rents a dozen mansions and ranches, snaps up eleven new cars, he sets up a money-laundering mechanism through Bitar Tafich, Hercules Ltd. Also he applies through Bitar Tafich for permission to run a construction—real estate business. He also buys people— allegedly including Chile's former ambassador to Great Britain. Carrillo impresses his servants at the various mansions. He is described as like "the heroes in old Mexican movies . . . with a big mustache, very good-natured."

Once the power fails in his rented house. He and his family immediately hit the floor while his bodyguards move into defensive positions. A maid notices that the family sleeps a lot. On Mother's Day, Carrillo throws a party for his wife complete with mariachis.

When he leaves on June 6, he allegedly goes to Cuba, where he has a two-year-old daughter by a woman named Marta. There he lives in an exclusive enclave for guests of the government.[75]

They never decide exactly when he dies, sometime on July 3 or 4, 1997. Or how. Or if it is actually him. Or who killed him. Or if anyone killed him.

He checks into a maternity hospital in Mexico City, one he is said to own, and uses the name of a cop in Sinaloa. He is the only patient or the only patient on his floor. He is to have plastic surgery and lipo-suction. They suck three and a half gallons of fat out of him. The operation takes nine or ten hours and later a sedative kills him. Or he dies on the table in a surgical theater with the doctors and his pis-toleros. U.S. agencies get prints off the corpse and they match ones from border-crossing documents in the mid-1980s. The attorney general's office in Mexico City hesitates in supporting any positive identification. His mother says simply that he died of a heart attack in Mexico City.

When Amado Carrillo dies, he is facing only a misdemeanor weapons charge in Mexico. His drug business, much like his life, might as well never have happened.

The body at first goes home to Sinaloa, then is hijacked by the attorney general's office and returned to Mexico City for more study. The press is allowed to photograph it, the face a mess from crude stitches such as no plastic surgeon would ever make. DEA suddenly reveals that Carrillo has been in Russia the previous winter, had brought his children back from school in Switzerland just a month ago. Other reports have him in Chile, or Cuba. DEA also argues the surgery was part of a desperate attempt to escape their pressure by altering his appearance. This is puzzling since DEA was not certain what Amado Carrillo looked like when alive. One DEA official says, "As we say in DEA, I would bet my badge to say it is him." The official refuses to give his name. A Mexican radio and news host recalls that he had a phone conversation in April with a man claiming to be Amado Carrillo. The man said, "I just want to ask you to say, when you see the news of my death, that I wasn't killed by anyone. The only person who can kill Amado Carrillo is Amado Carrillo."[76]

In Sinaloa they make ready. Bushes are pruned, tents set up for hundreds of guests. And men polish the marble on the chapel where Amado Carrillo's father and his brother, Cipriano, are buried. Eight-foot-tall wreaths line the walls. Relatives keep vigil over the silver cof-fin and eat posole. The Reverend Benjamin Olivas gives the funeral service. He tells the audience, "Who can be a judge if not only God?" Then he turns to the mother and continues, "Let her love not be changed by what the entire world says."

His mother, Aurora, wears black and a lot of heavy gold jewelry.

About 1,200 people attend, mainly locals. Two hundred of the guests arrive very late and appear to be deliberately dressing down.

Outside the house in Sinaloa, a cage holds deer, peacocks, geese, and a wild boar. One of Carrillo's sisters says, "As a family we love him and adore him. He always put us first." Another adds, "Mom always said that somewhere out there, God will take care of him."[77]

One local priest, Carrillo's confessor, adds, "He would ask me for advice. We don't only follow saints. I wasn't going to turn my back on him. I once told him, 'This is not right.' He told me, 'Father, I can't retire. I have to keep going. I have to support thousands of families.'"[78]

He is forty-one years old. Or some other age. He is alive and being protected by U.S. drug agents as he lives out his days on a Caribbean sanctuary. Or so Mexicans think.

A Tijuana newspaper says his successor will be Eduardo González Quirarte, the contact used by Carrillo for his dealings with General Rebollo. U.S. officials now peg Carrillo's fortune at $25 billion and think he smuggled four times as much coke as anyone else.[79]

Irma Ibarra Naveja is stunning, a former beauty queen. She is said to have been the mistress of General Jesús Gutiérrez Rebollo. She is worried about something. In May 1997 she writes and dates a note that says, "If something happens to me, I want to leave testimony that I accuse Eduardo González Quirarte . . . given that I have received constant threats." In her note, she says she learned of Quirarte's drug activities and reported them to the general. The general in turn told Quirarte what she had said. She is gunned down at a red light in Guadalajara on July 29, 1997. The killers ride a white motorcycle and pump 9mm rounds into her chest, head, and neck. Two days earlier she had been named in military documents made public as the key conduit between major drug figures and military brass.

Other links between the military and Carrillo begin to die. His jeweler and sometime accountant, Tomás Colsa McGregor, is arrested shortly after his employer's death. Or he is simply dragged from his home. He handled bribes to military officers. U.S. law enforcement personnel are allowed to talk to him. Colsa also says that Carrillo was annoyed by the constant demands for money he was getting from the governor of Chihuahua.[80] Then something goes wrong. Colsa turns up bound, gagged, tortured. And dead. Or does not turn up at all. It depends upon whom one believes.[81]

Press reports, based on secret Mexican military files, surface stating that Amado Carrillo had contact with the governors of Campeche, Quintana Roo, Sonora, Yucatán, Morelos, and Chihuahua.[82]

Quirarte, a key aide to Amado Carrillo, vanishes.[83]

The songs so long held back by the presence of Amado Carrillo now begin to come. For months, he has had a fleeting existence in the nation's tabloids for the poor where the omnipotent Lord of the Skies kept triumphing over mere governments and men. Dead, he can finally be a song in the cantinas and on the radios. A corrido appears suddenly that explains it is hard to say goodbye, but not to worry because "the mail is leaving on time."

Inside the agencies—DEA and U.S. Customs—a quiet revolt builds. For years, any effort to trace the link between the Mexican drug industry and the Mexican government has been shut down by U.S. officials. So in 1997, Operation White Tiger is secretly launched. The name comes from the penchant of Jorge Hank Rhon of Tijuana for illegally acquiring Siberian white tigers. The target of the probe is the Hank family and their billion-dollar fortune and their deep ties to all the presidents of Mexico since the 1970s. The operation reveals endless connections to cartels and to straight businesses. The Zaragosa family in Juárez, the same family Phil's sister Virginia was involved with, shows up. As does Amado Carrillo, Juan Abrego of the Gulf cartel, the Tijuana cartel, U.S. banks, and on and on. But like all secret operations, this one leaks.

One U.S agent tries to put the effort in perspective: "It would be like the Mexicans having tried to indict LBJ or Nelson Rockefeller, or both at the same time, and keeping it from us."

The operation is shut down. But the files are shared with the National Drug Intelligence Center, a federal dope think tank, and it cobbles together a report on the Hanks that paints them as a major criminal threat to the United States. This report is finally leaked to the American press in 1999 and briefly noted.

When the Hank family protests both the leak of the report and all of its allegations through its mouthpiece, former Republican U.S. Senator Warren Rudman, he gets results. Rudman at the time is a member of the president's Foreign Intelligence Advisory Board. Janet Reno, the attorney general of the United States, retracts the report by issuing a statement: "The analysis and any conclusions and inferences contained in the report have not been adopted as official views and positions of the NDIC, the Department of Justice, or the various federal, state and local law-enforcement and regulatory authorities that may have provided information to the drafters of the report."[84]

A small magazine in California, El Andar, prints material from the report. The Hank family through the agency of one of its U.S. banks threatens a $10 million libel suit against the publication. A college professor in Ohio, Donald Schulz, reads a copy of the report's summary and is slapped with a suit, even though he never publishes a word about it.[85]

On August 3, two well-dressed men enter the Max Fim restaurant in Juárez. They start firing at the table of Alfonso Corral Olaguez, said to be a member of the Juárez cartel. He dies along with five others, one the head of the guards at the local prison. The contract killers, sicarios, leave after spraying about a hundred rounds.[86] For the first time, people in Juárez start to think that Amado Carrillo might really be dead since he preferred to kill discreetly and dispose of bodies secretly.

Silvestre Reyes, the congressman representing El Paso, announces that former U.S. soldiers are now working for the Juárez cartel. For years, Reyes ran the Border Patrol in the El Paso sector. The former Green Berets are said by some U.S. intelligence sources to be earning up to a half million dollars a year. They are especially prized for their skills in communications and for detecting bugs. But they also help out in teaching firearms, explosives, and the benefits of night-vision goggles. Also, they help in breaking secret police and military codes. The U.S. government denies Reyes's claim.[87]

On August 22, four doctors are found strangled, the bodies dumped next to a peace park in Juárez. They are suspected of having treated a patient of a drug shooting some hours earlier. In all, August sees about twenty executions.

It is the third annual mass for Bruno and I am restless in the hard pew. The priest speaks in Spanish and his voice is certain. The regular church could not be used because of a celebration. The regular priest could not come for the same reason.

Most of the immediate family sits two pews in front of me—Beatrice and Antonio are erect and alert. The daughters, Virginia, still a beauty, and then Christina, hobbled by her arthritis. To the back the grandson, Sean, sits with his wife, and up by the altar is Tony, who has flown in from Las Vegas for his brother's memorial mass. Fifty or sixty people gather in the old church for what would have been Lionel Bruno Jordan's birthday. This is the third time we have gathered because Bruno Jordan died in a carjacking one cool El Paso night.

Finally the priest ends for a while and Tony walks to the pulpit. He unfolds a piece of paper from his pocket, brown paper irregularly shaped, something torn from a grocery bag. And begins to read. He says, "You leaving this earth as a person of living flesh marked the end of one journey and the beginning of another. As a bigger universe was unveiled, you learned all there is to know and to understand about what happened to you. To forgive those who are to blame for your death and to help those who are suffering because of it and without relentless doubt, you embraced that bright light onto the waiting arms of God, your first step into eternal life. Time at that point was forever suspended, and time was no longer your predator. You are where the sun never sets, where the wind is no longer cold, where peace of heart, soul, and mind are one. You are our future."

Then he gets to the meat of his message. "When this terrible thing happened to you," Tony tells the congregation and his dead brother, "I had no future. My life was engulfed with an instant dose of violence, hate, distrust, and an overwhelming sense of revenge. I could not think straight and I know at that point you asked our Lord to step in and show me that there is a future, and that revenge only gets in the way of the future."

Tony starts to sing and the song swells from the center of Tony's chest, floods out and sweeps across the church and soon the people in the pews begin to disappear beneath the waves of sound, the priest goes under, then the altar, Christ, everything and there is nothing but the sound of music pouring out of Tony as he stands rigidly in his black suit.

Outside the afternoon light is still brilliant as we gather on the sidewalk and trade embraces and make small talk. Tony works his way through the crowd of relatives and then he is in front of me and gives me an abrazo.

Hey, Tony and Sean are saying, come with us, come on out to the cemetery before we all go to the house, come and have a drink with Bruno. And I say yes, of course, yes, yes. Maybe it will stop the whirring in my mind. That first year I came to the mass, right afterward Phil and Tony disappeared and later they told me they stopped by the grave and drank beer with Bruno. That is when it started. So, of course, into the truck, down the old streets, past the house in the barrio, the house nestled amid warehouses and cheap cafés and little stores and all the signs in Spanish, on a ways under the bridge leading into Juárez, and then a left into the old burying ground, a cemetery almost complete and the family felt very lucky to nab a grave for Bruno—"so he could stay close to home." I park, walk over the humpy ground of the graves, and then comes the stone with a photograph of Bruno smiling, an oval image in color beaming out into the fading light as dusk comes down. A balloon emblazoned with the Washington Redskins logo floats above the headstone, a child's drawing for Uncle Bruno— the work of Tony's son—is taped to the cold stone. A dozen or more people stand around the grave with twelve-packs under their arms, sipping beer, talking, laughing, and from time to time pouring a little out on the grassy mound for Bruno.

As we slowly break up our party, someone turns his head and says calmly over his shoulder, "Hey, Bruno, see you back at the house."

The smell is of tamales and frijoles and chicken and enchiladas, as people fill the rooms and spill out into the front porch, the lawn, and then the street itself back at the house. I grab a beer, a plate of food, eat and talk and laugh. Antonio embraces me, and then Beatrice.

Virginia smiles, Sean whirls past, the noise buffets the walls. The television screen is on and Antonio has plopped a cassette into the VCR, the video of a cut from Sean's latest album. Suddenly a black guy is standing on a wall in the sun bopping to the music, look, there's Sean cruising with a bunch of dudes, Tony's voice booms on the sound-track, Antonio looks at the collage of images blurring on the screen and smiles in quiet contentment.

I walk out in front of the house and there is Tony standing and smiling with his old high school yearbook. He points to a full-page photo of the class beauty and says, "That was my first wife." And then he turns to another page and fingers a small picture of a guy a class or two behind him.

His finger points to the thumbnail photograph of the guy he remembers from his high school days, Eddie González Quirarte. He looks up at me and says, "See. That's him."

"The same guy?" I ask.

"Absolutely."

Eddie González went to the same high school as Tony and Virginia and Christina and Phil. And Bruno. He was really nothing back then, Tony remembers, just some guy, you know, not sports, not anything, a face in the hall. He always spent a lot of time in Juárez, he remembers that he liked to party, you know, in Juárez. And then Tony and every-one else left high school and found a life and suddenly it is the late 1980s, and my God a lot of water has gone under the bridge. Tony's the kingpin at the nightclub, the Costa Brava, and one night ol' Eddie González comes in with some guys and he's sitting at the table and hassling guys at the other table, good customers you know, so Tony throws his fucking ass out of the joint and that's that.

Then, Tony's in El Paso back for a visit and pops over to Juárez to play a round of golf. He'd heard from friends that Eddie was into the chips, "money, reaaaaaaaaaaal money," they said and he sees him out on the links and walks up to him and says a few words, just small talk.

Then there is the matter of negotiations in December of 1996 and January of 1997 when Eduardo González Quirarte approaches the drug czar of Mexico and offers $60 million for some peace and quiet and gives a message for the president of Mexico: leave us alone, or we will leave Mexico to writhe in bankruptcy. Or it is the spring of 1997 and Eddie González is in Chile with Amado Carrillo buying houses wholesale, and buying government protection and staking out a new base of operations. Or it is the summer of 1997 and a former beauty queen is at a red light in Guadalajara when she is blown apart and a few days later that note surfaces that reads: "I want to leave a testimony that if anything happens to me without a motive, I blame Eduardo González Quirarte because I have received persistent threats."[88] Or it is the day of Bruno's birthday mass and we stand out in front of the family home with beers and the yearbook and this gawky-looking nobody is rumored to be a main contender to take over the Juárez cartel and the billions that pour into its treasury each year.[89]

Drug czar Barry McCaffrey has his visit to El Paso somewhat altered in late August 1997 when U.S. intelligence discovers a missile may be used to kill him. The cartels are known to have various weapons including rocket-propelled grenade launchers.[90]

The drug czar also offers his take on the recent spate of murders in Juárez: "Some of these incidents are brutal and stupid and don't appear to contribute to a business-oriented, cold approach." Two days later, three more are gunned down at a fashionable Juárez restaurant, Geronimo's. The shooters, after firing 150 rounds, leave in a limousine. The mayor of Juárez goes on El Paso television to assure viewers that neither he nor the governor of Chihuahua works with drug traffickers. He adds, "This is something you cannot say about many mayors or governors in Mexico."[91]

• • •

In September a plane is seized in Mexico with 130 pounds of cocaine. It is a government airplane carrying nineteen pilots. They work for the Mexican attorney general's office in drug enforcement as part of the Special Aerial Interdiction Team.[92] They had been trained in the United States to read sophisticated radar so that they could track drug planes, all this as part of an $8 million U.S. program to enhance the Mexican drug effort. Days before their arrest, the attorney general had said that there was "not one iota of corruption" at the highest levels of his office. So far this year, 161 Mexican agents and detectives in the attorney general's office have been busted for bribes and other drug-related matters.[93] The attorney general tries a new tack and fires all of the agency's 2,300 cops and prosecutors and demands they take a polygraph to be rehired. Three out of four fail the test.[94]

Later in September General Rebollo appears before a judge in prison. He notes that President Zedillo's family and that of his wife were being investigated by him, when he was drug czar, for suspicious ties to drug people, among them Eduardo Quirarte. A day after making these statements, the general is threatened with the possibility of more charges being piled onto his indictment.[95]

Evidence comes up that suggests that President Zedillo's closest aide, José Liebano Saénz, lives in a house given by the Juárez cartel, and brokered a pact with Carrillo and other cartel figures for $60 million, a price that would ensure peace with the president.[96]

The general's attorney is one Tomás Arturo González Velázquez. He knows the general well, having been part of his operation when he was based in Guadalajara. He argues that the general is really the victim of a power fight in the military between generals who favor the Tijuana cartel and those officers who favor the Juárez cartel. He also insists that President Zedillo's brother-in-law is a big peddler of methamphetamines. Zedillo and his relatives have consistently denied such allegations.

González is a friend of Eduardo González Quirarte. He is eventually murdered by someone witnesses say had the bearing of a soldier or policeman. González was waiting at a red light.[97]

In Juárez, Sergio Roldan, thirty-five, represents Rafael Muñoz Talavera, the brains behind the huge Sylmar, California, cocaine operation exposed in 1989, and one of the pretenders to leadership of the Juárez cartel. Muñoz, during his Mexican incarceration after the DEA raid at Sylmar, had a cell equipped with a bar. But then, Mexico has five hundred judges and magistrates authorized to issue wiretaps and yet only one of this number is even trusted by the new Mexican anti-drug force. Roldan's office is in an old part of Juárez and is very nice. Roldan is executed in October 1997 as he strolls to his office.[98]

In Mexico, the pace quickens in one way. The CIA responds by hurling another two hundred agents and analysts into Mexico to get a fair share of the action.[99]

In early October, the Mexican government shuts down two hospitals in Juárez, the same places where the four doctors murdered in August had worked. It turns out the hospitals were owned by the Juárez cartel. On the documents, the owner is listed as Manuel Bitar Tafich, the same man who allegedly helped Carrillo set up business fronts in Chile in the spring of 1997. The Mexican attorney general's office suspects Bitar Tafich is the accountant for the cartel.

Eight other chunks of prime real estate are pounced on by the state at the same moment.[100]

On Monday, November 3, 1997, two barrels sit by the roadside of the highway from Mexico City to Acapulco. Inside are bodies encased in cement. The hands and feet are tied, the mouths gagged. Two had cables wrapped around their necks, a third had been shot. There are also signs of burning, beating, and nails yanked out. Two of the men in the barrels were doctors who had operated on Amado Carrillo in July in Mexico City at the time of his alleged death. Five days earlier, warrants had been issued for them by the Mexican government. There had been scattered reports about the doctors, that they had gone into hiding, or that they had gone about their business. One of the doctors is identified by his brother solely by the dental prosthesis he wore.[101]

One DEA agent in the U.S. gets a phone call from the newly made widow of one of doctors who operated on Carrillo.

She asks, "Why did they kill my husband? He did what they asked."
He can offer no answer to her question. And he does not ask her
who "they" might be.

In Juárez things continue apace. The state government issues a list
of one hundred people who have disappeared in the first ten months of
1997. Eight Americans are also missing. The police in Juárez are
alleged to have told an investigator that "the desert around Ciudad
Juárez is a vast cemetery."[102]

Marc Perron, Canada's ambassador to Mexico, causes a stir when he
tells a Mexican reporter that political life in Mexico is a "joke" and a
"barbarity." He includes in this joke the American War on Drugs. "I
think the pressure," he says, "on Mexico from the United States is just a
game that the American government uses for political ends, and serves
to hide a much blacker reality in that country [the United States]."[103]

One of the doctors, Pedro Rincón, flees with his family to the
United States on a U.S. government jet. Then he disappears into the
web of U.S. intelligence through the witness protection program. The
government says he really has nothing to say except that Amado
Carrillo died accidentally in surgery due to complications from hepati-
tis. Another doctor, Carlos Avila, is also in the United States but the
government implies it has not kept track of him.[104]

The killing rolls on for months and then spills into the new year. It is a
war for control of the Juárez cartel now that Amado Carrillo has apparently dropped out of the picture. By the time it winds down, sixty people have been executed in Juárez. But it is a war largely ignored by the
rest of the world and so the dead file dutifully to their graves like little
items on a to-do list. On Saturday night, January 10, eight people are
kidnapped in Juárez and one person is found Sunday morning, the
body tied up, gagged, and tortured. Five men had been kidnapped and
executed on December 28. Then on Tuesday, January 13, the federales
in Juárez revealed that this kidnapping talk was overblown since they
had located six of the people, who it turns out were in custody. On
January 19, a federale subcomandante is executed in Juárez. He takes
at least fifty-one rounds, ten of them in the skull, his killers shouting,

"This is to teach you to keep your word." On January 20, the governor of Chihuahua announces that the people behind all the killings in Juárez are known and arrests were being planned. A day later another federale takes six rounds in the head in southern Chihuahua. On January 26, two bodies are found in barrels just west of Juárez, one a man, one a woman. They had been beaten and the woman had cocaine stashed in her purse and bra. A coroner disputes that lime was tossed in the barrels to decompose the bodies. He says it was simply a gesture to cut down on bad odors. On the twenty-ninth, two more die in Juárez shootouts, one a cop. A local newspaper says that a U.S. drug agent believes Amado Carrillo is alive and well and living in Cuba. The mayor of the city takes out a big ad in various Mexico City dailies and beseeches the president to send in the army.[105]

Some Mexican law enforcement people claim that 100,000 people in Juárez work in the drug business. U.S. officials say they don't know. But mainly there is a sense that Carrillo is sorely missed.

George McNenney, a U.S. Customs agent in El Paso, explains, "Amado was an evil genius. He was considered a diplomat within and outside the organization. Everybody won. . . . He believed in a system of give and take, and he believed in negotiations. 'What does it take for you to be loyal?' That seemed to be his philosophy. There was no war. Drugs moved on time. He was amazing, a tremendous organizer."[106]

After the death of Carrillo, his right-hand man, Eduardo González Quirarte, and the man rumored to be the key to hits in the cartel's schemes, well, Quirarte also has this strange shadow life where he exists and does not exist. He is the one person who almost certainly knows what happened to Bruno Jordan because he is the one person who absolutely knew how important Bruno Jordan was to his family and what his murder would do to them and to the eldest son, Phil Jordan.

But Quirarte, a man who has helped move around billions, barely exists in the theater of the drug business. He is not a famous name. In fact, he is hardly a name at all. And yet he continues to pop up even though he is officially wanted for criminal charges in both Mexico and the United States.

On July 21, 1997, a chopper hovers overhead while twenty squad cars from Customs, Border Patrol, the IRS, DEA, and the sheriff's department, plus some dog units, hit the Royal Knights Transportation Company in El Paso. The business is rumored to be connected to drugs. It sits directly behind a business seized in 1994 because of links to Eduardo González Quirarte.[107] Quirarte himself has vanished and no one seems to know his whereabouts.

Eduardo's brother, Rene, is a civil engineer in Guadalajara and he has stayed technically out of his brother's business. When his brother makes the papers as a big drug guy, he is indignant and takes out a full-page ad in the Guadalajara newspapers insisting on Eduardo's innocence and giving his cell phone number should the president of Mexico wish to call him for details. President Zedillo never calls.[108]

A year later, a raid staged by Mexican soldiers and drug agents in Cancún picks up Eddie's trail. The Yucatán has become a drug platform for the Juárez cartel. Boats regularly ply the six hundred miles of water to Colombia and the local beaches have become landing sites for kilos. The raiders look for Eduardo González Quirarte, who has taken up residence in the resort. They fail to find him. He makes the Mexican attorney general's Web site as one of the most wanted men in Mexico.[109]

Quirarte surfaces briefly in 1999. He is partying in Mexico City's fancy Zona Rosa. He runs low on cash and goes to a nearby ATM machine where two men try to mug him. He kills one but takes a round in the head. The two thieves are off-duty cops. Quirarte spends the next three days in a coma in a hospital with no name. His friends track him down and he vanishes.

The thick sweet fumes float in the air when, on January 31, 2000, a scavenger finds a human head behind a chocolate factory in Guadalajara. For two weeks the cops keep the head in a freezer. Then a headless body turns up and they make a match. It is Rene González Quirarte, the brother of Eduardo. Apparently, Rene had drifted into drug deals and shorted some Colombians. When he did not pay up, they cut his head off. For a while, Rene had contemplated fleeing to Argentina, where his brother along with Amado Carrillo had bought up thousands of acres plus hotels and houses in 1997 when they were plotting out possible refuges. Rene did not leave soon enough.

The police in Guadalajara are rumored to be keeping Rene's body under heavy guard in hopes that Eduardo will try to steal it. Armed troops also keep this vigil. But the ploy fails. After the decapitation in Guadalajara, Eduardo González Quirarte disappears from view.

In the spring of 2001, the new government of Mexico, the one that has finally toppled the ruling party and run on a promise of revealing the truth about the past, begins to have second thoughts. Can Mexico be governed, some in the leadership begin to ask, if an endless stream of cops, generals, politicians, and businessmen are dragged into court? One member of the defeated PRI explains the problem simply: "It's a problem of political realism."[110]

A report surfaces of a meeting that took place January 26–28 in northern Mexico at Apodaca, on the edge of Monterrey. Apodaca is a center for Mexican smugglers, a place businessmen favor for meetings, and where residents can be trusted to keep their mouths shut. Men in suits and cowboy boots arrived in private jets, at least sixty in all. One of the men was supposedly on a kind of peculiar furlough from Mexico's highest-security prison, the same facility where Raúl Salinas, Jr., was incarcerated. For three days they dined and talked and decided several matters. There must be a joint strategy for moving drugs through Mexico and peddling them in the United States. They must pool their money to bribe Mexican officials. Two Mexican generals in attendance endorsed this new pool for payment. They must also stop killing each other, though they did agree to increase violence if they must to destabilize the Mexican government. The group grew quite friendly as the meeting progressed and swapped informants, bribe schedules, and the names of corrupt officials. And like all groups of merchants they agreed on one final point: to have more meetings in the future.

The newly installed government of Mexico denied that the meeting took place. Others said that this meeting took place in the back room of a restaurant as the leaders sat along a large wooden table and dined on steak, roasted goat, and carne seca soup. Every major cartel was represented except for the Arrellano-Félix clan in Tijuana. The two generals in attendance were said to be representatives of the attorney general's office. Colombians also attended as consultants.

Jorge Chabat, a drug expert in Mexico City at the Center for Investigation of Economic Development, knew nothing of the meeting. But he did offer that "this seems like a normal process to me. This occurs in all legal businesses and there's no reason it shouldn't in the illegal ones, too."

DEA refused to comment.[111]

The dreamtime ends with the murder of Cardinal Posadas Ocampo in May 1993. Or with the Zapatista revolt on December 31, 1993. Or the murder of presidential candidate Luis Donaldo Colosio in March 1994. Or it ends with the murder of José Francisco Ruiz Massieu in September 1994. Or with the collapse of the peso and the Mexican economy in December 1994. Or the murder of Bruno Jordan on January 20, 1995. Or the arrest of Raúl Salinas in February of 1995. Or with the flight of Carlos Salinas in March of 1995. Or the death of Amado Carrillo in July of 1997.

Or maybe the dreamtime never ends, just purrs along unnoticed and unremarked. That is part of the nature of dreams, the hesitation in recognizing them and then, if they are recognized, the widely varying explanations of them. In the late 1990s, General Augusto Pinochet, the dictator of Chile from 1973 until 1990, suffers the embarrassment of arrest in Britain. Then it comes to light that the general has over $1 million in a bank account in Washington, D.C. This is serious thrift for a man whose yearly salary as commander of the Chilean army was $16,000. Still, the general is a legend, a man who ruled with total power, asserting in 1981, "Not a leaf moves in Chile if I don't move it—let that be clear." What becomes clear is that Chile through its secret police was moving billions of dollars worth of cocaine into Europe in the mid-1980s. A former U.S. marine and CIA operative was the crucial element in this work. Eventually, Pinochet is released by the British for alleged human rights violations. He is said to be in poor health and returns to safety in Chile. The entire episode, the tales of billion-dollar cocaine shipments, disappear.[112]

The dreamtime has this core characteristic: that Mexico is on the march toward modernity, that there may be missteps, stumbles, digressions, and the like, but the path is clear and unmistakable. The economy is growing, the government is, well, changing.

Celia Reyes's little peso account, the one she stuffed in an account in 1988 and ignored by the bank, it purrs along also through these years. The banks collapse after the peso devaluation in December 1994, and still the little account purrs along. Then the government of Mexico pours $100 billion into the banking system to save it and assumes a huge number of the outstanding debts. The little account by the woman living on $109 a month, it just sits there in the bank growing.

Finally, there comes a day in April 1999 when a tally is made, and the money, maybe $24,000 in 1988 when President Carlos Salinas became president, back before all the murders and revolts, before NAFTA and the rise of the cartels to new heights fueled by the money of cocaine, back before the hyperinflation, well, this little sum is worth, with the compounded interest, $46 billion. The entire banking system only has reserves of $38.16 billion, not enough to pay off this one little debt. Cecila Reyes's lawyers enter into negotiations to maybe take over a half million in housing loans as payment. But the negotiations are very costly. The meter keeps running and by the summer of 2001, Mrs. Reyes's claim has risen to $2.3 trillion and keeps rising thanks to being compounded monthly.[113]

That is the nature of dreamtime, a place where even the hard numbers of accounting and ledgers become the thing of fable. If Amado Carrillo can run a criminal empire without obvious precedent in the history of the planet and still remain faceless and virtually unknown, who is to question Mrs. Reyes's bank account. In the lurch toward modernism that is Mexico, a feat of legerdemain that has been going on since the late nineteenth century, fantastic things become almost the norm. And the best way to deal with these unseemly eruptions of incident, finance, and death is to insist they do not exist. Or do not matter.

In dreamtime, anything is possible.

The corrido about Amado Carrillo explains that his work is not over, that the police are not part of his destiny. In fact, his destiny is not really over because his work of delivering things has no end.

> *I have made no will*
> *And the mail is still leaving on time.*

fantasma

bets

He drives in the night. The store comes up on his right, he can see the sign clearly, feel the warm, beckoning glow of the lights, but he is not going to do that, no, not this time. He is on the phone, trying to explain and yet at the same time struggling to deal with this tug, trying to put it into words and yet barely able to speak as he cradles the phone, keeps his eye on the road, sees the sign and the store coming up, fights the urge to pull over, and keeps rolling on.

He knows he needs help, and now, for the first time, he can almost say it out loud. It is December and Christmas is coming but the season is empty for him. The house is empty. The marriage is dead. The children are no longer children and they are gone and he senses they do not respect him.

He keeps talking over the phone, he says, "But you know, in my head I think: this could be the one." He is alone and he knows this is the dangerous time for him, when he is alone in the car and can just pull over. He will do it once, twice, three times, he loses count, he will do it often during the day. Still, he has a hard time admitting that he has a problem. He thinks, he is not like the others he has read about: the true addicts. He doesn't go to the places they go. He is different.

I have known what has been eating at him for a long time but I have said nothing. When we came out of a restaurant that time, and I was about to get in my truck and he said, hey, I'm in a jam, could you help me out? We went to an ATM and he stood there in the rain as I worked the machine and gave him $600. I let it pass.

Now his voice is anxious over the phone, another place is coming up, the lights are on, he could pull over. He is alone, all alone, this is

315

the hard time, the temptation. We keep talking, the phone goes in and out, but we wait out any interference and keep talking. He knows when it started almost to the minute: January 26, 1995, in the late afternoon.

He talks until he finally pulls into the driveway of his home, the solid brick building on that shady curved street in Plano, Texas. The house has a pitched roof that hints of a château origin, the big living room with fireplace, the dining room, the sunroom off the kitchen, the long kitchen with a big kitchen table, the family room and the little room off it with a bar. The laundry room and down a long corridor three bedrooms and three bathrooms. This is the basic house where the family is safe and kids can play in the street.

Now he is safe.

Phil Jordan has made it back to his empty house.

There are stories that come and go and no one speaks much of these stories. Here is one: He spent the night drinking in Juárez, which is something twenty-seven-year-old men like to do. Mario Alberto Valenzuela Arreola had U.S. citizenship but worked in Juárez selling used cars. He was with two friends on that night of September 25, 1994. All three vanished. Mario's Thunderbird turned up abandoned a few days later.

His sister says he was a good guy but maybe all of his friends were not good. His brother says, "We've tried to pretend that he's been on vacation so that we don't have to think of him as disappeared."[1]

A man drinking with two friends, he would feel safe.

The gray sky offers the first rain in months and the dry ground yearns. Floresville, Texas, lies about thirty-five miles south of San Antonio and is home to about six thousand people, a little over half of them are Mexican-Americans. Fields of peanuts cradle the town and a big statue of a peanut rests on the courthouse lawn.

The White House Cafe and Saloon has been tending to local thirst and hunger for 120 years. The streets around the ancient courthouse are clotted with stores saying Legacy, Recycled Memories, Heritage House, Twice Is Nice, and of course, the Promised Land Gift Shop.

Down at the White House, Rudy Sánchez, a Korean War vet, grills steaks from local beef and sausages stuffed by local butchers. After Korea, he returned with a bazooka and three live shells, went down to the river with a buddy, fired one round, and, Jesus, the fish jumped and the sound was something awful. "Not like," he notes, "when we did it over there."

Now, he's a city councilman. LBJ, John Connally, George W. Bush, you name them, all came to the White House and bellied up to the ancient bar to press the flesh.

Rudy leans forward on the table, looks across with clear eyes, and speaks to this guy sitting there, a man of thirty-seven, married, living for a spell in Floresville, and says to him in a very calm voice, "I've gone through many terrible things and the only thing that has got me through is my belief in God, in a higher power."

The young guy nods. He's fresh from mass this weekday morning. Earlier in the evening, the guy had been a kind of live wire, the voice bopping here and there like a set of snare drums, the sentences studded with "hey, bro," or "dude," the face flashing grins, the eyes friendly at a glance but on a second take cop eyes.

The younger guy is running out of time. He is Federal Criminal Case No. L-00-132. He now feels the tick-tock of every second, the glory of each dawn, the sweat of every night tossing in that bed. He hasn't slept solid for months. He's drinking scotch, and this thirst chases him now after each and every sunset. And yet the booze doesn't seem to work anymore. He's been slamming down shots for four or five hours and it's all been a waste, he's still stone-cold sober.

"You know what I think?" Rudy Sánchez continues. "I think you were more or less like a robot. You were trained to talk and act the way you did."

The younger guy says nothing. The stars shine through the budding live oak in the patio, and hang low enough so that a hand can reach right up and pluck one.

The young guy taps out a number on the phone, speaks softly for a moment as he tells the wife, who is over at her parents', that everything is fine, asks how she is doing because she just got back from the hospital and is wrestling with the pain from the surgery, says, he's okay, be home in just a little bit, don't worry.

After the arrest and the charges, he'd moved in with his in-laws. He was broke, unemployable, and for a while, wearing an electronic anklet. This one night, he'd been eating up a storm, and God, he knew better but the food was all so good, and what can you do? His mother-in-law is such a fine cook, and the judge, his father-in-law, is so rock solid and good to him, and so he just made a pig of himself, just couldn't help it, you know? So he wakes up in the night, the wife is sound asleep by his side, and his guts are just roiling, the cramps, the waves passing through him. He slips out of bed, quiet like, and paddles down the hall to the other bathroom, because he knows, he can feel it in his guts. He walks lightly so no one will notice or be bothered. And he's just settled on the toilet when the alarm starts blaring from the monitor his father-in-law keeps right by his bed. He looks down at the electronic anklet the federal prosecutors have attached to him, and thinks: I'm on a short leash. It's a loud alarm, a sound that cuts through doors, walls, and any prayer of sleep and suddenly the lights go on in the house, the doors fly open, and the judge is shouting, where's Sal? and his mother-in-law is crying out, where's Sal? and now his wife is awake and feels the empty place in the bed by her side, and she's up looking for Sal. The electronic anklet is set so fine, so exactly at one hundred feet, that Sal realizes he can't even roam everywhere within the walls of the home. Sal calls, "Hey, it's okay, I'm right here, right here, don't worry." That is the moment—not the arrest, not the terrible stories in newspapers across the country, not even the shackles, the nights in jail, none of those really did it—that gave him a taste of what he had done and what he'd become.

He's looking at eighty-seven months in the federal joint. He's pled guilty to that matter of arranging a contract to having Miguel Angel Flores killed. He is Salvador Michael Martínez, the cousin of Phil Jordan and of the late Bruno Jordan.

Jordan finally focuses on what he can do: he can solve the crime if he has enough money to pay for detectives. He can become his own agency. He can be a good son, a good father, a good husband. And finally, he can be a good brother. All it takes is money, once he clearly understands the problem. And the problem is simple, a murder at a K-Mart at 7:00 P.M. on January 20, 1995. Someone drove the killer into the lot. Find that person. Someone disposed of the truck and gun after the killing. Find that person. Someone is keeping Miguel Angel Flores from speaking. Find that person. It all gets concrete once you see it this way and then, the only barrier to an answer is money to finance the investigation. Round-the-clock detectives, perhaps some snitches in Juárez. Who knows?

When he thinks, he sees his mother and father and their grief and his brother and sisters and their impatience. He is the oldest son, the cop. Fix it. And sometimes when he cannot block it out, he sees his grandfather. His grandfather's brother was murdered. And his grandfather fixed it.

He cannot quite block it out, his grandfather's voice, then his face, the eyes are the hardest part because his grandfather always saw things clearly.

Jordan keeps these moments largely to himself. He'll say nothing. Just as he's sat on airplanes for years and no one in the next seat ever knows that he is a narc. He is trained in silence, in keeping what matters to him under wraps.

It is all about luck. He sits there and draws two numbers on a piece of paper: $100,000, $200,000. That is the range, he thinks. With that kind of money, he can fix it, fix everything, the family problems, the bills, and Bruno's death. Right there, those two numbers. He has lucky numbers and he knows them cold. 627 is very lucky because his first son, Sean, was born June 27. 207 is lucky, that was his DEA badge number. 213 is good because his second son, Kenny, was born February 13. And he was born at 127 A.M., so of course 127 is good. But 127 is better than good, 127 is wonderful. All of Phil Jordan's life he has had a feeling about 127, that it is his lucky number. Once he went to the track in El Paso with Bruno and Tony and Phil picked his horses off the numbers 1-2-7 and he won over $800. Just like that. 127, his number.

He knows he can fix this with money. And he must get the money and he must fix it. Or he will break.

• • •

Here is another story: The morning paper explains that in January 1998 Eddie Barragan and Matthew Baca of El Paso stopped in a Juárez bar and were never seen again. When he was in high school in the 1980s, he drove a DeLorean. His sister argues this does not prove he was part of a drug cartel and that she knows nothing but good things about him.[2] *But she's been nervous since the grave sites were announced about ten days ago. She'd like to think the two men are alive and not in a hole in the desert.*

He'd been Phil's little secret, his DEA cousin buried deep in Mexico. Now suddenly Sal Martínez has been in all the papers. Beatrice, Bruno's mother, has made me a plate of tacos, Bruno's father has pressed cold beer on me. The old couple move around their house on Frutas Street like ghosts. They cannot find the words for dealing with this latest thing that has happened. They suggest that it is all some kind of mistake.

Sal shows up more than an hour late. He is a vigorous, solid man, I discover, his black hair flecked with gray. His face is animated, his voice full of life. But he cannot talk. He'd just gotten a phone call from his lawyer in Dallas and a deal is on the table: go to court and the fall could be twenty-five years hard time, take the deal and, with good time, it is seven years and three months. He has forty-eight hours to decide or the deal will go off the table. His lawyer has told him he'll get him a good book on how to survive in prison, one written by another lawyer who had taken a fall.

Sal sits at the end of the table with sun pouring over him from the south window. His chair is pulled back, his arms rest on his knees. He begins to speak, then stops, says he should not talk. Then begins to talk again. He smiles at his aunt and uncle, he tries to laugh, he looks down at the floor again and the sun pours over his face.

He drifts off into his work, how once he would pop right over the bridge into Juárez, go alone in a fancy truck all tricked out, a veritable billboard shouting drug dealer, go over there with long hair, an earring, the whole costume, and hang out in drug bars with the guys, his machine pistol hidden under his shirt, go there alone. Four times he'd faced down AK-47s shoved into his face.

And now they are going to lock him up in a federal prison.

He focuses on the truck, the maroon finish, the felt top, tinted windows. DEA had seized it from a trafficker and Sal had used it as his war wagon during his days of masquerading in Juárez as a heavy dude, hanging out with the vatos and talking shit and picking up those little crumbs of information that give federal agents a contact high. He says he's busted hundreds of guys, some of them guys he'd gone to high school with. But that was business.

They have him cold.

His aunt and uncle move in and out of the room Bruno dreamed of building. It is January and Sal Martínez is almost sweating. His eyes are anxious. Cops are very particular about their eyes, about the belief of all people in the life that cops can be made by their eyes, by the darting, quick looks they take. Not to have cop eyes is essential if you are going to make those deals and bust people. Now Sal Martínez's eyes are beyond his control.

He stands, tells his aunt and uncle he is going to stop by and see Bruno.

The house on the shady side street in Plano is piled high with magazines still fresh in their plastic wrap. He can hardly sell any of them. Except the stroke books, *Genesis, Club,* and the like, for those he can get $3 a copy from mom-and-pop liquor stores. They never age, the month or year does not matter. He has a connection, he can make some money dealing these magazines. He had them in that storage unit, but then he lost the space.

On the refrigerator, there is the newspaper photograph of his daughter Kelly when her high school basketball team played in Europe. And there is a photograph of his son Kenny when he did a hoop tour in Europe also. And there are Brigitte and Sean, his two other children, hugging. And photos of their children, his grandchildren. And there is a photograph of Bruno.

He has kept one clear place, the reclining chair that faces the television with full cable service. The blinds are closed, always, the house looks sleepy-eyed. The chair and the television link him with the world. The phone has caller ID to screen out people.

Right beside his chair he keeps his scrapbooks from DEA on a broken stereo speaker, especially the early years in Phoenix when he was making bones and chasing Pedro Pérez Aviles, the godfather of all the cartels and all the cartel leaders. He'll flip them open sometimes and there he is. It is February 27, 1973, and one guy stands to the left, a Mexican soldier with an automatic rifle crouches down below, and to the right is Phil Jordan in a trench coat holding a twelve-gauge pump. Behind all three figures is a mountain of burlap sacks, ten tons of marijuana taken down in San Luis, Sonora.

Or he sits in his backyard. He has buckets out to gather rainwater for a palm tree that once belonged to Bruno, a memento he brought back from El Paso after the murder. The palm has died.

He is not sure of the amounts. He is puzzled by this, not being sure of the amounts. He has trained himself to keep things in compartments, in little boxes. But the boxes, while secret, are not supposed to be empty.

He has never been drunk in his life, not once. So why is it so hard to remember the amounts?

There is a moment that stands clear in his memory: he drives to the El Paso airport the day after Bruno's funeral in January 1995 and suddenly pulls over at a 7-Eleven mart and plays six birth dates—his wife's, his four children's, and his own. Before Bruno's murder playing the state lottery was his one entertainment. The games ran six days a week and he dropped maybe $100 a week buying tickets. He told himself that he did not drink or smoke or do much of anything but work so this hundred bucks was his allowance for pleasure. But this day, as he wheels into the 7-Eleven on his way home to Dallas after the funeral, he can feel a change in his play. He knows something has been altered within him. Then, this sensation passes and he simply buys some tickets in a convenience store, loses, and continues on to the airport and his flight.

By the spring of 1995, Phil Jordan is playing $140, maybe $150 a week on the lottery. He tells himself, "I am not a gambler. I never go to casinos, I've hardly ever played the horses. Besides, I'm having results, especially with the birth dates of my two daughters."

When he wins, he throws the money at his household bills. When he wins with his wife's birth date, why then he'll give her maybe $500. Of course, when he wins, he always holds out some money for future bets, but then, that is simply plowing more money back into the business.

He is a rational man, having rational pleasures. He has taken out bank loans for $20,000 to $25,000 to finance his hired investigators who look into Bruno's murder. He tells the wife none of this, he intercepts the bank statements before she sees them. He will replace the money, pay down the debt with winnings.

He tells himself that "I'm not superstitious. But I do believe in God, in the saints, and in Catholicism. Whether I practice my faith or not. My grandfather told me never, never give up the Church."

Sometimes, he wins. But he never seems to gain on his debt, on that bank loan for his failed investigation of his brother's murder. Still, he keeps the debt from his wife. He retires in January 1996, takes a fat pension, and gets a consulting job based on his career and lifetime connections. His credit rating is excellent. He owes maybe $99,000 on the house in Plano, and his other debts on cars and stuff might run $75,000. He's got $15,000 in savings. He'll be okay. Especially if he just gets one decent score at the lottery.

"Now I need to explain what happened, explain it to me," Sal blurts out. "And I don't know how to do it. Before I had regular forms and outlines to fill in and file, agency case reports, a system of order."

I ask, "Does your wife feel betrayed by you? Does she feel she married this man and now this man is a stranger?"

He falls silent and then after a while, he says, "You should ask her that."

The stories seem not to stop: he hears a voice, that's what happens. Alfonso Magaña Chávez is in his late thirties when he hears a young guy calling and he goes out of his house to talk to the guy over the fence. It is November 10, 1994, and Magaña is a comandante with the federales. Then, nobody sees him again.

• • •

The marriage is cold. Phil Jordan knows this fact but he cannot give up. He has never recovered from the failure of his first marriage, from being an absentee father to Brigitte and Sean. Not that he regrets his career, he lives for his work. But still, he has this guilt and so in this second marriage with two more children, he is determined to keep things together and raise up the kids. Debbie, his wife, struggles with this fact. She is devoted to the children but not to the marriage and she scornfully tells people she is Phil's trophy wife.

Early 1997, Debbie finds one of the bank statements in the mail. She realizes her husband has buried them in a secret debt. A failure of trust, she tells him. He has no response.

The children are off to college and they live there under the same roof in legal separation. There is not enough money for one of them to move out.

Sal has a brother and two sisters, and when he is a child the family lives in the lower valley of El Paso near the oil refinery.

The father works driving a government bus full of workers to White Sands Missile Range just north of El Paso in New Mexico. He also cuts meat, a traditional skill in the Martínez clan. In El Paso, relatives market their own brand of pork skins. The father is often gone during the week and leaves his wife a simple instruction: tell the children I will deal with any failures in their conduct when I return. Sal's mother tends her brood and her church, holds down a job also, and so the family thrives. He is the quiet boy, sometimes prone to stuttering, the kid who seldom says anything and stands on the edge of things. His mother never spanks him, not once.

The thing that sticks in his mind is Sunday and Sunday is always blue. His dad and older brother would be off for softball, and Sal just didn't like being in the park while the men played and drank beer. His mother and sisters would be off to visit her people. He'd be home alone, left with his chess board, and that made Sunday something to dread, made it the blue day when even the smallness of his normal El Paso closed in yet more and seemed to choke him. His body becomes rigid as he remembers those Sundays.

Though he is not large at 165 pounds, he excels at football and in high school makes all-city as defensive halfback. His life is odd jobs and football. He is spooked by women and does not have a girlfriend until the last month of his senior year. In his studies, he has a knack for math, scores very high on the SATs, and his high school counselor points him toward a career in accounting. Sal looks into that field and learns that accountants have a very high suicide rate. He decides to study criminal justice. He hangs out with buddies, has a few beers after the big game but never touches marijuana, not even when he goes to those heavy metal concerts.

His grades are good and he gets into college at Sam Houston in Richland. But after a year of odd jobs and a full class load, he is sinking financially and returns home to attend the University of Texas at El Paso, sometimes called Taco Tech. He washes dishes, bags groceries, buses tables, and graduates in law enforcement in May of 1984. He has a degree and no job and so he continues bagging groceries.

One day he helps a lady to her car and she gives him a 10 cent tip. He's working in his own neighborhood and he realizes there is no money and the tip is all the woman can spare and this is going to be it, degree or no degree, unless he does something. By January 1985, he has offers from military intelligence, the El Paso police department, and the Texas highway patrol. He speaks Spanish, he fulfills quotas in the era of minority recruitment, and he's got those grades. The highway patrol academy lasts eighteen weeks. They instantly cut his hair off and Sal loves every minute of the training. There are about 120 in his class but only eighty-four make the cut and get the badge and the gun.

By the summer of 1985, Sal Martínez is a trooper with the big hat, the Magnum on his hip, and his own new turf, Floresville. He is the law for a town of six thousand and he relishes entering cafés and having everyone fall silent as he walks past.

He is twenty-two years old, out cruising in his squad car, and there is an accident, busted metal, broken glass, people reeling with injuries, blood streaming, and Sal rolls up and gets out of the car with that big hat and he takes control, he calms the panic, gives the orders, has the power. And this sense of control, this force flowing from him, gives him self-confidence for the first time in his life. He thinks: I can do this. He is the man.

He accepts a transfer to El Paso because he has friends working for the big DEA intelligence center there, EPIC. After two years he jumps to U.S. Customs—better pay, better pension, and best of all they teach him how to fly a plane. He flies along the border for eight or nine months looking for smugglers and then, suddenly, his ticket is punched. DEA wants him and he starts at $36,000 a year in May 1991.

Their academy lasts thirteen weeks. He grows comfortable with a machine gun at his shoulder. They teach him various scenarios for a life underground, a rich background in role playing. He takes to this part of the work.

Law enforcement feeds off snitches and cops generally lean on informants to make their cases. DEA often raises this game to a different level. They become the informant. They go into the room and walk the walk and talk the talk and the talk is bad shit talk. They live the life, the hair long, that earring, the clothes, the tricked-out pickup, the stance. And this can last an hour, or a day, or weeks. Don't tell the wife, don't discuss it with friends. Everyone armed, talking that shit, the rich border Spanish studded with English words, a language almost choking on slang, talking bad, dirty, talking big, making the deal, being a heavy guy, and drinking, so much drinking but somehow staying alert. Angling for the buy, the money on the table, the dope right there, angling for that moment of trust and this trust has grown like a weed, been nurtured for hours, days, weeks, months, been handled tenderly so that the forbidden ground of budding friendship is reached and then when it is kickback time, when everyone feels safe, then the betrayal, the gun at the head, the handcuffs, the ride to jail and long mandatory sentences falling down and sending everyone away for decades until they cannot even remember their youth, can barely recall that time when they trusted and relaxed.

He's good at this jive. He loves making buys, talking up the dude, going to the deal, then taking the motherfucker down. Once, God he smiles at the memory, once he did a twelve-ounce heroin deal in four minutes flat from the first hello to the cuffs.

Then comes the next step, across the river and into Mexico. Move this south, move it just a little ways across that bridge into Juárez and suddenly there is no real backup, the Mexican cops working with DEA, well, everyone knows they are on the pad to the cartel. And the room is electric now, there is no call to make, no place to run, now the acting had better be good, be better than good, be the performance of a lifetime, this is the place where people disappear all the time, hundreds of people, poof! gone just like that, vanished into vapor. Or bodies turn up, their hands and ankles tied, holes in their heads, signs of attention dancing on the bodies, marks where an ice pick has been shoved in again and again, shoved in deep to the bone, a custom called bone tickling. Or the genitals have been severed and shoved into the mouth. Or a vat of acid has devoured all the flesh. Or a dose of milk, quicklime, has been dolloped on the hide. Or the body has been tossed onto a stack of mesquite and burned like a roast. Or the grave has been dug and the person tossed in alive. Or the body is left on a public street, hands and ankles tied, bullets in the brain, and graced with a bow of yellow ribbon, a gift to the authorities from the people who despise the authorities.

Sal Martínez loves this part of the work, loves the culture of DEA. The rush flooding him from pretending, from being in control, from being the only one who really knows what is going on.

Once Sal finds a warehouse stuffed with ten tons or more of cocaine. He watches it, sees the trucks roar in and out, and finally calls in his Mexican counterparts in Juárez. They say, ah, yes, we will put it under surveillance. So Sal goes back to El Paso leaving the Mexican drug cops in charge. He calls the next day and asks when they are going to hit the warehouse. They say be patient, we are getting everything in place. He gets the same response the next day and the day after that. Finally, the Mexicans are ready to move and they hit the joint. It is empty. Not even a scrap of paper. It has been vacuumed. All the glass from the windows has been removed lest any fingerprints be left behind.

He marries Suzie, the girl he met back in Floresville when he was a green state trooper. She's got a degree in political science, her dad is a respected man in the community, eventually becoming the local justice of the peace. And now Sal is in DEA, a kick-ass organization.

He stumbles into things where he does not belong and he learns to leave such things alone. There is the guy who goes down hard and gets serious time in the States. He decides to talk to Sal. He tells him of a trip he made in '94 at the time of a Mexican presidential election, drove a Suburban for Amado Carrillo, a vehicle with armed guards riding before and after it on the road, drove all the way to near Mexico City. The Suburban allegedly held millions. DEA decides not look into the matter.

There is no way to talk about this stuff at home. Or with friends. The business is complete, a finished thing humming along on money, gore, murder, and dope. The bodies come and go, the loads get taken down now and then, the big money flashes and then vanishes.

DEA needs Mexican-Americans because they know Spanish and can physically pass in the drug business. And DEA does not trust Mexican-Americans for precisely the same reasons. Once the then agency head, Thomas Constantine, hits the El Paso office on a flying visit, gives a spiel, and then asks if there are any questions. Sal is the only one to speak and he wants to know when they're going to get more agents that can cross the bridge and blend into Juárez for the deals. Constantine says that's why we're hiring Mexican-Americans and this simple answer burns Sal because he can't stomach the notion that his only merit is his color and background.

He decides to try skydiving, just like that, in the spring of 1997. The thought frightens him but he senses that anything as simple and clear as stepping out of an airplane into thin air might straighten out his head. The plane drops him near the line, just north of the border, a little west of El Paso, and at first he hears a roar from the air streaming past him as he falls, and then, he pops the chute and there is this sudden silence, a peace floods his body as he drifts down to the brown earth below, Mexico just a mile or two away, the world shut down without a murmur or a cry or a gunshot or a shout, a world of tranquillity, and just before he slams into the earth, he hits that thin skin of life that wraps the planet and scent fills the air. The dive fixes him, he thinks, flushes the poison out and clears his mind.

He stands on the ground after the jump and suddenly believes that he will be okay, that if God wanted him He would have taken him during the dive. He can face his work again, he's been spared for some reason.

In August 1997, Sal is offered a transfer to Monterrey, Mexico. Carrillo is dead. Bruno would have been thirty. The world is moving on. After the jump, he has no hesitation and he goes for the transfer because Mexico is the big show in DEA. He must go for three years but there is that salary boost fattened with danger pay. Plus, now he gets free housing and a cost-of-living bonus and all this amounts to a 25 percent raise. Monterrey will be his next step up the ladder.

He and Debbie go to a marriage counselor in 1997. There is this chart on the wall about compulsive gambling and as Phil Jordan reads the signs, he feels uncomfortable. But still, he does not really feel it. He's playing $200 a week, and the bills keep piling up. His business ventures since leaving DEA have gone sour and he now has more loans outstanding that financed those ventures. But in his head, he thinks he can pull out of this temporary financial pocket. For a while, he cuts back on his play.

But then it creeps up again. One big score will solve everything: the case, the marriage, the bills. He is simply one number away from a solution. In late 1997, he takes a trip to El Paso and all day this one number burns into his brain: 481. His daughter, Kelly, was born in April 1981. So he plays it and he wins $15,000, enough to pay back most of one bank loan he made for the investigation. But by now, the debts have grown. Still, it is a beginning, and a sign that things can be turned around. He just has to have the right number.

In 1998, his sister Virginia has a dream. Bruno comes to her and tells her to play two numbers: 835 and 746. She tells Phil. So he adds them to the birth dates he is playing. And of course, he does not cut back on his betting, this is hardly the time to do that when he is so behind in payments. He's got to win and solve the case and save his marriage and pay the debts.

He tells himself, "I have to bring justice before my parents pass away."

• • •

In early 1998, U.S. Customs agents are deep into a money-laundering investigation of Mexican cartel players. They have already washed $60 million for drug merchants as a way of getting entrée into this hidden financial world. Apparently, the drug merchants are impressed by the undercover agents. Early in this probe, a voice claiming to be Amado Carrillo calls them on the phone. At one meeting, the drug merchants show up with sixteen federales acting as bodyguards. At another meeting, a man says he is from the Mexican attorney general's office and has simply dropped by to pick up $1.7 million in cash, a sum that includes $415,000 from Amado Carrillo. The drug merchants explain that Carrillo faked his death in 1997. They come with a new laundry order: $1.5 billion. They say the money must be cleansed for the general who heads Mexico's Ministry of Defense. The drug representatives are worried at times about the money, since, they explain, some of the take belongs to the president of Mexico, Ernesto Zedillo. The CIA denies that the general is in league with the drug business, as does the Mexican government. Within weeks of this offer, the Clinton administration shuts down the investigation, once called Operation Casablanca. The probe is decried by the secretary of state, Madeleine Albright, and by the U.S. drug czar, General Barry McCaffrey. The Mexican government also denounces the probe. In the end, a herd of Mexican bankers are arrested at a sting meeting in Nevada. Though they have funneled money through numerous U.S. banks, none of the cooperating U.S. financial institutions are charged or held culpable for moving drug money. It is assumed that they did not know who their clients really were.[3]

During his five years as head of the DEA in the Clinton administration, Thomas Constantine is never asked to brief the president. He never receives a single phone call from the president. He has one regret about the Mexican drug merchants: "We underestimated their importance."[4]

Sal lived off the rush. He told himself, "Doing undercover, arresting people who were making millions of dollars in an illicit activity, and knowing I was making a dent in the organization, all that made me feel good."

He helps in busts in Monterrey. He is in the police station. The suspects are silent. The Mexican cops put plastic bags over their heads and they begin to suffocate. Or they beat them. Or they shoot soda water laced with pepper up their noses. Or they put their heads in a toilet clogged with shit and piss. Or sometimes, the Mexican cops say, hey, Sal, how about making a beer run? And off Sal goes and when he comes back, the suspects have confessed to everything and Sal knows better than to ask what persuaded them.

He thinks, "I could see getting killed in my line of work, but to see a guy like Bruno who sold suits for a living, and he was such a nice guy and he wasn't confrontational, he wouldn't even fight when we were kids, he'd have handed over the keys to that kid, and to have him killed over a pickup truck, that's where my deepest anger is."

He still has a black sport coat Bruno sold him and sometimes he wears it and then he thinks of Bruno.

Phil Jordan can't believe it. Slowly but surely, he raises the reward offer for any information leading to a conviction in the murder of Bruno Jordan. He calls in favors from men in Dallas, men whom he has helped in the past. Finally, he has pledges of $100,000. The phone never rings. Not a single call comes in with a tip. Nothing.

The stories look so small in the newspapers, as if they never happened at all: he took the phone call and then left his supper on the table, told the wife he had to meet someone. Raúl Alarcón Sánchez is thirty-three, and he owns a hardware store in Juárez. He'd done a little time for moving drugs but now he's got a good business. His mother still hopes he is alive. He left supper on the table May 3, 1995.

The heating system never really works. Two years and constant calls to repairmen and still they are always cold in the winter. Nothing works. Mexico, Sal discovers, is fucked up. The poverty, the begging. He's living in a two-story, four-bedroom house with marble floors. The woman comes and scrubs it top to bottom. Sal gives her fifteen bucks for busting her ass all day. And when he tells people what he paid the woman—the Americans in the federal community in Monterrey, the rich Mexicans who are his neighbors—they jump on him, they say, what are you doing paying a cleaning woman that much? You will spoil them.

He gets to know a local guy and the guy hasn't got any money and is sick with diabetes. Eventually, they cut his leg off. And there is no care, nothing. What is this place? He lives amid the rich but they want nothing to do with Americans. His neighbors only speak to him to ask favors. Can you get me these papers? We want to take the maid with us to the States, can you arrange her visa?

He can't believe it. First, he has to face the fact that Miguel Angel Flores, a thirteen-year-old kid, would rather do time than take his deal of freedom, be reunited with his family, and given sanctuary in the United States. But in his head, Phil Jordan is sure the kid will crack in prison, and start talking. But he does not. He brags to his fellow juvenile inmates about his connections to la familia Carrillo in Juárez, but he gives up really nothing. This little kid does his time, goes to the prison school, learns English, prospers.

And then he wins that appeal. And then in October 1998, there is a new trial and the whole case comes back to life. His parents, Phil, and Virginia go down there each day and sit in a row and watch that jury. They are confident as the witnesses tell their tales—as Israel Reyes recounts following Bruno into the parking lot and seeing Miguel Angel kill him at close range—that the verdict will be guilty. Justice will be done.

The jury, though, cannot decide and is hung at ten for conviction and two for acquittal.

A new trial is ordered for May 1999.

In Monterrey, DEA works out of the consulate and four agents handle four Mexican states in the north. Work means the office, a stack of folders, a flow of information with no time to pursue it or really think about it. Sal has his own office and he pretty much stays in there shuffling papers. He hates the work. He feeds a string of confidential sources, people who have been investigated, photographed, fingerprinted, and get paid regularly. Plus a herd of other snitches (SOIs) who are not checked out and get paid too. As part of the constant effort to placate the American government, the Mexicans keep inventing new drug task forces that will be incorruptible and stand up to Yanqui standards. The latest incarnation in this effort is FEADS (Fiscalía Especializada para la Atención de Delitos contra La Salud), a group of federal cops created in 1997, recruited and trained to be untouchables. The Mexican government, however, pays them only $200 a month and then drags them north to the border far from their families. So DEA regularly gives them money for information. Sal is the contact with about twenty guys in the local unit and four times a year he shovels them $20,000 or $25,000 to divvy up among themselves. And he thinks what the hell is this? This is the new, clean drug force and our policy is to regularly bribe them for some information?

The Mexican cops work until eight, nine, ten at night and then Sal gets together with them to pick up some tidbits and suddenly it is three or four in the morning. One club has three separate stages, with three different brands of music wailing. Another has the women tending the bar working on a kind of platform so that when they serve a drink, man, they have to really bend over and bam! tits right in the face. Nothing in these places is cheap and the crowd is rich businessmen, drug guys, Mexican cops, and Sal, all living life in a bubble of music and tits and high-class booze.

Suzie and Sal must talk in code because they both know the phones are tapped. Once Suzie notices three guys watching their house and she calls Sal at work and says, "There are three birds on the wire," and Sal can't figure out what in the hell she is trying to say and so they go back and forth over the phone talking in a code that even they can't decode. They never use the Internet. There is a computer in the house, but Sal and Suzie don't connect it. Somebody can read that stuff. And in the backyard, two big German shepherds. Always keep an eye on the rearview mirror also.

Chat it up with Mexican cops as they boast of their girlfriends, or toss pics in front of you of the latest bodies hacked, stabbed, or shot.

That face before it sinks below the shit and piss in a toilet bowl. Sit at the desk, booze through the night, everyone with their hand out—he wonders, what in the hell has he signed on for?

There is one other task, an SOI, Comandante Jaime Yañez of the Coahuila state police. He is a dark guy with a big beer gut and he's been selling information to everyone—dope guys, DEA, FBI, CIA—for years and years. Nobody in the office likes dealing with him so they dump him on the new guy, Sal. The guy drops by Sal's office, talks some shit, offers a few crumbs. And DEA needs him because Yañez has this one thing he can do, run plates through the Mexican computers and find out who the hell that car belonged to. For this DEA forks over a grand or two a month and for this Sal stays cordial and friendly with the comandante. So they bullshit together regularly, starting in August 1997 when Sal arrives in Monterrey, a thirty-four-year-old agent hot to make some bones.

Beatrice begins to see the blue light. It glows in the corner of the room at the back of the house, the large room with the television and couches right off the kitchen. The color is rich, the light warm. She finds it sometimes in the night and she knows without question that it is her son coming back to her.

Time stops existing in a normal sense for Phil Jordan. He has these tracks running through his mind, these pathways of stories. There is the murder of his brother, the lines of investigation, the case. That is one track. There is his troubled marriage, the children who must be put through college, the wife who is estranged. That is another track. There is his family, his parents in El Paso, his brother and sisters, the children from the first marriage. That is yet one more track, one more set of things to be tended. There is his living, his fees for calling judges or cops and fixing cases for people, these dribs and drabs of money that keep his world functioning. And there is the mountain of debt, God only knows how big this mountain is since Phil Jordan cannot stomach sitting down and doing any kind of tally. If he could arrive at the real number, he senses, he would collapse, break down. And he must not break down because there are these other matters, these tracks, these stories, these people that he must tend to.

He must play. The tickets for sale everywhere, in every store it seems. He can be driving, talking on his cell phone, and at a whim, he can pull over and buy a ticket. He has these numbers, all the birth dates, plus the numbers Bruno brought to Virginia in the dream. He has good numbers, he senses they will come around for him. He will win.

And then, he knows exactly what he will do.

Fix it.

We're riding in the car through the first hints of the Texas spring. The dogwood is blooming and here and there a few signs of bluebonnets. Sal is at the wheel and he says, "I woke up at 3:00 A.M. with the answer. My situation, my decision to pursue the effort, well, it could be because I was desensitized to murder. I saw murder, I had informants who were killed in Juárez. I experienced death in the extreme because I was working the border. A coldness sets in, sets in your mind and your heart and, eventually, it reached my soul. I went to my evil side. It's very easy to cross the line. And I did cross the line. And I crossed the line by letting the Mexican cop do an operation that is illegal in the U.S. But in Mexico anything goes."

The green countryside streams past, the horses graze, the little houses look safe with their neat yards and purple martin houses prim on tall poles, signs warn to watch for deer.

Sal remembers a time he went into Juárez to meet with a comandante. The guy wheels into a parking lot and the side of his vehicle is pockmarked with bullet holes. The comandante is edgy. He's a hard-driving guy, likes coke, regularly hosts orgies. But shit, he'd just been in the gym with his bodyguard and then they come out and bam! a goddamn drive-by rakes his fine four-wheel-drive machine. The comandante shakes his fist in the air, tells Sal he's going to find those fuckers and they will pay for this, goddamn right.

Phil Jordan first thought he would solve the case in one month. Then he told himself it might take six months. Yes, the bills were piling up, but he could do it, everyone was counting on him, he could do it. Six months, fix it. He'd tend to the bills later. He could answer the ghost of his grandfather, tell him that he, Felipe Jordan, had avenged the family and brought justice to his parents.

Then, as time went on, he decided this would take one year. But it would be done. No thirteen-year-old could hold out forever. Something would break in the case.

He had these rich friends in the Dallas area, people he had helped when he was the bureau chief for DEA. He felt sure they would kick in money to help his investigation. But he was wrong. He had left DEA, he was a private citizen, and now they were not interested in his problem, not a bit.

One day he realized something: "I knew I was going up against big money and that if I pledged $500,000 for the reward, Amado Carrillo could always outbid me."

And when Carrillo died, that did not matter either. The thing went on, the tracks in his mind. So did the organization across the river, the cartel, the business. Carrillo's death changed nothing.

A senior Mexican official concluded that of every ten judges in one border city, Tijuana, "eleven of them are on the [cartel's] payroll."[5]

In August 1999, the top drug prosecutor in the Mexican government barely survives an assassination attempt in Mexico City. A few weeks earlier, gunmen mowed down two members of the elite presidential guard near Los Pinos, the residence of the president.[6]

DEA is a warren of snitches and the average agent seems more spooked by co-workers who might snitch him off to internal affairs than by drug guys. But still, sometimes they talk, just to get it out. One tells of the time he and his DEA buddies were riding at night somewhere in L.A., and they pull up to a red light, and he leans out the window with his gun and blows the light away. He tells the other guys in the car, now the light is green. Or another time two agents are riding down a freeway in an unmarked car and some cholo punks come up beside them and give them some kind of sign to go fuck themselves. So the agent in the passenger seat leans out his window and blows the fucking tires off the car full of assholes.

Another DEA agent is talking. They'd trained, worked it all out, he explains, and then gone into Mexico for the killing. It was a hit squad, off the books, but real and they'd gone in to wipe out a whole group of guys and the plan was to just do it, not tell the Mex feds. He wants some record made of this war that goes on silently with no one the wiser.

In May 1999, Miguel Angel Flores is tried again in El Paso. He has the same excellent attorney who did the appeal and the first trial after the appeal. Jordan has learned through informants that money for the attorney is handed to the Mexican consulate in meetings at La Serata, the lavish club Amado Carrillo opened in December 1995. The informants say at least $50,000 has been handed over for the defense of this street kid who once juggled in El Paso on traffic islands for spare change. The attorney denies this.

During the closing arguments, Charlie Roberts, Flores's defense attorney, briefly wanders into this shadow land that cannot be part of the evidence phase of the trial. He says, "We don't have a videotape from God telling us what happened. . . . Let me tell you something, nothing, and I wish it were otherwise, nothing will bring Mr. Jordan back. . . ." Then he marches through the evidence and throws dust in the air about the identifications by eyewitnesses, the violation of the crime scene due to police negligence, the illogic of picking a thirteen-year-old who can't drive, handing him a $1,200 Uzi, and sending him on such a mission, and finally offers with a shrug, "Insane, ladies and gentlemen, absolutely insane. Well, they'll say they're all crazy out there."

For a small moment, he ventures into the ground that everyone has thought about for four years and almost no one has said out loud: "It's almost like an assassination. What's happening here? This is no carjacking. You don't need an Uzi in front of all those people in a parking lot to steal a truck in El Paso."

This time the jury hangs at eleven for acquittal and one for conviction. The county decides not to retry Flores, who is now eighteen years old, and fluent in English. He is deported back to Juárez.

Phil Jordan and his family cannot believe this turn of events.

Besides controlling the source, there is the matter of trust. The rule is simple: never trust anyone.

"Working in law enforcement," Sal Martínez explains, "you see things that most cannot imagine. You develop a cynical view and lose touch with people and their normal lives. You socialize with a small circle of people, the people you work with, and believe they are your friends."[7]

Besides control, besides trust, there is the matter of wanting, of wanting something. Never want something. If you want something, other people can feed your desire. And as they feed you and you consume what they offer, they take control.

Against all this street wisdom of the life there are pressures. And the big pressure is the deal. The drug guys have to make deals. And the agents have to make cases, lots of cases, get those stats up.

"After all," Sal continues with a smile, "I thought that I had accomplished everything I wanted to do in life: loved, career goals accomplished, traveled, lived on the edge of death, owned an original Jeep, and saw Led Zeppelin."

So you are out there and you are alone. You are the secret agent man. You bribe the new, clean force of Mexican narcs to get information. You carry a gun illegally and everyone blinks at this. You watch suspects being tortured. You see the killings, blood pooling by the head, seeping from the neat hole in the skull. You cut corners, you wiretap, monitor intercept stations, booze with Mexican cops, and hang out with narcos in their joints. Get home late, things a blur.

It is an appetite. "I remember," Sal says, "the time that I was assigned a new Ford Mustang pursuit vehicle when I was a trooper in El Paso. I wanted to make the trip from Austin DPS [Department of Public Safety—the highway patrol] headquarters to El Paso as short as possible so I 'broke in' the car by maintaining my speed at 100 miles an hour."

The day Miguel Angel Flores, Bruno Jordan's alleged killer, has his second hung jury in El Paso in May 1999 and the state decides to give up, cut him loose and deport him to Juárez, Sal fields a call from family. He learns the murderer of his cousin will walk free.

Comandante Jaime Yañez is in Sal's office in Monterrey. Sal blurts out, "They let that son of a bitch go, he's over in Juárez. My family's pissed."

The comandante picks up on the anger in Sal's voice. They talk. The comandante says, "Hey, I've got somebody in Juárez who owes me a favor. Want me to call him?"

"Okay."

A few days later, the comandante drops by and says, "My guy is going to check up on the kid."

Sal thinks, shit, I can't even remember the kid's name. He's erased it all like a bad dream.

The comandante grows ever more friendly. Here, a fine leather jacket with the official state police insignia, for you my friend. An official cap also. This stuff goes on all the time in the office, this tossing of little gifts between the agents and their sources and Sal doesn't think much about it. Except the jacket does not even fit him. And the comandante has questions. Sal, what do you want me to do? My guys are waiting.

Small stories flowing quietly: he peddles properties and on August 19, 1996, Richard Pfieffer is going home from a day at the office in Juárez. Three guys take him down in his house and tie him up and leave with him. He's thirty-six and has four daughters. He's got a pregnant girlfriend also, but she kills herself from the strain. Richard hasn't called home yet. His real estate business apparently languishes.

His business as a consultant is a failure and he loses the office. His credit cards, well, he just keeps jacking them up. His marriage, well, his wife is down the hall in that other bedroom. His roommate. They are both trapped by a lack of money.

They are going through the divorce proceedings finally. She has a lawyer. He does not. He thinks, maybe, this will bring her around, maybe, if he does not have a lawyer, does not argue, maybe then she will change her mind and the marriage can be saved. He has to have some kind of victory. This streak has to end.

In September 1999, the divorce goes through. His wife gets, as she is entitled to under the law, a portion of his pension that he accumulated while they were married. Plus, her equity in the house. He takes another bank loan to buy her out of the house. He surrenders the portion of his pension that is hers.

His credit rating is still excellent. His debts are large but they can be paid. Just one number.

The play accelerates.

He will win big. He will put all that money into solving the case. He will pay everyone back he owes. And on top of that, he will build a sports complex, yes, a sports complex in Plano. Kids will go there and learn sound ethics, the regimen of athletes. They will become immune to the lure of drugs thanks to lessons learned on the court. He will show them all.

He makes a change in the numbers he plays. His now ex-wife's birth date is off the list. She is no longer a lucky number.

The summer slides along. Sal is busy with all that busywork in the office. Comandante Yañez keeps calling, dropping by. One day, Sal shows him his new government-issue pistol. A small moment.

Later, when it all falls down it looks this way to Sal: "My mind is saying wait a second, we're talking about taking a life. But my heart is saying, I don't give a rat's ass what happens to this guy. There's my anger toward the kid, Miguel Angel Flores. And someone is pulling me toward my weakness. He is pulling me in like a fish. He's been setting people up for a long time. He is very good."

Toward the end of summer, the pace quickens. Yañez says he needs a photo of the kid for his people so they can be sure they whack the right guy. Sal says, shit, I don't have a photo, the case is well known in Juárez and El Paso, have your people get their own photo.

But then Sal remembers the file of clippings and the video his former partner had made from the television coverage when Bruno was murdered. He finds the thing, pops it into the VCR in his office, and watches on the little television there. He freezes the frame on the kid, a thirteen-year-old boy, small in stature, the look of a young punk caught on tape four years before. He gets out his Polaroid camera, snaps two shots. The first one is pretty bad, he tosses it in his desk. But the second shot is better.

On September 24, 1999, Sal Martínez meets with Comandante Yañez on the border at the Exxon station in McAllen, Texas. He hands Yañez an envelope and says it's about *el primo,* the cousin. When Sal leaves, the comandante opens it up and there is a Polaroid of Miguel Angel Flores with his name and address. The picture is blurry.

The record says that after this exchange, the comandante contacts the FBI.

The gun Sal once showed the comandante will become evidence of a promised payment. At the time Yañez is angling for the big payout—for ten or twenty grand, he promises to produce the database on disk for all the vehicles in Mexico. That will be seen as a ruse to mask payment in a contract for murder. The folder of clips, the video made by Sal's fellow agent in El Paso at the time of Bruno's killing, all grist for showing obsession, premeditation. But most of all the case will hinge on the tapes secretly made of Sal talking with the comandante over the phone.

Sal says, "You don't need anything right now?"

It is October 27, 1999, and it is precisely 9:10 P.M.

Jaime Yañez purrs, "Just for you to be okay, do you know why I've been calling you? My people went over there to the hospital where the sick guy was."

"Uh huh."

And then they meander awhile, and it doesn't seem to be going anywhere.

But Sal says, "It's . . . is it possible to complete the contract?"

"Yes, of course. Sure, it'll be contracted."

And a little later Sal says, "Very nice . . . very nice, partner. Really! Hey, look. I'm going to call here to my uh . . . to the people that are real interested over here. Okay?"

And the comandante's ears grow with this over here stuff.

"Where?"

"You know," Sal rolls on, "things are happening. No, I really appreciate, partner. That's something I know you don't have to do but you're helping the whole family."

Or there is a call at 12:30 P.M.

Sal says, *"No, sígale."* No, go ahead with it.

"Huh?"

"Give it everything you got. Give it your all." *Más ánimo. Echale ánimo.*

Sal loves the Miami Dolphins and now they are going to play in Dallas. So he calls his cousin Phil and asks if he can get tickets for the game. And Phil, of course, he says yes. Sal and Suzie come up from Monterrey for the big game in Dallas. It is a holiday, a relief from the pressure of life in Mexico.

They meet Phil in a restaurant-bar in Plano, one near his home. He brings the tickets he has gotten free thanks to connections. They sit there, talk and laugh and catch up with each other's lives.

It is all observed by the FBI.

The tape recorder is running again.

"But my kids," the comandante says, "want to go see . . . the . . . sick person."

Sal says, good, get on with it.

The comandante asks, "Do you have, um, a prettier, or better poster?"

No, no, Sal answers.

Sal says, "Well, I know. Well, fuck, well, uh, tell them that, well, we're always in the public eye. Everybody knows the dude."

"Living with an agent was like living with Dr. Jekyll and Mr. Hyde," she explains in a calm voice. "I was used to living in the dark."

Suzie Martínez met Sal in church two months after he hit Floresville as a green highway patrolman in 1985. They took in each other at a glance and after that moment in church they were a couple. They married in 1990. On the wall in her parents' home are wooden religious carvings that she and Sal got down in Mexico and brought back after the bust. There is a big bas relief of the Last Supper. Another of Christ being taken off that cross. A crucifix. And of course, Our Lady, the Virgin.

Suzie is thirty-two years old, and until their move to Monterrey, Mexico, she had worked as a middle-school teacher. Her Mexico was housework and cooking since she refused to have a maid. The normal tour of duty for an agent abroad is three years, and Suzie had decided to dedicate those years to having children. Two miscarriages ruined her plan.

"The first clue I had," she continues, "that something was going on was on a Fourth of July party in 1999 at the consulate. It was raining. Another agent came over and told Sal, 'I think they found your informant yesterday, or at least they found his legs.'"

She's not talking about the first clue to the murder contract, or the first clue that something was off with Sal—that moment never came. She means the first time she caught a whiff of what DEA actually did in Mexico. And then she continues in that calm voice, "The way I dealt with Sal's job was I never asked, and he never said anything."

That first call, the one from Sal after the FBI busted him, took her by surprise. "Sal said, 'Don't worry about it, it's bullshit, it'll be taken care of.' I didn't know a whole lot, it had something to do with Bruno's case, and what the hell was that about? That was five years ago."

She has just gotten out of the hospital after surgery to remedy the ravages of two miscarriages and she is in pain.

She is sitting at her parents' dining room table, her father, the judge, is outside mowing the lawn. She continues, "Sal wouldn't cooperate with the FBI unless they had him by the balls. I heard they had tape and video and I thought, Oh, God, he is guilty as sin. I'm thinking, we are going to need a sympathetic jury."

She sat in Monterrey and refused to leave for two days. DEA had instantly terminated Sal, and was pushing her to get out. She took control by refusing to go along with them. And when she left after this brief, quiet time she took three things: family photos, some videos, and food, lots of food she had bought for Sal's family's upcoming visit at Christmas, took the food because she'd been stockpiling it for the holidays and she was damned if they, the people in the agency who had suddenly cast Sal out, damned if they would eat a bite of it. She took down the Christmas tree also.

"I was disappointed," she offers, "that the thought would even cross his mind. But Bruno wasn't my cousin and I don't ask Sal what he does. And Sal had become so, so desensitized to death, to tortured people, to dismembered bodies."

The first feeling after Sal called from jail was shock. She cried every day for two months.

"I was angry," she explains, "because he's pissed away his career over this little boy. I asked him, what made you think you could do this? I know Sal didn't want that to happen. If the comandante had actually done it, Sal wouldn't have had rest."

And she is sure of one more thing: "The shit that they do now in Mexico, they should not be doing."

For years, she lived with the Work Sal and the Play Sal and then the Work Sal started crowding in on the Play Sal, as if he could not ever really break free of what he did out there on the streets. Now the man she fell in love with fifteen years ago has come home again.

"I don't know what DEA did to Sal," she says, "but how can you see these dead people, tortured people, dismembered people and not say it does something to you?"

Phil Jordan's world collapsed a little bit more on December 14, 1999, when Sal Martínez was arrested by the FBI for arranging a murder for hire.

He found a criminal attorney for his cousin and signed on to help pay part of the fee. He talked to the press and defended his cousin, saying the charges could not be true.

Back in 1996, DEA took down a big stash house in El Paso. They'd gotten a tip and then they'd taken a drug dog by the place, a business with a big vent pouring air out of the building, and the dog snorted the vent once and gave a canine high-five, and so the judge signed a warrant and they hit the joint and got tons of coke. Then the killing began, patrons in an El Paso bar mowed down, bodies popping up in Juárez, all part of the pattern after a big loss: simply kill everyone who knew to make sure the snitch dies too.

Sal was part of the case and the case became a part of me. I'd published a story in a New York magazine that touched briefly on this burst of killing and in it there'd been this photograph of a woman spread out fresh on the warm desert floor. After the story ran, the editor in New York got a call from the woman's brother and he said, you're going to get me killed and my wife killed and my children killed and my parents killed, my whole family killed. So the editor called me and asked what the hell I made of all this. I told him the guy had every right to be afraid.

Sal and I are sitting out on the Riverwalk in San Antonio and watching the world go by and somehow we hit on this old case and it turns out it was his case and he remembers the killing and the death of that one woman. She had nothing to do with it, he says, she'd been to the place the day before the bust and bought half a key, but she wasn't the source, she was innocent. Vicente, Amado Carrillo's brother, he ordered the hits. Hell, Sal says, and he's rolling now, Vicente was more bloodthirsty than even Amado. The guys in the cartel called the woman from Juárez, said come on over, let's talk, and she and some friends had gone over and been popped.

"Yeah, yeah, bro," Sal beams. "I remember."

I've got the photograph with me and so we look at it. She looks so good and fresh and clean and innocent with the sun dappling her face, all serene and dead on the brown dirt.

Sal says, "She was innocent, had nothing to do with it. Just bought a half key, for God's sake."

Stories: Salvador Méndez Barraza loves shooting pool at a cantina in the area of La Campana. He's nineteen and young guys, they like hanging out in joints. He left home saying he wanted some tripitas. He works in a maquiladora, loves to play soccer, a good boy, his mom says. He was last seen August 24, 1996.

•   •   •

November 6, 1999, has been a bitch. Sal has come up with other agents from Monterrey to play in a charity basketball game, and during the warm-ups before the game, his back went out, bing! just like that and the pain was terrible. Still he played. Then afterward the guys went to a bar where there were batting cages and Sal took the bat and tried to hit some sweet ones and that made his back even worse. He drove back to the motel, and grabbed his duffel bag from his car. Two doors away from his room, he went down on all fours and could not get up. Two women came along the hall and helped him up, took his bags also, and got him into his room. He looked out the window and saw the place had a Jacuzzi, so he called the desk and told them to turn the heat on. He hobbled down and got in, the water still cold, but even so he thinks the jets might help. His boss came along with a case of beer he'd gotten just for Sal, and so Sal sat there for an hour or so downing beers. Comandante Yañez called Sal's beeper but he blew him off. The comandante was also in Laredo, he kept his family stashed on the U.S. side.

Finally, Sal got out of the Jacuzzi and went out to dinner at Corona Charlie's with the guys. He could hardly sit in the chair, and he drank scotch hoping to blot out the pain. He was shitfaced when the comandante got ahold of him.

Sal said, "I don't understand."

"The seal," the comandante offered, "from the time they went to Ciudad Juárez, Chihuahua. The visit. The first time. He's already totally . . . what's it called?"

"Mmm humm."

"Identified and everything, the dude. The damn pictures are really . . . very blurry as shit."

Sal listened, tried to follow the patter, but the pain, the booze, hell, he was drunk.

"What do you want to do with him?" the comandante asked. "Honestly."

"Honestly."

"I'm scared," the comandante added.

"No, no, no, no, no, no," Sal said. "No, nobody else. It's you and me, dude."

"For sure?"

"For sure."

"Okay," the comandante said. "We have him very well located. What do you want us to do with him?"

"Terminate him, please." *Termínalo, por favor.*

"But to what extent? Do you want us to bring him to Monterrey?"

"Yeah. Terminate him. I don't want the dude to live. Honestly, dude. He killed my cousin for a damn car and we gave him an opportunity to speak with us about . . . about why did he do it? Who has . . . ? Look, do you know the situation?"

"All right. Do you want us to get out of him who sent him . . ."

"Yes."

" . . . or not."

"Just that. Yes. If you all can. If not, it's not worth . . . worth shit. Kill him. I don't want him to live. So then my family doesn't want this guy to live. He got . . . the system won. He killed my cousin that never had anything to do with drugs. He just wanted to be . . . go to school."

The comandante ran it by one last time.

"So then we don't bring him to Monterrey?"

"No. Terminate the dude already. I don't know . . . as long as it comes out in the newspaper . . . so the whole family finds out the dude already died."

"All right," the comandante said. "The dude's going down. There's no more. Okay."

"Yeah. Hey. I appreciate it . . ."

On February 5, 2000, Sal accepts a plea bargain and is widely denounced within his own agency. He cops a plea because the cost of his defense attorney has bankrupted him and his wife and gutted what few resources Phil Jordan has left. Sal also gives in because of the evidence— those taped conversations in which he talks about the plan to kill Miguel Angel Flores. Twice—once before the plea, once afterward—the FBI and DEA offer to lighten his legal charges if he will give up Phil Jordan. Twice, Sal Martínez refuses.

Sal tells himself and others that if he went to court, the attorney cost would be $150,000 he does not have. And that if he lost at trial the pile of federal charges could mean twenty to thirty years. He is thirty-seven years old and if he takes the deal, he can be out with good time in six years, when he is forty-four.

Phil Jordan is divorced.

The play goes up and starts touching $500 a day.

Suzie wants to make sure she gets it right. Of course, she was angry when she learned what Sal did, damned angry. But she wants this anger cushioned by another part of herself. The storm has lifted, last night tornadoes were spotted in a neighboring Texas town. But this is morning, and the air is cooler, and very fresh and smells like a drug to make us believe in spring. The flowers are poking out in the beds around her parents' house and Suzie stands out in the clean air and tries to get it right.

"I said," she explains about her and Sal, "it was for better or worse. And it couldn't get more worse than this. Marriage is a contract."

Sal listens. Then he asks a favor. Could I find him a used book? He hands me a slip with the author and title: Hurricane Carter, *The Sixteenth Round*.

Now, Phil Jordan has finished lunch. Outside the traffic of Plano roars by but in here it is quiet, the tables mainly empty, the lighting soft. He has savored baked ziti with four cheeses, had a salad. No wine.

He asks softly, "What do you think my grandfather would have done?"

And there is no question what he means, what he wants to know.

I answer, "Well, the easy thing is to say your grandfather would have killed whoever killed his own flesh and blood. But your grandfather was a survivor. When he murdered, he was a young man studying to be a lawyer, not a husband and father. And he was a realist. He made a fortune in Juárez and El Paso, but he never went to war with the corrupt governments in both cities. Your grandfather would have survived. He was a realist."

Phil Jordan says nothing.

There is a photograph in the house in Plano, one of the old man with Phil's daughter Brigitte and with another great-grandchild. It is framed with a letter from President Richard Nixon, a note thanking the old man for his columns in the El Paso paper before the 1972 election. Nixon thanks him for his "expression of support."[8]

In the photograph, the old man truly looks old, but he does not look his years. He is unsmiling, though surrounded by two very young great-granddaughters. He is brooding, unknowable, and adamantly silent.

Eugenio Forti was a lifelong Democrat. He warned his grandson Felipe back then about the danger of Henry Kissinger and the Nixon administration. At the time of Nixon's letter, he'd been living for years across the river in Juárez.

"He would have survived," I repeat.

Earlier Suzie had said, "It's so sad. Sal's a nice guy who was too trusting, who talked shit and he got caught."

I ask Sal, if the deal had gone down, if Miguel Angel Flores had been murdered by the comandante's men in Juárez as Sal had requested, would he have been able to go on with his life and career? Would he have been able to just file it away like a dead letter and not let this killing and his hand in this killing touch his life?

He looks at me and says, "Sure."

He doesn't really complain about what is happening to him. He regrets it, but still, it is not really a complaint. He loved DEA, loved the work. He crossed a line but hell, there were no lines in the life.

Phil Jordan turns to me and says, "I could do it like that," and then he snaps his fingers. Yes, he says, like that. He explains that he has the connections, he could set it up, have a murder committed in, say, Juárez, and no one would know, no one would trace it back to him.

When he says things like that, his face tightens, his eyes focus hard, his words become clipped. Then it passes, the face softens, the words purr along again and the eyes look vague, almost distracted, and Phil Jordan melts back into a blank face.

•   •   •

In 1999, there were five hundred moments characterized as violent assaults against federal officers on the Mexican border. Back in 1997, the last year with a breakdown of types of assaults, people tried to shoot federal agents ninety-seven times, rammed their cars sixty-four times, and sought to blow them up with bombs twenty times.[9] When Sal Martínez was talking up a storm with the comandante, he was also working a case, a big case that involved Mexican cops encircling an FBI agent and a DEA agent on the border and threatening them with machine guns, one gold-plated.

In 1998, Allana Martin, a border writer of mysteries, puts out *Death of a Saint Maker* and in this tale of holy men and desert color, there is a moment when one character erupts and says, "You people tolerate thousands of small drug dealers, then build up the agency's reputation by exposing one or two big ones. Do you think I don't know the kind of retaliation to expect from playing games with the . . . Cartel? Your own boss had a brother gunned down in El Paso—"

"That was a carjacking."

"—as a warning. We're on the line in more ways than one here. The border is not holding against the drug lords. They're taking it over."[10]

There are incidents that happen outside of novels. A contract, *el contrato,* goes out on the father of a federal agent. The agent leaves the city where he is stationed, travels a long distance, and comes to a place on the line. He knocks on a door. He shows his official identification. But he explains that this is not an official visit.

He says, "I know this house, I know the three stash houses, I know all the addresses. I am the one you are looking for. You understand? I am the one."

Of course, they know this is not true, that he is not the one, that he is not the right age, the right name, the right face. And of course, they don't have to ask what a stash house is, or what it means that this stranger knows all the addresses.

He repeats, "I am the one you are looking for. I want you to understand something: this is about family, *familia.*"

They understand. *El contrato,* the contract, becomes dormant.

•   •   •

When Sal Martínez was arrested by the FBI on December 14, 1999, the next day's papers were flush with accounts of his crime. Donnie Marshall, acting DEA administrator, instantly terminated Martínez without pay and said, "We condemn any attempt by DEA employees to take the law into his or her hands."[11] The U.S. ambassador to Mexico, Jeffrey Davidow, said, "This incident has nothing to do with the work of a DEA agent in Mexico."[12] Congressman Silvestre Reyes of El Paso and many others denounced the plot and Sal Martínez. The case was instantly opened and closed by officials. Martínez was faced with a $200,000 bond, later dropped to a $100,000 cash bond, which was put up by a friend.

Other stories keep coming: Geraldo Ortega, Salvador Ortega, and Manuel Hernández, all guys around forty, were taken by cops. The neighbors in Juárez got kind of alarmed but other police assured them it was okay, just a special detail working the War on Drugs. They were last seen January 11, 1997.

Beatrice leans over the stove making tacos as her daughter Virginia staples together copies of articles about a place called La Campana, the Bell. The FBI has announced in late November 1999 the discovery of mass graves in Juárez. All the people who have vanished for years in the kingdom of the late Amado Carrillo are now rumored to be coming back. The oil sizzles in the pan as the old woman turns tortillas golden and the scent of the meat fills the house in the barrio. Bruno stares from his picture frame, a granddaughter works away at her homework in criminal psychology for her university class, two great-grandkids are underfoot, a son-in-law scratches out a lottery card, the television plays faintly in the next room and announces that today two more bodies have been dug up. Phil is here, just in by plane from Dallas, and he's all over the phone setting up stuff for tomorrow when they cut the ribbon on the new addition to EPIC.

The reports would come into DEA of yet another informant snatched, tortured, and killed, and of course these reports came from yet other informants, part of that legion willing to tattle for money or tattle to cut a deal on a bust or tattle to fuck over a competitor in the life, well, these reports would come in and they would note who snatched who and where they took them for a little bone tickling or a taste of electricity or dismemberment or beatings, the menu varied. The result was constant: you talk and then you die and then you go into a hole in a ranch on the edge of town. Sometimes you would go into a hole alone, sometimes with colleagues, but you went into the hole and then the informant reported and you went into the file and the file went into the computer. Hundreds made this journey in this place, thousands made this journey all along the line, more thousands made this journey in the interior of Mexico.

Phil Jordan has been on network news and all over the newspapers talking about the mass graves and saying that DEA has known for years about these private burial grounds, has known that they are scattered all over Mexico, exist wherever the drug business exists, and that during these years of knowing, no one in the U.S. government wanted DEA to talk about these boneyards.

"We knew the locations of the ranches," he carefully explains to the media, "but we couldn't do anything about it. You can't turn to Mexico's federal police because they are the ones who buried some of these people."

He is saying that this new FBI discovery is old news and that it is not really a matter of a mass grave but of countless graves filled one by one as people disappear in the drug business. Phil Jordan is the man on television saying this new FBI headline is logically false in the matter of a mass grave, historically late in acknowledging the killing, and geographically restricted, since this is not a peculiar custom of Juárez but a fact of life in the drug business.

Initially, the Mexican attorney general announced the discovery of mass graves, four of them, just outside Juárez, and he also announced that one hundred to two hundred people were in these graves, twenty-two of them believed to be U.S. citizens. The world rushed in, television and press, reporters from Asia, reporters from Europe, and for a few days, there was talk of genocidal death on the border. The digging began. One hole gave up six men, another hole surrendered two. After about two weeks, the digging slowed and then, finally, one more set of bones came up. The FBI allowed that it would take three months, at least three months, to do the digging right. The press grew bored, and drifted away. The mayor of Juárez said the digging was bad for business and bought a $30,000, full-page advertisement in the *Washington Post* to celebrate the real nature of his city. He said, maybe the dead bodies were plants, things placed there to besmirch his fine city.

This investigation of the grave sites began in 1997 according to the Mexican attorney general's office. Or the investigation into the mass burials began in early 1999, according to the FBI, when an informant, a Mexican federale comandante, a man who had himself killed eighty other men in the line of his duties, confessed to the grave sites. Or it began ninety days before the digging when representatives of the missing approached the American drug czar in El Paso during one of his visits to the front lines, the same czar who had to flee during an earlier visit when U.S. intelligence learned the Juárez cartel had rockets and intended to use them on the selfsame czar.

The dead themselves, as they come up one by one and in bits and pieces, say nothing. Not even in most cases say their own names. The bodies are dug up in Mexico by a joint U.S.-Mexican team. The remains are examined in El Paso by experts. The head of the FBI and the attorney general of Mexico visit La Campana together as a show of unity in the war against the drug cartels.

When they come to the site—the Mexican official by Russian helicopter, the FBI chief by armored convoy—thirty hostesses in black miniskirts greet them and form a corridor of young pretty flesh leading to the pit. The two men look down and then retire to a large white tent for a press conference. The FBI says they know of four or five Americans missing in the area. The Mexicans have already announced that twenty-two Americans will be found in the holes. The differing numbers will not be reconciled or explained.

Some Mexican officials come to the site by ground transport, the license plates taped over, their faces hidden behind sheets of white paper. The soldiers and police on the site wear black ski masks to hide their identities.

It is a matter of safety.

•   •   •

It is late at night. Sal and I are sitting alone in the beer garden of the White House Cafe and Saloon in downtown Floresville. The clock is ticking, the cell door comes closer by the hour. The lights are out, the business is closed. Still we keep drinking.

I ask Sal, "Was there a point in all your talking with the comandante, in all this making Polaroids, talking about contracts, was there a point when you said, hey, this is crazy, a point when you backed off?"

He looks at me and says in a hard, fierce voice, "I never backed off."

It's Phil and Sal in the bar, Phil sipping iced tea, Sal slamming down some scotch. Phil was DEA brass before he retired a few years back, and he still has some connections. He's kind of a renegade, always shooting off his mouth to the press and television about dope and Mexico and corruption. Just a week or so ago, he testified at a congressional hearing and the people from the Justice Department first tried to get him barred from speaking and then buried the members of the committee with a stack of clips four or five inches high and the clips, every one of them, were about Sal and his contract to murder a citizen of Mexico.

Phil Jordan tells Sal Martínez that the two FBI people who made the case did not want to pursue it. That the prosecutor who is arguing the case did not want to pursue it. They all wanted the tapes and the evidence turned over to DEA and then have DEA woodshed Sal. But the orders came from on high, from Attorney General Janet Reno, from FBI head Louis Freeh, from DEA head Donnie Marshall, and the orders were to prosecute. And the reason for the orders was to fuck over Phil Jordan for shooting off his mouth about Mexico. That is what Phil thinks.

Sal falls silent over his drink.

The drive home is country roads in darkness, the trees pressing in from the side of the road. Sal does not talk much and his face is stone in the glow off the dash. He pulls over at a small country store.

"You want a beer, bro?" he asks me.

In the corner sits a bronze eagle, by the judge's bench the American flag, on the wall a huge print of the founding fathers with a tag line floating that says WE THE PEOPLE. It is Cinco de Mayo of the year 2000. The first two rows of benches are Sal's people, his mother, father, brother, sisters, his in-laws and other kin. He and Suzie sit off to one side and look straight ahead. He wears a gray-patterned suit with a pin on the lapel that says WWJD, What Would Jesus Do? Suzie wears black. Close by three windows bleeding north light, the two FBI agents that worked the case now huddle and wait. Scattered about are the press, the AP, *Houston Chronicle, Los Angeles Times.* In the back corner, all but unnoticed, are six men in orange jumpsuits awaiting arraignment in the federal district court of Laredo, Texas. A few blocks away, just across the Rio Grande, is Mexico.

Christopher Milner, Sal's attorney, wears a blue suit and red tie. He is a ramrod-straight man with close-cropped hair and for years he was the federal prosecutor in this district. He has come home and oozes confidence and deference. He is a born-again Christian and for $70,000 (eventually, more than $90,000) he has cut a plea agreement where Salvador Michael Martínez admits guilt in arranging a murder-for-hire contract and offers up eighty-seven months of his life in the bargain. The reporters are here because Milner has let it get about that he will make a powerful statement this morning. Judge George P. Kazen hails from a politically powerful clan that has won him a seat on the bench. He is a pale man with thinning gray hair. He enters, the bailiff says God save these United States, and Sal's mother makes the sign of the cross.

Sal and Milner approach the bench when the case is called. Kazen scratches his ear and asks, "Is there anything you'd like to talk about?" They say no. And all the family members lean forward.

Kazen notes he is looking at "a strong case of a calculated effort to hire an assassin," a scenario, he continues, "right out of the movies." He pauses and allows, "Lord have mercy on us if that's how our law enforcement are going to behave."

Kazen continues that there have been these letters, a torrent of letters, and they all say that Sal is a good man and that he should not go to prison. The judge sighs over these letters and says he answered two of them and then gave up as they kept coming, one after another. He's got a plea agreement admitting to this terrible crime, and then he's got the letters saying no, no, the defendant is a decent man. Kazen recalls T. S. Eliot's *Murder in the Cathedral,* the scene where the king says to his nobles, Who will rid me of this meddling priest? and then, after this offhanded remark, Thomas à Becket is slaughtered in his vestments. Kazen shrugs and tries another tack.

"You come in here," he points out, "without even waiting for an indictment." The judge wants to make a simple point: if the defendant thinks he is innocent, he can withdraw the plea agreement right now and go to trial. Otherwise, the judge continues, Sal Martínez should level with his family. And anyway, he notes, the defendant is getting light time, only eight years and change, whereas the probation arm of the court wants him to do nine, ten, or even more. The judge picks up his official federal sentencing card, a menu of punishments, and says, Sal is getting only a level twenty-nine sentence, and the rules suggest he should get a level thirty-one. So you see, Kazen says, "I'm being told to do something for him . . . it's essentially his deal."

Sal and Milner whisper into each other's ear, the court is tense as they consider the judge's offer to go to trial. Finally, Kazen tires of waiting and sends them off to the jury benches on the side where they continue whispering. Sal's face is blank, as it has been all morning. After three or four minutes, they are back.

The judge presses the issue, "Do you feel like this is a miscarriage of justice? Tell me now."

Sal says he wishes to go on. He reads a brief statement, one all but inaudible in the huge courtroom: "I come before you today to receive a sentence for circumstances surrounding the brutal death of my cousin that led me to think with my heart instead of my head. I have had a successful career in law enforcement for fifteen years that included saving many lives. Now, I will be considered a convicted felon for the rest of my life. Many people have been praying that you would impose the most lenient sentence possible. I hope these prayers have reached you because the lives of so many are in your hands."

The judge says, "You are apparently a very decent guy . . . and I'm sad for you. I'm sad for all of us."

He says he sits in this courtroom and hears endless drug cases, he is living in "a war zone" and he knows it.

"You obviously," Kazen purrs on, "believed with all your heart that this fellow murdered your cousin . . . [but] we're not in a freewheeling system anymore, not in a system like when I first got on the bench." He is a captive of the rules and the rules this morning say eight years and three months. He says, "With a heavy heart, I'm going to follow the deal."

The judge could fine Sal $250,000 but he notes that he is waiving the fine. And he is allowing Sal a month or so to put his life in order while the prison system tries to find a place for him.

"Well," Kazen closes, "Mr. Martínez, good luck to you. Time has a way of healing almost anything." Perhaps, the judge offers, he could use his time in stir to write his memoirs.

In the hall, Milner spins for the press, saying the judge's kind words about Sal were an extraordinary gift, that Sal showed far greater courage by taking the deal than going to trial, and he extols the court's "salute to a fallen comrade."

Phil Jordan tells the reporters that the whole thing represents a failure of customary agency policy. "When the FBI first got wind that Sal was talking recklessly," he explains as the pens scratch across the notebooks, "they should have notified the DEA, and Sal should have been ordered to return immediately to the United States, where he would have been disciplined and received counseling. The FBI should have handled this much like they have for their own agents—keeping the matter internal."[13] Just six weeks before the sentencing, DEA came to Sal and offered to help him if he would implicate Phil Jordan.

Later that day, we sit in the White House Cafe in Floresville. Sal dives into two orders of chicken wings. And then it is off for nine holes of golf with family members. But he fails to calculate the tension knotted beneath his smiling face. His back muscles lock out on the greens and he is poleaxed by pain.

Very little stories: José Luis García Maldonado likes to walk his small son. He works on a ranch. A police patrol scoops him up on January 10, 1998, in downtown Juárez. People selling cigarettes and flowers watch it happen. Then they stop talking also.

Suzie had the dream weeks before the sentencing in Laredo and the dream was very real to her. In the dream, she is divorced from Sal and he's got his arm around some chick and Suzie can tell the chick is really hitting on Sal. And in the dream, Suzie does not care. She looks up at the sky and sees seven and a half tornadoes, she counts them off one by one, and she thinks this is odd, seven tornadoes and then over there, a half a tornado. She must get her purse, that is what she thinks, the tornadoes are coming and I have to get my purse. And then they all find shelter, Sal, this chick hanging off him, and Suzie with her purse. And in the shelter Sal puts his arm around her and suddenly Suzie feels real peace.

She knows the dream cold, she has no questions about it. The purse is money, security, everything that has been destroyed by Sal's arrest. The chick is the blows against the marriage. And the seven and a half tornadoes are easy for Suzie. Sal was in DEA exactly seven and a half years.

She has never read the transcripts of the tapes. They are in a folder, just down the hall from the dining room, resting there in the folder in the house on the quiet street in Floresville, Texas. But she does not need to read them. They are details. She knows all that she needs to know.

Seven and a half tornadoes.

About the time of Sal's sentencing, DEA announces that since the summer of 1999, Mexico has ceased to give lie detector tests to members of its new anti-drug force. The Mexican government denounces this statement. It explains that it has simply decided not to let U.S. agents witness such tests.[14]

Gerardo de la Riva is hungry, and hell, when you are twenty you get hungry a lot. He works at his dad's bar in Juárez. So he goes out to eat something. Later, a body identified as his came out of yet another mass grave. Maybe. Nobody's heard from him in a good long while.

•   •   •

He will get cool, the bounce will leave his voice, the hi! dude energy of his normal speech vanishes, and then, when he is in that special place where he can feel the walls closing in on him and the cell door clanging shut, he says things like this: "I have not slept since December 14. Imagine you are out on the ocean and bam! this big wave comes up and bam! it hits you. I've always been religious and I think, Lord, why is this happening to me? I was always the good guy in high school. And why is this happening to me? And I'm in DEA and we're a very proud agency and why are my fellow agents ignoring me and where are the top guys who should have stopped this case cold. They trained me to talk in this garbage language and now . . . I'll be stigmatized as a felon, me who has arrested hundreds of people. And shit, what've we got here: a convicted felon, the kid, the kid who murdered my cousin, and he's free living in Juárez. And a corrupt Mexican cop who will be over here probably, a protected witness with a new life, with his whole family. And me in prison. But I'll do fine."

Beatrice has someone come in to do the family ironing on Frutas Street. The woman is new and never met her late son. One day the woman is in the back of the house near Bruno's old room. She spies a man, an intruder, and rushes out to get Beatrice. The two women return to the hall where the intruder was spotted and find nothing. The ironing woman explains how the intruder was dressed, the kind of slacks, the shirt, and the brown shoes. Beatrice takes her to the closet where Bruno's clothes still hang. The woman recognizes everything, especially the brown shoes.

Sal carefully takes up a shirt, smoothes it with his hand, and then holds it away from his body. Afternoon light seeps through the east window and catches the particles of floating dust in the storage room of his parents' home in El Paso. Before him stands a mountain of brown boxes. A woman's hand has clearly written on one box: UNIFORMS. GUEST BOOKS. HONEYMOON STUFF.

The shirt, white with black stripes, is short-sleeved. He fetches a hanger from a big moving carton, the kind with a built-in-rod, and

carefully places the shirt on the hanger. Yes, he decides, he will want
this shirt in seven years and so he carefully stores it in the box.

He finds the snapshot that has him in camouflage pants, black
sleeveless T-shirt. He crouches in the dirt behind a car, the semiautomatic pistol holstered on his hip, the submachine firing at his shoulder.
The hair is long. His body shows the ease of an athlete.

Sal's talking a steady patter.

On August 28, in four days, he will enter prison. On August 31,
he will be thirty-eight years old. He must report with nothing, not
even his contact lenses, will earn 15 cents an hour, and must pay for his
own plane ticket, $238, one way.

He still has the smooth skin of a boy. A log called TRIGGERFISH
rests on the boxes. The transcripts whisper about a guy who killed
someone named Reuben. Or they capture a voice calling Colombia, a
voice reciting numbers, one number after another, a code floating into
the jaws of TRIGGERFISH. The name coming from a device that listens in on private cell phone conversations. In one transcript, a man is
in Juárez. He reports that he has been taken down a cobblestone street
and is now inside some house without furniture. There are eight guys
in the house, he continues, but he can't tell if they are armed. The man
whispering is an FBI snitch.

The agents never find the place where the man is calling from, they
can't triangulate the signals fast enough. The man's body turns up
later.

Sal no longer is interested in the intercepts. He is busy figuring out
what shirts he will still want in eighty-seven months.

He holds up a plastic milk bottle of water. The thing is leaking
onto his shirt.

"Shit," he says.

This is a bad sign. And he knows it.

I ask him idly about his informants.

"One got shot in the head a couple of times, bro," he explains of his
Mexican informants, "another was knifed a bunch of times in the
heart." He stops this inventory with a shrug that says people die all the
time in the work.

"Did you ever tell Suzie?"

"No, bro," he answers.

He points to a book he wants to take with him to prison: *The Way of the Pilgrim.*

It's on a box that says: JOGGING SUITS. WINTER STUFF.

Raúl Salinas, Jr., is serving a twenty-seven-year sentence for murder. He is on the phone. Or he is not on the phone. The conversation is recorded and broadcast in 2000 and purports to be between Raúl Salinas, Jr., and his sister, Adriana. The voices talk about money, apparently the hundreds of millions of dollars that once flowed through Citibank and then came to rest in Swiss vaults. The government of former President Ernesto Zedillo asserts the tape is authentic.

The voice identified as Raúl says, "I think it's very stupid on his part to say that he's going to demand a precise clarification [of the funds], and I'm going to give it to him, Adriana, I'm going to clarify everything—where the money came from and where it went. I'm going to say what funds came from the public treasury so that they're returned."

The other voice, the one assumed to be Adriana, starts to argue but the voice identified as Raúl cuts her off and says, "Carlos shows gigantic cowardice. The money is his. And then he says he doesn't know anything about it."

Who this Carlos might be is never made clear. At the time of the release of tape, Carlos Salinas happened to be visiting Mexico to tout his memoirs, which he has written to clear his name. Press reports indicate he was stunned by the release of the taped phone conversation. Since 1996, Citibank itself has been rumored to be the focus of two grand jury investigations. But these alleged probes never produce indictments.[15]

There is a new song in the air now, one called "El Corrido de Amado Carrillo Fuentes."

> *He was the "Czar" of cocaine*
> *the master of the Mafia,*

He didn't respect the Mexican government
nor the American authorities.[16]

The box says WATERBED LINER/HEATER. A book rests on the box, *Zen for Americans,* and the first sentence reads: "To be free from passions and to be calm, this is the most Excellent Way." Sal plans eventually to get this book into prison, along with a Catholic Bible. He has scribbled on his bookmarker, "I must cut off my passions, emotionally detach myself and discover the limits of my mind."

The room keeps getting smaller as the boxes press in but Sal never skips a beat in his careful sorting and hanging of his clothes. He talks without turning his head, he talks right into the boxes stacked floor to ceiling.

"I had that tunnel vision," he offers, "that tunnel vision every cop has. I was always thinking things are black and white. I need to explore the gray areas."

I ask, "How often did you do it?"

And he knows what I mean, knows I'm talking about how DEA agents in Mexico take care of some of their problems. There is, say, a guy who is dirty, a fucking drug dealer and you can't nail him in the U.S. and the Mexican cops pretend they know nothing. And you get pressure from your bosses to get results. And so, finally, you go to the Mexican cops and you give them the plate numbers and the make of the guy's car, his address, a photo even, and you say this guy is causing me trouble, I'm hearing about him and I gotta do something. And that guy, if he's not too big and powerful, that guy disappears into an unmarked grave.

So how often?

"Maybe twice a year."

And then he pauses, he's giving it real thought.

"No, more like three or four times a year."

"And you had to know," I say, "what would happen to them."

This pause is longer and when the voice comes it is soft.

"Sure, we knew."

He picks up the small box and opens it and shows me the harmonica. He's been trying to learn to play the blues for years. But every time he gets going his practicing is broken off by his work. Now he thinks, he can really get down with the blues. Next to the harmonica, he's stacked a bunch of blues on CD. When things settle down in prison, he'll send for them. Sal holds the Vulgate Bible in his hand and riffles the pages, stares down at the holy words in this room where he packs away his life.

The light filters through the dust in the air, a plastic pouch with small objects to spur religious thoughts rests on a box. A cousin gave it to Sal for the good of his soul.

Sal says, "What I did was wrong, what I regret is the misery I've caused my family." But he never says he feels guilty.

A week or two or three earlier, a Mexican federal cop, one of those guys in the new incorruptible drug force that Sal tended to, well, this guy came to Juárez. Sal had ignored his calls. But the guy crossed the bridge into El Paso and runs him down.

They go to a bar. The guy tells Sal he'd been good to them. And Sal had been good to them. The Mexican government had shipped this new would-be band of drug warriors far from their families and paid them very little and sometimes forgot to pay them at all. Sal had been their handler and gave them money to keep them in line. The guy says, let's go somewhere private. They huddle in the men's room.

The guy reaches in his pocket, comes out with a thick wad of bills.

Sal is taken aback. The only source of this kind of cash for a Mexican cop is the drug business.

Sal asks, "Where'd you get this?"

The question hangs in the air. The Mexican agent knows Sal is going to prison. He has come up from Mexico out of loyalty.

The Mexican agent looks at him and says, "You know better than to ask."

Sal is finished with his sorting of clothes. His shirt is now dry from the spilled holy water that seeped out of the leaking bottle.

The water came from a church in McAllen, Texas. In the 1930s a plane crashed into the church and it burned to the ground. But the statue of the Virgin of Guadalupe survived and that was the miracle. So

Sal and Suzie made a pilgrimage and got the bottle of holy water in the hope that it would help.

"The clock," he says, "started at my sentencing hearing and my focus changed to preparation for separation: retirement benefits, storage of belongings, Suzie's welfare, and most importantly reassuring my family that everything will be all right, even though I didn't really know. I canceled credit cards, magazine subscriptions. My Day-Timer, which was once filled with appointments, telephone numbers, and notations of important meetings, including meetings I had with Yañez, is now blank. Not having a career goal, rushing for a meeting, or tending to someone in need was a helpless feeling. I had to deprogram myself: no pager, no cellular, no weapon, sitting with my back to the wall evaluating everyone, etc. I moved from the fast lane to the shoulder."

He packs a suitcase for prison, plus a dozen tamales his mother insists he deliver to a relative. His mother tells him to get on his knees, and then she blesses him with a prayer in Spanish and the sign of the cross. He flies to San Antonio to spend the last few days with Suzie.

He goes to evening mass with Suzie at the same church where they first met and where they were married. They cling to each other like young lovers. Later, the priest comes to the house and gives them a special blessing. Finally, they get to bed and he holds Suzie as she cries herself to sleep.

As he leaves his in-laws' house, his mother-in-law makes the sign of the cross on his forehead. Suzie drives him and he keeps things safe by pelting her with rhetoric from motivational stuff he has read. He tells her they will overcome. He insists she drop him at the front of the airport and not come in. He leaves her with a kiss, a hug, and the order to "get over the emotional shit. Focus on your responsibilities and suck it up!"

He does not cry. That is the key thing for him. He has made it through all the farewells without a tear.

At the ticket counter, the clerk asks, "One way? It would be cheaper if you purchased a round-trip fare."

He says, "I wish I knew when I was coming back."

When his plane lays over in New Orleans, he thinks of flight. But he cannot do it. He is not cut out for running away. He tells himself he can do time, that plenty of people have done time. He says to himself, this will be his biggest undercover role, a narc in prison.

He sits alone the night before he turns himself in and silently cries. At the prison, Sal sees the highest walls in his life and cannot stop staring at the razor wire. He rehearses his story in his head: he is a teacher who was arrested for conspiracy. Before he walks in, he takes a very deep breath and repeats his favorite scripture to himself: "I can do all things through Christ which strengthens me." (Philippians 4:13)

Then he asks Bruno to take care of him.

The mass graves of Juárez never really pan out. The digging goes on for weeks but hundreds of bodies do not emerge, just a mere handful. At one site, the authorities found a thousand gallons of chemicals handy for processing cocaine, plus some cartridges for AK-47s.[17] That same day the mayor of Juárez holds a fiesta that draws eighty thousand people. The mayor explains that the party "is to erase the poor image that has shaken our dear city with negative publicity."[18] A few weeks later, the local Juárez bar association asks for a new law that will permit citizens to carry guns in order to protect themselves in a city without any real police protection.[19]

Two of the bodies in the mass graves turn out to be a Colombian coke dealer and his attorney. The men vanished after crossing the bridge from El Paso on February 15, 1995, after the Colombian beat a criminal charge. They were both seen being picked up by Mexican federales in the employ of Amado Carrillo. Almost certainly, DEA and the FBI had alerted the federal police to their release and crossing point after the acquittal came down. Later, it was discovered that the attorney had left a message on his answering machine stating that the Mexican federales were holding him. The skeleton was partly identified by remnants of the dark slacks, gray shirt, and black loafers he was wearing that day.[20]

The FBI source for its grave search is alleged to be a former police commander who did contract killings for Amado Carrillo. His street name is El Animal.

•   •   •

Sal becomes a student in his new world. He meets a guy deep into a thirty-year stretch for killing two cops. The guy has ceased to speak. Sal reads his Bible. His cell was built when FDR was president. He watches the sun set each day and thinks that it is moving on to where his wife lives.

He picks up the little courtesies: knock twice on a cafeteria table before sitting down, knock twice when leaving. He learns not to think about the future.

Suzie is back teaching school in her hometown. She reads in the papers about all the last-minute pardons granted by President Clinton and she thinks, why not some mercy for a guy who risked his life for years for his country?

Sal is standing at the fence with another convict and watching traffic flow into the nearby town. The cars all seem to have their lights on and the convict says, "There must be a funeral."

Sal explains, "Vehicles are equipped with daytime running lights now."

The man falls silent and then offers, "I've been locked up so long."

bruno's song

In May 2000, the woman arrives in the Dallas–Fort Worth area. She
knew Phil years ago, when he was making bones in Phoenix and they
have kept in touch, sometimes close, sometimes not so close, over the
years. Now he needs help, he is divorced, the bills are climbing. She is
that answer to the question we always hesitate to ask: what does it mean
to be human? She leaves Arizona and moves to Texas for a new job.

Phil Jordan asks to borrow her credit cards to pay off a few bills.
Sure, she says.

In June, she finds $10,000 to $15,000 of new charges on her cards.
She tries to cut off Phil's access to her cards.

In July, the charges are higher.

In August, another $13,000 in charges appears.

She asks, "How can you do this to me?"

Phil says, "I have to survive."

He says he will give her his pension check, have it sent directly to a
joint bank account. They set up the account. She puts in $1,000, a
kind of beginning, a test. That day Phil overdraws the account by writing a check for $1,300.

He is playing at least $500 a day.

He visits his mother in El Paso and asks his sister Virginia if he can
borrow her card. She says sure. He runs up $11,000 in a few days. One
by one, he taps out every source.

And still the number eludes him, the number that will make it all
come out right.

Sal is made as a narc by another inmate within three weeks of entering prison. In June 2001, a story I've written about Sal comes out in

GQ. Within hours, the prison officials move him out of the general population into maximum security. Eventually, he is placed in another facility.

Jordan hustles around Dallas trying to use his connections to get Sal moved to a safe place within the prison system. He tells everyone an eighty-seven-month sentence is not supposed to be a death sentence. He has been to see his senators. He has talked and talked with their aides. He has made phone calls, written the letters. He can't help but remember his grandfather and those parties in the house on Frutas Street with the band and all the food and every local pol there, the cops too, down there by the junkyard, and his grandfather walking around, calm, and he is the center of this thing he has created out of nothing. Jordan sits in these waiting rooms and he can't help but remember favors he did in DEA because some relative was in a jam and when a congressman called he listened and said, sure I'll look into it and fix it. Send the kid to rehab, not jail. Or call up some friend in the cop network and massage that DWI or whatever. Or make radio commercials for this campaign or that. And now, on this Sal matter it is hard to get a meeting, hard to get a callback.

He feels angry.

And then on June 6, 2001, he goes to see the prison officials in Dallas and to warn them that they will be hearing from the senators. This visit is pro forma, a kind of courtesy drilled into him from decades of his own federal service.

They make him wait. He is used to that. They finally call him in and he offers them the sheaf of letters he has written to politicians. They say, mail them to us. He is seething. He knows the house must also go on the block. The kids won't talk to him. The divorce is cold now. He has begged from friends. And now: mail it, while he stands right in front of them with the documents in his hand.

They sense his anger and one says, "You seem to be taking this personally."

He says, "Yes, I take it personally, yes, you are right. If you can consider that my brother was murdered by the fucking Juárez cartel and that Sal by an error of judgment tried to deal with this murder and has landed himself in prison for seven years, and that now the guy who killed my brother has probably been promoted in the fucking Juárez cartel and yes, I fucking take it personally and now my cousin Sal is in danger and you won't protect him and you figure I will do nothing and I'll tell you if it was just some fucking punk I won't care if you tossed him into the general population where he could be raped every day but this is my cousin and he risked his fucking life for years in DEA fighting drugs and I'm not going to let you kill him, and even the fucking federal judge said he should be in a camp, not a prison, and you ignored the federal judge—"

And right then, one of them interrupts and demands to know the district of this federal judge and once he hears it is in Laredo, Texas, relaxes with the knowledge that it is a backwater and the judge cannot possibly matter.

Jordan wants to beat them and beat them and beat them.

He calls on his cell phone as he drives and goes over and over this conversation and he keeps getting angrier and angrier as he relives it and then he says he's got to pull over and take his high blood pressure medicine but he does not, he keeps talking and driving and getting angrier, and he thinks, they want to murder my cousin, they know what will happen to Sal, goddamn, they fucking well know he'll be raped every day or killed and they fucking don't care, they say mail the stuff while it is right there in my hand, right there in their office, they don't give a damn about people, my brother is dead, Quirarte is out there somewhere and living good and Bruno in his grave, Sal in a prison of cutthroats and he's a DEA agent and so he's doomed and they will do nothing and what in the hell must they do to people who have not given thirty fucking years to federal service.

And then he says over the phone, "If there is one thing, I can't . . ." and he starts to choke, almost stutters with rage and gasps out "I can't . . ." and fails again and he keeps gasping for air and words and saying, "I can't . . .

"I can't . . .

"I can't . . .

"I can't . . ."

and then the phone goes dead as he careens down a Dallas street.

•   •   •

Sal writes the prison system asking that he be transferred to a facility near El Paso. The request is denied. The authorities note that he tried to kill someone and that this is a severe action.

He remembers those last few hours of freedom. He went into the airport alone. He wished it that way. And as he entered the airport, and then boarded the plane, and finally, as he walked up to the federal prison and turned himself in, he felt, well, better, much better. He felt this weight lift off him, and he began to breathe again.

The relief came from no longer having to be brave, to pretend, to keep up a face for those around him. He is reading the Bible, talking with the prison priest, sorting things out. He is sad for the grief he has caused his family. But not for his intentions. He cannot renounce wishing the person dead who killed his cousin.

But now he can breathe.

Brigitte, Phil's daughter from his first marriage, returns to Frutas Street for visits with her grandparents and brings the children. She sleeps in the bedroom off Bruno's room, and two chambers are connected by an open doorway. In the night, she will look up and see a beautiful, swirling light on the ceiling. She is not frightened, the light feels warm and inviting. And in her heart and soul, she knows it is Bruno, near and comforting.

He keeps going back to those scrapbooks that he keeps by the chair in the house in Plano. He can open them and see his life. He is smiling on July 31, 1969. He poses with sixty-one kilos of marijuana in Phoenix, Arizona. The American flag is to his right, the suitcases with the kilos to his left. He wears a white shirt, tie, his pocket full of pens. The hair is trimmed, the face young, the smile winning.

In one photograph from Operation Cactus, that long-ago operation in San Luis Sonora where Phil Jordan led a team of Mexicans and Americans and almost nabbed Pedro Pérez Aviles back in the 1970s, is a patch of earth with a small open crack in the ground. This is the fabled slit that led to tons of marijuana, the one overlooked by Calderoni and the other federales and discovered by the DEA agents. The soil looks light and sandy, the slit looks dark and forbidding.

Phil Jordan's yearbook from his high school is full of young hopeful faces. The class of 1960 is mainly brown, the faculty is mainly white. Jefferson High School has Felipe E. Jordan on page thirty of the yearbook. He is a graduating senior. He is also: Student Body Pres., National Honor Society, Assembly Manager, J-Club, Cloak & Dagger Club, Varsity Basketball, Varsity Baseball, M.C. Mardi Gras, Vice-Pres. Senior Class, Senior Follies, Boys State, "All Jeff" Boy, FHA Beau, All District.

A yellow newspaper clip falls out from the 1960s. It reads: "FORTI: Mrs. Elisa Diaz Forti, 60, 3909 Frutas, died Monday in a hospital. She was a resident of El Paso 52 years and a member of El Calvario Catholic Church. Survivors, husband Eugenio L. Forti; two daughters, Mrs. Virginia Varela, Mrs. Beatrice Jordan; four sons . . . twenty-one grandchildren. . . ."

A photo falls out of Felipe Jordan, the All Jeff Boy, with Frankie Avalon, the singer.

His coffee cup rests by his chair. The seal of DEA is emblazoned on the cup's side with the words FIGHTING DRUGS WITH SPORTS. Phil Jordan poured his life into DEA. Over his career, he recruited five to six hundred agents, this out of an agency that finally employed four thousand. His agency spent not a single moment on his brother's murder. It was not a suitable case.

His debts exceed $300,000. His only assets are a little equity in his house and what is left of his federal pension. His other real property has little value. A dead brother in a grave in El Paso. A cousin in a federal prison. The worthless lottery tickets scattered around the house. And of course, the magazines full of naked women that he can sell to mom-and-pop liquor stores and earn some gas money with.

He files for bankruptcy in the first week of June 2001. There are forty-two messages on this answering machine. They come from creditors. The messages say that it is urgent that he call.

He has eased off betting. He thinks he can leave it alone now. He has lucky numbers, everyone does, but he is not buying tickets by the hundreds. He is no longer a player.

He says, "I finally won the lottery. I get a second chance at life."

He slowly relaxes. The pressure is declining. He has escaped, like Sal, into a prison that protects him. He cannot fix it and now he knows he cannot fix it.

He will be driving in the throng and noise of Dallas traffic and talking to me about something else and then this body appears in the car, Bruno's body. Phil Jordan will say, "You know, I'll be watching the news, and, I can't explain this, but here in Dallas there are carjackings all the time, and a carjacking will come up on the screen . . ." And then he pauses, gathers himself, starts to go on. And cannot.

He will be talking about how it is over, the case is over, justice is in the hands of God or someone, justice is not something to be found in courts. There will be no solution. How you can know what happened but never really know.

And suddenly he will say "if." If Miguel Angel finally talked about who drove him into the K-Mart lot that night. If someone else talked. Quirarte, Eduardo González Quirarte, he'd know. Carrillo's right-hand man, brother Tony's old classmate, the guy who fixed things for the cartel, dealt with the Mexican government, helped scout out Chile and other bases of operation, he'd know. If he could be found, he'd know. Quirarte. And then for an instant, the fantasy will be real again, the belief that answers can be found, facts verified, case solved.

He'll remember all the little connections, all faint traces of the cartel and Bruno Jordan's murder—the silence of the boy, the peculiar interest of the consulate, the money for a good attorney for the appeal and subsequent trials coming from the cartel. Remember the disinterest by DEA and FBI in examining the case. Run thousands of details through his mind, pretend it is a detective story or a movie and that persistence will get him to the last page or last reel where all is made plain. And then stop for a moment, and realize there is nothing more to understand, that there is no mystery. He already knows how the world works. He simply has to face it. Or refuse to accept it.

But what if he has it all wrong. What if Phil Jordan focused on the car theft, and on the guy who must have driven the black truck into the K-Mart that evening, and on his relative's new bride who once was involved with that guy, and what if they had nothing to do with it. What if they are innocent and that is why they would not talk and that is why they did not help. What if Phil Jordan was wrong, got off on the wrong trail. His brother has been underground for six years now and yet the people Phil Jordan once suspected, his relative's wife and her former boyfriend, have led blameless lives without a single action to indicate any guilt. He is left with memories of a conversation with her and nothing else. Even the alleged killer, Miguel Angel Flores, has had the charges dropped against him and is living again in Mexico without the slightest proof of any guilt.

It is hard for him to think this way after all that has happened, after all the losses. But still, what if. He must face the fact that he can always know what happened to his brother—that it was a hit, not an accident—but never definitely know anything more. He can simply note the silence around the death, the unusual interest of the Juárez cartel in the case of the alleged shooter, Miguel Angel Flores.

He can sit and think and know everything, know they, those people, the cartel, killed his brother. And that they want him to sit there and know that they did it. And be able to do nothing about it.

She has moved thirteen thousand to fourteen thousand kilos of cocaine. She is in her early forties. There was a stretch in a U.S. prison but that did not stop her. She flips open her phone directory and her finger races down the list of Colombian numbers. She still keeps in touch with Carlos Lehder, now technically retired from the Colombian cartels, free of the U.S. prison system and living in Cuba.

But she talks about El Señor de los Cielos, the Lord of the Skies. His mistress is a friend and they talk often. His mistress thinks El Señor is still alive. She leans across the table to me and says that in Mexico even the five-year-olds know that Amado Carrillo is not dead.

"He was too smart," she says softly.

Look, she explains, by the spring of 1997 he is notorious and is a problem for the Mexican government. He is hunted by DEA and other police forces. He has become the symbol of the drug business. So he checks into a hospital he owns, in a nation where he has his greatest human assets. And then, he officially dies.

"His best escape mechanism," she purrs on, "was death."

And now he is legally and officially dead, though on June 14, 2001, a Mexican daily reports a witness in an investigation asserts Carrillo still lives. In this testimony, the dead man substituting for Carrillo is one of his cousins.[1]

Dead men living on because of doubles is a tradition in Mexico. When Emiliano Zapata was murdered in 1919 the government took the precaution of filming his body, and organizing public viewings of his corpse. These efforts achieved nothing. Zapata was said to still be in the hills on a sorrel horse, or have shipped out as a sailor. The body was easily explained: Zapata had sent a double to the fatal meeting.[2]

Then she goes. She is moving some kilos of heroin to the Russian and Italian mafias in New York. She says her goal is to become a citizen of the U.S. She is giving her children, she says, a very good education. She makes a good living.

Cocaine, heroin, marijuana flow across the line and the prices keep dropping. By 1995, cocaine and heroin were, after adjusting for inflation, one third of their price in 1981. Marijuana had remained at its 1981 price but with much higher quality.[3]

In Juárez, Police Lieutenant Jesús Benavides explains, "We're realists. Corruption is never going to end. It's a culture going back generations. If you have someone in the back of your patrol car and he says to you, 'Take the money or I'll kill your family,' which one would you pick?"[4] The governor of Chihuahua comes to El Paso to receive the key to the city from the city council and mayor. He recently survived an assassination attempt from a federal police officer, a hit U.S. intelligence says came from the Juárez cartel. His director of public safety is rumored to be in the drug business but these charges are denied.[5]

Citibank, it is now discovered, somehow moved $300 million from drug dealers in Mexico to a financial institution in the Cayman Islands. The bank in the Cayman Islands had no physical office and its branch in Uruguay was the address of some accounting firm. Everything was tied into former government officials in Argentina. The money flowed from someone named Amado Carrillo. All this happened in the long ago, although it does not come to light until early 2001. Citibank says it had no idea the money was dirty.[6]

In Mexico City, the Defense Secretariat opens a museum on the top floor of its building. On a wall, 380 soldiers are listed who died in the War on Drugs. There are odd exhibits like a photo of a woman's ass full of heroin implants in a bungled smuggling attempt. There is a small model of a marijuana farm. A toy version of the truck owned by Amado Carrillo, the one that spewed clouds of smoke, nails, and oil slicks. Also, samples of jewelry and fancy guns seized from drug merchants.

The museum is not open to the public.[7]

On the refrigerator in the house in Plano, the big white, double-door machine that makes ice automatically and dispenses cold water at command, the one thing Phil Jordan has not touched or altered since the children left home, since the wife left his life, there is still that photograph of Bruno sitting on a couch back home in El Paso. He is smiling and wearing a T-shirt and his smooth face lacks the mark of a single lash from life. Stapled to the Xerox photograph are the two pages of handwritten lyrics for the song Tony Jordan composed in memory of his brother.

The song asks,

> *If he hadn't shot you—*
> *If he hadn't killed you*
> *Where would you be right now*
> *What would you be in life my son*
> *Where would you be right now*
> *Would you be sleeping*
> *Would you be dreaming or*
> *Eating Mom's apple pie . . .*

On January 20, 1995, a man goes down in El Paso, Texas. His killer is arrested, tried, convicted, and sentenced to twenty years. The killer is thirteen years old. Four years later, the killer becomes the alleged killer, and after two hung juries is released and extradited to Mexico. That is all there is to it.

The case is closed.

The case remains unsolved.

Brigitte's boy plays in the sunlight. The house is old and brick and surrounded by trees and shade. Inside, there are many toys and rooms. His sister stands near him. The air fills with laughter and bright voices.

Brigitte remembers as the child plays. She is Phil Jordan's daughter from his first marriage and now she is married and has children. She is interested in the arts. She is interested in civic improvements. She is active, the person who files the grant application, attends the meetings, gets things done. She is almost the same age as her Uncle Bruno, or the same Bruno would be if he had not been murdered in a K-Mart parking lot. She cannot believe what has happened to her relative Sal Martínez. She cannot fathom that Bruno is dead.

In the old photograph with her great-grandfather Eugenio, the one framed with that thank-you note from President Nixon, she looks up. His right arm hangs down from his shoulder slumped with more than eight decades of life and he clutches her tiny hand in his. She is cradled against his hip, her eyes squinting in the bright sunlight, her dark bangs riding like a helmet on her face. She wears pink shorts, a pink top, and the old man wears a pink shirt and slacks. Another great-grandchild is cradled by his left arm. The old man stares unsmiling at the camera and looks like a wolf with his young.

At the time of the photo, Phil Jordan has been in drug enforcement six or seven years. He is at the precise point where decades later, he decides he should have left, taken his federal experience and gone off to law school and another life. But he hesitated, the agency kept altering its name and booming and growing, the opportunities for advancement were so great, and so he stayed with narcotics enforcement. Just as his parents also changed their plans with the birth of Bruno, then a child like his daughter Brigitte. They also adjusted to a different future, closed their used clothing store and focused on raising this new boy, the one named after Eugenio's late brother, slaughtered so long ago in some village in Calabria down on the boot of Italy.

For Brigitte, her father's life is almost rumor, the DEA, the drug busts, the work. He left when she was very young, and her link to him were the summers when she lived with her grandparents on Frutas Street and stood by her great-grandfather's side in the glare of sunlight for a photograph. For Brigitte, Bruno was not an uncle but a fellow child. For Brigitte, El Paso was not a distant city but a force. The old house with cooking aromas, the lilt of Spanish in the air, the constant coming and going of relatives.

The rumor is that Amado Carrillo lives, that he sacrificed his brother Vicente in faking his own death, all this to satisfy the North Americans with their passion for DNA. Another rumor floats up that a succession of people have been murdered in Juárez. Each of the dead made a fatal mistake, this rumor says: they all claimed Amado Carrillo was still alive.

Phil Jordan dips his hand into old waters. He fields a phone call for a local narc investigation in Dallas and pretends to be a man named Enrique, a man who sells stolen cars and seeks drugs in payment. The woman on the phone is a member of the Juárez cartel and claims connections with the Mexican consulate in El Paso. She seeks Durangos, Lincolns, Mercedes, and this new American craze, the PT Cruiser.

Ah, Enrique says, if only you had called me yesterday, I had ten Mercedes. Now, at this moment, I have only two, one white, one black. The others, the Lincolns, Durangos, and PT Cruisers, they are no problem, Dallas is rich in such cars.

The woman has much to report. There is a new group in Juárez, don't you know, that calls itself Grupo Orion and its membership is comprised of state and local police. They have two business services. First, they protect drug dealers. Second, they have nine hundred hectares under cultivation in southern Chihuahua, the field green with marijuana. Seven hundred campesinos work these fields. Ah, yes, Jordan thinks to himself, it is another Rancho Búfalo like the plantation Kiki Camarena stumbled on so long ago when the drug business was wonderfully innocent.

And then, there is a moment that is unsettling. The woman insists, this woman from the bowels of the Juárez cartel, that Miguel Angel Flores is innocent, that he had no part in that shooting so long ago.

Why is she saying this? Phil Jordan wonders. Can it possibly be true?[8]

He cannot get away from this uncomfortable notion. He goes to a restaurant where the woman is dining and watches her from the bar. He has his girlfriend tail her into the restroom for a closer look. He is safe from detection since he is simply a voice named Enrique on the phone, not a face. But still, he knows he should not be there. But he has to see and get a sense of this woman from Juárez. He has to sniff the air and take in her scent and somehow decide if she is speaking truth or lies.

Later, he watches a videotape made of the woman, one taken by the narcs as part of the sting. He leans into the screen, tasting the body language, looking for some deep feeling that will tell him yes or no about this woman.

Six years after his brother's murder, Phil Jordan cannot get through a day, not a single one, without talking about him.

He leans into the screen looking for a message.

Former President Carlos Salinas keeps testing the waters in Mexico. In June 1999, he suddenly visits Mexico for the first time since his flight in March 1995. The day he departs a 6.7 magnitude earthquake kills seventeen. He returns in September. A 7.5 magnitude quake kills twenty-seven. In late December 1999, a 5.9 magnitude quake hits sixteen hours after he lands.

A Mexico City housewife announces, "even the Earth doesn't like him."[9]

U.S. congressional investigators conclude that U.S. and European banks launder between $500 billion and $1 trillion a year of what is called dirty money. No one really knows the real number. But they think that in the 1990s American banks laundered something like $2.5 trillion and $5 trillion. This is just the money count and skips real estate transfers, bogus security titles, and wire fraud. During the same years, the U.S. trade deficit keeps growing until it hits $300 billion a year. Dirty money flowing into U.S. banks helps make up this deficit.

Once in a while, like in the case of the Salinas brothers or in the case of Amado Carrillo, a small rivulet in this torrent is made known and decried.[10]

Two months into the administration of President Vicente Fox, the opposition leader who finally ended seventy-one years of rule by the PRI, a cabinet member explains how this new reality of a transfer of power must deal with an older reality of real power. He says in January 2001, "All of our phones, faxes and e-mails are monitored by the narcos. We are surrounded by enemies. We cannot attack corruption unless Washington ends its indifference to wrongdoing by the Mexican elite."[11]

If Bruno died in a contract murder, then why was Israel Reyes the first person asked to deliver the truck? Or was Reyes asked first simply as a ruse because it was known he would almost certainly refuse the request? And if the killing was an accident incidental to a simple carjacking, why did the boy, Miguel Angel Flores, refuse to consider a deal that bought him freedom and a reuniting with his family in the safety and affluence of the United States? And if the Juárez cartel had nothing to do with the death, if it was simply a non-event to Amado Carrillo as he went about the business of building his empire, then why did that same cartel allegedly funnel tens of thousands of dollars into financing the defense of the boy? And why in a place of such poverty as Juárez and El Paso has no one, not a single soul, ever called to try to earn the $100,000 reward, not even a crank? There are, by 1998, 72,000 people living around El Paso in 180 wildcat colonias, U.S. communities lacking water hookups, sewer connections, paved streets.[12] The city's substance abuse centers admit more people for heroin problems than for alcohol.[13] Over in Juárez, things do not look good. Wages in the maquiladoras, the largely American-owned foreign factories, pay about one fifth to one fourth of what a person needs to meet the basic needs of a family of four.[14] Still, the phone remains silent.

And then there is another matter, the rumor fluttering up from the drug business that Miguel Angel Flores, now free in Juárez, is working for the cartel. And that he is rising in the ranks.

In DEA circles, there is this belief that Phil Jordan lost his judgment, could not accept the simple truth and pain of a brother's death and blew it into something larger, into a fantasy of murder caused by a cartel. And there is a belief that Sal Martínez was a bad agent, a reckless agent, the rotten apple who simply got what he deserved.

Phil's daughter Brigitte goes over a part of her past. It is morning and the light is brilliant in the yard, the fire of summer has returned. She is talking about that last time in El Paso, that time just before Bruno's murder, when she had such a good time with him. Bruno has been dead six years.

"I was there," she says, "for two weeks and I hadn't been there in a long time. I was seeing Bruno as his own man. He'd always been protected by his mother and now he had his own things."

It is early January 1995, Brigitte is twenty-seven years old, Bruno the same age. The days are a blur for Brigitte. A relative has died and there is the funeral. Bruno is deep into a new girlfriend, and he fusses constantly to please her and worries about getting her upset.

One night they are all at a disco and Brigitte looks over and catches a glimpse of Bruno on the dance floor. The strobe light is blasting his face and he is looking "in this incredible knowing way." It is a second, two seconds, and then it is gone and Brigitte has this desire, this need, to know what Bruno knows, to learn what she sees in those flashing seconds. But the feeling passes and they dance and drink and she does not ask.

When the regime falls after seventy-one years, and the new government takes power in Mexico, there is a feeling of cautious hope in the air. Not optimism, just a glimmer of hope that things will start to improve. Or at least stop getting worse. The new government promises to end corruption. And to take on the drug cartels and start a new day in Mexico.

In 1996, future president Vicente Fox told a newspaper that everyone knew there were cabinet officials tangled up in the drug business, that "everyone knows that there are people involved with drugs at the highest levels of power."

After his inauguration, a DEA agent tells a U.S. reporter, "The good news is that Mexico has a new leader committed to fighting corruption. The bad news is that Washington has been unwilling to act against the top people who protect the cartels. The leading Mexican families are longtime friends with key U.S. political leaders: summit meetings, fishing and hunting trips, friendships among the wives and kids. They use the same clubs and lawyers."

Three months after the new presidency begins, Joaquín "El Chapo" Guzmán escapes from prison. He had done time with private cooks, whores, visits from fellow merchants, cell phones, alcohol, periodic hits of Viagra, a dictated daily menu, guards functioning as his servants, and other staff making shopping trips for him. He is alleged to have escaped in a prison laundry van. The government responds by arresting most of the staff and the warden, seventy-three in all. The president admits that the country has a problem in the law and order area. Guzmán had been imprisoned for suspected involvement in the murder of Cardinal Posadas Ocampo.[15]

And then seven months after it is in power, the new government arrests one of Amado Carrillo's key henchmen, a man reputed to have moved at least $200 million worth of cocaine and marijuana at wholesale values. For years he has lived and operated around Cancún. Formerly, he was state police commander in Juárez. He has a bas-relief of Don Quixote and Sancho Panza carved into his mansion. His partner, Eduardo González Quirarte, lived in the same area of mansions and the very rich.

There is talk of extraditing the man. And surely, since he was a key capo in Juárez from 1994 to 1998, he will know something about Bruno Jordan's murder. If he can be reached and if he wishes to talk. It is suddenly all conceivable. But of course, it is not. Phil Jordan is out of the agency. And Phil Jordan knows that neither his agency nor the FBI nor any other federal agency ever cared to look into his brother's murder.

On July 9, 2001, Comandante Jaime Yañez drives through Matamoros with his aide. At half past three in the afternoon five bullets enter his body, mainly his head. Two other bullets enter his aide's body. They are instantly killed. When the police arrive they find $20,000 in $20 bills in a black briefcase by Yañez's side. The state police where Yañez served say he was a model officer and is a victim of his relentless war against the drug cartels. The FBI announces that he was the fellow officer who cooperated in building the case against Salvador Martínez and, for this work, he received not a penny. Other opinions surface, namely, that he received somewhere between $30,000 and $200,000 for delivering Sal Martínez. And that he was murdered by the Mexican federal police for his greed in taking drug money, an avarice that naturally cut into the income of fellow officers. As for the Mexican state police, they insist the $20,000 found in his briefcase was planted by the Gulf cartel in an effort to smear Comandante Yañez.

Two days later Juan N. Guerra, the founder of the Gulf cartel and intimate of the Salinas family, dies peacefully at age eighty-six. A Mexican magazine runs a portrait of Guerra. He is baldheaded and seated at a table in a café. At each of the old man's shoulders is a young woman, blouse open and breasts spilling out. The women smile fetchingly at the camera.

Around 1:00 A.M. on July 25, 2001, a man and his daughter are machine-gunned to death in Juárez. A son survives. They were riding in a green Dodge Ram pickup when about a hundred rounds from AK-47s tore through their vehicle. Two cars had followed the Dodge for blocks before opening fire. The mother happened to be away at a conference in Mexico City. Her name is Dr. Irma Rodríguez and she was the Mexican forensics expert who identified the few bodies eventually recovered from what were once called the mass graves of Juárez in late 1999. She had also worked on the curious string of three hundred women murdered in Juárez since 1993. The police note that the slaughter of the family has nothing to do with her participation in the uncovering of the cartel graveyards. The authorities contend initially that the deaths were an accident resulting from loose rounds fired in some gangland dispute. There is no report of the killers or of their alleged target. A special Mexican police unit, Grupo Zeus, is investigating.

Dr. Rodríguez says of her work that in Juárez the dead can whisper things the living are afraid to say.[16]

Brigitte can still feel the joy of that night in January 1995 when they go out and buy lottery tickets, a few bucks at a time, and they keep winning and so they wind up going to ten or fifteen different 7-Elevens and other convenience stores and the streak holds.

"We weren't going to stop until we stopped winning," Brigitte explains.

And then they are back at the house on Frutas Street. Everything feels good, lighthearted. The world is like a song and the lyrics are obvious.

She is going out with a guy she has always known, her first lover. And that is past but still, they are friends. Bruno first introduced them when Brigitte was fourteen and now years later, they still like each other's company. She is over at the guy's place and his brother and sister are there. They are all sitting at the table talking about which movie they should go out and see. And suddenly, Brigitte says to the guy, let's go to your room. And so, they just stand up and go there.

They make love. And afterward, when Brigitte is lying there, she has this feeling, this absolute feeling and she knows she has conceived.

She is standing by the dining room table in the house on Frutas Street. Bruno is rushing about getting ready to go to work, grabbing his shoes, looking for socks, making sure of his necktie, a flurry on his way to the clothing store. She feels this urge to tell him how much she loves him, how much he means to her. But she cannot do it. The hurry of getting ready, the awkwardness of saying such things out loud, somehow it does not get said. And then he is gone.

She gets back home and makes plans to move to Colorado, take some classes, get on with her life. And she comes back to her house one evening and there are these messages on her answering machine from her father and the messages say that Bruno has been shot. She thinks, he can't be in real trouble, he must have been partying in Juárez at a club and maybe got caught in the crossfire of some gang shooting. That's it, maybe he took a round in his leg from accidental fire.

She calls her father and listens and says, "I'm going to bed now. Why don't you call me back in the morning."

And then, a while later, he calls back and tells her Bruno is dead. She becomes hysterical. Two hours later, she is on a bus to El Paso.

Her lover, Bruno's friend, picks her up.

She says, "I'm late." And he says nothing.

They stop, get the newspapers, which are headlines about Bruno's murder, and then go to Frutas Street. A day or two after the funeral, she buys a pregnancy test and the results are positive. She will carry the child to term.

"For me," she explains, "you can't have a life taken and then create a life in the same thirty days without there being a connection. While I was pregnant, the first time I came back to El Paso, I slept in Bruno's room.

"And I didn't want to close my eyes because I have always been afraid of seeing too much and not being able to handle it.

"But finally, I did close my eyes. And I felt a hand going down my side and then I heard the whisper of prayers, indistinct, but I could tell they were prayers, that they were some chant. And I knew it was Bruno. And he took his hand and opened my mouth and then his other hand is putting pressure on my abdomen.

"Finally, I open my eyes and then I see him. He is smiling and he is wearing a basketball jersey. He is fourteen, maybe sixteen years old.

"He begins floating backward, getting smaller and smaller. And then he vanishes."

When the new president ran for office, he promised to expose the sins of the former regime during its seventy-one long and dark years of rule. He would bring to justice the murderers of Cardinal Posadas Ocampo in Guadalajara. He would bring to justice the murderers of presidential candidate Luis Donaldo Colosio. He would bring to justice the murderers of José Ruiz Massieu. In his inauguration, he said, "I propose to open what has remained closed in sensitive episodes of our recent history and investigate that which has not been resolved, through a body that attends to the demands for truth by the majority of Mexicans."[17] Every Mexican had a private list of things to be exposed and made right, of justice that must be exacted for the sins and crimes of this long and dark past. The slaughter of the university students in 1968. The real truth of all the people who disappeared over the years.

And there are gestures toward a new kind of government. The new president, for example, denounces torture as a police tool. Confessions obtained through torture are legally admissible in Mexican courts. Between 1997 and 2000, Mexican law enforcement spent $15 million on shock batons, stun guns, straitjackets, and shackles, supplies useful for torture. Of course, the common methods—water laced with pepper sprayed up the nose, electric cattle prods to the genitals, head dunking in a toilet full of feces and urine, a file cabinet slammed on the head— hardly require special purchases. Generally, confessions obtained under torture are the only evidence in Mexican courts since it is felt the police lack the investigative skills to produce other kinds of evidence.[18]

But once in office and as the months roll past, the new president begins to hesitate in probing too deeply into Mexico's past. There is a growing reluctance in the new government to explore the killings of the past and it becomes an open question whether the government can even rule if it looks into the past. The families of the missing sue and demand that federal prosecutors file charges against all the ex-presidents. The new attorney general cautions, "We're not magicians. If we have the chance to clarify cases, we'll do it. But if not . . . well, no."[19]

The FBI hides a former federale comandante who is a legend in Juárez. He personally is credited with fifty to sixty executions for the cartel. Now he has crossed the river and cut a deal with the U.S. government because if he stays in Juárez he will die. But no one really asks him about the dead, about his own little graveyard on the line. In the end, the dead are left to take care of the dead.

In August 2001, Carlos Hank González dies of cancer at age seventy-three. Thousands attend his funeral, just as for years thousands attended

his annual birthday party at his estate outside Mexico City. He is suddenly someone that can be discussed. The U.S. press has brief notices
that mention his charm and power and how he was seen as the leader of
traditional and conservative elements in the government of Mexico. No
mention is made of his alleged association with drug merchants or of the
recurrent and thwarted U.S. investigations of him and his family.

A leading Mexican magazine headlines the death by saying,
"Goodbye Godfather." The magazine makes clear it means its use of
Godfather "to be in the style of the mafias in Sicily."[20]

At the end of August 2001, Phil Jordan's bankruptcy petition is
granted.

But first the judge asks him a question: "Have you won the lottery
in the last sixty days?"

She pauses here, she does not want to make too much of these
moments. She does not want to make claims, no claims at all. It is just
that she knows, she was there, certain feelings are not to be denied.

When the baby is born, Brigitte takes the child to El Paso. She carries him through the front door, he can't talk yet, and he sees a photograph of Bruno. And points firmly at it. Then, the family starts to listen to him, to watch him. They look for signs and yet cannot really
admit what they are looking for. The boy will be in another room, and
he's talking to himself the way small children do. He will see a photograph of Bruno and he will tell himself out loud, "He's an angel."

The child always wants to go to El Paso. And whenever he enters
the house on Frutas Street, he says, "I'm home." He never wants to
leave. Out of the blue, he will bring up Bruno.

I am drinking in my yard with a retired DEA agent. He spent years in
Mexico, survived gun battles, and then spent more years tracking the
huge flows of money. Night has fallen, and he sits in the shadows sipping a Pacífico, the beer of Sinaloa. He likes to talk at these moments
but he never wishes these conversations to go on the record because, he
explains to me repeatedly, they cannot be beaten. And this "they" he
refers to is the CIA.

So, he gives an example. He tracks drug money out of Mexico to a Swiss account, hundreds of millions of dollars. Maybe a billion, he offers. He prepares to move on the account.

But by the time he receives clearance to move, the account is empty. I look up and wait.

Yes, he continues, they vacuumed it. And he makes clear that he means the CIA.

He refuses to explain how he knows. He refuses to go on record.

He repeats that they cannot be beaten.

I let it go. It is part of the erased times. Amid all the Salinas family problems, amid all the Amado Carrillos, amid the pain of Bruno Jordan's murder, among the boneyards that dot the border, it must be mentioned. We have the files, the agencies have carefully taped and noted many things. Our history sleeps in cabinets and vaults.[21]

For the sixth anniversary of Bruno's murder, Beatrice and Antonio place an announcement in the El Paso newspaper. A photograph captures a young businessman with a white shirt, tie, good suit, and the glasses of a banker. The text runs:

> If I could I would try to change the world I brought you to and never let the harm that came to you this I'd do if I could. If I could, I would keep you safe from that fateful night and would never leave you from my sight this I'd do if I could. If I could, I would keep you from the time & place you were going to be and keep you next to me. This I'd do if I could.
>
> We miss you Bruno.
> Love,
>
> *Mom & Dad*

But it is so hard to let it go. On November 24, 2001, the bodies of four men are found in Juárez. They'd been partying at Hooligan's, a nightclub favored by the stylish set. One of the men had asked a woman to dance and then her boyfriend threw a punch. The people who worked at the club warned the men to leave and offered to forgive their bar bill. Later, they were pulled over in their car by the Juárez city police. The squad car left when five other cars arrived, complete with ten armed men and federal police. The four men were beaten to death and this incident would have been erased—except that there were five men and one of them, David Sánchez Santacruz, was left for dead and yet somehow lived.

The El Paso paper notes, "The boyfriend's identity has not been revealed."

The whole incident has an eerie echo of what Memo once told me about Bruno dancing with one of Carrillo's women in a Juárez club and that being the reason for his death. Of course, Memo vanished and his tale led to nowhere.

In this recent incident, there is one tiny detail that bubbles up in Juárez, though it is never published. The boyfriend who throws the punch and then has city police round up the men and then apparently has armed federal police beat them to death, well, his name is whispered. He is a relative of Amado Carrillo. A week later, he is married in Sinaloa.[22]

I let the story go. You learn to let things go.

He was framed, as was his brother. It's like this. When Carlos Salinas became president, he sought to modernize Mexico. The old guard, the nomenkultura in his account, fought him. His successor as president, Ernesto Zedillo, destroyed the economy and the peso through a colossal blunder and then blamed Carlos Salinas. His brother was set up through the bribery and torture of witnesses. His chosen successor, Luis Donaldo Colosio, was murdered by evil forces and then some had the gall to blame him for this catastrophic killing. Mexico suddenly became a gangster state, a place without law or rights where men are framed, reputations are smeared, and government responsibility is shifted onto the shoulders of the innocent, namely Carlos Salinas. The thirteen-hundred-page defense, *Mexico: The Policy and Politics of Modernization,* causes a stir when published in 2000 (appearing in English in 2002) and goes through several printings. Running summaries dot the margins and the pages are deeply footnoted with news clips and asides about the real history of his accusers. Carlos Salinas is blameless, save for trying to bootstrap Mexico out of a doomed economic strategy of high tariffs and state industries and into its only possible future as part of a global economy.

For the first time, Carlos Salinas describes a Mexico remarkably like the one he governed, a place of vast illegal enrichment, of secret torture, of law being a farce, of a PRI party saturated with privilege and corruption. Only he places this Mexico in the administration of his successor, Ernesto Zedillo. And it is difficult not to believe many of his charges since they sound like the background music to the world of Amado Carrillo, of the thousands murdered in the drug trade, of the police and generals so easily bribed to look the other way. Salinas's deconstruction of the murder case against his brother Raúl playfully points out the farcical moments, the *bruja* locating the body in Raúl's garden, the bogus nature of the corpse, the sleazy features of the investigation. It all sounds like the farcical investigation of the murder of the cardinal in the Guadalajara airport produced by his own administration in 1993. Or the stuttering response and explanation of the revolt in Chiapas by the Zapatistas on New Year's Eve of 1994. Or the trial in secret of the alleged killer of Colosio while Salinas was president. But his account of his brother's travails offers no real explanation for the hundreds of millions of dollars Raúl secretly stashed away in foreign accounts while toiling as a civil servant in the government of Carlos Salinas—"I must admit that I did not pay enough attention to Raúl's activities," he allows finally on page 1306. But he is adamant that the money did not come from the drug world.

Dreamtime has finally reached the highest levels of society, and in this unreality, Carlos Salinas must try to use facts against a world of shadows and rumors and smears and lies. He must finally, perhaps for the first time, become a Mexican and know what it is like to be at the mercy of power that answers to no one. Born and raised in an elite, in that sheltered group known as the untouchables, he is now finally part of *la gente,* the people, those who can be touched. And mauled.

•   •   •

Phil Jordan hardly ever has this dream and in ways he is grateful for
that fact. But still the dream comes. He is alone in bed in his home in
Plano and has shut the door to his room lest the cat leap on him in the
night and ruin his sleep. In this dream, Jordan feels someone pushing
and pushing against him. He senses he is being tossed about on the
bed. He worries because Bruno is sleeping in the next room and he
does not want anything to disturb his brother. He finally gets up in his
dream and walks quietly to the next bedroom and finds with relief that
his brother is still slumbering in peace.

In the morning, Jordan awakens with a start. The dream is still
firmly in his mind. He leaps out of bed and goes to the next room to
find his brother.

The room is empty.

He is the kind of child who is alert and bright and happy and yet
somehow circumspect. He has this gravity as if he were watching
things. He is a lot like Lionel Bruno Jordan was as a small child, the
child who is happy and yet somehow older than his years. The child
who said when spanked, "Thank you, I needed that." The youngest
child who slowly but surely became the counselor to his much older
brothers and sisters.

The new child's middle name is Lionel.

He is given two kittens, and he names one, a black cat, Shadow.
Then suddenly, he begins calling Shadow, who is of course black,
Brownie. The family is taken aback. Phil Jordan wonders what it
means. Brigitte is at a loss to explain the new name. Brownie was the
name of Bruno's dog, an animal that slept in his bed every night and
looked for him ceaselessly after his murder.

Some things are beyond questions, especially since years of questions have brought the family nothing but ruin. No one in the family
asks why the water glass monitored by Beatrice in Bruno's old room,
the glass by the candles forever kept burning, keeps going up and
down depending on, well, depending on what one makes of it. There is
always of course a choice to be made. The story can be about the lies
made by governments to protect their economic interests and further

their foreign policy goals. The story can be about the war on drugs. The story can be about the rise of the Mexican cartels, a major readjustment in global capitalism that occurs at the end of the twentieth century. The story can be about one Mexican family's rapacious rise to the presidency of the nation. The story can be about one poor Mexican's innovations in escaping the poverty of village life in Sinaloa. The story can be about one narc's career and the collateral damage that comes from the life. Or the story can be about not having a story, about not understanding, about simply accepting a kitten whose name shifts as some kind of consciousness flows from a place beyond simple knowing or telling.

Brigitte remembers the viewing of the body in the funeral home, those first few days when she sensed she was carrying a child, and this guy came in with a big camera, one with a flash and everything, and he was from Juárez, she could tell this fact at a glance from the clothes, the body language, it was stamped all over him. And suddenly, he is up at the coffin snapping pictures of Bruno—Bruno lying there with his Washington Redskins cap, his DEA badge, his red ribbon memorializing Kiki Camarena that says "Proud To Be Drug-Free" (and he was, not even a trace of Tylenol in the autopsy report), his little DEA flashlight tucked in his suit pocket—and the guy keeps snapping pictures, leaning right over Bruno's body, and she flipped, she thought, what is this? And she went up to the guy and asked, "What are you doing?" and the guy just scurried off and left the building, left just like that, and she ran and got her father and they went out in the parking lot, her father in a kind of daze, asking, what? A guy taking pictures? And the guy is moving off and she points and her father stops the guy, and he has no press credentials but yes, he is from Juárez. And that ends it. She never asks her father what the strange moment meant. Or who wanted the pictures. Because, she knew, deep down inside, and the photographer was gone and was across the bridge with his images, a trophy for someone who wanted a photograph of Bruno dead, a corpse framed and ready to mount. You learn to stop asking because you know and what you know is all you are ever going to know. And Bruno is murdered, cut down, a carjacking they say, something that happened down by the river, near that line, back then, in one of those places.

The child is in the sunlight. Brigitte is talking.

She knows better than to think there are answers. She knows better than to believe in vengeance.

What she knows is this: the child is in the sunlight.

our country

I'm with a friend, a photographer. We've gone to La Campana, one of the private graveyards of Amado Carrillo, and looked at the holes in the ground. I am struck by how the site was open to view from the highway.

My friend gently admonishes me, "The work is done at night."

Across the river as night falls, I know there is a candle burning. And beside the taper rests a glass of water that goes down according to the thirst. And I know Beatrice at times has been out hanging clothes on the line to dry in the yard beside the house on Frutas Street. And suddenly she has heard Bruno calling, "Mom, Mom." This has happened to her twice and she is certain that he is telling her that he is all right.

Here the feeling is different. My friend shows me another compound, one very near a burning man he once encountered. He'd gotten this call about a body and gone to take a photograph. The night before two kids out fooling around had noticed a small fire but they'd not taken a close look and gone home. In the morning, they ambled over and found a man about sixty, charred but with some sense of his face still apparent despite the blaze. Nearby there were sixty empty packets that had held cocaine. The photograph had been terrific, a shot worthy of a poster for the *Friday the 13th* movie series. But the paper had run the image very small and now he'd lost the negative. He loses most of his negatives and does not seem to care about this loss.

Suddenly, he turns down a rutted track, wanders a bit past a warehouse, and then there it is, the high walls, the concertina wire, the stout steel gates, the few windows covered with a film that blocks curious eyes.

He says, "Everyone knew this belonged to the cartel. Everyone always knows. The police are always the first to notice, it is their business to notice, to collect their money. But everyone, when they see these places, knows they are narco. Sometimes I would go in and ask questions and no one could ever give real answers. You always know."

The huge complex sits on a corner. It has been seized now by the city and my friend does not know what goes on there. Just as he does not know what went on there. He knows just one thing: you always know.

The sky is an angry gray, the walled compound looks lonely under this sky. Maybe there is someone buried within. No one is going to ask. There is a fistful of narco sites in this neighborhood alone and they are left to slumber unnoticed and undug.

There is a line dividing the two nations. It is official and marked. But it has been erased in this pain.

"What about the burning man? What was his name, what happened?"

My friend cannot remember, he is not sure the case was ever pursued. He just recalls the photograph he made, how the body was burned and yet the face still held in a vague way, the lips curled back from the heat, the teeth gleaming up at him. He never mentions the smell. There is talk that people living around La Campana noticed bad smells. I'm skeptical of this point since the graves were six feet deep. But no coffins were used in the work. Sometimes quicklime, what Amado Carrillo called "a dose of milk," but no coffins. The smell seems to have been lost to my friend's memory. Just as the negative is now lost. And the man's name is gone.

When I landed in the republic of conscience
it was so noiseless when the engines stopped. . . .

At immigration, the clerk was an old man
who produced a wallet from his homespun coat
and showed me a photograph of my grandfather.

—SEAMUS HEANEY, "THE REPUBLIC OF CONSCIENCE"

afterword / dead men not talking

He is on the phone and very upset. Recently, the comandante had told Phil Jordan to clear out of Texas and watch his back. And now, Phil Jordan hurriedly continues, a single bullet has snuffed out the comandante's life. I hang up and I know I am going. There is suddenly a huge hole in this alternative universe and I want to taste this void before night falls and this gaping wound disappears from view. The Mexican press is claiming that the FBI beat local cops to the murder scene. A rumor hits the U.S. press that a drug leader paid $3 million for the hit. A Mexican magazine announces the comandante was getting ready to return to Mexico and tell all. What can I say? He allegedly made hundreds of millions of dollars, he allegedly killed more people than anyone can count, and he absolutely beat two governments into submission. He lived and thrived in obscurity except among those who had also tasted the life.

And I am going because the comandante coursed through this book like a shadow and his death underscores the silence this book sought to end when it was first published in the fall of 2002. The book argues that the drug industry is buried alive in a secret history and that this hidden history is demanded by the political needs of the United States and Mexico. The death of the comandante chokes off forever the knowledge of one of the great players in this unauthorized history. It is like hearing a match strike in some great library and reeling back as a wall of flames devours all the records.

So I hear the comandante has at last fallen, put down the phone, and I go to the killing ground to say goodbye to part of my past and part of his past. But I know this past is not past, that it is buried but not dead, that it is out of sight but still swaggering down the corridors of power and growling in some of the hardest streets in the world.

The small metal statue of a steer and mounted cowboy sleeps on the huge wooden conference table in the dead man's office. It has been only five days since the execution briefly barked out terror at the comandante's lawyer's office on the northern edge of McAllen, Texas, and yet everything has already slipped far into the past. The son's voice purls out soft words as he sits at his father's oak desk in the trading company near the border. He is explaining that his father lived an honorable life and died an honorable death. Just one bullet to the neck and he was gone as he entered his Mercedes-Benz on a sunny February day. The son sweeps his arms as if holding a machine gun, goes ack! ack! ack! as he demonstrates the alternatives, the disfiguring results possible from a barrage of high-velocity rounds. But in the case of Guillermo González Calderoni, death came swiftly, almost tranquilly. The dead man's office seems almost unoccupied as the son softly continues. A huge conference table with no chairs for a meeting. A large side table with a sculpture of an eagle, the big desk with little on it to show any kind of work. And a phone which in the course of the hour only rings once and that with a call from the boy's mother, Calderoni's first wife.

In a day or a week, surely in a month, Calderoni and his life and his death will all but be erased. The footprints of his life will blow away as the ground shifts in the secret world where he thrived. He will become a figure known by a few old cops and agents and analysts savoring twelve-year-old scotch, a story told in some murderous cantinas, a memory to some beautiful women as they rest their heads against their fine pillows in those special moments just before sleep comes. He was the man who knew everything and his death means—and of this I am certain—that now certain things will never be known. That is the way of the world that produced him and that world was not simply Mexico or the border or the drug wars but more accurately a world of spies, secrets, agents, networks, the basic tissue governments have increasingly found so necessary as events overwhelmed simple customs and laws. I have never met an American who even knew Calderoni's name unless they had entered certain rooms and certain conditions and tasted certain pains. On the other hand, I know a drug dealer in Dallas who reacted to his death as if a fire bell had tolled in the night.

The son explains that his father and he lived separate lives, that his father's business was his father's business, and the son has followed a different path. He has deliberately spoken to no one in the press, he rolls on, because he wants his father to rest in peace. But then everyone wants his father to rest in peace, and especially to stay silent. *Epoca,* a Mexican magazine, runs a simple graphic to explain the murder: the face of his father with a gun to his head and imprinted on the mouth the universal symbol of a circle with a slash across it. The *New York Times* at first dismisses the killing with seventy-odd words and then after a pause of thirteen days, finally runs an article explaining that Comandante Calderoni was a creature from the past, a footnote to an era that is now "as remote and romantic as cowboys and Indians."[1] The world, the paper asserts, has moved on into a new time of terror and bombs and the highjinks of a Calderoni are now both quaint and irrelevant. The son in his utter calm seems to agree. He wears a soft cotton shirt with a plaid pattern, slacks, loafers, and has a bookkeeper quality. Ah, he explains, he knows nothing of his father's activities, he simply runs the family business, this trading company where the phones never seem to ring. The large building is full of offices and yet nothing seems to go on in them. Men mill about, burly men, and underneath their jackets the outlines of barrels push against the fabric. One man opens a desk drawer as if looking for a file, and there gleaming is a machine pistol.

Just what does the firm export? Ah, an oil, yes, an oil, the son explains, a special oil, though he cannot quite remember what it is at the moment. And drinks, yes, some wine and vodka, things like that also, he continues. There are no samples in the silent building, nothing that indicates activity except numerous squat paper-shredding machines. The office is down by the Rio Grande, right across from Reynosa, Mexico, where the comandante was born and raised. McAllen itself has a hundred thousand people and is a border boomtown eager for the riches of NAFTA to shower down.

His father perished at 11:54 A.M. on Wednesday, February 5, 2003. The funeral was Friday, followed instantly by a cremation because, the son continues, his father had always expressed a wish to be free of the grave, to be part of the wind and the world. So as we sit on Monday in the late afternoon, everything is over, the era of cowboys and Indians has ended. Why just last week, his father had gone deer hunting in the scrub around the city. And on the day of his death, he had called his lawyer, a relative, and said he must see him immediately, he was excited about buying a ranch, and so he would be in early against all habit and custom that had governed his life. And then, suddenly, the murder. And now the desire for tranquillity, a desire shared by people in many places, in the FBI, in DEA, in the highest reaches of the Mexican government, in the largest drug organizations on earth, in the vaults of American secrets where clerks quietly bury unseemly sections of the history of the United States.

I nod at the son, say that I understand. And I do.

When the Mexican government sought to extradite his father from the United States in the early 1990s, they pegged his wealth at $400 million, hardly a remarkable sum since the Juárez cartel, just one part of the industry, was at the time earning $200 million a week. The comandante while walking down the corridor of the federal courthouse in San Antonio during the extradition hearings offered that if he was hounded much more, he might begin to remember things—a warning aimed at the Mexican government. The court decided to let him remain in the U.S., gave him permanent residency and then he largely slipped from notice. Until one round of a 9mm cracked in the parking lot of his lawyer. Calderoni knew too much and now that knowledge is safely committed to the furnace and that fabled ash bin of history.

It is worth a few moments to review the bones of Calderoni's career that are scattered throughout this book. He was born March 26, 1948, in Reynosa, Mexico, to a rising official in Pemex, the nationalized Mexican oil industry. His heritage was part Italian and in adult life he used his mother's name. Calderoni grew up with the García Abrego family, the clan that would rise to dominate the Gulf cartel, the premier drug organization of the late 1980s and early 1990s. Juan García Abrego, now serving eleven life sentences in the U.S., called Calderoni his brother in a tape secretly made by the U.S. government. Calderoni became a Mexican cop.

By the 1970s, he appears in Phoenix to participate in an early U.S.-Mexican drug raid along the border. After days of being wined and dined and heavy visitations at the Playboy Club, the group crosses the line and takes down tons of marijuana in San Luis, a Mexican town on the Arizona line, a bust that helps launch Phil Jordan's career. The DEA notices several things. Calderoni, a young agent, was careful not to let the Mexican army know of the raid lest they warn the drug dealers. And after the raid, they witness another facet: Calderoni and his colleagues took the prisoners into another room and then the screams began. The Americans in the sweet joy of victory ignored a third thing: all the big guys escaped.

Calderoni's reputation begins as a Mexican cop who can get things done. He joins the federal police in 1983 and is a protégé of Florentino Ventura, a man who eventually rises to run the federales. Ventura is part of the blur of Mexico that U.S. officials can never quite comprehend. He ends his career this way: he is in his car with his wife and two guests. Ventura is driving, his wife nagging. He shoots her and then blows his own brains out.

Calderoni cuts an image. He's about five-foot-seven, knows English, Italian, Spanish, French, travels to Europe for holidays and to buy breeding stock for his kennel which specializes in rottweilers, dresses very well, and is a crack shot with a .45, which he wears strapped to his boot. He sometimes helps U.S. agents, a minor miracle for a Mexican federal cop. He is stationed in Matamoros, the ground zero of the Gulf cartel and of his boyhood friend, Juan García Abrego, and yet he is viewed as oddly clean by his American counterparts because sometimes he gives up criminals to them. He loves women and marries Miss Mexico. He is said to be independently wealthy thanks to his family.

When U.S. DEA agent Enrique Camarena is kidnapped, tortured and murdered in Guadalajara in 1985, Calderoni cooperates with DEA and earns their eternal gratitude and trust. He tells agents that he is "the greatest cop in the world," and they like to believe him.

A legend begins to trail him, one that strikes awe in American agents and terror in Mexican citizens. Rumors spread that he interrogates with a bolt cutter, the ultimate twenty questions. Or sometimes it is said he uses pliers on the teeth, allegations he always denies. When a capo in Juárez roughs up a member of the American press, Calderoni is sent in to placate U.S. protests. He does several things. He tells the previous comandante that he has twenty-four hours to get out of town. He goes to the mansion of the offending capo, nimbly getting past the pet tiger, alligators and boa constrictors, and hauls the guy and his pistoleroes off to prison.[2] Then he goes down river to Ojinaga, Chihuahua and murders Pablo Acosta, at that moment the major conduit of Colombian cocaine through Mexico into the U.S. In the last action, the FBI arranges helicopter transport from Fort Bliss to Mexico. Calderoni is that stand-up guy to U.S. agents.

But to their consternation, the agents keep hearing of a different Calderoni from the snitches, one noted earlier in this book. They promptly bury this information in their secret files. In part, because Calderoni is the kind of Mexican connection that can make a narc's career, a man who can hand them the big case all wrapped up in a ribbon with a bow. And in part, because they cannot believe the truth since it means their Mexico is not the real Mexico.

At the very moment the FBI is cooperating with Calderoni in his plan to murder Acosta courtesy of U.S. military helicopters, they possess a report from a snitch who has recently been with the comandante and his colleague Chato in Mexico. The Calderoni of this report, and it is one worth recalling now that Calderoni is dead and silenced, is miffed because some of his men have been busted in El Paso for selling cocaine. He explains the matter has been fixed and that if necessary, he can get more coke. Also, the comandante notes that he has a man who crosses his drugs into El Paso. Ah, the comandante allows, the DEA agents are all sonsofbitches, as are the FBI.

In this meeting with the FBI snitch, Calderoni is told that the head of the Gulf cartel is funneling his payments through a certain intermediary to Calderoni's boss and patron, Florentino Ventura, the head of the federal police and Mexico's Interpol representative. The comandante also learns that Juan García Abrego wishes to see him and give him a gift. Calderoni says that he will be in his mansion in Reynosa in a few days and ready for such a visit. A gift of course would be nice since García Abrego's drug business is earning $10 to $20 billion a year. The comandante explains that Juárez is awash with marijuana, cocaine, heroin and barbiturates but there is really no problem because the local DEA and FBI "were not worth a damn, and a bunch of assholes."

That memo goes into a file and is buried for years and years. As is the information that Calderoni, the hero of the raid that murders Pablo Acosta, got a million-dollar fee from Amado Carrillo Fuentes, the eventual boss of the Juárez cartel, for wiping out his competitor. The image of Calderoni that persists is of him riding back from the killing ground with the body of Acosta at his feet like a bagged deer.

For the U.S. agencies, the comandante is the man they can go to, the Mexican cop that makes their careers. The file is only rare in one way: in 1998 it slips into the hands of Terrence Poppa, an American writer and he publishes it. No one pays the slightest attention to this fact. Nor does the American press clamor for the opening of the tens of thousands of secret files strangled in various U.S. agencies, files detailing day by day the absolute partnership of the Mexican government, the Mexican army, the Mexican police and the Mexican drug cartels.

Calderoni deals with the FBI, DEA, the heads of the Mexican government, the heads of the cartels, he is the man who lives in the space between loyalties and exploits the needs of others to be loyal to something.

The FBI brings him to conferences in the U.S. as a model of their kind of cop. DEA hosts him at its secret intelligence center in El Paso and then takes him to Washington for more briefings and accolades. When Calderoni boards the planes with the DEA agents, he has a hot woman on his arm. The agents show him his seats in the back of the plane. He waves them off, takes his woman up front and buys two first-class seats on the spot.

Flowers drench the air in McAllen in early February, the bougainvillea is a riot of bloom, the trees lush and green, the sun tropical. The lawyer's office on North Tenth Street is called Nightingale Plaza and the building is secreted from the busy street by a wall and vegetation. The lobby is leather-covered Victorian furniture, a marble floor and a receptionist with fine bones, brilliant teeth and eyes that do not whisper statute numbers. She goes in to get Calderoni's lawyer, the next-to-last man to see him alive. He is an easy six feet, gray hair, generous gut and he looks at me with hostility. I can smell fear rising off him. He has only told the press one thing: that the late comandante was not thinking of talking to any agencies about anything. Why are you asking about this murder? his eyes say. We get past this moment and he explains what happened.

It was this ranch thing, the comandante had all but become crazed about buying a ranch. Maybe it was the second marriage to yet another beauty queen, and the two young children, one now a year and a half, the other six. The comandante at fifty-four was beginning yet another life. He lived quite well, secure in his mansion in his gated community and played golf regularly. But he never called before, say, 11:00 A.M., and yet that day he phoned early and was at the office by 10:00 A.M. He wanted that very day to go with his lawyer to look at ranches but the attorney's schedule made this impossible so they agreed to make their inspection the coming Saturday, a day when it turned out Calderoni would be reduced to ash and bone.

When they came out of the office, the comandante flirted with the receptionist, then went out to his Mercedes, which was about ten feet from the door and parked facing the building. Suddenly a car wheeled up pinning the Mercedes, a man leapt from the passenger side, there was one shot, and then the car sped away. Calderoni was pronounced dead in the hospital emergency room. Only Chato, his companion, witnessed the murder. He was sitting beside Calderoni in the car, and yet no one sought to harm him. At first, he gave police a description—two men with dark skin, a Chrysler with Louisiana plates. Then he recanted, said he was too emotionally upset to recall what he had seen. He had violent diarrhea for three days. The next day the police found the car he described about thirty blocks away. The Louisiana plates were stolen. On the window was a decal for the Mexican Red Cross. At that the trail went dead, though the police did offer that they suspected it was a professional hit and came from Mexico. McAllen only averages ten murders a year and this is the very first one for 2003.[3]

The baffled lawyer speculates to me that the hitters simply circled the block and then rushed in when the comandante emerged. When I try this out, it takes me slightly over a minute to go around the block and during that minute it is impossible to see into the lawyer's parking lot. On the other hand, anyone parked in the lot could perform the execution easily.

I go to the trading company to visit with the son. The address I'm given does not exist so I enter an office building near it. There is no such company listed in the building directory. I ask a woman entering the elevator. Turns out she is the daughter of the landlord and says, I know that name, Calderoni, they are tenants, I get their checks. She takes me to a firm with a different name, one also specializing in import-export. It is one huge room with no windows. A small lovely woman sits at a desk and tends the phone. No, she says, she has never heard the name Calderoni. Back in the corner of the huge office is one other desk, and a coffeemaker. I have a drink next door at a barbeque joint. Ah, Calderoni? yes, they had a wedding reception here, everyone came from the office next door. Which is what the hairdresser across the street told me. In fact, she was the one who originally steered me to the office since she remembered the big party the day of the wedding.

When later I meet Calderoni's son in yet another family office and ask him about this strange phantom business, his face becomes blank and he politely tells me he knows nothing about such an office. I tell him I must have made a mistake.

Life, of course, was success after success for the comandante. He bonds deeply with U.S. law enforcement, deepens his ties thanks to help in rounding up some of the killers of Camarena, and then in 1989, takes down Miguel Angel Félix Gallardo, the brilliant leader of the Guadalajara cartel, uncle of the boys who become the Tijuana cartel, and a former policeman to boot. Calderoni becomes famous for putting the muzzle of an AK-47 into Félix Gallardo's mouth and for turning

down a $5 million bribe for letting him go. Félix Gallardo retires qui-
etly to a luxurious prison suite where according to DEA he continues
to run his flourishing drug business.

Calderoni is dubbed the Eliot Ness of Mexico, an Untouchable. He
is though touched by a million-dollar bribe when he helps get the
brother of a cartel leader released from prison.[4] He helps in other ways.
In 1988, Mexico's ruling party, the PRI, is in a fight for its life.
Cuauhtemoc Cárdenas, son of a revered former president, has broken
with the party and is running for president. Three days before the election, his three key aides are murdered in Mexico City. Calderoni later
tells the FBI that his friend García Abrego did it. But the suspicion
lingers that the comandante delivered the order for the hit.[5] On election night, Cárdenas is clearly winning when the computers break
down for over thirty hours. When they come up, the PRI candidate,
Carlos Salinas de Gortari, has won. Calderoni is credited with stealing
the computer passwords. He becomes the top cop under President
Salinas, his personal hitter. Salinas has consistently denied that he was
involved in any election fraud.

Once when I ask a DEA agent how many people he thinks
Calderoni has murdered, he says, "Who cares? If he has killed two hundred, I'll guarantee a hundred and ninety-nine of them are assholes."

In the fall of 1991, the comandante begins having secret debriefings with U.S. prosecutors who had indicted Juan García Abrego. He
tells them that Raúl Salinas, the brother of the Mexican president, col-
lects the drug money for the president. President Salinas is the Great
White Hope of the United States at the time, the proponent of free
trade and the man who has officially increased Mexico's anti-drug budget seven-fold.[6] As Calderoni reveals his information, the debriefings
are ended on orders from Washington and the information falls dead
into files.

In February 1993, the comandante seeks safety in the United
States when the Mexican government suddenly accuses him of torture
and illegal enrichment, the charges coming because of fears he is talking to U.S. officials. Allegedly, the FBI wants to ship him back but is
stopped by DEA. In the hearings, Calderoni admits to a fortune of

about $7 million, one he accounts for through inheritance and various wise investments.

It is easy to lose sight of reality in this blur of events. Things get forgotten. For instance, when the U.S. wanted Calderoni to get Juan García Abrego (who is now serving multiple life sentences in a U.S. penetentiary) to turn himself in, the comandante failed because García Abrego told him that the Salinas family, meaning the president and his brother, should protect him considering all the business they'd done together. This statement seems to disappear from consciousness and when the president, Carlos Salinas, ends his term at the end of 1994, he proudly sits on the board of the Dow Jones Corporation, the company that owns the *Wall Street Journal.* Salinas has consistently denied any involvement with the drug cartels.

People come from Mexico for the comandante's funeral and the church of Saint Joseph the Worker in McAllen is packed. Some retired DEA agents show up, along with a lot of other people who do not advertise who and what they are. In the border press some accounts of Calderoni's career emerge but in general there is a vast desire to forget it. One former DEA agent even denies that the comandante ever took dirty money or played both sides against the other. Or did murder for hire.

Back in 1997, Calderoni had mysteriously erupted in a huge story in the *New York Times,* complete with a photo of him posing with President Carlos Salinas. In the story, U.S. officials explained that Calderoni's charges were dismissed because "back in 1993, it was very unpopular to say anything against Mexico, basically because of NAFTA. Who was going to go and do a direct investigation against the president's brother? You just put it away, and it goes into the batter."[7] The story was a kind of explanation of how the U.S. government had failed to notice that the Mexican government was in cahoots with a $30 billion a year Mexican drug industry, and by implication helped explain how the *New York Times* had also failed to notice this fact.

The comandante once again left public notice and became a man left to his golf game in McAllen, Texas. For years, I heard rumors that the comandante had not truly retired, that he retained his network in

Mexico, that he continued to help in contract killings and other house-keeping matters. When I would mention these rumors to people in DEA, I'd receive a shrug and silence.

After the funeral, the mists slightly clear. Someone talks to me but has no name or face, not even a city or an agency. Simply, someone talks to me who for years tracked Comandante Calderoni for the U.S. government, someone who never would talk to me before. When I spent seven years on this book, I could not get the time of day from the voice. I had adjusted to living in some Twilight Zone of lies and slippery facts. Now the door opened and the stale air blew away.

"He backed us a hundred percent," he explains to me. "He did his thing on the side. He went up the ladder because he was sharp. And because he kept lots of recordings of people in power. He had his shit together."

In time, the comandante knew who was taking drug money or other illicit riches, the names of everyone's girlfriends. He came into the federal police from some assignment in the federal car registration force. But he soon learned what he needed to know. He remembers an early heroin case, when Calderoni looked at the seized drug and asked, "What in the hell is this?"

He soon learned.

And thought ahead. By the early 1970s, the comandante kept a house with a swimming pool in McAllen, as a kind of fallback invest-ment in the United States. In the 1980s when flights of cocaine began to flood Mexico, the comandante prospered. In one year, the voice explains, his agency tracked 185 planeloads of cocaine into Mexico, and as Calderoni rose, so did his share of the action. Under Salinas, he continues, they tried to pin down the comandante's assets but gave up the work when they hit $1 billion. As of the spring of 2002, the United Nations pegged the global narcotics trade as $400 billion a year, a sum that exceeds the global oil and gas trade and is double the global trade in motor vehicles.[8] How unbelievable is it that a smart comandante dipped his hand into this flow and captured a billion?

But here the feeling of unreality returns as it always does concern-ing wealth and Mexico: a billion dollars flowing into the hands of a man who lived and died largely unknown to the American press and government? I mention this, and the voice takes note. He describes a briefing he once gave to the U.S. State Department, just a normal kind of dog-and-pony show. And in this briefing, he flashed on the screen the picture of a house in San Luis, Sonora, a dusty border city. The house cost maybe $250,000, nice, but was no mansion. After the briefing he got angry memos from the State Department that it was ridiculous to claim some Mexican drug trafficker could have such a house. And that is what surprised the voice because the house belonged to what is known as a gatekeeper, a small cog in the machine who simply helped get things through at that one U.S. crossing. Not a big fish, barely a fish at all. And yet this cog in San Luis had other houses and bank accounts around the world. How could the U.S. government grasp the torrent of illicit money flowing through Mexico if it balked at this one house belonging to almost a clerk in the organization?

The comandante flourished in this world of disbelief. The voice explains that Calderoni "had a reputation for taking the money and then fucking people over." He would work with DEA, seize loads left and right, and do this because a part of him wanted to be this super-cop. And then the comandante would blame the seizures on DEA, even at times when they had nothing to do with them. But he was careful never to give the U.S. agencies everything. If they had wished to notice, they would have discovered he generally arrested no one except the pilots. And then, the pilots, being useful, seemed to be released. The drugs were of course destroyed but then no one really checked up on this destruction.

DEA made busts, got headlines, had a valiant anti-drug comandante to celebrate. The billion dollars stashed away? A detail. The voice waves away my question by simply saying, "DEA never looked for Calderoni's money. DEA was in love with him."

And what was not to love? the voice continues. Calderoni was well spoken, wore button-down collars, came across as a gentleman. He was controlled, careful about his drinking. A thoughtful man. When he told the world during the effort to extradite him from the U.S. that he had but $7 million, the statement was true since he had transferred his holdings into the names of others.

Retired to his mansion in McAllen, he continued to do what he had always done, the voice explains. He sold intelligence to everyone. He consulted with traffickers on how to bring drugs into the United States, he smuggled things into Mexico, he blackmailed leading Mexican politicians with his tapes and archive. He flourished as if the flight from his police post and nation had never occurred.

Did you like him, I finally ask.

"No. He was an asshole. Pompous, arrogant. Here's this coman-dante making $500 a month and he's talking about his cars and houses. He treated people under him like shit."

The voice stops speaking. He tells me one more time: remember I do not exist.

And then the rub comes, the sense of stepping off something solid into thin air. This sensation shimmered throughout the world of Comandante Calderoni, a man doing deep deals with the FBI and DEA and most likely, given the logic of information desires, the CIA. And also arresting, killing and, at the same time, billing multibillion-dollar drug cartels, and carrying out the crimes and desires of the leaders of Mexico. And betraying all of them to each other and somehow keeping his footing, never spinning out of control, never twirling off into space, never flinching as one thing led to another. Living in McAllen, Texas, playing golf, right there on the banks of the Rio Grande where he faced a nation of harsh and corrupt power that held warrants on him and faced large organizations of cutthroats whom he had beaten, tortured, arrested, and of course, charged generously for the experience.

Down by the river, you get to understand but not to know in the definitive sense treasured by courts. Months after Calderoni's death, Phil Jordan learns through a golden source that the late comandante had been the one who ordered the July 9, 2001 murder of Comandante Jaime Yañez, the Mexican who had talked for months with Sal Martínez about a contract murder of the alleged killer of Bruno Jordan. Calderoni had ordered the hit, according to this source, because Yañez had gotten greedy about his share of the border drug money. But more important, because Yañez had been heard speaking disrespectfully of Calderoni. Other cries from the past also briefly broke the silence of the line. In November 2002, the same month this book was initially published, the head investigator of the El Paso county attorney's office was arrested for illegally using the law enforcement databases in various computer probes. For years, he had allegedly told his fellow employees that a close relative in Juárez was connected to the Juárez cartel. He earned $27,000 a year and at one point was planning to build a four-thousand-square-foot house. He was in charge of the investigation of the murder of Bruno Jordan in Miguel Angel Flores's third and final trial, the one ending in a hung jury and his release and deportation. And then in July 2003, the FBI arrested one of its own employees in El Paso, a man who for five years had been assigned the translation of various electronic intercepts made of communications between members of the Juárez cartel. He allegedly was paid by the cartel for his FBI labors. At the same time, disgraced former president Carlos Salinas de Gortari has returned to Mexico and is feted at banquets by the rich. This is the world where the murder of Bruno Jordan occurred and this is the world where that murder was supposedly investigated. And this is the world where Comandante Calderoni thrived until the very last minute of his life.

Now he becomes ash and dust, becomes a footnote in a few American newspapers, becomes a file sealed in various American agencies. He becomes part of the hidden history we all know so well now, the hidden history that hides within our very governments. He defied the government of Mexico and lived. Calderoni beat the Mexican effort to extradite him back to Mexico and certain death—an effort supported by the then disenchanted FBI and fought by a still loyal DEA. He cheated agency after agency and yet they remained in some kind of thrall to him. A double agent is hardly work. Try being the comandante, dealing with two or three U.S. agencies plus the various cartels plus two governments, plus the Mexican army, plus—who can really say how many forces he dealt with? And winning.

The son walks me out past the offices where the phones never ring, past all those paper shredders, past the help with those outlines of gun barrels probing through their clothing, past the young secretary in tight jeans, the one right over there bending over a file with a swatch of skin blooming over her ass as her blouse slips ever so softly up. He maintains his even tone. I ask him if he feels safe and he says he feels very safe.

He explains how he saw his father late on Monday and then of course, he had to be off to Houston on business and then, alas, the bullet, that single bullet cut its path on Wednesday morning. He says three masses will be said. He says he wants no vengeance, that his father had his life and he has a different life.

And I guess he does. I know his father the day before he died reached out on a business matter—some problem with Nigerian oil and getting it exported from there to here and I know nothing about oil export but marvel that he called a retired DEA agent about facilitating the matter, not that Nigeria's major exporting of heroin could be an issue. I am impressed by the son, by his quiet and courteous manner and by how well he handles his grief. One would think his father had been slaughtered a year ago, not about a hundred twenty hours ago.

We are outside now, the son and his colleagues and my God, there is Chato, the very man who was sitting next to the comandante but, praise the Lord, was spared when the assassin swung into view and fired the round. The very man who first gave a description of the car and killers and then recanted. The luckiest man in the world, one left deliberately alive it seems as an eyewitness to a murder. Chato is short, sixty-something and still not at peace. But my questions to Chato are instantly stopped by the son. Chato looks down at his boots and falls silent.

I can feel the long night falling, a recurrent sensation whenever one ventures into this terrain we call the War on Drugs. Soon none of this will have ever happened. A new day will dawn and its rays will obliterate our memories and our ability to read the few scraps of records that have escaped the inferno of our desire to incinerate the actual past.

The son says he wants his father left in peace, in serenity. And then he places both of his hands before him, palms down, and swirls them like a plasterer smoothing over the final sealing of a grave.

acknowledgments

I sit in the office chair of an old narc who has passed away, Arturo Carrillo Strong. Once, when we were at a drug gathering in Sonora, the host, a dealer who worked for cartel leader Amado Carrillo, heard Arturo's name and jokingly said, "Carrillo? *Muy pesado!* Very heavy." I don't know what Arturo would have thought of this book but I know I've thought of him as I wrote it. He was a man typical of the border, a person raised in a barrio, a man with an appetite for whiskey and at times cocaine, and a man who chose the law and spent many years arresting the same guys he'd been raised with and sending them to prison. And a man who often introduced me in his home to men he'd sent to prison. I know he watched with horror the growth of the drug industry in the 1980s and 1990s, read with disbelief the press silence on this growth, and went to his grave angry over the slaughter in Mexico and the United States that was largely unrecorded. He also warned me not to go to Juárez and to never trust DEA.

I ignored his advice, inherited his chair, and cherish his memory.

Many people have helped me with this book. Most of the Mexicans and almost all of the American officials would not wish their name in this book or any thanks. So I shall pass them by with a tip of my hat for their help. Two people in El Paso and Juárez were instrumental in my education: Julian Cardona and Carlos Vigueras. Also, the entire—and enormous—Jordan clan must be thanked for allowing me into their life and their sorrow. Phil Jordan and his siblings and parents and Phil's children have been a family to me. None of them has read a word of this book, truly a testament to faith. They have changed my life, as has the late Lionel Bruno Jordan, whom I never met. Also, I cannot forget the kindness and decency of Sal Martínez and Suzie Martínez, who

415

spoke to me at their moment of greatest peril. I cannot alter facts but I know I have seldom met two people as decent as they are. Sal is in prison for a felony but I know I am not a better man than he is. And this knowledge is a gift for me in the miles ahead.

I must note a few of the many books I've read that mattered to me: Dan Baum's *Smoke and Mirrors*, Friedrich Katz's *The Life and Times of Pancho Villa*, Terrence Poppa's *Drug Lord*, Elaine Shannon's *Desperados*, and Gary Webb's *Dark Alliance*. The scholarship of Peter Lupsha and Luis Astorga has also been crucial for me.

I wrote the first draft of this book in Marfa, Texas, a singular town besotted with late-twentieth-century art. I want to thank the people of Marfa, whom I hardly met as I scribbled, and the Lannan Foundation, which made my time there possible. I have seldom dealt with a foundation as thoughtful as the Lannan, which provides a house, stipend, and then lets their guests work out their own damnation. I also want to thank the foundation for stocking my domicile with an excellent CD collection, particularly a disc by Sarah Vaughan.

And I want to especially thank my cousin Cheryl Beerman, who pitched in when a family crisis carpet-bombed my careful plans and by that act she made my stay in Marfa possible. Blood counts, as this book amply shows.

My publishers have changed as I worked on this book. I began it at Random House with the peculiar notion that I could do it in eighteen months. That was almost seven years ago. So I want to thank the people who fortified my erratic efforts: Ruth Fecych, David Rosenthal, and my editor at Simon & Schuster, Geoff Kloske. Also, my agent, Kathy Anderson, who I'm sure has had many second thoughts about me.

Some of the material on which this book rests was research that materialized as articles in various magazines: *Harper's, Esquire, GQ, Talk, Aperture,* and I'm sure others I can't remember. I want to thank these publications for those checks that kept my satanic mills grinding away and for their willingness to finance stories about the one nation Americans studiously ignore: Mexico.

I could not have written this book without the love and tolerance of Mary Martha Miles, God help her. I know she wishes I had never entered into the world it contains. Which makes her support all the more important.

No one is responsible for a word in this book, save myself.

Every man who writes needs a dog. The resident beast is named Sam Spade and, not surprisingly, he kicks me rather than the traditional arrangement celebrated in folklore. I'd like to make a nod to the birds and plants in the yard, but hell, I realize this is beyond custom.

—CHARLES BOWDEN

notes

ANOTHER COUNTRY

1. "The Importance of the Drug Trade in the Mexican Economy," *El Diario de Juárez,* June 25, 2001.
2. Todd Robberson and Douglas Farah, "Mexican Cartels Expanding Role in Trafficking," *Washington Post,* March 12, 1995.
3. Diana Washington Valdez, "Juárez Violence Continues," *El Paso Times,* July 30, 2001.
4. "Tables Turn as Town Opts for Mugshots of Cops," *The News,* Mexico City, August 17, 2001.
5. Edward Humes, *Buried Secrets: A True Story of Serial Murder,* Dutton, New York, 1991.
6. Tim Golden, "Head to Head in Mexico: DEA Agents and Suspects," *New York Times,* November 24, 1999.
7. Julie Watson, "Mexico Police Raid Causes Fear," Associated Press, June 22, 2001.

CRIME

1. Michael Christie, "Old Habits of Silence Die Hard in Mexico," Reuters, March 30, 1999.
2. *El Imparcial,* Hermosillo, Sonora, June 1, 1995.
3. Andres Oppenheimer, *Bordering on Chaos,* Little, Brown, Boston, 1996, p. 138.
4. Diego Cevallos, "Publishing Industry Stuck in the Doldrums," InterPress Service (Peace Net), May 21, 1995.
5. Mark Fineman and Sebastian Rotella, "The Drug Web That Entangles Mexico," *Los Angeles Times,* June 15, 1995.

6. Tracey Eaton, "Drug Gangs in Juárez Follow Morbid Routine," *Dallas Morning News,* July 9, 1995, p. 1A.

7. David Fisher, *Hard Evidence,* Simon & Schuster, New York, 1995, p. 249.

8. Stephen Power, "Unsolved Killings Highlight Cross-Border Police Tension," *Dallas Morning News,* August 21, 1995.

9. Confidential DEA summary.

10. Peter Reuter, "Economics of the Narcotics Industry," Conference Report Sponsored by Bureau of Intelligence and Research, November 21–22, 1994.

11. Thaddeus Herrick, "Job Seekers Overwhelming Border Cities," *Houston Chronicle,* July 16, 1995, p. 21A.

12. Associated Press, "Accused Fiscal Villain Rises to Defend Self in Mexico," *Houston Chronicle,* July 15, 1995, p. 28A.

13. Anthony De Palma, "After the Fall," *New York Times,* July 16, 1995, p. 1F.

14. President Ernesto Zedillo Ponce de León, State of the Nation Address, September 1, 1995.

15. Paul B. Carroll, "Zedillo Lays Out Economic Forecast," *Wall Street Journal,* June 1, 1995.

16. Testimony, Thomas A. Constantine, head of DEA, Senate Foreign Relations Committee, August 8, 1995.

17. Mike Gallagher, "Beaten at the Border: Part One," *Albuquerque Journal,* October 22, 1995.

18. Rául Hernández and Leticia Zamarripa, "FBI Links Federales, Drug Lord," *El Paso Times,* July 4, 1996.

19. Mike Gallagher, "Beaten at the Border: Part Two," *Albuquerque Journal,* October 23, 1995.

20. "Mexico's Choice of Silver or Lead," *U.S. News & World Report,* October 14, 1996.

21. Fineman and Rotella, "Drug Web."

22. Andrew Reding, "Narcopolitics in Mexico," *The Nation,* July 10, 1995.

23. Peter Lupsha, secret DEA briefing to the State Department, November 1994.

24. Alfredo Corchad, "Troubled by Temptation," *Dallas Morning News,* June 25, 1995.

25. *New York Times,* Sunday, March 29, 1998.

26. Oppenheimer, *Bordering on Chaos,* p. 232.

27. Tim Coone, "Money Laundering in Mexico," *Latin Trade,* Vol. 5, No. 9, pp. 56–60.

28. Fineman and Rotella, "Drug Web."

29. Carlos Vigueras, *La Jornada,* October 6, 1994.

30. Oppenheimer, *Bordering on Chaos,* pp. 269–70.

31. Tim Golden, "Newark Case Is Keeping Mexico Rapt," *New York Times,* June 19, 1995, p. 9A.

32. Donald E. Schulz, "Between a Rock and a Hard Place: The United States, Mexico, and the Agony of National Security," Strategic Studies Institute, U.S. Army War College, Carlisle Barracks, Pennsylvania June 24, 1997.

33. Eduardo Molina y Vedia, "It's Official—Crisis Is Long Term," InterPress Service (PeaceNet), May 16, 1995.

34. Ken Flynn, "Waiting for Justice," *El Paso Times,* February 27, 1996.

35. Elaine Shannon, *Desperados: Latin Drug Lords, U.S. Lawmen, and the War America Can't Win,* Viking, New York, 1988, pp. 181–82.

36. Jamie Dettmer, "Family Affair," *Insight Magazine,* March 29, 1999.

37. Tim Golden, "An Investigator in the Killing of Mexican Cardinal Is Slain," *New York Times,* May 11, 1995, p. 4A, and Juanita Darling, "Tijuana Cartel Linked to Killing of Ex-Investigator," *Los Angeles Times,* May 22, 1995, p. 4A.

38. Juan Resendiz, *El Paso Herald-Post,* August 14, 1997.

39. Dudley Althaus, "Mexican Judge Dies, Adding to the List of Slain Officials," *Houston Chronicle,* June 21, 1995.

40. Joel Simon, "Mexico's 'Untouchable' Family," *San Francisco Chronicle,* June 12, 1995, p. 8A.

41. Dettmer, "Family Affair."

BLOOD

1. Enrique Krauze, *Mexico: Biography of Power,* HarperCollins, 1997, pp. 636–37.

2. Sam Quinones, *True Tales from Another Mexico,* University of New Mexico Press, 2001.

3. Robert Collier, "Mexico's New Emperor of Narcotics: Amado Carrillo's Rise Shows Growing Clout of Drug Lords," *San Francisco Chronicle,* February 26, 1996.

4. Molly Moore, "Drug Legend Is Buried in Mexican Village," *Washington Post,* July 12, 1997.

5. Sam Dillon, "Canaries Sing in Mexico, but Uncle Juan Will Not," *New York Times,* February 9, 1996.

6. Luis Astorga, Discussion Paper 36, "Drug Trafficking in Mexico," UNESCO, p. 3.

7. Krauze, *Mexico,* pp. 730–31.

8. Background on Pérez Aviles in Elaine Shannon, *Desperados: Latin Drug Lords, U.S. Lawmen, and the War America Can't Win,* Viking, New York, 1988, pp. 59–60.

9. Dan Baum, *Smoke and Mirrors: The War on Drugs and the Politics of Failure,* Little, Brown, Boston, 1997, pp. 75, 91.

10. Quinones, *True Tales.*

11. Interview June 13, 2001, informant X.

12. Krauze, *Mexico,* p. 755.

13. Ibid., p. 760.

14. Ibid., p. 772.

15. Luis Javier Garrido, "The Narco System," *La Jornada,* June 11, 1993.

16. Gary Webb, *Dark Alliance: The CIA, the Contras, and the Crack Cocaine Explosion,* Seven Stories Press, New York, 1998, p. 72.

17. Astorga, Discussion Paper 36.

18. Interview with DEA head of Mexican intelligence.

19. Shannon, *Desperados,* p. 257.

20. From Terrence Poppa, *Drug Lord: The Life and Death of a Mexican Kingpin,* Demand Publications, 1998, Chapters "Search and Rescue" and "North South Dialogue."

21. Fox Butterfield, "Drug Research Inadequate, White House Panel Finds," *New York Times,* March 20, 2001.

22. Shannon, *Desperados,* p. 294.

23. Ibid., p. 318.

24. Poppa, *Drug Lord,* p. 215.

25. Ibid., p. 254.

26. Baum, *Smoke and Mirrors,* p. 233.

27. Carlos Marin, *Proceso,* February 16, 1997, based on U.S. court documents which are heavily censored.

28. Assertion of Eduardo Valle, former drug enforcement leader under Carlos Salinas. In Christopher Whalen, October 7, 1994, Report.

29. Shannon, *Desperados,* pp. 58–59.

SONG

1. Sebastian Rotella, *Twilight on the Line,* W. W. Norton & Company, New York, 1998, pp. 137–38.

2. Andrew Downie, "Lawyers in Drug Cases Risking Death in Mexico," *Houston Chronicle,* August 10, 1997.

3. Dudley Althaus, "Zedillo Hit on Drug War Results," *Houston Chronicle,* July 30, 1995.

4. Christopher Whalen, "Mexico: What's Next?" remarks at the Council on Foreign Relations, New York, March 6, 1995.

5. Tim Weiner, *New York Times,* August 3, 1995, p. 5A.

6. Paulino Vargas, "El Zorro de Ojinaga," *The Devil's Swing,* Arhoolie Records, 2000.

7. Jo Bedingfield, *San Francisco Chronicle,* October 18, 1995, p. 1C.

8. Mark Fineman (*Los Angeles Times* wire) in *Austin American-Statesman,* June 18, 1995, p. 7A.

9. Nancy Nusser, *Austin American-Statesman,* September 3, 1995.

10. Mark Stevenson, "Mexico Plans U.S.-Style Freedom Act," Associated Press, September 8, 2001.

11. Juanita Darling, "Mexico Seen Expertly Silencing Voices of Dissent," *Los Angeles Times,* July 30, 1995, p. 4A.

12. InterPress News Service, September 2, 1995 (MNP).

13. "82 Children Die Daily Due to Malnutrition," InterPress News Service, September 16, 1995. The study is by the National Institute of Nutrition (INN).

14. Andres Oppenheimer and Lucy Conger, "Narco-Culture," Knight-Ridder Newspapers, December 2, 1997.

15. Jamie Dettmer, "U.S. Drug Warriors Knock on Heaven's Door," *Insight Magazine,* April 21, 1997.

16. "Mexican Drug Kingpin Among Heirs to Cali Cartel," Reuters, August 7, 1995.

17. *Global Habit,* pp. 1–2.

18. *El Financiero Internacional,* February 12–18, 1996, p. 17.

19. InterPress News Service, December 29, 1995, (MNP).

20. Jim Landers, *Dallas Morning News,* October 11, 1995, p. 16A, (MNP).

21. Jorge G. Castañeda, *The Mexican Shock,* New Press, 1995.

22. "Bruno's Song," all lyrics copyright by Tony Jordan.

23. Andres Oppenheimer, "Salinas Brother Stash Tip of Iceberg," *Miami Herald,* November 29, 1995.

24. Mike Gallagher, "King of Kingpins," *Albuquerque Journal*.

25. Ibid.

26. Robert Collier, "Mexico's New Emperor of Narcotics: Amado Carrillo's Rise Shows Growing Clout of Drug Lords," *San Francisco Chronicle*, February 26, 1996.

27. John Ward Anderson, "After Death, Kingpin's Life Is an Open Book," *Washington Post*, November 25, 1997.

DREAMTIME

1. James F. Smith, "Woman Banking on $46 billion—If Courts Give the OK," *Los Angeles Times*, July 1, 2001.

2. Andrew Reding, "Mexico Under Salinas: A Façade of Reform," *World Policy Journal*, Fall 1989.

3. Ibid.

4. Andres Oppenheimer, *Bordering on Chaos*, Little, Brown, Boston, 1996, p. 24.

5. John Ward Anderson, "A Mexican's Mystery Millions," *Washington Post*, October 12, 1998.

6. Mexico City's twenty-three dailies have a combined circulation of 500,000. During the election the PRI paid $800,000 each to the leading papers—*Excelsior, El Universal*, and *La Jornada*—to keep Zedillo's campaign on the front page. Other government payments made the election worth about $3 million for each paper. Basically a reporter covering the Zedillo campaign for a major Mexico City daily made about $12,000 a year but during the campaign received an additional $80,000 from the PRI. *La Jornada*, the leftist and widely viewed as independent paper, printed potted government-paid Zedillo stories with headlines in italics to signal the cognoscenti. Oppenheimer, *Bordering on Chaos*, pp. 135–36, 138.

"We are optimistic. We don't see any evidence of a pattern of systematic irregularities or abusing of the system. There may be operational glitches, but {there is} no systematic pattern of irregularities."

—U.S. AMBASSADOR TO MEXICO, JAMES JONES, AT BRIEFING FOR U.S. REPORTERS AUGUST 19, TWO DAYS BEFORE THE ELECTION. JONES, FORMER HEAD OF THE NEW YORK STOCK EXCHANGE, HAD BEEN CLINTON'S POINTMAN IN LOBBYING CONGRESS FOR NAFTA. IBID., P. 160.

7. Jack Blum comments based on telephone interviews.

8. See William Greider, *One World, Ready or Not: The Manic Logic of Global Capitalism*, Simon & Schuster, New York, 1997, pp. 32–33: "'Choke points in the world's financial system,' the IMF [International Monetary Fund] calls them. Big money hides in the global economy. Respectable capital mingles alongside dirty money from illegal enterprise (drugs, gambling, illicit arms sales) because offshore banking centers allow both to hide from the same things: national taxation and the surveillance of government regulators. Major governments, including the United States, are not likely to help IMF get these financial entrepôts to open up their books since major governments actively encouraged the rise of offshore banking as a convenience for global companies and investors."

9. Anthony De Palma and Peter Treul, "A Mexican Mover and Shaker and How His Millions Moved," *New York Times*, June 5, 1996.

10. Andrew Wheat, "Mexico's Privatization Piñata," *Multinational Monitor*, October 1996.

11. Personal interview in the United States, May 6, 2000.

12. Tim Golden, "In Breakthrough, Mexican Official Testifies in Texas Drug Case," *New York Times*, July 15, 1998.

13. "Aide to Ex-Mexico Leader Had Fortune," Associated Press, May 4, 1998.

14. "Mexico Seeks to Arrest Top Salinas Aide—Report," Associated Press, July 16, 1998.

15. De Palma and Treul, "Mexican Mover and Shaker."

16. Tim Golden, "Mexico and Drugs: Was U.S. Napping?" *New York Times*, July 11, 1997. Also, same day, Tim Golden, "Salinas: Plenty of Smoke, No Smoking Gun."

17. Bill Lodge, "Hide and Seek," *Dallas Morning News*, March 13, 1996.

18. Christopher Whalen, *The Mexico Report*, Vol. III, No. 20, October 7, 1994.

19. Oppenheimer, *Bordering on Chaos*, chapter entitled "The Banquet."

20. Sam Dillon, "How Mexican Drug Lord Set Up Shop Under Not Too Watchful Governor," *New York Times*, March 20, 1998.

21. Christopher Whalen, "Mexico Drug War Has a U.S. Front," *Insight Magazine*, April 2, 2001.

22. Tim Golden, "U.S. Report Says Salinas's Banker Ignored Safeguards," *New York Times*, December 4, 1998.

23. From an interview with Carlos Hank Rhon for a *Frontline* broadcast in 2000. The interview can be found online at www.pbs.org/pages/frontline/shows/drugs/special/hank.html.

24. De Palma and Treul, "Mexican Mover and Shaker."

25. Alma Guillermoprieto, "Murder, Mexico & the Salinas Brothers," *New York Review of Books,* October 3, 1996.

26. Craig Torres, Joel Millman, and Diane Solis, "Raúl Salinas Probe Touches Mexico's Top Businessmen," *Wall Street Journal,* August 7, 1998.

27. Andrew Wheat, "Mexico's Privatization Piñata," *Multinational Monitor,* October 1996.

28. David Adams, "Mexican Drug Lord Had Account in U.S." *The Times* (London), September 15, 1997.

29. "Mexican Denies Role in Citibank Laundering," *Wall Street Journal,* September 11, 1997. In this account, Bitar Tafich denies being a member of the Juárez cartel.

30. Molly Moore, "Where It All Begins with 'Narco,'" *Washington Post,* January 10, 1999.

31. Jorge G. Castañeda, *The Mexican Shock,* New Press, 1995, p. 79.

32. Tracey Eaton, "Customs Inspectors Say Bosses Ignoring Border Corruption," *Dallas Morning News,* June 16, 1996.

33. Jamie Dettmer, "Family Affair," *Insight Magazine,* March 29, 1999.

34. Matthew Cooper, "Fools and Their Money," *Washington Post* national weekly edition, January 29–February 4, 1996.

35. Andres Oppenheimer, *Miami Herald,* "Death Squads Are Stalking the Streets of Mexican Border Town," in the *Arizona Republic,* November 2, 1997.

36. Mary Beth Sheridan, "Narco Charity Makes Saints Out of Drug Traffickers," *Los Angeles Times,* in the *Arizona Republic,* October 26, 1997.

37. Oppenheimer, *Bordering on Chaos,* pp. 186, 187; *Time,* February 1, 1999, International Section.

38. Julia Preston with Craig Pyes, "Secret Tape Deepens Mystery of Murder in Mexico," *New York Times,* January 14, 1999.

39. "Ex-Official: Salinas Gave Bonus," *Los Angeles Times* wire in *El Paso Times,* August 4, 1995.

40. Tim Golden, "Mexican, in U.S. Suicide Note, Blames Zedillo for Death," *New York Times,* September 17, 1999.

41. *La Jornada,* December 7, 1994, pp. 12, 13.

42. Whalen, "Mexico Drug War."

43. Julia Preston, "How Cartel Tried to Buy Bank Group in Mexico," *New York Times,* March 29, 1998.

44. Anthony De Palma, "Salinas in New York for Dow Jones Meeting," *New York Times,* April 18, 1996.

45. Tim Golden, "Tracing Money, Swiss Outdo U.S. on Mexico Drug Corruption Case," *New York Times,* August 4, 1998. David Lyons, "U.S. Cali Cartel Accountant, Key U.S. Witness, Gets 7 Years," *Miami Herald,* December 16, 1998.

46. Tim Golden, "Salinas Brother Is Tied by Swiss to Drug Trade," *New York Times,* September 19, 1998.

47. Golden, "Mexico and Drugs: Was U.S. Napping?"

48. Michael Erard, "So Far from God: Irishman Carlos Salinas O'Gortari," *Texas Observer,* August 6, 1999.

49. John Ward Anderson and Molly Moore, "Following the Paper Trail: Not Everyone in Mexico Wants to Find Out How Deep the Official Corruption Runs," *Washington Post* national weekly edition, August 12–18, 1996.

50. See Dan Freedman, "Cocaine Bribery Crosses Border," *San Francisco Examiner,* Sunday, October 13, 1996. Or wire reports at the same time, in one of which, Daniel Knauss, assistant U.S. attorney in Tucson, Arizona, offered, "The numbers? That's one of the things we're trying to get a handle on. Maybe I'm optimistic, but I'm willing to stick my neck out and say a majority [of agents and inspectors] are honest." Few who live on the border share Knauss's optimism. The simple rule on the line is: never trust anyone in INS, Customs, DEA, or the Border Patrol.

51. Molly Moore, "It's All a Show, Says Ex-Agent," *Washington Post,* July 30, 1996; letter of Christopher Whalen to James R. Jones, U.S. ambassador to Mexico, August 2, 1996.

52. The background on Rocio's rip-off of the cartel was told to me in the summer of 2001 by a Mexican drug dealer who is part of the cartel.

53. Steve Fainaru, "An Old Killing Has Offshoots in Mexico," *Boston Globe,* May 20, 1997.

54. Tracey Eaton, "Obstacles Increase Probe," *Dallas Morning News,* August 28, 1996.

55. "Despite the nationwide recession, Juárez—along with many of its sister cities along the border—is growing, if not prospering. Employment

is up, glitzy new office buildings are under construction, and its bars and restaurants are packed. While much of the city's economic success is the result of legitimate business, a strong industrial base, and the cross-border tourism from El Paso, city residents from all walks of life say drug money has become so entwined in their local economy that above-board businesses and those financed by narco-dollars are difficult to separate. . . . [T]rucking businesses and car dealerships . . . a petroleum company . . . small airlines." Molly Moore and John Ward Anderson, "Where the Drug Lords Hold Court: In Northern Mexico, the Cartels' Billions Distort the Economy of a Booming Industrial Region," *Washington Post* national weekly edition, May 6–12, 1996.

56. Julia Preston, "Body Bizarrely Found in Mexico Telling No Tales," *New York Times,* October 27, 1996, p. 3.

57. Anita Snow, "Journalist Couple, 3 Children Found Slain in Mexico," Associated Press, December 7, 1996.

58. Christopher Whalen, *The Mexico Report,* Vol. V, No. 4, February 29, 1996.

59. Molly Moore and Douglas Farah, "Confounding Predictions, Juárez Cartel Carries On," *Washington Post,* December 1, 1997.

60. Molly Moore, "Drug Legend Is Buried in Mexican Village," *Washington Post,* July 12, 1997.

61. Robert Collier, "Mexico's New Emperor of Narcotics: Amado Carrillo's Rise Shows Growing Clout of Drug Lords," *San Francisco Chronicle,* February 26, 1996.

62. Golden, "Mexico and Drugs"; Carlos Fazio, "Mexico: The Narco General Case" in *Crime in Uniform: Corruption and Impunity in Latin America,* Transnational Institute and Acción Adina, December 1997.

63. John Rice, "Alleged Mexican Drug Lords Evade Capture, Conviction," Associated Press, January 8, 1997.

64. "Major Drug Tie Suspected in 26 Arrests in Mexico," *New York Times,* January 7, 1997, Internet edition.

65. "PGR Officials Goofed in Murder Probe,"Reuters, January 10 and Michael Stott, "Creditability of Mexican Prosecutor Takes Fresh Knocks," Reuters, January 10.

66. "Cartel Boss Gives Mexico the Slip Again," "Top Mexican Prosecutor Killed in Tijuana," Reuters, January 5.

67. Fazio, *Crime in Uniform.* Carlos Marin, "Documentos de Inteligencia Militar Involucran en el Narcotráfico a Altos Jefes, Oficiales y Tropa del Ejército," *Proceso,* No. 1082, July 27, 1997.

68. Originally reported in *La Reforma* (Mexico City) and then placed on the wire by Reuters out of Mexico City, "Fugitive Drug Lord Said to Live Near Capital," January 16, 1997. Also, Fazio, *Crime in Uniform.*

69. *La Jornada*, September 19, 1997.

70. John Ward Anderson, "Drug Kingpin's Life Is an Open Book, Now That He's Dead," *Washington Post*, November 25, 1997. Fazio, *Crime in Uniform.*

71. Sam Dillon, "Mexican Drug Dealer Tried to Buy Way Out," *New York Times*, September 20, 1997.

72. "Dead Mexican Drug Lord Was a 'Narco-Nationalist,'" Reuters, April 1, 1998.

73. Michael Christie, "Witnesses Die, Vanish in Mexico's Anti-Drug Czar Case," Reuters, January 12, 2000. Fazio, *Crime in Uniform*, "Mexico: The Narco General Case," at tni.org/drugs/folder3/fazio.

74. Sam Dillon, "Mexico Remodels Anti-Drug Unit in Time for Clinton Visit," *New York Times*, May 1, 1997.

75. Reuters, August 18, 1997. John Ward Anderson, "Drug Kingpin," *Washington Post*, November 25, 1997.

76. Julia Preston, "U.S. in Spat with Mexico over Identity of Drug Lord," *New York Times*, July 9, 1997.

77. Niko Price, "Mexico Buries Top Drug Lord and Opens Battle for Cocaine Trade," Associated Press, July 11, 1997.

78. Molly Moore, "Drug Legend Is Buried in Mexican Village."

79. Martha Brant, "Liposuctioned to Death," *Newsweek*, July 21, 1997.

80. Diana Washington Valdez, "Cartel Paid Off PAN Official, Warrant Says," *El Paso Times*, October 15, 2000.

81. Tim Golden, "Mexican Military Helps Drug Traffickers, U.S. Reports Say," *New York Times*, March 26, 1998.

82. Anthony De Palma, "Ex-Beauty Queen Slain," *New York Times*, July 31, 1997.

83. "Murdered Woman's Letter Accuses Drug Trafficker," Associated Press, August 6, 1997.

84. Jamie Dettmer, "Reno Contradicts U.S. Drug Report," *Insight Magazine*, July 3–10, 2000.

85. Thomas Francis, "White Tiger Unleashed," *Cleveland Scene*, May 17, 2001.

86. UPI, "Probe Continues in Juárez Café Massacre," August 6, 1997.

87. Christopher Goodwin, "Mexican Drug Barons Sign Up; Renegades from Green Berets," *The Times* (London), August 24, 1997.

88. Reuters, Mexico City, August 5, 1997; Mark Fineman, *Los Angeles Times,* August 8, 1997.

89. Associated Press, August 14, 1997, *El Universal,* Mexico City.

90. Molly Moore, "Threat to U.S. Anti-Drug Czar Causes Alarm on Border Trip," *Washington Post,* August 29, 1997.

91. Douglas Holt, "Multiple Slayings in Juárez Strike Terror," *Dallas Morning News,* September 12, 1997.

92. Tracey Eaton, "Mexican Agents Accused of Using Plane," *Dallas Morning News,* September 5, 1997.

93. Andrew Downie, "Drug Smugglers Learn U.S. Radar, Paper Says," *Houston Chronicle,* September 5, 1997.

94. Sam Dillon, "One Mexican's Daunting Task," *New York Times,* December 12, 1997.

95. "Rebollo Threatened with Further Charges," *The News* (Mexico City), September 20, 1997.

96. "Review: The Lost Battle Against Drugs," *Proceso,* December 3, 2000.

97. Sam Dillon, "Accuser of Top Generals Slain in Mexico," *New York Times,* April 23, 1998.

98. Sam Dillon and Craig Pyes, "Alleged Drug Kingpin Benefits from Mexico's Inept Justice System," *New York Times,* April 15, 1998.

99. Tim Golden, "Mexico and Drugs."

100. "Mexico Closes Hospitals Tied to Juárez Cartel," Associated Press, October 9, 1997.

101. Molly Moore, "Dead Drug Lord's Doctors Found Embedded in Cement," *Washington Post,* November 7, 1997.

102. Sam Dillon, "Disappearances Mount in Mexico's War on Drugs," *New York Times,* October 7, 1997.

103. Linda Diebel, "Country Corrupt, Ambassador Tells Magazine Writer," *Toronto Star,* October 6, 1997.

104. Douglas Farah and Molly Moore, "Doctor in Drug Lord's Operation Sheltered in U.S.," *Washington Post,* April 11, 1998.

105. All from stories in the two Juárez dailies of January 1997.

106. Alfredo Corchado, "Bloody Battle Rages for Drug Lord's Empire," *Dallas Morning News,* February 16, 1998.

107. Juan A. Lozano, "Royal Knights Raided," *El Paso Herald Post,* July 22, 1997.

108. José DeCordoba, "Head Trip," *Wall Street Journal,* May 10, 2000.

109. Diana Washington Valdez, "Alleged Drug Dealer Won't Be Arrested, Official Says," *El Paso Times,* September 20, 2000.
110. Andrew Hurst, "Mexico's Fox Treads Lightly Through the Past," Reuters, June 15, 2001.
111. Amparo Trejo, "Mexican Drug-Lord Summit Reported," Associated Press, *San Diego Union Tribune,* April 9, 2001.
112. Hugh O'Shaughnessy, "Pinochet's Drug Link Comes to Light," *Guardian Weekly,* December 14–20, 2000.
113. Reuters, "Mexico Court Orders Bank to Pay Back Woman $48 Billion," May 7, 2001; James F. Smith, "Woman Banking on $46 billion—If Courts Give the OK," *Los Angeles Times,* July 1, 2001.

BETS

1. *El Paso Times,* December 5, 1999, p. 8A.
2. Christina Pino-Martina, "El Pasoan Hopes Brother, Husband Not Among Buried," *El Paso Times,* December 8, 1999, p. 1A.
3. Tim Golden, "Top Mexican Off-Limits to U.S. Drug Agents," *New York Times,* March 16, 1999. On April 16, 2000, *60 Minutes* broadcast a segment on Operation Casablanca. The following transcript is between Ed Bradley and William Gately, the agent in charge of Casablanca:

(Footage of President Bill Clinton; Madeleine Albright; Barry McCaffrey)

MR. GATELY: (Voiceover) There was a hue and cry, not only from the Mexican government at every level, including the president, but our own secretary of state, Madeleine Albright, our drug czar, General McCaffrey. Both took the side of the Mexican government, also hammering the operation. So I believe that everyone thought that that meant Mexico gets a pass, "You don't follow up on this stuff. Nobody cares. We don't want to hear about it." So they didn't follow up on it.

(Footage of Janet Reno)

BRADLEY: (Voiceover) Attorney General Janet Reno even signed an agreement which assured Mexico that the U.S. would never again mount an undercover operation in Mexico without first telling the Mexican government. In other words, no more Casablancas, even though the attorney general and Commissioner Kelly acknowledged that Operation Casablanca had accomplished something unprecedented in U.S. law enforcement.

4. Tim Golden, "U.S. Brushed Aside Mexican Role, Ex-Drug Chief Says," *New York Times,* November 26, 1999.

5. Tim Golden, "Mexican Gang Still on the Loose Despite Search," *New York Times,* January 10, 2000.

6. CNN, "Mexico's Anti-Drugs Chief Unhurt After Assassination Attempt," August 16, 1999.

7. Personal letter, February 12, 2002.

8. Letter, Richard Nixon to Eugenio L. Forti, December 20, 1972.

9. Esther Schrader, "War on Drugs Taking Toll on Border," *Los Angeles Times,* Sunday, March 12, 2000.

10. Allana Martin, *Death of a Saint Maker,* Worldwide Library, 1999, pp. 151–52.

11. Madeline Bario Diaz, "Drug Agent Charged in Murder-for-Hire Plot," Associated Press, December 16, 1999.

12. Sam Dillon, "Drug Agent Charged in Murder-for-Hire Plot," *New York Times,* December 16, 1999.

13. Mark Smith, "Ex-DEA Agent Apologizes for Plot: 7-Year Sentence for Seeking Hit Man to Avenge Cousin's Death," *Houston Chronicle,* May 6, 2000, p. 1A.

14. Sam Dillon, "U.S. and Mexico Are at Odds over Truth about Lie Tests," *New York Times,* March 2, 2000.

15. Christopher Whalen, "Mexico Drug War Has a U.S. Front," *Insight Magazine,* April 2, 2001.

16. Copyright Tradition Music Co., On *The Devil's Swing: El Columpio del Diablo,* Arhoolie Records, 480, 2000. The song was recorded November 1, 1997, four months after Carrillo's alleged death.

17. "Hunt for Graves Digs Up Drug Labs," Associated Press, December 15, 1999.

18. *El Diario de Juárez,* December 15, 1999.

19. *El Diario de Juárez,* "Cd. Juárez Bar Association Wants Citizens Armed," January 25, 2000.

20. Sam Dillon, "Mexico Ties a Mass Grave to Abduction and Cocaine," *New York Times,* May 14, 2000.

BRUNO'S SONG

1. Interview informant X, June 13, 2001. *El Mercurio,* "Amado Carrillo Está Vivo, Asegura Testigo: 'El Señor de los Cielos' Fue Sustuido por un Primo de Igual Parecido,'" Ciudad Victoria, Tamaulipas.

2. Frank McLynn, *Villa and Zapata: A History of the Mexican Revolution,* Carroll & Graf, New York, 2001, p. 361.

3. Richard Lowry, "This is a Bust—The Futility of Drug Interdiction," *National Review,* July 9, 2001.

4. Julie Watson, "Fight to End Corruption Meets Up with Reality," Associated Press, *El Paso Times,* March 8, 2001.

5. Diana Washington Valdez, Embattled Chihuahuan Governor to Visit," *El Paso Times,* June 5, 2001.

6. Tim Golden, "Citibank Criticized for Slow Response to Money Laundering Scheme," *New York Times,* February 27, 2001.

7. Lee Romney, "Museum Dedicated to Mexico's War on Drugs," *Los Angeles Times,* March 3, 2001.

8. Phil Jordan, August 6, 2001.

9. "Disgraced Former President Visits Mexico," Reuters, December 29, 1999; Josh Tuynman, "Another Salinas Visit Greeted by Uncanny Quake," *The News* (Mexico City), December 30, 1999.

10. James Petras, "Dirty Money, Foundation of U.S. Growth and Empire," *La Jornada,* May 21, 2001.

11. Christopher Whalen, "Mexico Drug War Has a U.S. Front," *Insight Magazine,* April 2, 2001.

12. Cindy Ramírez-Cadena, "HUD Chief Vows Aid," *El Paso Times,* July 25, 2001.

13. Cindy Ramírez-Cadena, "Heroin Deaths Prompt Action," *El Paso Times,* July 24, 2001.

14. Based on the study *Making the Invisible Visible: A Study of Maquila Workers in Mexico—2000.*

15. "Escaped Drug Lord 'Owned' Prison—Mexican Probe," Reuters, February 20, 2001.

16. Rafael Núñez, "Jaime Yañez Cantú, un 'Doble Agente' Ejecutado," *El Norte de Ciudad Juárez,* July 16, 2001, p. 6A; Alison Gregor and Bonnie Parker, "Violence Increases on Border," *San Antonio Express-News,* July 16, 2001. Orquídea Fong, "Muere 'El Padrino,' Juan N. Guerra," *Proceso,* No. 1289, July 15, 2001. *The News* (Mexico City),

July 27, 2001. Diana Washington Valdez, "Forensics Expert's Kin Slain in Juárez," *El Paso Times,* Thursday, July 26, 2001.

17. James F. Smith, "Mexico Is Still Waiting for Human Rights Probe," *Los Angeles Times,* August 16, 2001.

18. Tim Weiner, "Mexico Vows to End Impunity for Torture in Justice System," *New York Times,* March 18, 2001.

19. "Mexican Families File Complaints," Associated Press, August 30, 2001.

20. "Adiós Padrino," *Proceso,* No. 1293, August, 2001.

21. The conversation took place in the summer of 1997 with the most decorated agent in the history of DEA. At one point in his career he had a $3 million annual budget for his informants in Mexico.

22. Diana Washington Valdez, "Juárez Police Accused of Role in Deaths of 4 Men," *El Paso Times,* Sunday, November 25, 2001.

AFTERWORD / DEAD MEN NOT TALKING

1. Tim Weiner, "Mexican Drug Agent Crossed the Line Once Too Often," *New York Times,* February 18, 2003.

2. Terrence E. Poppa, *Drug Lord,* (Demand Publications, 1998), pp. 277–80.

3. Christopher Lee and Kevin Sullivan, "Former Mexican Police Official Shot to Death in Texas," *Washington Post,* February 6, 2003.

4. Christine Biederman, "The Comandante," *Texas Monthly,* July 1997.

5. John Ross, *Mexico Barbaro* (newsletter), August 14–20, 1998.

6. Craig Flakus, "Mexico: Of the Success Stories in War Against Drugs," Voice of America, May 5, 1993. In the story, the exposure of Calderoni as corrupt is seen as proof of Salinas's intent.

7. Tim Golden, "Misreading Mexico," *New York Times,* July 11, 1997.

8. Thalif Green, "Global Drug Trade Reaches Staggering Proportions," International Press Service, March 2, 2002.

Index

About the Author

CHARLES BOWDEN has written sixteen books of nonfiction, including *Blood Orchid, Trust Me, Desierto, The Sonoran Desert, Frog Mountain Blues,* and *Killing the Hidden Waters.* Winner of the 1996 Lannan Literary Award for Nonfiction, he lives in Tucson, Arizona.